Bonhoeffer's Christocentric Theology and Fundamental Debates in Environmental Ethics

Princeton Theological Monograph Series

K. C. Hanson, Charles M. Collier, D. Christopher Spinks,
and Robin A. Parry, Series Editors

Recent volumes in the series:

Andrew R. Hay
God's Shining Forth:
A Trinitarian Theology of Divine Light

Peter Schmiechen
Gift and Promise:
An Evangelical Theology of the Lord's Supper

Hank Voss
The Priesthood of All Believers and the Missio Dei
A Canonical, Catholic, and Contextual Perspective

Alexandra S. Radcliff
The Claim of Humanity in Christ:
Salvation and Sanctification in the Theology of T. F. and J. B. Torrance

Yaroslav Viazovski
Image and Hope
John Calvin and Karl Barth on Body, Soul, and Life Everlasting

Anne C. Miller
Corinthian Democracy:
Democratic Discourse in 1 Corinthians

Thomas Christian Currie
The Only Sacrament Left to Us:
The Threefold Word of God in the Theology and Ecclesiology of Karl Barth

Charles C. Twombly
Perichoresis *and Personhood:*
God, Christ, and Salvation in John of Damascus

Bonhoeffer's Christocentric Theology and Fundamental Debates in Environmental Ethics

Steven C. van den Heuvel

☙PICKWICK *Publications* · Eugene, Oregon

BONHOEFFER'S CHRISTOCENTRIC THEOLOGY AND FUNDAMENTAL
DEBATES IN ENVIRONMENTAL ETHICS

Princeton Theological Monograph Series 217

Pickwick Publications
An Imprint of Wipf and Stock Publishers
199 W. 8th Ave., Suite 3
Eugene, OR 97401

www.wipfandstock.com

PAPERBACK ISBN: 978-1-4982-9619-9
HARDCOVER ISBN: 978-1-4982-9621-2
EBOOK ISBN: 978-1-4982-9620-5

Cataloguing-in-Publication data:

Names: Van Den Heuvel, Steven C., author.

Title: Bonhoeffer's christocentric theology and fundamental debates in environmental
ethics / Steven C. van den Heuvel.

Description: Eugene, OR : Pickwick Publications, 2017 | Princeton Theological Mono-
graph Series 217 | Includes bibliographical references and indexes.

Identifiers: ISBN 978-1-4982-9619-9 (paperback) | ISBN 978-1-4982-9621-2 (hardcover)
| ISBN 978-1-4982-9620-5 (ebook)

Subjects: LCSH: Bonhoeffer, Dietrich, 1906–1945. | Bonhoeffer, Dietrich, 1906–1945—
Ethics. | Ecology—Religious aspects—Christianity. | Jesus Christ—Person and offices.

Classification: BX4827.B57 V36 2017 (paperback) | BX4827.B57 V36 (ebook)

Manufactured in the U.S.A.   05/03/17

Contents

Preface

I was introduced to Dietrich Bonhoeffer during my first year as a student in training for Christian ministry at Ede Christian University of Applied Sciences. Bonhoeffer was mentioned in class one day, and the reference sparked my curiosity. After purchasing a copy of a Dutch translation of Bonhoeffer's *Discipleship*, I started to read it. This reading had a profound impact on me personally—indeed, it proved to be a formative experience for my own spirituality, an experience that, as I later found out, is shared by many readers of Bonhoeffer. As I came to desire to know more about him, in the Summer following that first year, I borrowed a copy of a Dutch translation of *Letters and Papers from Prison* from the local library. Day after day I cycled the twenty kilometers from my home city of Elburg to the rustic city of Kampen, by the river IJssel. There, I would sit on a bench located on the green dike, near an old mill, enjoying the scenery of the river while reading Bonhoeffer's letters from prison.

Though I could sense that these letters contained important thoughts, I didn't yet grasp what they were about. Coming from the context of the conservative Dutch Reformed tradition, his thoughts on living in the world *etsi Deus non daretur* sounded quite strange, and even heretical, to me. But for the most part, I simply couldn't connect with Bonhoeffer's prison writings, for they represented a world far too different from my own. Therefore, after a few days, I gave up on his prison writings and started reading his more familiar sounding *Life Together*. While I was much better able to connect with Bonhoeffer's devotional writings, throughout my student years, I kept wanting to explore the other aspects of his theology as well.

This opportunity presented itself when I was accepted into the doctoral program of the Evangelische Theologische Faculteit. Under the guidance of my promotor, I came to hone my intitial desire to "do something with Bonhoeffer" on the question of the potential contributions that his theology could make to the field of environmental ethics. The project later transformed into a joint-doctorate with the Theologische Universiteit Kampen, which required that I return to the city of Kampen, no longer for a leisurely reading of Bonhoeffer, but for a deeper study of his theology; and instead of doing so surrounded by nature's beauty, I read through his theology, much more systematically, in light of the ecological crisis. Despite these differences, I still managed to enjoy myself as I worked on exploring the intersection between Bonhoeffer's theology and environmental ethics. This not only helped me to come to understand Bonhoeffer better as a theologian, but to further open my eyes to the importance of bringing Christian theology to bear on the many challenges that we face in our contemporary world in general, and the challenges of ecology in particular.

I have a number of people I would like to thank for their involvement in this project. First and foremost I want to mention both of my promotors in this regard. My first promotor, Prof. Dr. Patrick A. Nullens, helped me sharpen the focus of my research project (as indicated above), and also spurred me on through his continual enthusiasm for the project. His ability always to keep the bigger picture in mind was quite refreshing whenever I happend to get bogged down in the details of my research. I am also grateful to my second promotor, Prof. Dr. Ad L. Th. de Bruijne. Not only was he also quite enthusiastic about the project, but he kindly and carefully read through the drafts of the chapters and made many suggestions for improvement. I also want to thank Prof. Dr. Barend Kamphuis for his willingness to read most of the chapters. From his perspective as a systematic theologian and a scholar of Bonhoeffer, he offered me valuable advice. I am also grateful to Dr. Edward van 't Slot, president of the Dutch section of the International Bonhoeffer Society. In meeting with me to discuss my research plans, he kindly recommended some valuable resources that I should use for the section on Bonhoeffer's conception of the divine mandates. Also, I would like to mention Dr. Brian Robertson, who, as a native English speaker, made many helpful suggestions in correcting and improving the English.

After having defended my dissertation in January 2015, I subsequently contacted Wipf & Stock, who agreed to publish a revised version of it in the Princeton Theological Monograph Series. Preparing the manuscript for commercial publication meant cutting down on footnotes and bibliographical references—while it felt painful to do so, I hope these changes have improved the readability of the book. I am very grateful to the editors who were involved in this process—I'd like to specifically mention Dr. Charlie Collier and Brian Palmer in this regard.

It is my wish that this book will contribute to a positive and thorough Christian engagement with ecological concerns, thereby contributing to a fuller answer to the call of Jesus Christ to be his disciples in this world.

Leuven, July 2016

Abbreviations

DBWE   Dietrich Bonhoeffer Works. Edited by Victoria J. Barnett and Clifford J. Green. Vols. 1–16. Minneapolis: Fortress, 1995–2013.

DBWE 1   *Sanctorum Communio: A Theological Study of the Sociology of the Church*. Edited by Clifford J. Green. Translated by Reinhard Krauss and Nancy Lukens. Minneapolis: Fortress, 1998.

DBWE 2   *Act and Being: Transcendental Philosophy and Ontology in Systematic Theology*. Edited by Wayne Whitson Floyd and Hans-Richard Reuter. Translated by H. Martin Rumscheidt. Minneapolis: Fortress, 1996.

DBWE 3   *Creation and Fall: A Theological Exposition of Genesis 1–3*. Edited by John W. de Gruchy. Translated by Douglas Stephen Bax. Minneapolis: Fortress, 1997.

DBWE 6   *Ethics*. Edited by Clifford J. Green. Translated by Reinhard Krauss, Charles C. West, and Douglas W. Stott. Minneapolis: Fortress, 2005.

DBWE 10   *Barcelona, Berlin, New York: 1928–1931*. Edited by Clifford J. Green. Translated by Douglas W. Stott. Minneapolis: Fortress, 2008.

DBWE 12   *Berlin: 1932–1933*. Edited by Larry L. Rasmussen. Translated by Douglas W. Stott, Isabel Best, and David Higgins. Minneapolis: Fortress, 2009.

CD   *Church Dogmatics*. Translated by G. W. Bromiley et al. Edinburgh: T. & T. Clark, 1936–77.

CD I/1   *The Doctrine of the Word of God. Part 1*. Translated by G. W. Bromiley. Edinburgh: T. & T. Clark, 1936.

CD 2/2 *The Doctrine of God. Part 2.* Translated by G. W. Bromiley et al. Edinburgh: T. & T. Clark, 1957.

CD 3/1 *The Doctrine of Creation. Part 1.* Translated by J. W. Edwards et al. Edinburgh: T. & T. Clark, 1958.

CD 3/4 *The Doctrine of Creation. Part 4.* Translated by A. T. Mackay et al. Edinburgh: T. & T. Clark, 1961.

CD 4/4 *The Doctrine of Reconcilliation. Part 4 (Fragment).* Translated by G. W. Bromiley. Edinburgh: T. & T. Clark, 1969.

I

Introduction

THE AIM OF THE PRESENT MONOGRAPH IS TO BRING THE THEOLOGY OF Dietrich Bonhoeffer to bear on the developing field of environmental ethics. Here in the first chapter, the following, initial section will begin by offering a broad, introductory account of the subject and its relevance. On that basis, the second section will put forward the research question, followed by a brief overview of previous research that has been carried out on the topic under discussion (the *status quaestionis*). Following the third section, which deals with the methodology that shall be employed (namely, that of correlation), the fourth and final section will chart out the course that the monograph will follow.

The Subject and Its Relevance

When Dietrich Bonhoeffer's life came to an end at the gallows on April 9, 1945, he left behind a work—and a life—in fragments. This fragmentary nature of his work is perhaps best exemplified by his *Ethics*: though Bonhoeffer considered this collection of disjointed manuscripts to be his main work, he never managed, in the end, to bring it to completion.[1]

Following the war, the enigmatic "fragment" of Bonhoeffer's work—which was catalysed both through and in conjunction with his moving and inspiring biography—became a major source of inspiration for theological

---

1. He himself was well aware of the fragmentary nature of his life and his work, as is evidenced in a letter that he wrote to his friend, Eberhard Bethge, from Tegel prison on February 22, 1945 (DBWE 8:304–6). In that same letter he expresses the hope that this fragment will nevertheless testify toward the "whole." In his own words: "What matters, it seems to me, is whether one still sees, in this fragment of life that we have, what the whole was intended and designed to be, and of what material it is made." DBWE 8:306.

reflection. After some initial confusion about his perceived departure from classical theology in his writings from prison, it quickly became apparent that there was much more to Bonhoeffer's writings than a mere collection of catchphrases describing a world "after God"—indeed, scholars soon discovered a rich and robust Christology underlying his work. At present, decades after his untimely death, a much clearer and systematic understanding of his theology has been achieved, even though debate over the interpretation of certain aspects of his thought continues.

One of the defining features of the research carried out on Bonhoeffer's work is not only an ever-deepening understanding of his theology, but the repeated attempts to bring his theology into conjunction with a wide variety of different contexts and debates, such as on the political struggle for a new South Africa,[2] on the ethics of resistance,[3] and on debates in the biosciences.[4] Although Bonhoeffer is certainly not the first or the only theologian to be studied in this way, attempts of this sort are comparatively more frequent in his case, even in spite of the apparent gaps between the world in which Bonhoeffer lived and worked and the contemporary world in which the problems in question are being raised.[5] Beyond the general attractiveness of Bonhoeffer's biography, one important reason for this has to do precisely with the fragmented nature of his life and work, combined with the open and searching character of his thought.[6] Another reason relates more directly to the content of Bonhoeffer's theology, specifically to his desire to speak to the *world*—throughout his work he developed multiple concepts by which to overcome what he perceived to be a false distinction between "Christian" and "secular" concerns, the most famous of which is his proposal for a non-religious Christianity. Notions such as these have led interpreters to perceive in Bonhoeffer a public theology *avant la lettre*.[7]

This monograph aims to continue this research-tradition by critically correlating Bonhoeffer's theology with contemporary environmental ethics.

2. See de Gruchy, *Bonhoeffer and South Africa*; and ibid., "Bonhoeffer, Apartheid, and Beyond," 353–65.

3. See Rasmussen, *Dietrich Bonhoeffer: Reality and Resistance*.

4. See Wüstenberg et al., *Bonhoeffer and the Biosciences*. A recent account of how Bonhoeffer's work has been applied to various debates over the years is offered by Clark and Mawson, "Introduction," 1–18.

5. This gap has been eloquently described by De Lange, *Waiting for the Word*, 4–5.

6. This, however, also gave rise to many misinterpretations of Bonhoeffer's theology, the most famous example of which is perhaps Robinson, *Honest to God*.

7. See Green, "Bonhoeffer's 'Non-Religious Christianity,'" 275–81; De Lange, "Against Escapism," 141–52; and Nullens, "Towards a Spirituality of Public Leadership," 91–113.

Rather than being born out of pure and simple academic interest, the basic motivation for the project is the widespread recognition that an adequate theological response is greatly needed in light of the current ecological crisis. Lynn White Jr. was the first to make the case that Christianity is at least partly responsible for the present environmental crisis and that, as such, in order to address this crisis, resources from the Christian tradition are needed.[8] Although the particulars of his argument have been seriously criticized, the fact that a relation exists between religion and ecology is nowadays widely acknowledged.[9] Ecotheology can be seen as a conscientious attempt to reflect on this relationship and to transform it into a mutually constructive one, although it is true that, at present, no consensus has been reached on how such a fruitful correlation should be brought about.

One specific way of working in ecotheology is to research the theology of one or more individual theologians whose work is thought to be capable of contributing to the current environmental debate, even though these theologians themselves may not have explicitly written on environmental issues. Many examples of this approach are readily available, and more often than not, they take shape in the form of articles published in scholarly journals or of essays printed in edited volumes. One recent example is *Ecological Hermeneutics: Biblical, Historical and Theological Perspectives.*[10] In the second part of this book, the theologies of, among others, Thomas Aquinas, Martin Luther, Karl Barth, Hans Urs von Balthasar and Jürgen Moltmann are redirected towards the field of environmental ethics. With the exception of Moltmann, none of these theologians expressly addressed ecological concerns in their work. As such, various hermeneutical procedures and methods are employed in order to transpose their theologies, or to make them relevant, in the context of ecology.[11] Many other examples of this approach abound, and some of them will be mentioned further on. This study fits within this research tradition.

---

8. White, "The Historical Roots of our Ecologic Crisis," 1203–7.

9. See Gottlieb, "Introduction," 3–21.

10. Horrell et al., *Ecological Hermeneutics.*

11. In his essay on Barth, for instance, Thompson makes the case that, among other aspects of his work, Barth's resistance against "anthropocentrism"—or more specifically, against "a Christianity tailored to the capacity of the human"—can be used to criticize an anthropocentric approach to nature, even though Barth himself did not make this application (Thompson, "'Remaining Loyal to the Earth,'" 183). Barth's theology is also transposed into the field of environmental ethics by Gabriel, "Beyond Anthropocentrism in Barths Doctrine of Creation," 175–87.

The Research Question and the *Status Quaestionis*

In this study, I seek to answer the following research question: "In which way can a number of concepts from the theology of Dietrich Bonhoeffer be transposed and made relevant for contemporary discussions in the field of environmental ethics?"

There have been various attempts to transpose Bonhoeffer's theology in the direction of environmental ethics. In what follows, I will address the *status quaestionis* in this regard. It will become clear that, in spite of the research previously carried out, a thoroughgoing study of the subject has yet to be made.

The first scholar to draw a connection between Bonhoeffer's theology and environmental ethics was Hans Dirk van Hoogstraten.[12] Specifically drawing on James Burtness's interpretation of Bonhoeffer,[13] he discerns a christological teleology in Bonhoeffer's assertion that it is Christ who structures reality, and directs it towards himself. Van Hoogstraten places this teleology over against the teleologies of market capitalism and gaiacentrism, claiming that instead of these, Bonhoeffer's christocentric teleology provides us with a goal that can really be aspired to.

The second one to relate Bonhoeffer's theology with ecology was Patrick A. Nullens. He did so in his doctoral dissertation, submitted in 1995.[14] Although it does not focus exclusively or even primarily on Bonhoeffer's theology, Nullens does clearly indicate certain contributions that Bonhoeffer's theology can make to the field of environmental ethics.[15] Concretely, he takes note of Bonhoeffer's deft navigation between the extremes of radicalism and compromise, the christocentric bearing of his ethics (which concentrate on Christ's incarnation, crucifixion, and resurrection), as well as his twin concepts of the ultimate and the penultimate. The connections between these elements of Bonhoeffer's theology and environmental ethics that Nullens calls attention to are undoubtedly important and will certainly need to figure as elements of any serious project dealing with the link between Bonhoeffer and environmental ethics. They could, nevertheless, be worked out in much greater detail than Nullens, in the context of his dissertation, was able to devote to them; in addition, they could be further complemented by other elements and concepts found in Bonhoeffer's theology.

The third scholar to tease out connections between Bonhoeffer's theology and the ecological crisis is Larry L. Rasmussen. Rasmussen is both

12. Hoogstraten, "Fundamenten voor een theologische milieu-ethiek," 42–64.

13. Burtness, *Shaping the Future*.

14. Nullens, "Leven volgens Gaia's normen?"

15. Ibid., 199–206.

a well-known scholar of Bonhoeffer and a noted authority in the field of environmental ethics; as such, he is ideally equipped to address the subject. A number of his works deal specifically with the theme presently under consideration. The first of these texts can be found in a chapter entitled "Song of Songs," in his celebrated book *Earth Community, Earth Ethics*.[16] In this chapter, Rasmussen uses Bonhoeffer's theology in order to call out for and foster a greater Christian love for the earth. He offers a detailed account of Bonhoeffer's personal affirmation of the earth, and he provides a sensitive commentary on some key texts in Bonhoeffer's corpus dealing explicitly with nature. He nevertheless does not engage with everything that Bonhoeffer has to say about nature; he devotes no sustained attention, for example, to Bonhoeffer's exegetical lectures on Gen 1–3, which, as we shall see later on, are clearly pertinent to the topic. Despite its relatively limited scope, the chapter does develop an account of crucial elements in Bonhoeffer's approach to the earth. Later on, Rasmussen also published further essays on the same subject, expanding his argument.[17]

After Rasmussen, the next scholar to take up the challenge of connecting Bonhoeffer and environmental ethics was Peter Manley Scott. Like Rasmussen, Scott also wrote about the subject on more than one occasion. In his first publication on the matter,[18] he consciously seeks to build upon Rasmussen's argument and to engage more directly than Rasmussen had done with Bonhoeffer's writings on nature. He focusses much of his attention on Bonhoeffer's anthropocentric approach to nature, which he perceives to be inherently problematic. After endeavoring to show that this approach fails to do justice to Bonhoeffer's theology of sociality, he accordingly tries to correct it by means of that self-same theology of sociality. Apart from the question of whether or not it is possible, let alone necessary, to correct Bonhoeffer's anthropocentrism, it is Scott's limitation to the subjects of the theology of sociality and anthropocentrism that keeps him from examining other contributions that Bonhoeffer has to offer to environmental ethics. More recently, Scott wrote another article on Bonhoeffer's concept of nature where he further develops the arguments made in his earlier article.[19] He

---

16. Rasmussen, *Earth Community*, 295–316.

17. Rasmussen, "Bonhoeffer's Song of Songs," 186–93; ibid., "The Whole of Earthly Life," 68–78; and ibid., "Bonhoeffer and the Anthropocene," 941–54.

18. Scott, "Christ, Nature, Sociality," 413–30.

19. Scott, "Postnatural Humanity? Bonhoeffer, Creaturely Freedom, and the Mystery of Reconciliation in Creation," 111–34. This essay has since been reprinted with a different title: ibid., "Postnatural Humanity? Bonhoeffer on Freedom and Order in Creation," 11–35.

also introduces Bonhoeffer's concept of the divine mandates into the discussion and draws out the latter's relevance for environmental ethics.

The next author to write on Bonhoeffer in the context of environmental ethics is Stephen J. Plant.[20] His contribution appears in the context of a compendium gathering together the work of major theologians on the themes of creation and salvation in the context of the current ecological crisis. His article is significantly shorter than any of the attempts listed above, which is easily understandable, given that Plant set out only to provide an overview of these in Bonhoeffer's work. After a short introduction to Bonhoeffer's biography, the text proceeds to examine how, in his thought, creation and redemption are closely linked; it deals in particular with the text of Bonhoeffer's book *Creation and Fall* (to which, in what follows, I will refer as *CF*), as well as themes from Bonhoeffer's *Ethics*, and closes with a reflection on Bonhoeffer's thoughts on living *etsi Deus non daretur* ("as if God does not exist").

Another attempt to describe the promise of Bonhoeffer's theology in the context of the ecological crisis has been made by Benjamin Burkholder, in an article published in 2013.[21] It is a long article and represents the most thorough transposition of Bonhoeffer's theology into ecology to date. Burkholder's aim is apologetic in nature: in opposition to those claiming that much of the content of the Christian faith would need to be dispensed with before one could arrive at an ecologically friendly faith, he argues that it is possible to continue adhering to the Christian tradition, even (and especially) in light of the environmental crisis. He focuses on Bonhoeffer's theology as a case in point, arguing that "Bonhoeffer crafts his theology in an ecologically sensitive direction . . . while retaining large portions of the Christian tradition and remaining faithful to the biblical texts."[22] Specifically, he identifies Bonhoeffer's concept of Christ-reality, as well as other concepts from his anthropology, soteriology, and eschatology, as valuable resources for current environmental ethics. His approach, then, is a very broad one, which precludes him from engaging critically either with Bonhoeffer's theology or with environmental ethics; indeed, the framework of his study only allows him to arrive at brief indications of the value and possible applications of the various concepts of Bonhoeffer's theology. Due to its engagement with a number of key concepts, it nevertheless constitutes an important and very serious attempt to transpose Bonhoeffer's theology into environmental ethics.

---

20. Plant, "Dietrich Bonhoeffer (1906–1945)," 92–96.

21. Burkholder, "Christological Foundations," 338–56.

22. Ibid., 340.

Also in 2013, Newton Millan Cloete finished his—unpublished—ThM thesis, entitled "Hamartology and Ecology: A Critical Assessment of Dietrich Bonhoeffer's View on the Nature of Sin," written under supervision of well-known ecotheologian Ernst M. Conradie.[23] In this thesis, Cloete focuses primarily on the question what contribution Bonhoeffer's view on sin might make to contemporary ecotheology. Like Scott did before, he proposes a reinterpretation of Bonhoeffer's anthropocentrism in the context of ecology. At the same time, he finds value in Bonhoeffer's thoughts on human bodiliness and in his specific outworking of human dominion over nature.

In 2014, Willem Roskam wrote an article on the subject—he too considers Bonhoeffer's theology to be a valuable resource for ecotheology.[24] He focusses on his concept of Christ-reality as a means of coming to see human beings and animals as one, interconnected community. In addition, Roskam discusses the contribution that Bonhoeffer's theology of responsibility can make to human behavior towards nature, and animals in particular. Also in 2014, Dianne Rayson, and Terence Lovat, wrote an article on Bonhoeffer, specifically in the context of global warming.[25] They argue that Bonhoeffer's Christology harbors an implicit eco-theological ethic, which they then compare with the "natural theology" offered by Gandhi.

The most recent effort to bring Bonhoeffer's theology to bear on environmental ethics was made by Adrian Langdon.[26] Accepting the charge often made that (Christian) anthropocentrism lies at the root of the ecological crisis, he seeks to overcome this anthropocentrism by focusing attention to the theological anthropologies of Barth as well as Bonhoeffer. Regarding Bonhoeffer, he argues that particularly his account of human embodiment proves helpful as it stresses human beings' connection with, and dependence and interrelationality with the rest of nature.

Apart from these specific engagements with Bonhoeffer's theology in the context of environmental ethics,[27] Bonhoeffer's name is also often mentioned in passing in works dealing with the connection between theology

---

23. Cloete, "Hamartology and Ecology."

24. Roskam, "Bonhoeffers posthumanistische christologie," 110–20.

25. Rayson and Lovat, "'Lord of the (Warming) World,'" 57–74.

26. Langdon, "Embedded Existence," 59–77.

27. While no sustained engagement, noteworthy in this context is also the way Moltmann connects Bonhoeffer's theology with environmental ethics, specifically focusing on Bonhoeffer's appeal to remain loyal to the earth. See Moltmann, "Theologie mit Dietrich Bonhoeffer," 19–25; and ibid., *Ethics of Hope*, esp. 118–19.

and environmental ethics.[28] This speaks to the wide appeal of Bonhoeffer's theology and, at the same time, stimulates more sustained attempts at developing a thoroughgoing connection between his theology and environmental ethics.

Methodology

Bonhoeffer lived and worked in a time when there was no awareness of the environmental crisis that was then in the process of taking shape, and, as a consequence, no ethical or theological disciplines were devoted to addressing it. As such, any effort to apply his theology to the field of environmental ethics requires a hermeneutical process, namely, a *translation*, both between Bonhoeffer's historical context and that of our own, and between his theology and contemporary developments in environmental ethics. The method that I shall adopt for making this translation is a particular form of the general method of correlation. Here in this part of the introductory chapter, I will outline a broader description of this method. Firstly, I will detail some of the different methodologies used in other attempts to translate the thought of individual theologians into the field of ecology. As I shall argue, these proposals each use one form or another of the general method of correlation. In the second part, I will enter into this method's background, as well as some of the criticisms that have been formulated against it. In the third and final part, I will outline a particular variant of the method of correlation, which I shall apply in the present monograph; if I find this variant to be helpful and advantageous, it is on account both of its critical interaction with other authors and of the way that it addresses the criticisms that have been levelled against the method.

Translating the Work of Individual Theologians Towards Environmental Ethics: Different Proposals

There is by no means a consensus—let alone very much discussion—concerning the method of translating the theological concepts and ideas of particular theologians into current discussions in environmental ethics. Indeed, the entire field remains relatively uncharted at the moment. At times, the necessity of developing a thoroughgoing methodology of translation—particularly insofar as the thought of theologians writing *prior* to the

---

28. See, for example, Conradie, *An Ecological Christian Anthropology*; McFague, *A New Climate for Theology*; and Northcott, "Perils and Dangers," 75–88.

emergence of awareness of the ecological crisis is concerned—even seems to be expressly denied. For example, as we saw above, in Burkholder's application of Bonhoeffer's theology to environmental ethics, he asserts that "Bonhoeffer crafts his theology in an ecologically sensitive direction."[29] And a bit further on, he argues, along much the same lines, that Bonhoeffer makes "ecologically amenable emendations."[30] Burkholder's claim is formulated rather precisely—he does not actually claim that Bonhoeffer crafted his theology with ecology in mind, only that he *happened* to craft it in a direction that is ecologically sensitive. Yet while that indeed is the case, it is still necessary to take methodological steps to bring this theology into current discussions in environmental ethics.

This process is often neglected in proposals to make the theology of individual theologians relevant for ecology. This is especially true of the conceptual translations proposed in many essays and articles.[31] In contrast, when authors bring the work of individual theologians to bear on environmental ethics in the context of monographs, they often give much more thought to their methodology.

Jame Schaefer, for example, develops her own methodology for translating the theology of patristic and medieval theologians into the context of ecotheology. Indeed, she already indicates the general direction of her methodology by the subtitle of her introductory chapter: "Reading the Catholic Theological Tradition through an Ecological Lens."[32] As she explains in that chapter, "[t]he ongoing degradation of Earth requires the fullest possible examination of our tradition in the quest for expressions of faith that are *relevant* to the condition of Earth, *coherent* with current knowledge about the world, and *helpful* for addressing the ecological concerns that plague our planet."[33] In concrete terms, she proposes a five-step methodology. Her first step consists in exploring concepts in the theology of patristic and medieval theologians that, to her mind, possess ecological promise. Secondly, she describes the philosophical and, on occasion, historical background in which these concepts took shape. Given the unavoidable existence of vast differences in background and context—particularly those separating the patristic and medieval periods—Schaefer's third step is to seek what she refers to as "coherence." Interestingly, according to her understanding of coherence,

29. Burkholder, "Christological Foundations," 340.

30. Ibid.

31. As cases in point, see the interpretative essays in the second part of Horrell et al., *Ecological Hermeneutics*.

32. Schaefer, *Theological Foundations*, 1–16.

33. Ibid., 2; italics original.

it should not be found internally (i.e. in the writings of the different patristic and medieval authors whom she treats), but externally. As she explains, "[T]he coherence of their concepts for our time must be determined by their ability to appeal intellectually to the faithful today."[34] In other words, to give an example, it is in terms of the way in which the theological conception of creation's praise of God can be made intelligible in the context of contemporary science that the concept's coherence is established. She accepts as a matter of course that, in order for this coherence to be attained, these concepts will have to be "reconstructed" or "enhanced"[35] in certain ways. The fourth step concerns the concept's relevance. In this case, Schaefer endeavors to show how the reconstructed concepts, derived originally from patristic and medieval theology, are relevant to environmental ethics "on the ground,"[36] that is, for the practice of environmental action. The fifth and final step consists in identifying the "helpfulness" of the concepts for ecology. In her own words, "this step leads to the identification of a *basic behavior pattern* that a reconstructed patristic/medieval concept suggests."[37]

Another approach is set out by Willis Jenkins in his frequently referenced *Ecologies of Grace*.[38] He starts off by investigating how Christian practitioners and leaders engaged in environmental ethics draw on their Christian traditions as resources for this engagement. Specifically, he focuses on how Christians relate different perspectives of salvation to their environmental action. In his own words, in his work he "follows three major contour lines, showing how several distinct strategies make environmental issues matter for Christian experience by situating them within one of three ecologies of grace: redemption, sanctification, or deification."[39] Jenkins lists a number of reasons for his focus on soteriology, one of which is the fact that soteriologies often form the underlying roots of many religious (and other) worldviews. The reason that this matters, as he argues (in quoting from Rasmussen) is that "ethics and cosmology are inextricable, indissoluble."[40] In total, he discerns three "practical strategies" used by environmental practitioners, namely, 1) the strategy of nature's standing, 2) the strategy of

34. Ibid., 6.

35. Ibid.

36. In the actual outworking of her presentation, Schaefer devotes minimal attention to this step in order to keep her project from overspilling its bounds. However, she does commend her readers to engage in it. See ibid.

37. Ibid.; italics original.

38. Jenkins, *Ecologies of Grace*.

39. Ibid., 4.

40. Rasmussen, "Cosmology and Ethics," 178. Quoted in Jenkins, *Ecologies of Grace*, 12.

moral agency, and 3) the strategy of ecological subjectivity. Having outlined these three secular strategies, he then identifies three Christian strategies that have been developed in response to these, namely, 1) the strategy of ecojustice, 2) the strategy of Christian stewardship, and 3) the strategy of ecological spirituality. Jenkins refers to these as "ecologies of grace" because he recognizes soteriological concepts at work in them. In the first strategy (viz., ecojustice), he recognizes a soteriology focused on redemption. He sees the second (viz., Christian stewardship) in connection with the soteriological concept of sanctification, and the third (viz., ecological spirituality) with that of deification. In his work, Jenkins seeks to strengthen these three strategies by bringing the thought of some major Christian theologians to bear on them. He correlates the strategy of ecojustice with the theology of Thomas Aquinas, that of Christian stewardship with the theology of Karl Barth, and that of ecological spirituality with the theologies of both Maximus the Confessor and Sergei Bulgakov.[41]

Another important contribution in this regard is made by Sigmund Bergmann. In his monograph, Bergmann translates the theology of Gregory of Nazianzus into the field environmental ethics, focusing specifically on the latter's conception of salvation.[42] His approach consists in three parts. In the first part, he outlines the ecological challenge to theology. Secondly, he focuses specifically on Gregory's theology, dealing both with its context as well as Gregory's description of the relationship between God and the world. In the third part, he correlates Gregory's theology (or more specifically, his soteriology) with concepts issuing from a number of different ecotheologians. In particular, he focuses on the ecotheologies of John B. Cobb Jr., Günter Altner, Jürgen Moltmann, Christian Link, Gerhard Liedke, Ulrich Duchrow, Sallie McFague, Rosemary Radford Ruether, as well as authors writing within the traditions of Modern Orthodoxy, and African theology (most notably K. M. George and Harvey Sindima).

All three of the approaches outlined above rely on a form of correlation—either implicitly or explicitly, they all claim that Christian traditions, crystalized in the work of individual theologians, can contribute answers to the questions raised by the ecological crisis.[43] The present monograph will

41. Jenkins is not the only scholar to approach environmental ethics within the perspective of salvation. Ernst Conradie follows a similar track in a book dealing with the potential contributions that the theology of Abraham Kuyper could make to ecotheology. Conradie focusses specifically on Kuyper's concept of "common grace" (a soteriological concept) in this regard. See Conradie, "Creation and Salvation," 95–135.

42. Bergmann, *Creation Set Free*.

43. This particular way of bringing Christian theology into relation with environmental ethics has been made explicit by Bergmann. See Bergmann, *Creation Set Free*, 323–52.

also apply one form of the method of correlation. Before outlining how this method will be employed in the following pages, however, it is imperative first to describe it more fully, to indicate both its background and its developments, and to engage with it critically.

The Method of Correlation: Background and Criticisms

The method of correlation first originated in the "Vermittlungstheologie" of the 19th century. As Francis Schüssler Fiorenza summarizes, the goal of this movement was "to mediate between the traditional theological starting point of Scripture and Schleiermacher's starting point of religious experience."[44] However, it was primarily through the use that Paul Tillich made of the method that it came to be known in systematic theology. Indeed, it figures as one of the defining features of Tillich's theology and functions as an important cornerstone for it. A clear and concise statement of the method can be found in the first volume of his *Systematic Theology*.[45] In this text, Tillich argues that the method of correlation "makes an analysis of the human situation out of which the existential questions arise, and it demonstrates that the symbols used in the Christian message are the answers to these questions."[46] Tillich also makes the further point that theology had, in fact, always employed some form or another of correlation. To illustrate this, he refers to the opening lines of Calvin's *Institutes*, where Calvin makes the point that the knowledge of God and the knowledge of humankind are interrelated.[47] Tillich then goes into an explication of the ins and outs of the method. He makes the case that, before all else, it should begin with

44. See Fiorenza, "The Method of Correlation," 55. Fiorenza refers to Holte, *Die Vermittlungstheologie*.

45. See Tillich, "The Method of Correlation," 59–66. These pages can be seen as representing a further development of an earlier form of Tillich's thoughts on theological methodology. See Tillich, "The Problem of Theological Method," 16–26.

46. Tillich, "The Method of Correlation," 62.

47. Calvin, *Institutes of the Christian Religion*, § 1.1.1. Tillich's observation that Calvin discerns a correlation between God and the human being is correct. The existence of this kind of correlation can be observed in the work of many other theologians. Within the Dutch Reformed tradition, one can point, for example, to Berkhouwer (for a description, see Van Keulen, "G. C. Berkouwer's Principle of Correlation," 97–111; and Berkhof, *Christian Faith*). It should be noted, however, that the way Tillich uses the method of correlation is very different from its use by Calvin and others. Whereas Calvin uses it to describe the relationship between God and human beings, Tillich uses it to describe the relationship between theology (Scripture and tradition) and humanity's contemporary existence. This different application certainly has no antecedent in Calvin.

an analysis of the "human situation," which should draw on all realms of human self-expression. Among these different realms of self-expression, he specifically mentions philosophy, psychology and sociology. Next, according to him, the theologian must formulate an answer to this situation from the perspective of the Christian faith. In a key citation, for instance, he notes that "[t]he Christian message provides the answers to the questions implied in human existence. These answers are contained in the revelatory events on which Christianity is based and are taken by systematic theology *from* the sources, *through* the medium, *under* the norm."[48] Tillich gives particular emphasis to this latter point, asserting that such answers aren't immediately available in human existence; instead, they are spoken *to* this existence. It should nevertheless be noted that this doesn't in any way imply that the Bible or the Christian tradition are pure and simple resources capable of delivering timeless truths to be applied to ever-shifting historical situations. Instead, Tillich insists that "[t]here is a mutual dependence between question and answer. In respect to content the Christian answers are dependent on the revelatory events in which they appear; in respect to form they are dependent on the structure of the questions which they answer."[49]

Tillich's overriding intention with his work on the correlation method was apologetic in nature, namely, to endow theology with greater relevance in an increasingly secular world. In setting out both the shape and the bearing of the method, he can be seen as one of the fathers of contextual theology. His understanding of the method also implies that, when the course of human experience takes a different turn, the specific theology that was articulated by means of the method loses its relevance. This point is noted by John Powell Clayton, who observes that, "[b]y incorporating the present cultural situation into his methodology, Tillich gave to his theology a planned obsolescence which precludes his system's having direct relevance for any but the cultural context in which and for which it was constructed."[50]

Despite Tillich's insistence on the shifting, dialogical nature of the relationship between the human situation and the Christian faith, his method of correlation nevertheless remains rather static in form. In particular, it implies that the Christian faith (embodied in the Christian tradition) contains answers for the human situation; it therefore fails to take into account that the tradition itself is also shaped by the contexts it addresses.[51]

48. Tillich, "The Method of Correlation," 64; italics original.

49. Ibid.

50. Clayton, *The Concept of Correlation*, 5.

51. This is also noted by Bergmann, who writes: "[B]y polarizing question (situation) and answer (tradition), he [Tillich] fails to consider that *every* form of expression

Tillich's method of correlation has been taken up and further developed by David Tracy.[52] In particular, Tracy proves himself capable of overcoming the static nature of Tillich's model by pointing out that the correlation between the contemporary situation and the Christian tradition works both ways: according to him, the Christian tradition doesn't only contain "answers" but *questions* as well—and the same applies to the contemporary situation. What the method of correlation gives shape to, then, is a "model of conversation" between the situation and the tradition, recognizing both the questions and the answers arising from either pole. This slightly revised model is succinctly outlined by Tracy in his well-known definition of the task of theology: "Theology is the attempt to establish mutually critical correlations between an interpretation of the Christian tradition and an interpretation of the contemporary situation."[53]

The method of correlation has not been immune to criticism. While this is not the place for a fully developed critical discussion of the method, I would like to draw attention to some of the key criticisms that have been raised against it. Towards this end, I would like to focus on the presentation of the method put forward by Schüssler Fiorenza, who raises three major criticisms.[54] First of all, Fiorenza argues that the method rests on a faulty distinction between reality itself and the language used to describe that reality. According to him, this erroneously presupposes that, while the language used to describe reality may change, reality itself does not. Secondly, he argues that the method wrongfully assumes the presence of a stable continuity within the pole of the Christian tradition. In his own words, "[i]t does not sufficiently take into account change and non-identity in the development of faith and theology."[55] Thirdly and finally, he points out that the method fails to adequately criticize the Christian tradition, for while it may take issue with certain theological formulations, it does not criticize the underlying "experiences and affirmations" which these formulations express.[56]

In order to ensure that the method of correlation can serve us as a helpful and reliable tool in the work that I have set out, these criticisms need to be addressed. Within the context of this monograph, this applies especially to the second and third points of contention raised by Fiorenza.

---

of the Christian message is also shaped by the historic situation of its origin." Bergmann, *Creation Set Free*, 325; italics original.

52. As examples, see Tracy, *Blessed Rage for Order* and *The Analogical Imagination*.

53. Tracy, "Theological Method," 36. Quoted in Bergmann, *Creation Set Free*, 326.

54. Fiorenza, "The Method of Correlation," 61.

55. Ibid.

56. Ibid.

By articulating a particular form of the method that responds to these criticisms (see the following section), I equip myself with a tool capable of critically relating Bonhoeffer's theology with environmental ethics.

The Application of the Method of Correlation in this Monograph

The form of the correlation method that shall be employed in the present monograph is one in which mutually critical and constructive connections are drawn between Bonhoeffer's theology and environmental ethics.[57] This means that, contrary to Tillich's conception of the method, Bonhoeffer's theology is not conceived of as a pure and simple "answer" to the contemporary problem of the ecological crisis. On the contrary, my use of the method recognizes that, while the contemporary situation does indeed pose a rather pressing question (in the form of the ecological crisis), it also contains certain answers to this question (e.g. in various philosophical proposals put forward by environmental ethicists, or again, in the work of certain eco-theologians). Similarly, while I shall primarily treat Bonhoeffer's theology as a resource for the articulation of certain answers to this question, I also recognize that his theology contains questions—or rather *problems*—in the form of elements that prove to be less helpful, or even potentially harmful, as far as environmental ethics is concerned.[58] However, as the use of the word "primarily" indicates, I shall focus in large part on the ways in which Bonhoeffer's theology can *contribute* to environmental ethics.

In response to the criticisms that Fiorenza raises against the correlation method, it is first of all necessary to indicate the *limitations* of this project: my goal is not to research every single aspect of Bonhoeffer's theology that could potentially contribute to environmental ethics. Even less is it an attempt to develop a full-blown approach to environmental ethics on the basis of Bonhoeffer's theology. In essence, the project's aim is simple: to correlate a number of major themes in the thought of an important, modern theologian (viz., Bonhoeffer) with a number of major debates in

57. It is important to note that I use the method of correlation specifically in the context of relating Bonhoeffer's theology with contemporary environmental ethics. That means that I do not accept it as a more general framework of relating the Christian faith with the contemporary world, nor do I suggest that Bonhoeffer advocated this position. Rather, I use the method of correlation as a heuristic device, for specific use in this context.

58. For example, in chapter 4, I draw attention to the inadequate formulation of certain differences that Bonhoeffer calls attention to between human and non-human animals.

environmental ethics. This is quite similar to Bergmann's aim, which he describes as follows: "I relate the local theology deriving from a *single* situation (in late antiquity) to various local theologies deriving from a *different* situation (in late modernity)."[59] The present project is much the same, aside from one minor difference: instead of the initial "single situation" being that of late antiquity, I shall be focusing on that of Western (or more specifically, German) modernity in the first half of the twentieth century, namely, the context in which Bonhoeffer lived and worked.

As already made clear, the contributions to environmental ethics cannot simply be "read off" of Bonhoeffer's theology, as if they were somehow already present in his works. Rather, the contributions need to be sought out on the conceptual level. In particular, Bonhoeffer's discourses on the relationship between God and the world (which he conceives primarily through Christ) and on the relationship between human beings and the world provide a number of concepts that can contribute to discussions going on in environmental ethics. In order for this process to be carried out appropriately, it is first mandatory to pay careful and critical attention to the three constitutive elements of this correlation: 1) the interpretation of Bonhoeffer's work, 2) my interpretation of a number of texts in environmental ethics, and 3) the perspective from which these two poles are brought into correlation. I shall deal with each of these elements in the following three subsections.

Principles for Interpreting Bonhoeffer

The first pole of the correlation targeted in this monograph is the theology of Bonhoeffer. As many valuable introductions to Bonhoeffer's life and work are already available,[60] I shall forgo giving a similar introduction here. In light of the history of misunderstandings and misinterpretations of Bonhoeffer's theology, it is necessary, however, to lay down a number of guiding principles for my interpretation of his work.

In this monograph, Bonhoeffer will not be taken as a sort of "proto-evangelical" in the way that Georg Huntemann[61] and, more recently, Eric

---

59. Bergmann, *Creation Set Free*, 327; italics original.

60. As for biographies, the most thorough work to date remains Bethge, *Dietrich Bonhoeffer*. For a more concise and recent biography, see Schlingensiepen, *Dietrich Bonhoeffer*. General introductions to Bonhoeffer's theology abound. A few relatively recent examples are those of Dramm, *Dietrich Bonhoeffer*; Plant, *Bonhoeffer*; and Lawrence, *Bonhoeffer*.

61. Huntemann, *The Other Bonhoeffer*.

Metaxas have done.[62] Apart from the fact that it would be anachronistic to label Bonhoeffer's theology in this way, it would also fail to sufficiently take stock of Bonhoeffer's "otherness," as can be seen, for example, in his acceptance of the use of the historical critical method in his reading of the Bible.[63] In the context of my research, elements such as these are neither denied nor reinterpreted, but rather accepted as integral parts of Bonhoeffer's theology. My focus is concerned, rather, with the way that this theology, when taken as a whole, can contribute to environmental ethics.

In the research process leading up to this monograph, I formulated the following principles in order to guide my interpretation of Bonhoeffer:

1. Take Bonhoeffer's entire corpus into account as a whole, without granting more importance, or weight, to one particular work or period of his development over another.

2. Give due consideration to the developments in his work.

3. Read Bonhoeffer's theology in close connection with his biography.

4. Take into account the philosophical and theological background of his works, as well as the political and social context in which he lived and worked.

5. Place the specific concepts into relation with other concepts.

6. Remain in critical dialogue with other Bonhoeffer scholars.

7. Leave room for unresolved tensions within Bonhoeffer's theology.

While these principles do not figure as part of a formalized or "official" way of interpreting Bonhoeffer, they can be seen as explications of a general consensus that has arisen in research into his life and work.[64]

Addressing the Field of Environmental Ethics

Secondly, there is the pole of environmental ethics.[65] While there is a general conception of what this discipline consists in and what it is about, there

62. Metaxas, *Bonhoeffer*. A critical review of Metaxas's book has been written by Green, Review of *Bonhoeffer*.

63. This "otherness" of Bonhoeffer (not only vis-à-vis evangelicalism but also in relation to liberalism) is succinctly sketched out by Zimmerling, *Bonhoeffer als Praktischer Theologe*, 18.

64. See Clark and Mawson, "Introduction," 1–18.

65. Throughout this book, I deliberately choose to transpose Bonhoeffer's theology to environmental ethics, not limiting myself to drawing out the contribution he can make to ecotheology. This choice is based on the directionality of Bonhoeffer's

is remarkably little agreement among scholars over even so basic a question as to what the definition of the discipline should be. My aim here is not to provide a new taxonomy through which to approach the field as a whole or to understand the different, baseline positions that various scholars have adopted.[66] Nor is it the aim of this monograph to develop a novel, full-fledged environmental ethic. On the contrary, my aim is simply to make constructive contributions to a number of debates within this field from the perspective of Bonhoeffer's theology.

A number of different approaches can be adopted in interacting with the field of environmental ethics. Bergmann, for example, correlates the concepts that he identifies in Gregory's theology with the thought of a number of specific ecotheologians. This book will follow a different approach: instead of focusing on the specific formulations of this or that ecotheologian, or ecologist, it focusses on a number of different concepts used throughout the field as a whole, or at least among a number of different writers. In other words, I shall draw much more attention to different issues and problems arising within the field than with the work of any given author. That being said, the work of certain scholars does feature on a consistent basis through this monograph, such as that of Northcott, Moltmann, Conradie and Rasmussen.

Correlating Bonhoeffer's Theology with Environmental Ethics

When correlating Bonhoeffer's theology (or that of any other past theologian) with the current discipline of environmental ethics, two interrelated but distinct processes need to take place. The first is the formal identification of concepts in Bonhoeffer's work that could potentially be correlated with concepts in environmental ethics. This is an "objective" process[67] insofar it can be convincingly shown that the concepts in question bear a certain

---

theology, indicated above: he wanted to speak to the *world*, and not just to Christians. While it is undoubtedly the case that most of the concepts studied in this book apply primarily or even exclusively to Christians, some have a broader relevance, such as his thoughts on technology (see chapter 5).

66. Work along these lines has been undertaken by a number of scholars. See Northcott, *The Environment*, 86–123; and Cochrane, "Environmental Ethics."

67. I am using the word "objective" here on account of the lack of a more suitable alternative. If I place the term in quotation marks, this is to reflect the difficulties surrounding the Cartesian subject-object divide, which has had a significant negative effect on the relationship between human beings and nature. For this reason, I shall carry out a critical analysis of the term in chapter 3 of this monograph.

resemblance to those used in environmental ethics, and thus they present the *possibility* for drawing a correlation.[68] For example, I shall argue later on that a possibility exists for correlating Bonhoeffer's thinking on human relationality and freedom with the debate in environmental ethics concerning the distinction between human and non-human nature. In order to bolster my account, I shall also examine the work of other authors who have drawn attention to such a correlation. This is, however, a purely *formal* identification: it simply notes the possibility of a correlation without going so far as to specify the process itself or its outcome.

The correlation itself is then set out in detail in the related, second process. In contrast to the first, this second step is guided by criteria applied by the interpreter; as a consequence, it is influenced much more strongly by his or her personal, philosophical and theological commitments. This will become clear in the various discussions that I shall enter into with other authors in this book: the critical interaction with other proposals to translate Bonhoeffer's theology into the field of environmental ethics will show that the differing results of these proposals depend on the choices made by the interpreters. Concerning Bonhoeffer's thoughts on human relationality, for example, it will become clear that one interpreter in particular makes the choice to extend this relationality to non-human beings as well. In contrast with this interpreter's proposal, I shall argue that Bonhoeffer's thoughts on relationality only bear relevance for ecology when it is treated as an interhuman concept.[69]

The divergent nature of the results of this correlation process do not imply that the method of correlation itself is unsound—rather, it forms an integral part of the method insofar as it allows for different results to be arrived at in different situations, or based on the differing commitments of the interpreter under consideration. Instead of figuring in modernity's search for the holy grail of "The Truth," the method of correlation reflects the cultural shift to postmodernity, in which the former search is replaced by a general recognition of the contextual nature, not just of specific theologies—such as feminist theology—but of all theological enquiries.[70]

68. Bergmann makes a similar argument when he writes the following: "Insofar as its form is objectively oriented toward specific problems, the method of correlation also accommodates the rational demands made on any hermeneutical undertaking." Bergmann, *Creation Set Free*, 330.

69. It is important to note that in the actual correlations made in chapters 2 through 6 I will only explicate the methodological steps taken when necessary, i.e. when I challenge the choices made by others in correlating Bonhoeffer's theology with environmental ethics.

70. To offer at least one account of this shift, viewed from an evangelical perspective, see Smith, *The Fall of Interpretation*.

At the same time, it is important to point out that this recognition by no means implies that rigorous scholarly standards no longer apply, or that everything boils down to an incommensurable stalemate between different "points of view." Instead, these standards take on a different form: rather than arguing for the "objectivity" of this or that correlation, it is the researcher's responsibility to argue his or her case step by step, explaining the reasons for the choices that he or she makes. In one way or another, each of the three authors treated above take on this responsibility. Schaefer, for example, explains (and thereby seeks to justify) the choices that she makes in correlating specific concepts from patristic and medieval writers with present-day discussions. In those cases where she sees a need to reconstruct a theological concept, such as the goodness of creation, she explains her choice and why she makes it. In doing so, her Roman Catholic background—as well as her personal interpretation and evaluation of it—come clearly into view. Jenkins and Bergmann each follow a different route. Jenkins, on the one hand, uses not one, but three different soteriologies as lenses through which to correlate the work of certain theologians and the field of ecotheology. On the other hand, Bergmann, as we saw already, explicitly constructs his correlation of Gregory's theology with ecotheology through the perspective of liberation theology.

Unlike Jenkins and Bergmann, who make a choice for a particular framework, the present monograph follows the approach chosen by Schaefer in correlating Bonhoeffer and environmental ethics from a specific theological perspective. The perspective used here can best be described as "open evangelical," a term used primarily in the Anglican community (specifically in the UK). In particular, open evangelicalism is committed both to the authority of the Bible and to the centrality of Jesus Christ. At the same time, it is committed to ecumenism and to dialogue between Christianity and other (faith) traditions. It is open to biblical criticism and has a holistic approach to life.[71] This perspective will inform the correlation between Bonhoeffer's theology and environmental ethics. It shows itself, for example, in the acceptance of the theory of evolution as currently being the best available explanation of the origins of species. But it also appears in the choice for a (weak) anthropocentrism in the relationship between human beings and non-human nature—although, as will become clear, this choice too can reasonably be argued for.

The emphasis on the particular nature of this correlative process could be seen to raise the question of just how much relevance this proposal could

---

71. For a description of open evangelicalism, see Kings, "Canal, River and Rapids," 167–84.

bear for those who do not share the author's presuppositions. As already indicated, however, the postmodern turn in theology has led to the insight that all theology is essentially contextualized. Rather than leading to a scattered theological landscape of small, unconnected islands, the recognition of this fact can instead lead to a sort of bricolage—that is, to a mosaic of different, contextual theologies which, in their diversity, give expression to the essential unity of the Christian tradition. In other words, my underlying expectation is that, in Bonhoeffer's theology, as well as in current ecotheologies, the same Christian tradition is expressing itself. As Bergmann puts it in his book on Gregory and ecotheology, he "presuppos[es] that the Christian tradition—as the social memory of interpretations of faith—will come to expression in both poles of the correlation."[72]

Overview of the Monograph

Here in this introductory chapter, I have formulated the research question and outlined the methodology. This final section specifies how I shall present my response to the research question in the following chapters.

Apart from this introduction, the book is composed of six chapters in total. Five of these (viz., chapters 2 through 6) contain the actual correlations between Bonhoeffer's theology and environmental ethics. Although the concepts described there differ from each other in many respects, they can be grouped together under two overarching themes: chapters 2 and 3 deal with concepts from Bonhoeffer's theology concerning the relationship between God and the world, and chapters 4, 5, and 6 treat concepts concerning the relationships between human beings and the natural world, and between human beings themselves. Each of these chapters is composed of two parts: in the first part, a specific concept (or a group of related concepts) from Bonhoeffer's theology will be expounded using the tools of critical scholarship. This will be carried out according to the principles of interpretation formulated in this chapter.[73] Then, in the second part of each chapter, these concepts will be correlated with concepts and debates in environmental ethics.

Chapter 7 will bring the monograph to a close. There, I take stock of the findings of the research project. In addition, I will describe their relevance for environmental ethics, and indicate further prospects for research.

---

72. Bergmann, *Creation Set Free*, 327.

73. While for practical reasons I am making a distinction between different sets of concepts in Bonhoeffer's theology, it will soon become clear just how interconnected they are.

2

Care for the Natural in Light of Christ-Reality

IN THIS CHAPTER I TURN MY ATTENTION TO A NUMBER OF CONCEPTS IN Bonhoeffer's theology that find their fullest expression in the manuscripts of his *Ethics*, which will therefore be at the heart of the discussion in this chapter. What these concepts have in common is their christological orientation—Bonhoeffer orders his ethics around the assertion that, in Christ, God decisively enters the world and directs it towards himself, towards the ultimate. This will be described in the first part. The way Bonhoeffer works this out is unique, and—as I will argue in the second part of the chapter— opens up promising perspectives for ecology. There I will indicate concrete ways in which the concepts in Bonhoeffer's *Ethics* provide direction for the elaboration of an environmental ethics.

Bonhoeffer on Living in Accordance with Christ

In this first part, I describe a number of key concepts in Bonhoeffer's *Ethics*. These are: 1) the concept of Christ-reality, 2) the distinction Bonhoeffer makes between three moments in the relation between Christ and the world, 3) the twin concepts of the ultimate and the penultimate, and 4) the concept of the natural. Each of these concepts will be described in a different section. Although my focus lies primarily on Bonhoeffer's *Ethics*, I will take his other work into consideration as well. In presenting these concepts, I will pay special attention to the inherent eschatological dimension that permeates them.

Bonhoeffer's Concept of Christ-reality

If one had to summarize Bonhoeffer's lifelong theological concerns in one word, then "Christ-reality" ("Christuswirklichkeit") would be the best candidate. It is the most fundamental concept of his theology and forms the—often implicit—foundation of all his theological work. First its central formulation in the *Ethics* will be described. The second section will focus attention on the context in which Bonhoeffer developed it. Thirdly and finally, the concept's eschatological direction will be described.

CHRIST-REALITY AS A FOUNDATIONAL CONCEPT OF BONHOEFFER'S THEOLOGY

Bonhoeffer offers the most explicit and thoroughgoing treatment of Christ-reality in the first manuscript of his *Ethics*, entitled "Christ, Reality, and Good: Christ, Church, and World."[1] It sets out with a critical assessment of the underlying presuppositions behind the basic questions of Christian ethical thinking, namely "'How can I be good?' and 'How can I do something good?'"[2] According to Bonhoeffer, these questions presuppose that the ultimate goal of Christian ethics is the betterment of the human person or the world as a whole. Instead, an entirely different question must be asked: "What is the will of God?"[3] This question presupposes that the ultimate goal is that the reality of God manifests itself everywhere as the ultimate reality. Bonhoeffer further clarifies his thought by insisting that the statement that God alone is the ultimate reality is not meant to sublimate the actual world, or to bring about the perfection of a profane worldview, but instead to voice a faithful "yes" to God's revelation in Jesus Christ. According to him, "God" should not be understood metaphysically, but as revealed in Christ: "*In Jesus Christ the reality of God has entered into the reality of this world.*"[4] All conceptions of reality that ignore Christ, as Bonhoeffer says, are abstractions. Christ is not an ideal or an ethical norm—rather, he is reality itself. This means that recognizing God as the ultimate reality is seeing the world as it is—it is only through this recognition that we can see things as they are.

Bonhoeffer is quick to point out that this in no way leads to a Christ-centered monism in which every difference collapses into Christ, and where ethical thinking ends up losing its function. Instead, he asserts that, although the contrasting realms of "worldly" and "Christian," or "supernatural" and "natural," give the impression of being static opposites, they are fundamentally one in Christ, even though, at the same time, "Christian" reality is not *identical* with worldly reality, nor the natural order with the supernatural

1. DBWE 6:47–75.
2. DBWE 6:47.
3. DBWE 6:47.
4. DBWE 6:54; italics original.

order, or the profane with the sacred. On the contrary, their unity is "given only in the Christ-reality, and that means only as accepted by faith in this ultimate reality."[5]

In this light, the task of Christian ethics is to let God's reality, as revealed in Christ, manifest itself in God's creation. So instead of seeing Christ as an "idea" to be realized by the ethical action of human beings, Bonhoeffer formulates the ethical task as follows: "What matters is *participating in the reality of God and the world in Jesus Christ today*, and doing so in such a way that I never experience the reality of God without the reality of the world, nor the reality of the world without the reality of God."[6]

With his concept of Christ-reality, Bonhoeffer makes a unique contribution to ethical thinking. As already indicated, this is the most fundamental concept in his theology. It is a rich concept with quite a complex history of development, which has been treated by many able commentators.[7] In the context of this chapter, I would like to expound upon two aspects of the concept in particular: 1) the intricate relationship between Christ-reality and the context of the historical period in which Bonhoeffer lived, as well as, more specifically, his activities in the resistance, and 2) the often overlooked eschatological dimension of the concept.

CHRIST-REALITY AS A POLEMICAL CONCEPT IN THE CONTEXT OF NAZISM

First of all, it is important to consider that Bonhoeffer's concept of Christ-reality is—at least in part—an answer to the pressing problem of his time: the lack of Christian resistance against National Socialism in Germany, which was theologically justified with reference to Luther's two kingdoms doctrine. This has been pointed out, among many other commentators, by the editors of *Ethics*, who note that, although the two kingdoms theory itself nearly disappeared after Luther, it regained a great deal of attention during the German church struggle in 1933, when the Lutheran churches made it a confessional issue.[8] This happened in two ways. The "German Christians" ("Deutsche Christen"), on the one hand, interpreted the doctrine in such a

---

5. DBWE 6:59.

6. DBWE 6:55; italics original.

7. See, for example, Mayer, *Christuswirklichkeit*, 195–97; Feil, *The Theology of Dietrich Bonhoeffer*, 84–90; and Kang, "Von der 'Nachfolge' zur 'Ethik der Verantwortung,'" 110–19.

8. DBWE 6:60, editorial footnote 48.

way that they could actively support the Nazi government.[9] On the other hand, for other Lutheran churches, the two kingdoms doctrine served to reject responsibility for injustices in the political realm: "The argument that the church is not allowed to obstruct worldly government, *Obrigkeit*, became a means of self-justification and excuse by all those who without protest accepted open governmental injustice."[10] Bonhoeffer refused both the sanctioning of the Nazi state by the German Christians and the retreat inside the church by the other Lutheran churches. In this light, Bonhoeffer's insistence on the *one* Christ-reality appears in its proper context.[11]

It is nevertheless important to point out that he does not criticize the two kingdoms theory as such, so much as the misuses to which it was applied in his time. Reality, as he insists, is undivided in Christ, even though there is still adequate room to establish relative distinctions. A properly conceived two kingdoms doctrine is one of these distinctions, and in another manuscript of his *Ethics*, "Heritage and Decay," Bonhoeffer employs it explicitly.[12] It is therefore false to claim, as James Burtness[13] and An Il Kang[14] have done, that Bonhoeffer categorically refutes any kind of two kingdoms theory.

There is not only a clear relation between Bonhoeffer's concept of Christ-reality and the historical context of his time, but also between the concept and his own resistance activities. The concept personally motivated Bonhoeffer to take responsibility in the public sphere, that is, in the dark times of National Socialism. As Rasmussen points out, "Dietrich Bonhoeffer's resistance activity was his Christology enacted with utter seriousness. Bonhoeffer's resistance was the existential playing out of christological

---

9. See esp. Moses, "Bonhoeffer's Repudiation of War Theology," 354–70; and Nicolaisen, "'Anwendung' der Zweireichelehre," 15–26.

10. DBWE 6:60, editorial footnote 48; italics original.

11. See Prüller-Jagenteufel, *Befreit zur Verantwortung*, 290. See also Wiebering, "Zwei Räume—Zwei Reiche?," 73–85; and Klemperer, "Beyond Luther?," 184–98.

12. He says there: "There are two kingdoms [Zwei Reiche], which, as long as the earth remains, must never be mixed together, yet never torn apart: the kingdom of the proclaimed word of God and the kingdom of the sword, the kingdom of the church and the kingdom of the world, the kingdom of the spiritual office and the kingdom of worldly authority." DBWE 6:112. The distinction that Bonhoeffer makes between the two kingdoms theory as such and its misuse is skilfully described by Mayer, *Christuswirklichkeit*, 200–204. For a good overview of the two kingdoms theory in the context of its historical development, see Honecker, "Zweireichelehre und Königsherrschaft Christi," 14–31; and Wolf, "Köningsherrschaft Christi," 75–97.

13. Burtness, *Shaping the Future*, 38–43.

14. Kang, "Von der 'Nachfolge' zur 'Ethik der Verantwortung,'" 110–19.

themes. Changes and shifts in his Christology were at the same time changes and shifts in the character of his resistance."[15]

CHRIST-REALITY AS AN ESCHATOLOGICAL CONCEPT

Secondly, a clear eschatological dimension underpins Bonhoeffer's concept, a fact which has often been overlooked. That is indicative of a more general tendency to downplay the importance of eschatology in Bonhoeffer—indeed, the theme has received relatively scant scholarly attention.[16] Some even claim that Bonhoeffer does not even outline an eschatology.[17]

On this count, it is both helpful and important to give a brief sketch of the development of eschatology in Bonhoeffer's theology.[18] At various points throughout his theological career, Bonhoeffer wrote specifically on the theme of eschatology. As a theology student, he wrote two papers on the subject.[19] And in his two dissertations, he focuses in a sustained fashion on the eschatology of the church. In *Sanctorum Communio* (to which, in what follows, I will refer as *SC*), for instance, he asserts: "Christian eschatology is essentially *eschatology of the church-community [Gemeindeeschatologie]*. It is concerned with the fulfillment of the church and of the individual within it."[20]

Bonhoeffer further qualifies this claim by adding that the Kingdom of God encompasses much more than the church alone; as he insists, it incorporates culture and nature as well. If he focuses specifically on the eschatology of the church, this is simply because the church occupies the central

---

15. Rasmussen, *Reality and Resistance*, 15.

16. Although the theme is mentioned in major Bonhoeffer-studies (see Mayer, *Christuswirklichkeit*, 99–103; and Abromeit, *Geheimnis Christi*, 93–95), it is rarely worked out in a systematic fashion. An exception on this point is found in Rasmussen, *Dietrich Bonhoeffer: His Significance*, esp. 75–88. A major study of Bonhoeffer's eschatology has also been carried out by Manrodt, "The Role of Eschatology," but, due to the fact that his dissertation has not been published, it has received little attention. It seems that Bonhoefer scholars have only very recently begun to pay more sustained attention to the theme of eschatology in his work, as will become clear further on.

17. Schmidt, for example, says: "Eschatology remains all the more the total horizon, both near and far, of a world which itself is no longer the place and content of God's saving deeds, rather it seems to be devaluated to a redemptive-historical no-man's land." Schmidt, "The Cross of Reality?," 223. See also Honecker, *Die Kirche als Gestalt und Ereignis*, 156. For an overview of other critics, see Mayer *Christuswirklichkeit*, 100.

18. See also Lindsay, "Bonhoeffer's Eschatology," 290–302.

19. "Paper on Church and Eschatology," DBWE 9:310–24; and "Paper on Early Lutheran Eschatology," DBWE 9:385–94.

20. DBWE 1:283; italics original.

focus of *SC*. Considering the scope of *SC*, this choice is entirely understandable. There is nevertheless one other problem with the eschatology that Bonhoeffer develops in *SC*, which Mayer correctly points out, namely that it appears to be merely added on to his ecclesiology, and does not form an intrinsic and necessary part of the work.[21] This changes already in *Act and Being* (to which, in what follows, I will refer as *AB*), however. This highly abstract, philosophical work culminates in a definition of being-in-Christ as a future-directed becoming, in which the fundamental dichotomy of faith as either an *actus directus* or an *actus reflexus* is overcome. There, Bonhoeffer points to the child as a paradigm of the future: "To-let-oneself-be-defined by means of the future is the eschatological possibility of the child."[22] Of this work it is incorrect to see the section on eschatology functioning as a mere addition, as Mayer maintains,[23] because without it the entire book would lose its focus. "The new heaven and the new earth" are still not a topic in *AB*, however. This changes in his lectures on Christology, where, as we shall see in chapter 3, Bonhoeffer describes Christ not just as the center of human existence, but also as the center of history and nature, and where he looks forward to the redemption of nature in the eschaton.[24] It is this broad vision of the eschaton that again features in his *Ethics*.

Bonhoeffer explicates this eschatological dimension of Christ-reality further on in his *Ethics*, in the manuscript entitled "History and Good [1]."[25] There he notes: "The world remains world. But it only does so because God has taken care of it and declared it to be under God's rule. The world must end before the kingdom of God can come. However, this very world that has been condemned in Jesus Christ is in Christ also accepted and loved and is promised a new heaven and a new earth."[26] This is a key citation, which proves that, for Bonhoeffer, reality as Christ-reality does not do away with the tension between the "already" and the "not yet," but in fact presents Bonhoeffer's own theological appropriation of that tension. Christ, in his coming to this world, has established his lordship over it. We presently live in a time of expectation of the definitive fulfillment of his kingship, at the end of times. This clearly shows that his conception of the one Christ-reality is eschatological through and through.

21. Mayer, *Christuswirklichkeit*, 101.

22. DBWE 2:159.

23. Mayer, *Christuswirklichkeit*, 101.

24. DBWE 12:327. See also the reference to Jesus' coming at the end of the lectures: DBWE 12:360.

25. DBWE 6:219–45.

26. DBWE 6:224.

This was already discerned by Benjamin Reist, who noted that, in Bonhoeffer's *Ethics*, "[a]n ethically presented eschatology replaces a mystical one."[27] Reist outlines the content of this "ethical eschatology" as follows: "To discern the God who is real in Jesus Christ in the midst of the fast-approaching tomorrows is an ethical task . . . The theme of the ethics of the reality of Christ is therefore always comprised of the search for an ever-renewing fulfillment. The Kingdom of God is always at hand."[28] By formulating the eschatological dimension in this way, it seems as if, according to Reist, Bonhoeffer has a purely actualistic Christology. This impression grows even stronger when Reist writes that "the fulfillment of the purposes of the God who is real in Jesus Christ coincides with the liberation of the men who are commanded to be free before him."[29] In this instance, Bonhoeffer's Christology appears as a program to be carried out, rather than as a gospel of liberation already realized on the cross. Further on in this chapter, I will critique this interpretation of Bonhoeffer in more detail. For the moment, let it suffice for me to point out that, in spite of the actualistic fallacy of his interpretation, Reist is right to bring out the eschatological dimension of *Ethics*.

This eschatological dimension is described in a more nuanced fashion by Hans Pfeifer, who notes that, for Bonhoeffer, "ethics is also concerned with eschatology. In a Christian act, it is a question of Christ's taking shape in the world. Bonhoeffer uses this concept to express Christ's act of expiation; it is not primarily an ethical concept, for representation or deputyship is impossible for mankind."[30] Recently, Philip Ziegler has also made an interesting contribution to the study of Bonhoeffer's eschatology. He relates the concept of Christ-reality to recent New Testament scholarship, which asserts that, for Paul, "apocalypse" stands for the redemptive inbreaking of Christ into the world, an event in which the world, reality as such, is fundamentally remade.[31] Ziegler makes reference to J. Louis Martyn, J. Christiaan Beker, Martinus de Boer, and others in this respect. "Apocalyptic, on this view," as he writes, "is more than mere rhetoric; it is a mode of discourse fit to give voice to the radical ontological and epistemological consequences of the gospel, consequences intensely relevant to the doing of Christian

---

27. Reist, *The Promise of Bonhoeffer*, 120.

28. Ibid.

29. Ibid.

30. Pfeifer, "The Forms of Justification," 35. See also ibid., "Dietrich Bonhoeffers 'Interim' Ethik," 104.

31. Ziegler, "Dietrich Bonhoeffer," 579–94.

ethics."[32] According to Ziegler, this is exactly what Bonhoeffer attempts to describe with his concept of Christ-reality.[33] The eschatological dimension of this concept, as well as its consequences for Christian ethics, are further specified by Bonhoeffer in his twin concepts of penultimate and ultimate, which I discuss further on.

Three Moments in the Relation between Christ and the World

In the previous section we have seen how, for Bonhoeffer, Christ is the ground of all reality. We saw how this does not mean that "Christ" is just another name for all that is, such that all differences are collapsed into a single Christ-centered monism. Instead, Bonhoefer discerns three different moments in the relation between Christ and the world. As with Christ-reality, firstly the central formulation of this threepartition in *Ethics* will be described. Secondly, the development of the three different moments in Bonhoeffer will be narrated. This is followed, thirdly, by an explication of how the three moments relate to each other and, fourthly, by an elaboration of the underlying Christology. Fifthly and finally, like with his concept of the one Christ-reality, the eschatological dimension to the threepartition will be expounded.

Christ's Threefold Relationship to the World: Its Central Formulation in the Ethics

In the second manuscript of his *Ethics*, "Ethics as Formation,"[34] Bonhoeffer discerns three moments in the relation between Christ and the world: incarnation, crucifixion, and resurrection. Christ's relation to the world—of which he himself is the ground—can be summarized in these three moments and, as the title of the manuscript implies, human beings are to be formed in relation to these moments.

Concerning Christ as incarnate, he says that Jesus, the God-man, steps directly into the middle between God and the world. This is an act of God's

---

32. Ibid., 580.

33. See also Ziegler, "'Voices in the Night,'" 115–45; and ibid., "Eschatology and Secularity," 124–38. Ziegler's thoughts have been picked up by others, for example by Christopher Holmes, who—referring to Ziegler—notes: "Recent Bonhoeffer scholarship has demonstrated the extent to which his Ethics is funded by a rich christological realism replete with eschatological resonances." Holmes, "The Indivisible Whole of God's Reality,'" 283.

34. DBWE 6:76–102.

immeasurable love. Only this love can overcome reality, as Bonhoeffer says. It is not ideals or ethical programs that overcome the fallenness of the world, but the embrace of God: "In an incomprehensible reversal of all righteous and pious thought, God declares himself as guilty toward the world and thereby extinguishes the guilt of the world. God treads the way of humble reconciliation and thereby sets the world free. God wills to be guilty of our guilt; God takes on the punishment and suffering that guilt has brought on us."[35] Bonhoeffer stresses most emphatically that God cuts through our distinctions between piousness and godlessness to embrace human beings as they are. He makes clear that the ground for God's love for human beings does not reside in human beings themselves, but in God alone—it is the unfathomable love of God for human beings that is the sole reason for the incarnation.

The second way in which Christ relates to the world is through reconciliation, and thus through his crucifixion. Bonhoeffer stresses that, as the crucified one, Christ stands over against all thinking that revolves around success or failure. According to him, neither the triumph of the successful nor bitter hatred of the successful by those who fail can finally cope with the world. Christ's concern is entirely different. As Bonhoeffer says: "His concern is neither success nor failure but willing acceptance of the judgment of God. Only in judgment is there reconciliation with God and among human beings."[36] This does away with all idealism, with "programs and ideals," as he had said earlier on. He concludes his discussion of Christ's crucifixion by stating: "Only in the cross of Christ, and that means as judged, does humanity take on its true form."[37]

The third moment in Christ's relation to the world is that of the resurrection. Christ's resurrection, as Bonhoeffer asserts, conquered death, and, as a consequence, overturned the idolization of death. There are barely veiled references here to the Third Reich, in which striving for earthly eternity was combined with a careless play with life. As Bonhoeffer puts it: "Nothing betrays the idolization of death more clearly than when an era claims to build for eternity, and yet life in that era is worth nothing."[38] In contrast to this, thinking in terms of the resurrection brings with it a very different attitude towards life and death. In this case, one does not demand eternity from life, but takes from life all that it offers, the good as well as the bad. It means that one neither clings to life nor throws it away carelessly; instead,

35. DBWE 6:83.
36. DBWE 6:90.
37. DBWE 6:91.
38. DBWE 6:91.

one is content with the measured time of one's life. Bonhoeffer makes clear that, with the risen Christ, a new humanity has been born, and the final Yes of God has been spoken to that new human being. Human beings continue to live in the old, in a world of death and sin, but at the same time they also live beyond this world: "The night is not yet over, but day is already dawning," Bonhoeffer writes, citing an Advent hymn.[39]

THE DEVELOPMENT OF THE THREEPARTITION IN BONHOEFFER'S THEOLOGY

A few comments are in order if we wish to better understand Bonhoeffer's threefold partition. First of all, it is important to note that *Ethics* is not the first work in which Bonhoeffer uses this formula. Its first occurance can be found as early as 1931,[40] when he was doing a postdoctoral year in the US, at Union Theological Seminary. In a seminar paper entitled "The Theology of Crisis and Its Attitude toward Philosophy and Science,"[41] where he presented Karl Barth's theology to the American public, he describes the three moments in Christ's relationship with the world as follows:

> The meaning of the proper presupposition of christian [sic] theology is, that God entered history in Jesus Christ, made himself known to the world in this revelation. The word or will of God, God himself was made flesh. But the revelation of God in Christ was a revelation of his judgement as well as of his grace. Christ's cross is the judgment of God upon the world. Christ's resurrection is his grace.[42]

In the lines immediately following these remarks, Bonhoeffer unpacks this terse statement in somewhat more detail. First of all, he specifies Christ's incarnation as a moment in which the "you ought," the imperative, is overcome by the "you are," the indicative. And yet already in the very fact of the incarnation, the condemnation of the world is implied, because it convinces the world of the impossibility of coming before God "is its condemnation,

---

39. DBWE 6:92. The title of the hymn is "Die Nacht ist vorgedrungen." The editors of *Ethics* point out that this hymn was written in 1938 by Jochen Klepper. See DBWE 6:92, editorial footnote 67.

40. In *AB* he only mentions the cross and resurrection, see Abromeit, *Geheimnis Christi*, 237.

41. DBWE 10:462–76. This manuscript was written in English as a presentation for an oral seminar, see DBWE 10:462, editorial footnote 1.

42. DBWE 10:464.

its sin and its guilt."[43] Bonhoeffer interprets the resurrection in a similar way. Christ's resurrection reveals to the world that God alone is righteous, and that it can itself only become righteous through God's action. Abromeit points out that, although Bonhoeffer did give expression to Barth's version of the "theology of crisis," as was his intention in this paper, the threepartite form of Christ's incarnation, crucifixion, and resurrection is not typical for Barth. For that reason, "[o]ne must judge . . . that Bonhoeffer summarized in one simple formula what in his estimation was the baseline of Barth's christology."[44]

Bonhoeffer employed the same formula recurrently in his theology from this point onwards. It returns again in 1932, for instance, in the lecture course "The Nature of the Church."[45] Later on in the development of his theology, Bonhoeffer continues to use the same threefold divionsion. In *Discipleship*, for instance, in the section entitled "The Image of Christ,"[46] he writes: "Christ does not cease working in us until he has changed us into Christ's own image. Our goal is to be shaped into the entire *form* of the *incarnate*, the *crucified*, and the *risen one*."[47] Bonhoeffer's *Ethics* can be seen as a culmination point of his use of the formula, but is not the last point where Bonhoeffer uses it—it comes back again in his *Letters and Papers from Prison*. There Bonhoeffer defines faith in the following way: "Faith is participating in this being of Jesus. (Becoming human [Menschwerdung], cross, resurrection.)"[48] On this basis, Abromeit's conclusion is justified: "Bonhoeffer has given the threepartite christological formula an ever more prominent position in his thought . . . In the *Ethics*, this positive christological grid has become the structuring principle of the entire ethical design."[49]

43. DBWE 10:464.

44. "Man wird . . . urteilen müssen, daß Bonhoeffer in einer einfachen Formel, die er selbst bildete, das zusammenfaßte, was nach seiner Einschätzung Grundzüge Bartscher Christologie waren." Abromeit, *Geheimnis Christi*, 230.

45. DBWE 11:269–332.

46. DBWE 4:281–88.

47. DBWE 4:285; italics original.

48. DBWE 8:501. And also: "What is beyond this world is meant, in the gospel, to be there *for* this world—not in the anthropocentric sense of liberal, mystical, pietistic, ethical theology, but in the biblical sense of the creation and the incarnation, crucifixion, and resurrection of Jesus Christ." DBWE 8:373; italics original.

49. "Bonhoeffer hat der dreigliedrigen christologischen Formel in seinem Denken einen immer größeren Stellenwert eingeräumt . . . In der 'Ethik' ist das positive christologische Schema zur Strukturprinzip des ganzen ethischen Entwurfes geworden." Abromeit, *Geheimnis Christi*, 230. The divine mandates that Bonhoeffer develops in a later manuscript in his *Ethics*, for example, can be seen as a concretion of the threefold partition. See Abromeit, *Geheimnis Christi*, 231.

Secondly, it can be observed that the way Bonhoeffer conceptualizes the three different moments in the relation between Christ and the world changed over time in his writings. This is most notably the case with the incarnation. A common misunderstanding holds that the incarnation in Bonhoeffer's theology stands for the indicative, that is, for the *acceptance* of human life. Green, for example, states: "To be formed in the gestalt of the Incarnate is to be really human before God—not less and not more."[50] This is indeed the interpretation that Bonhoeffer gives to it in his *Ethics*, as we saw above. In his earlier theology, however, the incarnation consisted in a primarily negative event that concerned the *condemnation* of human beings. This can be seen clearly in a sermon that he delivered on the first Sunday in Advent, during his vicariate in Barcelona.[51] The theme of the sermon is "waiting": waiting for Christmas, for Christ. Remarkably, Bonhoeffer stresses that this waiting is not so much a joyous, expectant waiting, but rather "horrifying news for every person with a conscience."[52] He wonders how one can calmly contemplate God's coming, "whereas earlier peoples trembled before the day of God and the world quaked when Jesus Christ walked among us."[53] The incarnation, as Bonhoeffer makes clear here, is God's judgment of the evil in us and in the world.

He makes essentially the same point in another Advent sermon two years later, in 1930, in Havana, Cuba.[54] There he preached on Deut 32:48–52, where it is narrated how Moses died on Mount Nebo and was not allowed to enter into the promised land. Bonhoeffer compares the entry into the promised land with Christmas, when God's great promise is to be fulfilled, and he asks: "Are you prepared for God?"[55] This question should lead one to penitence, Bonhoeffer asserts, pointing out that throughout early Christendom the Advent season was not a time of joy, but a time of penitence. He admonishes his listeners to work out their salvation with fear and trembling. Yet another example of how Bonhoeffer understood the incarnation in a primarily negative way is found in his lecture course "The Nature of the Church," in 1932. There he formulates the incarnation as follows: "*Incarnation*: God becomes human. In order to destroy humans, God becomes human. Here [the] human being is judged in [his] ethical

---

50. Green, *Bonhoeffer*, 310.

51. DBWE 10:542–46.

52. DBWE 10:544.

53. DBWE 10:544.

54. DBWE 10:585–89.

55. DBWE 10:587.

self-responsibility."[56] Already in *Discipleship*, however, the way Bonhoeffer speaks about the incarnation changes—in this case, it is first and foremost a positive moment. He writes: "God accepts humanity . . . also in the body of Christ. God's mercy sends the Son in the flesh, so that in his flesh he may shoulder and carry all of humanity. The Son of God accepts all of humanity in bodily form . . . In the body of Jesus Christ humanity is now truly and bodily accepted; it is accepted as it is, out of God's mercy."[57] This line is continued by Bonhoeffer in his *Ethics*.[58] That shows itself strikingly in the fact that Bonhoeffer does not use the word incarnation there, but instead he consistently speaks of "becoming-human" ("Menschwerdung").[59]

Also with regards to the cross and the resurrection, Bonhoeffer changed the emphasis over the course of time, though less significantly than with regards to the incarnation. In his sermons in Barcelona, for instance, the cross functions, as Feil puts it, as "a simple sign of salvation which is said to be a salvation in another world."[60] This changes already in 1932, however, when Bonhoeffer's preaching becomes more oriented towards the incarnation and soteriology. As Feil notes: "The basic difference between the sermons of 1932 and those of Barcelona lies in the relevance the cross is said to have for the world. The cross . . . is what brings about salvation in the world and for the world. This accent gives those sermons of 1932 an orientation related more concretely to the incarnation and the economy of salvation."[61]

Thirdly, a close connection can be observed between Bonhoeffer's use of the threepartite formula and his thoughts on Christ as being the only real. It is not without reason that, in his *Ethics*, this formula is an outworking of the statement that, in Christ, God and the world are one. This means that the formula is not "preached onto" reality, but is rather an explication of how reality already *is* constituted through Christ.[62]

56. DBWE 11:297; italics original.

57. DBWE 4:214.

58. Günther Thomas is therefore incorrect when he asserts that it is only in the *Ethics* that the incarnation is seen in a primarily positively light, that is, as a confirmation of the world as God's creation. See Thomas, "Christus als Konnex," 352n19.

59. See the comments by Green, DBWE 6:6.

60. Feil, *The Theology of Dietrich Bonhoeffer*, 115.

61. Ibid. Elsewhere, Feil says: "The Incarnation, cross, and resurrection are characterized by universality and world-relatedness—not by partiality and withdrawal from the world." Feil, "Dietrich Bonhoeffer's Understanding of the World," 245.

62. This is noted by Ott, for example, when he writes: "This is how the existence of the man who has been conformed with Christ appears. It is a description, admittedly again very terse and abbreviated, of existence in the Holy Spirit, of being *kata pneuma*. It is the behaviour of a humanity with nothing unnatural about it, of a humble

THE INTERNAL ORDERING OF THE THREE MOMENTS

In addition to sketching the development of the threepartition in Bon-hoeffer's corpus, a comment is in order concerning the internal interplay and ordering of the three moments of Christ's relationship with the world. One quickly gets the impression that, for Bonhoeffer, the incarnation is the fundamental and most important relation between Christ and the world, with the elements of crucifixion and resurrection being ordered around that central given. This is Mayer's position, who states that Bonhoeffer made the incarnation the foundation of his theology. He notes that Bonhoeffer does not do away with the crucifixion and the resurrection, but, according to him, "[Bonhoeffer] includes . . . their function in the event of the incarna-tion. Jesus is human being as the humiliated one on the cross as well as in the resurrection and the exaltation. The incarnation includes the cross, as well as the resurrection, which results in the new creation, as well as the rule of the exalted Lord. . . ."[63] The same opinion is also shared by Bethge.[64]

Abromeit, however, takes a strong stand against such an interpretation by pointing to the strict distinction that Bonhoeffer makes, in his lectures on Christology, between Christ's incarnation and his humiliation. The dis-tinction is important, for if the element of humiliation were not there, the incarnation would turn sin into part of a creation theology. As Abromeit notes: "God joints himself then indissoluble with his own creation."[65] With the element of humiliation, however, the incarnation looks towards the lib-eration of human beings from sin, which Christ brought about through his death on the cross. This does not make "humiliation" identical with "cruci-fixion," but there is nevertheless a close relation between the two elements—they stand in an equal, reciprocal relationship. Abromeit points out that a similar reciprocity exists between the crucifixion and the resurrection. The cross is thus at the center of Bonhoeffer's threefold partition (without for that matter becoming the most important element): the incarnation looks towards the cross, and the resurrection looks back to it. This ensures that Bonhoeffer's theology is well and truly a theology of the cross, and as such

---

openness which has renounced every form of self-justification, a joyful confident openness towards an ineffable future." Ott, *Reality and Faith*, 187; italics original.

63. "[Bonhoeffer] schließt . . . ihre Funktion in das Inkarnationsgeschehen ein. Je-sus ist Mensch als Erniedrigter am Kreuz sowie als Auferstandener und Erhöhter. Die Menschwerdung umfaßt sowohl das Kreuz wie auch die neue Schöpfung der Aufer-stehung und die Herrschaft des erhöhten Kyrios." Mayer, *Christuswirklichkeit*, 197–98.

64. Bethge, *Dietrich Bonhoeffer*, 718.

65. "Gott verbindet sich dann unauflöslich mit der von ihm geschaffenen Schöp-fung." Abromeit, *Geheimnis Christi*, 232–33.

it keeps his ". . .'theology of life,' which is founded both in the incarnation as well as in the resurrection, from collapsing into vitalism; moreover, it also keeps Bonhoeffer's theology in the reality of the world, in which suffering, death and sin takes place."[66]

The question of whether or not any particular relation between Christ and the world is primary (and if so, *which* relation) is not just a theoretical one. One of the earlier interpreters of Bonhoeffer, Heinrich Müller, in his controversial dissertation on Bonhoeffer, written from a socialist perspective, recognizes the crucifixion of Christ as the most central moment in Bonhoeffer's threefold partition. He calls it the *key signature* ("Vorzeichen") of all theology and asserts that it has to be understood as a foundation both of the incarnation and the resurrection.[67] As Abromeit notes: "As a matter of fact, Müller absolutizes the cross of Christ and becomes radical, by, in political ethics, opting unilaterally for the form of Socialism as it exists [in the Soviet bloc at the time]."[68] Further on in this chapter, I will show that, in the current debate between theology and ecology, the tempation is to prioritize the incarnation over against the crucifixion, which brings its own dangers along with it.

THE CHRISTOLOGY UNDERLYING THE THREEPARTITION

It is important to establish the character of Bonhoeffer's Christology, which underlies his threepartite formula. In this formula, we can clearly see that his Christology is an act-Christology as opposed to a Being-christology. He

66. "[Die kreuzestheologie Bonhoeffers] . . . bewahrt . . . die sowohl inkarnatorisch wie auferstehungstheologisch begründete Lebenstheologie vor Vitalismus und halt die Theologie Bonhoeffers in der Wirklichkeit dieser Welt, in der gelitten, gestorben und gesündigt wird." Abromeit, *Geheimnis Christi*, 234. This is also pointed out by Burtness: "It sounds as though Bonhoeffer's ethical theology could be described as incarnational. Such a designation would not be inaccurate, but it would be inadequate. Incarnational theologies can very easily be set adrift from the person of Jesus Christ, using 'incarnation' merely as an interpretive principle." Burtness, *Shaping the Future*, 39. Pointing to Bonhoeffer's use of the threepartite formula, Burtness notes: "Incarnation as a principle will not do for Bonhoeffer. His insistence throughout is that God and world come together in the babe in the crib and the man on the cross. Not Christology, not even incarnation, but Jesus Christ himself requires the rejection of two-sphere thinking." Ibid., 39–40.

67. Müller, *Von der Kirche zur Welt*, 385. In making this assertion, Müller posits a contrast between *Ethics* and *Letters and Papers from Prison*.

68. "In der Tat verabsolutiert Müller das Kreuz Christi und wird radikal, indem er in der politischen Ethik einseitig für den real existierenden Sozialismus optiert." Abromeit, *Geheimnis Christi*, 234n44. He refers to Hübner, Review of *Von der Kirche zur Welt*.

diverges on this point from the views of the early church. The danger of such an act-Christology is that it can lead to a diminishing of the historical person of Christ. In this case it is no longer the personal, exalted Christ who relates to the world, but these relations themselves, which, forming a program of how Christians should relate to the world, constitute a sort of immanent Christ-principle.

Abromeit opposes himself strongly against such a suggestion by pointing to Bonhoeffer's revelation-theology, which asserts that the baby born of Mary in Bethelehem truly is God. It, namely the incarnation, *has* happened, just as the crucifixion and the resurrection are historical events. And these factual events altered the very course of world history in fundamental ways. This remains a rather unsatisfactory answer to the problem, however, for it fails to explain how this "positivistic" assertion relates to concrete, Christian formation in the three moments of Christ's relation to the world. The work of Heinrich Ott proves to be quite helpful on this point. Like Abromeit, he refutes the error that human behavior coincides with the reality of Christ. He points out that, for Bonhoeffer, human behavior in accordance with Christ is only possible "because Jesus is present in person as the essential form of man, the form of the incarnate God to whom we are conformed."[69] It is thus Jesus Christ himself, as a person, who is the primary reality. Ott asserts: "The person of Jesus Christ is not 'resolved' into some human behaviour which then men have to make their own. There is always first presupposed his being himself as the Incarnate, Crucified and Risen."[70]

THE ESCHATOLOGICAL DIMENSION TO BONHOEFFER'S THREEPARTITE FORMULA

Finally, it can be discerned that each of the three moments bears an eschatological direction in Bonhoeffer's work. If the concept of Christ-reality is eschatological through and through, as I argued, then one could expect that, in the threepartite formulation of his Christology, this eschatological dimension is also visible. This is indeed the case, and it can be seen most clearly with regards to the incarnation. As Bonhoeffer argues, it is precisely the incarnation that brings about a longing for the completion of Christ's coming to the earth in the eschaton. He illustrates this in the sermon that he preached on the first Sunday of Advent in 1928. The text that the sermon focuses on is—remarkably—Rev 3:20a: "Behold, I stand at the door, and knock" (KJV). In the sermon, he skillfully mixes the expectation of the

69. Ott, *Reality and Faith*, 188.

70. Ibid., 188–89.

festive Christmas season with the expectation of the return of Christ. Toward the close of the sermon, Bonhoeffer brings the point into the sharpest focus when he says: "The time of Advent is a time of waiting, though our entire life is a time of Advent, a time of waiting for that final time when a new heaven and a new earth will emerge, when all human beings will be brothers and will rejoice with the words of the angels: Peace on earth and goodwill among people. Learn to wait, for he has promised to come."[71]

The eschatological dimension at work in the moments of the cross and the resussection is less apparent. Yet in *AB* Bonhoeffer casts these moments in an eschatological light as well. He says there: "It may be said of Christian revelation that the proclamation of cross and resurrection, determined by eschatology and predestination, and the occurrence effective within that proclamation, lift even the past into the present, or paradoxically, into something 'in the future.'"[72] Therefore, Bonhoeffer argues, Christian revelation must not primarily be interpreted as relating to a past event, as something that has already happened, but instead to something coming in the future. In his own words: "[T]he Christian revelation must not be interpreted as 'having happened,' but that for those human beings living in the church, in each present, this once-and-for-all occurrence is qualified as future."[73] Bonhoeffer illustrates this in a sermon he delivered in Barcelona. There he writes that, in the cross, God himself extends his hand unto us, into time, in Jesus Christ, to pull us into his eternity. He comments: "This is the miracle of the revelation in Jesus Christ. Here amid all transitoriness and darkness stands a sign from eternity, serious and mighty, bathed in the radiance of the divine sun of grace and light—the cross."[74]

The Distinction Between Ultimate and Penultimate

Related to the concepts of the one Christ-reality and Bonhoeffer's threepartite formula of Christ's relationship with the world are the twin concepts of ultimate and penultimate. These concepts will be explored here. Firstly, again, their central formulation in *Ethics* will be described, followed by

71. DBWE 10:546. The eschatological dimension of the incarnation in Bonhoeffer's theology has also been noted by Dumas, *Dietrich Bonhoeffer*, 254–57. His account doesn't offer much in the way of interpretation, however.

72. DBWE 2:111.

73. DBWE 2:111.

74. DBWE 10:519. An interesting parallel exists on this point between Bonhoeffer and Moltmann. Like Bonhoeffer, Moltmann perceives the three moments of Jesus' life, death, and resurrection as being eschatological in nature. See Plasger, "Hope in Our Lord Jesus Christ?," esp. 249–52.

an overview of the development of the concept in Bonhoeffer's thought. Thirdly and finally, criticisms concerning these concepts will be addressed.

THE CENTRAL FORMULATION OF THE DISTINCTION BETWEEN ULTIMATE AND PENULTIMATE IN ETHICS

In the *Ethics*-manuscript entitled "Ultimate and Penultimate Things,"[75] Bonhoeffer, as the title itself indicates, makes an important distinction between ultimate and penultimate things. The ultimate he defines as "the one event that the Reformation has called the justification of the sinner by grace alone."[76] He illustrates this event in colorful terms: the dark tunnel of human life is broken open and the word of God bursts in. This event places a person's past under the word "forgiveness" and his or her future is preserved in the faithfulness of God. It is an event of grace, accessible only by faith.[77]

Bonhoeffer points out that the ultimate bears at least two distinct senses. First of all, the event of justification is *qualitatively* ultimate, meaning that it is not in any way attainable by following a certain method. Since justification is spoken by God himself, it excludes any and every method of reaching it; it involves a complete break with everything penultimate, the penultimate being that which is *aimed* at the ultimate, but not the ultimate itself. As examples of the penultimate, Bonhoeffer mentions Paul and Luther, both of whom sought out justification in different ways (Paul by glorifying in the law and persecuting those following Christ, and Luther by being broken by the law, in desperation in the monastery). When they were justified by God's inbreaking, ultimate word, both their former ways were ultimately condemned.[78] The second sense in which God's word is ultimate is *temporal* in nature. Justification, as Bonhoeffer says, presupposes that the creature being justified once became guilty, or took on guilt. There is thus a road to travel, or a path to follow. Even though the ways of Paul and Luther were ultimately condemned, they still had to travel along their respective

75. DBWE 6:146–70.

76. DBWE 6:146.

77. DBWE 6:146. A bit further on, Bonhoeffer then gives a description of the justified person, written in the third person singular. As Clifford Green points out, this is a linguistic sign of the autobiographical dimension of this passage. See DBWE 6:148, editorial note 9. This emphasis on justification as the core of Christian faith is typical for Protestant theology, as the preceding quote from Bonhoeffer also made clear.

78. There is an interesting parallel here between Bonhoeffer and Barth, who writes: "[T]he last thing . . . is a radical break with everything that is next to the last." Barth, *The Word of God and the Word of Man*, 324. This has been pointed out by the editors of *Discipleship*. See DBWE 4:239, editorial footnote 49.

ways in order to come to the point of sinking to their knees under their respective burdens. There is therefore a place for the penultimate: for the ultimate word to be heard, there must be a penultimate to which this word is spoken.

Bonhoeffer points out that it is difficult for Christians to live in the tension between the penultimate and the ultimate. As a consequence, they often choose one of two extreme solutions in order to get rid of the tension: either *radicalism* or *compromise*, which, despite its name, is also an extreme solution. The radical solution, on the one hand, sees only the ultimate. It wants to break completely with the penultimate. As an example in literature, Bonhoeffer mentions Ibsen's stage play *Brand*.[79] In the solution of compromise, on the other hand, the opposite takes place. In this case, as Bonhoeffer says, the ultimate word withdraws beyond the scope of daily life, and thereby comes to serve as an eternal justification of all that exists. Here, the penultimate is not threatened or endangered at all by the ultimate. In this case too, Bonhoeffer offers an example from literature, namely that of Dostoyevski's Grand Inquisitor, in his classic novel *The Brothers Karamazov*.[80]

Bonhoeffer makes clear that both solutions contain truths, but that both, because of their extreme nature, also contain falsehoods. The problem is that, in their extremism, they both make the penultimate and the ultimate mutually exclusive of each other, either by destroying the penultimate through the ultimate (in the case of radicalism), or by destroying the ultimate through the penultimate (in the case of compromise). Bonhoeffer further specifies the problem with both approaches by placing them in relationship with Christ. Both extremes are ideas, or abstractions from the God-man, Jesus Christ, who is not radical in the sense of radicalism, and who also does not make compromises: only in him, as Bonhoeffer asserts, is the relationship between the ultimate and the penultimate resolved. Bonhoeffer then invokes the distinction of the three moments in Christ's relationship with the world, made earlier on in his *Ethics*. In the context of battling both radicalism and compromise, he, once again, strongly opposes himself to efforts that tear these moments apart. Because "[a] Christian ethic built only on the incarnation would lead easily to the compromise solution; an ethic built only on the crucifixion or only on the resurrection of Jesus Christ would fall into radicalism and enthusiasm. The conflict is resolved only in their unity."[81]

79. DBWE 6:155.
80. DBWE 6:155.
81. DBWE 6:157.

Bonhoeffer then moves on to a more detailed investigation of the penultimate. As he argues, when a human life is deprived of the conditions that are part of being human, this, at the very least, seriously hinders the justification of such a life by grace and faith, or if not, it makes it impossible. As a concrete example, he mentions the case of slaves who have been so deprived of control over their time that they simply have no opportunity even to hear the proclamation of God's word. What this means, as Bonhoeffer claims, is that they cannot be led, by the word of God, to the faith that justifies. He concludes that, in addition to proclaiming the ultimate word of God, namely the justification by grace through faith alone, it is necessary to care for the penultimate, so that the ultimate is not hindered. Quite sharply he states: "Those who proclaim the word yet do not do everything possible so that this word may be heard are not true to the word's claim for free passage, for a smooth road. The way for the word must be prepared. The word itself demands it."[82]

Bonhoeffer offers the feeding of the hungry as an example of the task of clearing the way for Christ's coming. He clearly states that, if the hungry do not come to faith, then guilt falls on those who denied them bread. Feeding the hungry is not, however, a proclamation of the grace of God and of justification. And it is also not the case, as he says, that the hungry must have been given bread before they can become Christians: it is not a part of the ultimate itself, but is strictly preparational. It is important to point out that Bonhoeffer is not speaking about social improvement in general. Instead, he asserts that the visible deeds done to prepare people to receive Jesus Christ must be deeds of humility, deeds of *repentance* before the coming Lord.

This links up with what Bonhoeffer had already set out in his earlier theology of social reform. He had first been confronted with the Social Gospel movement in America during his studies there. A few years later, he then reacted to this movement in a Memorandum that he wrote for the German branch of the World Alliance entitled "The 'Social gospel' (Soziale Evangelium)."[83] In this text, he gives a critical evaluation of the idea that human action can help to establish God's kingdom of the earth. According to him, "The optimism, the ideology of progress does not take God's commandment seriously (Luke 17:10). It is modern enthusiasm [Schwärmerei]. It fails to recognize human limits; it ignores the fundamental difference between a kingdom of the world and God's kingdom."[84] At the same time,

82. DBWE 6:160.

83. DBWE 12:236–42. Larry Rasmussen points out that at Bonhoeffer's request, Paul Lehman wrote a draft of this essay. See DBWE 12:236, editorial footnote 2.

84. DBWE 12:241.

it is also important to point out that he had great appreciation for the social gospel. He commends it in particular for taking seriously the fact that God's kingdom is a kingdom on earth. But in doing so, as he says, it does away with the eschatological understanding of the kingdom.[85]

HISTORY OF THE DEVELOPMENT OF ULTIMATE AND PENULTIMATE IN BONHOEFFER

It is important to note that *Ethics* is not the first place where Bonhoeffer develops his thoughts on the ultimate and the penultimate. Instead, the pair of concepts has quite a long history in his thought. As Bethge says, it "had existed for a long time in his theology without his being aware of it."[86] One finds him employing it as early as 1928, for instance, in a sermon that he gave, during his vicariate in Barcelona, on 1 John 2:17.[87] There he defines the ultimate as Christ reaching out from beyond the border of life, that is, from death. What human beings perceive at the end, Bonhoeffer says, is essentially the beginning of something new. This fact transforms what first seems to be the ultimate, namely death, into something penultimate. Also in his *Discipleship* one finds the distinction between ultimate and penultimate present, specifically in the discussion of the rich man who wants to follow Jesus (Matt 19:16–22).[88] As a response to his desire, Jesus tells him to give away his riches. Bonhoeffer asserts that giving away his riches is "not identical with discipleship itself. It is not even the first step of discipleship. Rather, it is the obedience within which discipleship can then become real. *First* the young man must go and sell everything and give to the poor, and *then* come and follow Jesus. The goal is following Jesus, and the way in this case is voluntary poverty."[89]

The idea of the penultimate also appears in Bonhoeffer's lecture "The Führer and the Individual in the Younger Generation."[90] In this case, he warns about mistaking the service of a political leader, or the office that he or she holds, as an *ultimate* authority, instead of as a penultimate one. The leader, he insists, ought to act in respect to the authority of God, and to point to this authority, "before which Reich and state are penultimate

85. DBWE 12:241: "The eschatological understanding of the kingdom, as one that God can create and brings in contrast to the world, has disappeared."

86. Bethge, *Dietich Bonhoeffer*, 718.

87. DBWE 10:516–21.

88. DBWE 4:69–76.

89. DBWE 4:73–74; italics original.

90. DBWE 12:268–82.

authorities. Leader and office that turn themselves into gods mock God and the solitary individual before him who is becoming the individual, and must collapse. Only the leader who is in the service of the penultimate and ultimate authority merits loyalty."[91] Also in Bonhoeffer's later writings, the distinction retains its importance.[92] Apart from explicit treatments of the concepts of the ultimate and the penultimate, there also are many places in Bonhoeffer's work where the terms, though not explicitly mentioned, can nevertheless clearly be seen at work.[93] This long history of the pair of concepts in Bonhoeffer's thought indicates, as Burtness points out, the importance of these categories for Bonhoeffer: "What is certain is that they are extremely important for Bonhoeffer, that they occur in some very early literature, and that they are essential for an understanding of the *Ethics*."[94]

Bonhoeffer's concepts of the ultimate and the penultimate can be seen as an outworking of the eschatological dimension of his concept of Christ-reality. Despite the fact that the terms "ultimate" and "penultimate" suggestively allude to eschatology, this dimension has not always been fully recognized by Bonhoeffer scholars, mainly on account of the fact that Bonhoeffer was not thought to have had a genuine eschatology, as we saw earlier.[95] At the same time, there have been some interpreters who recognized this fundamental dimension. This is true of Georg Huntemann, for instance, who states: "This presence of the kingdom now is the penultimate of the ultimate. And for its part, this present-day kingdom is an ultimate to the penultimate of social-practical and ethical actions."[96] Huntemann is right in arguing that Bonhoeffer's use of the terms penultimate and ultimate offers a different way of describing the New Testament tension between the *already* and *not-yet* of the Kingdom of God, as inaugurated by Jesus. John Panteleimon Manoussakis has made the same argument. As he observes, "It is precisely this Johannine tension between the not-yet and the already (Jn 4:23, 5:25) that Bonhoeffer is interested in preserving and uplifting by

91. DBWE 12:282.

92. One finds it mentioned in his letters from prison, for example. See DBWE 8:365.

93. This has also been pointed out by Burtness, *Shaping the Future*, 72, who, to give an example, mentions the discussion in *Discipleship* of Luther's commendation to Christians to sin boldly, but to believe more boldly still.

94. Burtness, *Shaping the Future*, 72; italics original.

95. Remarkably, in their recent studies of Bonhoeffer's eschatology, neither Thomas nor Ziegler recognize the eschatological dimension of the concepts of the ultimate and the penultimate.

96. Huntemann, *The Other Bonhoeffer*, 177.

his discussion of the eschatological."[97] The one problem with both these interpretations, however, is that they do not take into account the fact that Bonhoeffer consciously described the ultimate as the event of the justification of the sinner by faith. This must be recognized first and foremost before making the case that the ultimate is a broader concept as well.

A more cautious and detailed conceptual analysis of this sort has been undertaken by Hans Vium Mikkelsen.[98] As he points out, Bonhoeffer uses the concepts of ultimate and penultimate to broaden the doctrine of justification to include not just the individual sinner, but the whole of creation. He argues that a strictly individual interpretation of Bonhoeffer's thoughts on justification in his *Ethics* go directly against his criticism of such an individualistic understanding of justification. This, then, seems the right way to appropriate the eschatological dimension of Bonhoeffer's distinction between the ultimate and the penultimate: it originates in the doctrine of justification by faith, but is then given a wider scope.

Criticism Concerning the Twin Concepts of Ultimate and Penultimate

Recently, Bonhoeffer's concepts of the ultimate and the penultimate have been criticized by Edward van 't Slot.[99] While he recognizes the eschatological character of the distinction between the two concepts, according to him Bonhoeffer does not succeed in clarifying how the penultimate can really prepare the way for the ultimate, that is, for the eschatological coming of God. He writes: "He [Bonhoeffer] poses some important *questions*: is the faith that justifies (. . .) 'realizable' in everyday life, or does it happen only when 'the ultimate' strikes as a flash of lightning? But Bonhoeffer gives no other *answer* than that the order 'ultimate—penultimate' is irreversible."[100] What is lacking, according to Van 't Slot, is an explanation of how the ultimate can be a precondition for faith as obedient concentration on the penultimate. Barth proves to be helpful on this point, particularly when Van 't Slot says: "Here, I suggest, *Barth's 'christological concentration' may offer more perspective. For this concentration creates the possibility to stress the continuity and credibility in God's election, to anchor the 'being' of the believer therein,* and, at the same time to safeguard the eschatological character of

---

97. Manoussakis, "'At the Recurrent End of the Unending,'" 231.

98. Mikkelsen, "Kun den lidende Gud kan hjælpe," 266–87.

99. Van 't Slot, *Negativism of Revelation?*, 242–44.

100. Ibid., 243; italics original.

revelation."[101] I do not agree with Van 't Slot on this point. There are multiple aspects of Bonhoeffer's theology that clearly describe how, in light of the ultimate, life in the penultimate can be ordered; this is true in particular of his doctrine of the divine mandates, as well as his thoughts on Christian formation in the threepartite relationship between Christ and the world. These aspects of his theology stand in close relationship to the ultimate, that is, to (the justification through) Christ, and it is therefore not necessary to try to "correct" Bonhoeffer on this point by means of the theology of Karl Barth.

Bonhoeffer's Concept of the Natural

The fourth and final concept treated in this chapter is the category of the natural in Bonhoeffer's theology. Like the preceding concepts, the discussion will start out with the description of this concept in Bonhoeffer's *Ethics*. Then, the development of the concept in Bonhoeffer's other writings will be followed. Thirdly, the concept will be placed into context and its significance will be indicated. Fourthly and finally, the criticisms which have been formulated against this concept will be engaged.

The Concept of the Natural in Ethics

In the next manuscript of his *Ethics*, entitled "Natural Life,"[102] Bonhoeffer consciously sought to work out in greater detail what he meant by the penultimate. In this long manuscript, he begins by noting that the concept of the natural has, in Protestant ethics, fallen into disrepute. He notes a difference between those theologians for whom the concept was lost in the darkness of general sinfulness, and those for whom the natural took on the brightness of the primal creation. According to him, "Both were grave misuses that led to the complete elimination of the category of the natural from Protestant thought; it was left to Catholic ethics."[103] He identifies this as a heavy, substantive loss for Protestant thought because an orientation with regards to the question of natural life was lost. Compared with the brightness of the light of grace, everything human and natural seemed dark, and the relative differences within the human and the natural were not seen as significant. Bonhoeffer concludes that this confusion arose on account of the failure to recognize the right relation between the ultimate and the penultimate. The consequences, as he notes, are far-reaching: "If there were no longer

101. Ibid., 244; italics original.

102. DBWE 6:171–218.

103. DBWE 6:171–72.

any relative differences within a fallen creation, then the way was clear for any kind of arbitrariness and disorder, and natural life, with its concrete decisions and orders, could no longer be considered responsible to God."[104]

In this light, Bonhoeffer states that the concept of the natural must be recovered from the gospel itself. He then introduces an important distinction. According to him, the natural is both distinct from the created, such that it includes the Fall into sin, but it is also distinct from the sinful, so as to include the created.[105] At this juncture, Bonhoeffer restates what he had said in the preceding manuscript concerning the penultimate, but now in relation to the natural: he states, firstly, that the *un*natural does not make Christ's coming impossible, and secondly, that the natural cannot compel him to come. As such, the natural is the penultimate, and is therefore directed towards Christ, even though it does not lead to him. However, even in light of the ultimate coming of Christ, these relative differences continue to exist—hence the distinction between *natural* and *unnatural*.

Bonhoeffer then asks how the natural can be recognized. As a response, he mentions human reason as the organ through which we recognize the natural. It does not stand apart from the natural, but forms an integral part of it. It is therefore, together with creation, a fallen reason. Bonhoeffer makes clear that, in this respect, he differs from Catholic theory, in which reason is thought to have retained an essential integrity. He also mentions another element of the natural, which he calls "basic will." This also must not be understood as a remnant of the divine in human beings, unmarred by the Fall, but instead as embedded totally within the fallen and the preserved world, just as reason is. Within this limitation of the natural, penultimate world, reason and basic will have a certain autonomous function in guarding life, fencing it off from the unnatural. In a key passage, Bonhoeffer argues:

> In the end, it is life itself that tends toward the natural and ever again turns against the unnatural and breaks it down. Here lies the ultimate basis of health and healing, both of body and soul. Life, whether of the individual or of the community, is its own doctor. It fends off the unnatural as life-destroying. Only when life itself is no longer capable of this necessary defense are the destructive powers of the unnatural victorious.[106]

104. DBWE 6:172–73.

105. In his own words: "The natural is that which, after the fall, is directed toward the coming of Jesus Christ. The unnatural is that which, after the fall, closes itself off from the coming of Jesus Christ." DBWE 6:173.

106. DBWE 6:176.

What is asserted here by Bonhoeffer is a certain independence of the realm of the natural, a realm which, though wholly and thoroughly penultimate, tends automatically to the preservation of life. The unnatural tries to corrode natural life, but because it is not natural itself, it needs *organization* to do so, as Bonhoeffer asserts. In this it differs from the natural, which simply *is*, and does not require organization. As a concrete example, Bonhoeffer mentions the undermining of respect for parents. According to him, this respect is simply practiced, without being organized. The undermining of it, however, must be organized.[107] In this way, in its organized form, the unnatural can temporarily overcome the natural.[108] However, "[i]n the long run every organization breaks down, while the natural persists and prevails by its own strength, since life itself is on the side of the natural."[109] Even great shocks and revolutions in the external aspects of life cannot, as long as life continues, destroy the natural—it will always reassert itself again.

This leads Bonhoeffer to a modest optimism with regards to human history considered within the limits of the fallen world. He immediately clarifies that this optimism has nothing to do with the idea of sin being gradually overcome. It is, rather, a purely immanent optimism situated within the realm of the natural alone. Bonhoeffer calls to mind the observation that, according to the Bible, the utter destruction of the natural order is among the signs foretelling the end of the world (Luke 21 is mentioned in particular), and he therefore concludes that this "end of the world," when it occurs, also means the end of immanent hopes. As such, Bonhoeffer limits the concept of the natural in two ways: firstly, it is *qualitatively* limited by the ultimate—by which it exists and to which it is directed—and secondly it is *temporarily* limited: in the eschaton, it will be thoroughly abolished. This marks the Christian's attitude towards the growing disturbance of the natural with a certain ambivalence; while such a disturbance is considered wrong and unnatural, it is also a tell-tale sign of the coming of the Lord Jesus in glory, and thus a profoundly hopeful sign for Christians. This ambivalence is only *noted* by Bonhoeffer, however, and not systematically addressed.

Bonhoeffer goes on to further define the natural as the form that both inheres in and serves life. Life misses its goal when it absolutizes itself,

107. It is no coincidence that Bonhoeffer makes use of the example of respect for parents. Clifford Green points out that, during the Third Reich, the Hitler Youth organization indoctrinated children to spy on their parents ideologically and to report their behavior. See Green, DBWE 6:177, editorial footnote 21.

108. Again, Green points out that, by using the term organization, Bonhoeffer has again the repressive organization of the Third Reich in mind. See DBWE 6:177, editorial footnote 20.

109. DBWE 6:177.

making itself into its own goal. Such a vitalism, Bonhoeffer says, inevitably culminates in nihilism, in the destruction of all that is natural. "In the strict sense, life as such is a nothing, an abyss, a ruin. It is movement without end, without goal, movement into nothingness."[110] Such vitalism consists in the absolutizing of an essentially correct insight, however, namely that life is not just a means to an end, but also an end in itself. From this perspective, Bonhoeffer also corrects another error that he perceives, namely that of the mechanization of life. "Here the individual is understood only in terms of usefulness [Nutzwert] to the whole, and the community only in terms of its use to an all-controlling institution, organization, or idea."[111] Both of these attitudes towards life essentially give expression to a despair over life—they are drawn away from life by the allure of the unnatural. Natural life as such stands between these two extremes, however, being, at one and the same time, both an end in itself and a means to an end.

This is recognized in Jesus Christ. Through him we come to see that life, as an end in itself, is a reflection of the createdness of life, and, as a means to an end, a reflection of its participation in the kingdom of God. As an end in itself, life is expressed in *rights*, and as a means to an end, it finds expression in *duties*. They are both given with life, and the natural life must be lived in accordance with them. Although both rights and duties form integral and equal parts of natural life, Bonhoeffer allows the rights of natural life to take precedence over its duties. He explains this theologically as follows: "God gives before God demands."[112] In the sections following this remark, he then gives a detailed account of these rights. He treats 1) the principle of *suum cuique*, 2) the right to bodily life, 3) self-murder, 4) reproduction and developing life, 4) the freedom of bodily life, and 5) the natural rights of the life of the Spirit. His work on the last of these sections was only begun, however, and never brought to full completion. Also, he never found time to write the complementary sections on the duties of natural life.[113]

History and Further Developments of the Concept of the Natural in Bonhoeffer

The concept is not totally new for Bonhoeffer, however—he had already written about the natural well beforehand, in his earlier theology. The emphasis in this case was quite different, nevertheless. As we will see in chapter

110. DBWE 6:178.
111. DBWE 6:179.
112. DBWE 6:180.
113. On this see DBWE 6:218, editorial footnote 162.

3, in *CF* he sees "the natural" primarily in its negative relation to "creation": there it denotes particularly the *fallen* creation. In the *Ethics*, however, the emphasis shifts from a relation to what was ("in the beginning. . .") to him who has come and still is yet to come again, namely Christ. "The natural," as we saw, is what aims at the coming of Christ, and, as such, is a positive concept.[114] An even more notable difference concerning "the natural" arises in the interval between *Ethics* and *Discipleship*. In *Discipleship*, the natural stands over against the obedience of the disciple—it belongs to the world, not to the church, and Bonhoeffer strongly emphasizes the difference between the two. As a result, in *Discipleship*, "the natural" does not possess a positive function for the community of the disciples. According to An Il Kang, the divergence that Bonhoeffer brings about in *Discipleship* is not an absolute one, and should be understood in light of the church struggle in which he was involved.[115] While reference to historical context is indeed important and quite helpful, it still appears that Bonhoeffer, bowing to the pressure of the time, identified "the natural" too hastily with "the world." In *Ethics*, however, this changes—as we have seen, the natural transforms into a fundamentally positive category.

The category's positive dimension remains in effect in Bonhoeffer's later theology as well. His essay "After Ten Years," for instance, contains a paragraph on "Immanent Justice" in which Bonhoeffer further elaborates his thoughts on the natural.[116] In this text, he asserts that evil often very rapdily reveals or betrays its own folly, thereby defeating itself. As he says: "[T]he suspension of God's commandments on principle in the supposed interest of earthly self-preservation acts precisely against what this self-preservation seeks to accomplish."[117] According to Bonhoeffer, his group of co-conspirators experienced this for themselves. Recognizing evil by its self-defeating folly, and then acting accordingly, is wisdom, as he says—he interprets this as a virtue. According to him, "in the common life of human beings, there are laws that are stronger than everything that believes it can supersede them, and that it is therefore not only wrong but unwise to disregard these laws."[118]

114. This has also been pointed out by Green. See DBWE 6:171, editorial footnote 2.

115. An Il Kang, "Von der 'Nachfolge' zur 'Ethik der Verantwortung,'" 42–44.

116. DBWE 8:45–46.

117. DBWE 8:45.

118. DBWE 8:45.

Context and Significance of Bonhoeffer's Concept of the
Natural

It is important to draw attention to the uniqueness of Bonhoeffer's concept
of natural life. Clifford Green commenting on the *Ethics* manuscript on
"The Natural," remarks that it "is the first theological-ethical doctrine of
basic human rights developed by a twentieth-century German Protestant
theologian. Despite many similarities, it differs from American and West-
European traditions."[119] This novelty is also recognized by Feil, who says
that it is a special merit of Bonhoeffer to have reclaimed the concept of the
natural for Protestant theology.[120] Bethge indirectly alludes to the possibility
that Bonhoeffer may have been prompted to write the manuscript by his
stay in the Catholic monastery of Ettal, where he was at the time of writing.[121] However, although Bonhoeffer's Catholic surroundings at that time
may have influenced him in part, this certainly was not the only reason
for him to write the manuscript. As Green points out, "[t]he category of
nature, along with spirit, was a central and consistent part of his theological
anthropology from the beginning."[122]

In addition, it is important to note that Bonhoeffer's conception of the
natural differs significantly from the role that the natural plays in Catholic
theology. Bethge asserts that Bonhoeffer derives the natural not from an
analogia entis or from natural law, but from the revelation in Christ and
the doctrine of justification.[123] Feil too sees a marked difference between
Bonhoeffer's concept and that of Catholic theology: "Bonhoeffer's pleas for
the natural should not be interpreted as concealed rehabilitation of the kind
of natural theology that Karl Barth had attacked with such vigor."[124]

119. DBWE 6:218, editorial footnote 162.

120. Feil, *The Theology of Dietrich Bonhoeffer*, 145. See also Tödt: "As far as I know,
this is the only ethical elaboration on this theme by a theologian in German-speaking
Protestantism before the end of the Second World War, the only systematic Protestant
attempt to conceive of human rights." Tödt, *Authentic Faith*, 144.

121. Bethge, *Dietrich Bonhoeffer*, 718–19. See also Daub, *Die Stellvertretung Jesu
Christi*, 477.

122. Green, *Bonhoeffer*, 325. Related to the concept of "the natural" in Bonhoeffer is William Connor's work on the "laws of life" in Bonhoeffer. See Connor, "The
Natural Life of Man and Its Laws." A summary of this work is ibid., "The Laws of Life,"
101–110. See also the related work of Neugebauer, "Die Theologische Lebensbegriff
Dietrich Bonhoeffers," 147–65.

123. See Bethge, *Dietrich Bonhoeffer*, 719.

124. Feil, *The Theology of Dietrich Bonhoeffer*, 145. See also Burtness: "[A]s with all Bonhoeffer's formulations, the recovery of the natural has to do specifically with Christology or, better, with Jesus Christ." Burtness, *Shaping the Future*, 105.
See also Rasmussen, "Preserving the Natural," esp. 211–20.

Apart from that, the historical context also plays a decisive role in the concept's development. Bonhoeffer's emphasis on natural life in *Ethics* has to be understood in light of the attacks on life carried out by the Nazis, such as forced sterilizations and euthanasia. As the editors of the *Ethics* make clear, there was a fatal inadequacy in Protestant theology at the time in dealing with natural life. As such, it had little means to mount a strong opposition to forced sterilizations and euthanasia.[125] It is in this context that Bonhoeffer finds Catholic theology to be helpful, and that he starts working on his own thoughts on "the natural."

CRITICISMS CONCERNING BONHOEFFER'S CONCEPT OF THE NATURAL

Bonhoeffer's thinking on natural life has recently been strongly criticized by Günther Thomas.[126] As he notes, Bonhoeffer's concept of the natural was influenced by certain elements stemming from the philosophy of life ("Lebensphilosophie") as well as from Nietzsche's thinking. Thomas of course recognizes that Bonhoeffer explicitly opposed vitalism, not simply by saying so himself, but also by limiting his concept of the natural in various ways. He notes, for instance, that when writing about "The Right to Bodily Life," Bonhoeffer explicitly opposes himself against the notion that, following the proper use of rationality, a new, healthy humanity can be created.[127] He also indicates that the "Yes" that Jesus Christ speaks to affirm strong, healthy life, is linked by Bonhoeffer with the "Yes" that Christ speaks to suffering, self-renunciation, and humility.[128] Indeed, Bonhoeffer explicitly takes a stand against the false dichotomy that would set vitalistic ethics in opposition to the so-called ethics of Jesus.[129] And yet, according to Thomas, these "checks" are still not enough to secure a workable, theological conception of the natural.

In particular, he lists four problems with the concept. First of all, he notes that there is a certain ambivalence in Bonhoeffer's use of the term "the natural": while on the one hand, it comes into existence through revelation, being the penultimate, on the other hand, it denotes the biological-natural

---

125. DBWE 6:171, editorial footnote 5.

126. Thomas, "Christus als Konnex," 351–54.

127. DBWE 6:195. By saying this, Bonhoeffer indirectly aims against the new laws being introduced in Nazi Germany at that time. See DBWE 6:195, editorial footnote 83.

128. DBWE 6:252.

129. DBWE 6:252.

life. This is nevertheless only an apparent contradiction, as I would argue: according to Bonhoeffer, the biological-natural life *is* "the natural" that came about through Christ. Their unity is to be found in the concept of the one Christ-reality that underlies them both.

The second problem that Thomas sees is that, in the concept of the natural, it remains unclear how elements from the philosophy of life and theological-christological arguments relate to each other. This is, however, a problem that Bonhoeffer explicitly addresses in his *Ethics*. In the manuscript "History and Good [2]," he lists a number of life's ambivalences, such as life and death, sickness and health, and happiness and renunciation. He then notes that these contrasting elements are inextricably intertwined in a living, dialectical unity, which does not resolve the contradiction between them: "Any attempt to isolate one from the other, to play one off against the other, or to appeal to one against the other is an unholy destruction of the unity of life."[130] An essential aspect of living in the penultimate is that it is not only imperfect, but fundamentally ambivalent, and thus open to multiple interpretations, of which vitalism is one. A "purer" concept of life would not describe life itself, but, perhaps, the ultimate towards which it is oriented; aside from that, it would only be an unhelpful abstraction.[131]

Thomas' third objection expands upon the second. According to him, Bonhoeffer's assertion that life is its own healer stands in irreconcilable tension with his statement that, in Christ, the unity of life is given.[132] According to Thomas, Bonhoeffer himself opened up other ways to discuss the reality of the world, namely in light of his thoughts on Christ's resurrection. According to him: "Starting from the resurrection of Christ, one can speak about the reality of the world in a consequentially christological perspective."[133] Thomas doesn't seem to realize that Bonhoeffer *does* in fact connect the resurrection of Christ with the world as it is, as we saw already. The reason that Bonhoeffer also speaks of the natural, in *addition* to discussing Christ in the three moments of his relation to the world (incarnation, crucifixion, and resurrection), is that the three moments, in themselves, are not yet enough to describe the fullness of life adequately. There is more to life than can be explained by Christ's incarnation, crucifixion, and resurrection. What remains to be explained in particular is how the (imperfect) life, in the

130. DBWE 6:252.

131. Also, Prüller-Jagenteufel asserts that Bonhoeffer does not divinize or mythologize natural life. See Prüller-Jagenteufel, *Befreit zur Verantwortung*, 327.

132. Thomas, "Christus als Konnex," 357.

133. "Vom Christusereignis herkommend kann ja von der Weltwirklichkeit nur noch in einer konsequent christologischen Perspektivierung gesprochen werden." Ibid.

penultimate, is ordered. In order to do this, Bonhoeffer uses the concept of natural life, though in a strongly theologically qualified way. In particular, he does *not* understand the natural as being independent of Christ, as Green recognizes when he writes: "Describing Scripture, mandates and offices, and natural rights and duties as components of Bonhoeffer's everyday ethic is not to set up alternate bases of ethics independent of Christ. It is rather to point concretely to the process and ingredients of ethical formation within the church-community and society by which Christ takes form in human life."[134]

Thomas' fourth and final objection to Bonhoeffer's understanding of the natural alleges that Bonhoeffer fails to adequately incorporate biological nature into his concept. He points out that, although biological nature does contribute in certain ways to the concept, when Bonhoeffer discusses the fight between the unnatural and the natural, he only mentions cultural, political and organizational processes. This is indeed the case, but this lack of attention to biological nature should not be seen as deliberate; on the contrary, it is the direct consequence of the fact that, in the serious, historical situation of his time, Bonhoeffer was focused on the problems at hand, such as eugenics programs, and the artificial determination of who can or cannot sexually reproduce. Moreover, there was, at the time, no general awareness of the growing ecological threat that industrialization posed to nature. There therefore appears to be no intrinsic reason why Bonhoeffer could not have addressed such a threat with an appeal to his understanding of natural life, provided of course that he had been aware of the problem. In fact, as I will show in the second part of this chapter, the concept of natural life proves to be particularly helpful precisely insofar as the ecological crisis is concerned—it provides a concept by which to criticize the destruction of nature on a rather "neutral," immanent basis.

Apart from these problems, Thomas poses yet another objection to the concept of the natural in Bonhoeffer, namely an objection concerning the immanent eschatology inherent in Bonhoeffer's concept.[135] There he points out that, according to Bonhoeffer, the process of natural life itself is responsible for safeguarding the rights of the individual. Bonhoeffer realizes that the time that life processes need in order to repair the injustices done to individual life is longer than an individual's lifespan. This means that an individual who is oppressed in the present might never receive any restitution for that oppression in his or her lifetime. According to Thomas, this is far too meager a recompense: "That this process itself—eventually—repairs

134. Green, *Bonhoeffer*, 327.

135. See esp. Thomas, "Christus als Konnex," 358–60.

its own damage, is little more than a vague hope and offers no comfort to people who are suffering right now."[136]

I agree with Thomas that, as an eschatological concept, "the natural" does not suffice: there is no guarantee that the natural process will right the wrongs of history, and even if it were to do so, it would not last forever. The natural world, at least in its present form, is bound for destruction and decay. However, Bonhoeffer never intended the concept to be eschatological in nature—on the contrary, it belongs to the penultimate, which presupposes the ultimate, namely the return of Jesus Christ and the creation of a new heaven and a new earth. Bonhoeffer himself knows pefectly well that the process of life is incapable of righting the wrongs of history. In the manuscript "Ethics as Formation," he narrates how the successful direct and give shape to history: "The successful create facts that cannot be reversed. What they destroy cannot be restored. What they construct has, at least in the following generation, the right of existence . . . [T]he success remains and determines history."[137] The final justification and vindication of history's victims is therefore not to be expected from the natural process—which only seeks to return to a state of equilibrium when it is violated—but from God, at the end of history, in the eschaton.

The Relevance of Living "In Christ" For Environmental Ethics

In the second part of this chapter, I will transpose the concepts described above into the debates over environmental ethics. I will do this in four sections. In the first section, I will describe how the concept of the one Christ-reality can help justify environmental action by Christians. In the second, I will indicate the relevance of Bonhoeffer's distinction between ultimate and penultimate for discussions about the relation between eschatology and ecology. The third section will apply Bonhoeffer's threefold partition to the way human beings relate to nature, and, in the fourth and final section, I will describe how Bonhoeffer's thoughts on "the natural" can provide a theological response to the Gaia Theory.

---

136. "Daβ dieser Prozeβ selbst—à la longue—seine eigenen Schäden repariert, ist wenig mehr als eine vage Hoffnung und kein Trost für den Menschen, der jetztleidet." Ibid., 359.

137. DBWE 6:88.

The Concept of Christ-reality As a Motivation for Ecological Discipleship

Although Christian thinkers have generally recognized both the need for and the importance of developing a Christian environmental ethics in response to the ecological crisis, there have been and continue to be dissenters who contest the view that we ought to care for the earth. This is especially the case among evangelical Christians. At the same time, some evangelical leaders have been quick to respond to the ecological crisis by urging for Christian action.[138] Their plea has been answered by a growing number of initiatives, such as those developed by A Rocha,[139] The Au Sable Institute of Environmental Studies,[140] and the Evangelical Environmental Network.[141] Yet it is still the case that evangelicals fall behind the curve when it comes to showing concern for the environment, both practically[142] and theologically.[143]

One important reason why a great number of evangelical Christians remain averse to environmental ethics has to do with their eschatology. A clear connection exists between what one believes concerning the future and the way that one treats the environment.[144] If an eschatology emphasizes the transitoriness of the world and stresses the discontinuity of the new creation with the old, it is much less likely that such an eschatology will lead to an active attitude with regards to caring for nature. As Al Truesdale sharply states: "[E]vangelicals are predominantly committed to an eschatology that

138. See Schaeffer, *Pollution and the Death of Man*. A contemporary example is McGrath, *The Re-Entchantment of Nature*.

139. www.arocha.org (accessed July 21, 2016).

140. www.ausable.org (accessed July 21, 2016).

141. www.creationcare.org (accessed July 21, 2016).

142. See Truesdale, "Last Things First," 116–22.

143. The lack of attention to ecology in Christian eschatology is mentioned, among others, by Davis, "Ecological 'Blind Spots,'" 274n8. Specificaly evangelical theological support of environmentalism is growing, however. See Simmons, "Evangelical Environmentalism," 40–71; and Bookless, "Christian Mission and Environmental Issues," 37–52.

144. See Tanner, "Beliefs, Actions, Attitudes," 1–34; and Maier, "Green Millenialism," 246–65, esp. 246. A particularly shocking example of this relationship is a comment made by megachurch pastor Mark Driscoll. According to many witnesses, during an evangelical congress he said: "I know who made the environment. He's coming back and he's going to burn it all up. So yes, I drive an SUV." Reported by Pierson, "Does God Love the World?" To put it in context, it should be noted that most evangelicals do not recognize Driscoll as belonging to mainstream evangelicalism, nor would most evangelicals agree with such a statement.

makes it religiously unnecessary and logically impossible to engage in the long-range commitments to the environment required by a truly serious attitude of ecological stewardship."[145] The same point has been made by others as well.[146] One should take care, however, not to make hasty generalizations. Harry O. Maier points out that important differences exist between the eschatological schemes that are adopted by different groups of evangelicals.[147] An eschatology like that of Douglas J. Moo, for instance, which emphasizes the continuity between the old and the new creation,[148] is decidedly more environmentally sensitive than some versions of dispensationalism. The latter perspective, in stark contrast, becomes particularly clear in what Todd Strandberg, a popular premillenialist, writes about environmentalism: "The main job of a Christian leader is to guide lost souls to redemption. I can only ask where the Bible even hints that saving the whales and fighting global warming are part of the Great Commission. Dealing with environmental problems needs to be left to the politicians."[149] In this citation we see a form of eschatology that leads to a renunciation of Christian responsibility for the environment. But we also see how it makes a distinction between the Kingdom of God (carrying out the great commission), and the kingdom of the world (caring for whales). Though often formulated more carefully and precisely, this distinction is visible in other evangelical theologies as well.[150]

It is here that Bonhoeffer's concept of Christ-reality can be helpful.[151] We saw that, with this concept, he fought both the theological justification of Nazism as well as the attempt to escape from taking responsibility and opposing it. In a similar way, this concept can be used today to criticize attempts to flee from taking responsibility for the environmental crisis by

145. Truesdale, "Last Things First," 116.

146. See Curry-Roper, "Contemporary Christian Eschatologies," 157–69; and Granberg-Michaelson, *A Worldly Spirituality*.

147. Maier, "Green Millenialism." See also Finger, *Evangelicals, Eschatology, and the Environment*.

148. Moo, "Nature in the New Creation," 449–88.

149. Strandberg, "Bible Prophecy and Environmentalism." There have been certain developments in dispensationalist circles, however. For a modified position, see Turner, "The New Jerusalem in Revelation 21:1–22:5," 264–92.

150. It should be noted, though, that a great deal of the resistance against environmental action, especially in America, has to do with differing political allegiances. See the older but still relevant article by Wright, "Tearing Down the Green," 80–91.

151. For a more general description of how Bonhoeffer's christocentric approach to reality opens up a "third way" of Christian social engagement (between the neo-Calvinism of Abraham Kuyper on the one hand and the neo-anabaptism of Stanley Hauerwas on the other hand), see Nullens, "Dietrich Bonhoeffer," 60–69.

appealing to doctrines that claim that it is not a Christian's duty to be involved in caring for creation.[152] Specifically, the eschatological dimension of Bonhoeffer's concept can help to refocus (especially evangelical) eschatology by making it less concerned with what will happen in the future (and, in particular, *how* it will happen) and more concerned with recognizing the biblical assertion that the eschaton has already been made present through Christ. Such a refocusing can empower Christians to take "the world" (the natural world included) more seriously; by allowing them to attribute more value to the way that they act in this world, they will no longer see it as a transitory order but, indeed, as the world that Christ lovingly entered and directed to himself, to his coming in glory.[153]

Bonhoeffer's Ultimate/Penultimate Distinction in Relation to Immanent Eschatologies

In the preceding section we saw how the eschatology of many evangelicals prevents them, at least to a certain extent, from involvement in environmental care. For many other Christians, it is quite the other way around: they perceive the environmental crisis posing a challenge, or an obstacle to be overcome, in order to create a better world. Their eschatology is much more immanent in nature: the kingdom of God must (at least in part) be realized by human beings in the here and now. Hope for a better world and for a brighter future energizes them to get involved in environmental action. This is the mainline position in liberal Protestant theology.

A good example can be found in the work of Jürgen Moltmann. In his recent book *Ethics of Hope*[154]—the long-awaited ethical outworking of his

---

152. This possibility of the eschatological dimension of Bonhoeffer's concept of the one Christ-reality to function as a motivation for environmental action has also been recognized by others, most notably by Burkholder. After shortly describing the concept, he argues that it "allow[s] Bonhoeffer to shape soteriology and eschatology in a way which emphasizes life in this present world." Burkholder, "Christological Foundations," 348. And further on he argues: "In making Christ the center of all reality . . . Bonhoeffer establishes Christ as the very one who leads human beings back to an appropriate valuing of this world and nature." Ibid., 350. While he notes that human beings are not responsible for establishing God's kingdom on earth themselves, he does recognize that Bonhoeffer's concept can help Christians to change their ways toward the environment. Specifically, he mentions refrain from using animals for food and scientific experiments as a means to preview the eschaton.

153. This can be seen as an addition to the biblical arguments offered by Bouma-Prediger, *For the Beauty of the Earth*, 81–110.

154. Moltmann, *Ethics of Hope*.

ealier *Theology of Hope*[155]—he argues that Christian hope empowers people to build a better world.[156] As a part of his argument, he describes different models of the relationship between eschatology and ethics: an apocalyptic eschatology (which he identifies in Lutheranism and conservative evangelicalism); a christological eschatology (manifest in Calvin and Barth, among others); a separatist eschatology (which Moltmann recognizes in the Anabaptists, but also in the postliberalism of Stanley Hauerwas); and finally his own proposal for a transformative eschatology.[157] He also refers to this as an eschatological Christology, which recognizes that the eschatological future has already begun in Christ, even though it is also still yet to come. In this scheme, ethics becomes ethics of anticipation, or more precisely, a *messianic ethics* through which the Spirit lays claim on the present from the perspective of the consummation. Ethics thus becomes oriented in relation to an anticipation of the final Kingdom. This plea for transformative eschatology is fundamental for Moltmann's theology in general. He is certainly not alone in his proposal, moreover; on the contrary, he stands in a broad stream of late-twentieth century theology also visible in the work of Van Ruler, Berkhof, and Schillebeeckx, as well as in the theology of the World Council of Churches.[158] Moltmann himself does not indicate clearly what the perspective of transformative eschatology means for environmental ethics.[159] However, others have labored within a similar vein of transformative eschatology and have applied it specifically to environmental ethics.

One such attempt has been made by Anne Marie Dalton and Henry C. Simmons in their book *Ecotheology and the Practice of Hope*. According

---

155. Moltmann, *Theology of Hope*.

156. In this context, Moltmann strongly opposes himself against the philosophy of Hans Jonas, who wrote the influential *The Imperative of Responsibility*. According to Moltmann, Jonas offers an ethics of fear instead of hope, fear for what perhaps will no longer be. Regardless of whether or not his criticism of Jonas is justified, it certainly is the case that a deep concern about the future of the natural world has been one of the main influences on the field of environmental ethics and ecotheology. This is clearly discernable even in the titles of some of the benchmark-books that have been written on the subject, such as Cobb, *Is It Too Late?*; and Weizsäcker, *Die Zeit drängt*. This is pointed out by Van de Beek, *God doet recht*, 297n11. In the arena of popular culture, anxiety about the ecological future of the planet had led to the creation of films such as *The Day after Tomorrow*, directed by Ronald Emmerich, 20th Century Fox, 2004, and the documentary *An Inconvenient Truth*, directed by Davis Guggenheim, Paramount Classics, 2006.

157. Moltmann, *Ethics of Hope*, 35–41.

158. See Van de Beek, *God doet recht*, 21–23.

159. Someone who does develop a line of thinking in this direction is Harvie, *Moltmann's Ethics*.

to them, "[p]ractices of hope resist despair even in the face of evident ecological degradation. As practitioners of hope, Christian theologians are sober in their judgments about the certain results of business as usual in our relationship to the earth; still, they do not give up their intense efforts to pull the world back from the brink of ecological disaster."[160] The writers narrate how, while reading the texts of ecologists working on the theme of impending ecological disaster, they were, at first, almost driven to despair; reading Charles Taylor's *Modern Social Imaginaries*[161] thereafter opened their eyes to the fact that the accumulated texts themselves constituted a sign of hope, because they helped ecology gain a place in the academy and helped constitute a cultural space for environmental ethics. As such, ecology occupies a position capable of influencing and re-creating the present social imaginary, or more broadly, of helping create a new moral order. It is still the case that "[t]he present social imaginary in the West has little in its repertory that is ecologically sane."[162] Yet, at the same time, they assert that "[t]he community of texts we examine in this book [17] participate in the process by which this repertory can be extended and changed to include ecological values and practices."[163]

These citations—while in no way underestimating the direness of the current ecological situation—speak of an optimism with regards both to the future of the world and to the human capacity to improve the world. However, the question is just how realistic this "hope" is, in the end. Not only are the signs of progress few and far between, but they stand in the context of ever growing ecological problems. Wouldn't the proper answer to the title of Cobb's book (*Is It Too Late?*) have to be a simple, unequivocal "yes"?

Even leaving these questions to the side, the underlying theology itself can be radically questioned. One of the most outspoken contemporary theologians in this regard is Abraham van de Beek. He strongly rejects theological thinking of the sort that Moltmann offers, in which Christian eschatology is taken as a program for societal transformation. On his view, there are no convincing signs that the world will be able to improve as a result of applying Christian ethics. The optimism at work in this approach—namely the dream concerning the possibilities of a just and peaceful world—is, according to him, a late expression of the grand narratives of modernity.[164] And not only that, but according to him, this way of thinking misinter-

160. Dalton and Simmons, *Ecotheology and the Practice of Hope*, viii.

161. Taylor, *Modern Social Imaginaries*.

162. Dalton and Simmons, *Ecotheology and the Practice of Hope*, 16.

163. Ibid., 16–17.

164. Van de Beek, *God doet recht*, 23.

prets the New Testament teaching concerning the Kingdom of God. In his own words: "In the New Testament, it is not about a gradual development throughout history, but about the inbreaking judgment of God."[165] This is a point that Van de Beek belabors extensively in full conversation with recent New Testament scholarship. According to him, the task of Christians is not to try to improve the world by means of developing programs or developing and following ideals. It not only doesn't work, but it also isn't even the Christian's task.

At first sight, it would appear as if Van de Beek shared the criticism voiced by Strandberg who, as we saw earlier, argues that Christians have no business being concerned with environmental ethics. That is not Van de Beek's position, however. As he says: "We are strangers in the world. But that doesn't mean that we are not interested in the world. Christ has died for this world, and so we share in his concern for this world."[166] His point, then, is not that Christians shouldn't care about the world, but rather that they shouldn't expect too much from their work. Taking responsibility is good, of course, but it should happen in modesty and humility, that is, without expecting or claiming too much. The Kingdom of God is not established by human beings, but only by Christ himself. Van de Beek is not alone in his criticism, moreover. Northcott also opposes himself against unrealistic expectations, both theologically (in his criticism of Moltmann, for example[167]) and scientifically. He notes that, in the modern scientific myth, "[h]istory is said to be characterized by an inevitable progression from the 'dark ages' to the modern present and posited future."[168] According to him, this is essentially "a secularized version of Jewish and Christian eschatology, in which hope in the future fulfillment of history through the return of the Messiah, or Christ, and the divine restoration of the creation after the judgment, is transformed into a humanistic futurism in which human and technological progress in history is substituted for divine action and the eschaton."[169]

---

165. "Het gaat in het Nieuwe Testament niet om een geleidelijke ontwikkeling in de geschiedenis, maar om het inbreken van het gericht van God." Ibid.

166. "We zijn vreemdelingen in de wereld. Maar dat wil niet zeggen dat we ongeïnteresseerd zijn in de wereld. Als Christus voor deze wereld gestorven is, dan delen wij in zijn zorg voor de wereld." Ibid., 225.

167. Northcott accuses Moltmann of overvaluing the dynamic and changing character of the cosmos. On his view, Moltmann relies too heavily on progressive modern philosophers such as Bloch and Hegel, "whose philosophies of progress are . . . deeply implicated in the roots of the ecological crisis of modern civilisation." Northcott, The Environment, 143.

168. Ibid., 67.

169. Ibid.

Nullens also formulates similar criticisms concerning the modern belief in progress.[170]

Does this mean that we have to return to an "ethics of fear," as Moltmann accused Jonas of offering? Not necessarily. In Bonhoeffer's theology, we are offered an alternative view of ethics in light of the eschatological inbreaking of God's Kingdom, according to which the need for ethics (including environmental ethics) is not abolished, but is placed in its proper context, not as "building towards" the Kingdom, but as "preparing the way" for it. The key lies in Bonhoeffer's distinction between the ultimate and the penultimate, as we saw earlier. Caring for the penultimate is important, not because it helps to transform the world into the ultimate, but because it helps create the conditions in which the ultimate word of justification by faith alone can be heard.[171]

One other problem with immanent eschatology has been brought to the fore anew in the debate over the viability of Christian eschatology in light of the natural sciences. As natural scientists have pointed out, the Earth will not and cannot exist forever: approximately five billion years from now, when the Sun burns out, it will come to an end. It is not the solar system alone that is bound to decay and break apart, moreover; as Arnold Benz observes, "all cosmic structures from galaxies to planets and even the matter of the universe itself are bound for decay and destruction. Life cannot continue forever . . . The history of all things ends intrinsically in tragedy."[172] Benz, as a Christian, nevertheless continues to claim that there is hope for the universe in spite of this, though this is a hope based not on science so much as on a religious plane. This begs the question, of course, how that religious hope is supposed to relate to scientific predictions—a question that Benz fails to answer.

What remains to be carried out, in other words, is a hermeneutical-theological task through which Christian eschatology is made intelligible in light of the natural sciences. This task has been described by Kathryn Tanner.[173] As she points out, in protology, the theories of the natural sciences concerning the origin of life have been largely accepted by theologians and incorporated into a re-interpretation of the doctrine of creation.[174] According to her, we have to do a similar re-interpretation of Christian eschatology.

170. Nullens, "Leven volgens Gaia's normen?," 184–85.

171. Mostert makes a similar point in "Hope as Ultimate and Proximate," 231–46.

172. Benz, "Tragedy versus Hope," 120.

173. Tanner, "Eschatology without a Future?," 222–37; and ibid., "Eschatology and Ethics," 41–56.

174. For an evangelical perspective, see McGrath, *Darwinism and the Divine*.

She asks "what a Christian eschatology might be like if scientists are right that the world does not have a future. Is it really the case that such an end is simply incompatible as it stands with Christian hopes for this world?"[175] What is required, as she asserts, is not a simple capitulation of Christian hope before the hard facts of scientific knowledge; on the contrary, what is needed is a way of understanding the cosmos that makes sense theologically, while not denying the sciences. In doing so, she proposes to broaden the understanding of eschatology by moving away from a limited temporal understanding of "the last things" to a more spatialized conception. She connects this with postmodern thinking, citing the work of Foucault in particular.

Tanner describes eternal life not as an endless extension of present existence into the future, but rather as a new dimension of life in God, stating: "Eternal life is less a matter of duration than a matter of the mode of one's existence in relation to God, as the calibre of relation shows itself in a new pattern for the whole of life."[176] And she goes on to assert: "At the most fundamental level, eternal life is ours now in union with Christ, as in the future."[177] For biblical support of her views, Tanner turns to the Old Testament, where, as she points out, very different notions of life and death are used. "Life," in the Old Testament, stands for fruitfulness, longevity and communal flourishing, whereas "death" denotes isolation, fragmentation, oppression. As Stephen C. Barton observes, summarizing Tanner's point from the Old Testament, "the most important senses of 'life' and 'death' have to do with *relation with God*."[178] According to Tanner, this line extends into the New Testament as well. She summarizes her views in the following key statement: "[T]he eschaton . . . has to do primarily with a new level of relationship with God, the final one surpassing what we are simply as creatures, beyond which there is no other."[179]

---

175. Tanner, "Eschatology Without a Future?," 224.

176. Ibid., 49.

177. Ibid.

178. Barton, "New Testament Eschatology," 275; italics original.

179. Tanner, "Eschatology and Ethics," 47–48. Tanner has not been the only one to develop this view. Ruether formulates a similar proposal, arguing that we, as human beings, should accept our finitude instead of absolutizing the individual ego as everlasting. In a key citation she notes: "It is not our calling to be concerned about the eternal meaning of our lives and religion should not make this the focus of its message. Our responsibility is to use our temporal life span to create a just and good community for our generation and our children. It is in the hand of Holy Wisdom to forge out of our finite struggle truth and meaning for everlasting life." Ruether, *Sexism and God-talk*, 258, cited in Conradie, *Hope for the Earth*, 264. Ruether's position has been criticized by Conradie, "Eschatological Dimensions," 182–83.

It is easy to form reservations about Tanner's position.[180] Barton points out three problems with her position in particular. First of all, in spite of Tanner's claim to the contrary, she does in fact surrender the "end" to the terms set out by scientific naturalism. This is problematic because "this kind of position threatens the hope in God that is at the core of Christian conviction precisely because the naturalistic account is deemed not to be the whole story or the best way of telling the story."[181] Secondly, Barton accuses Tanner of focusing exclusively on what she calls the spatial dimension of the eschaton and of omitting the strong biblical testimony for its temporal dimension. According to her, eschatology has to be de-temporalized entirely. She argues for "uncoupling the eschaton from hopes for the world's future. We have our hope in God whether or not things are likely to turn out well in the end."[182] For Barton, this stretches the notion of eschatology too far. Thirdly and finally, Barton doubts if Tanner's alignment with postmodernism is a fruitful one, since, according to him, it involves "downplaying temporality—especially in its past and future aspects."[183] He argues that as a consequence, it negates the necessity of repenting for mistakes made in the past and for taking responsibility for the future. Although one may easily wonder if Barton's assessment of postmodernity as downplaying temporality is justified, he is certainly right when he points out that Tanner does away too quickly with the temporal dimension of the eschaton.

Tanner's outworking of the "spatial" dimension, however, does offer a much needed enrichment of Christian eschatology. Her appeal to Old Testament notions of life and death as ways of life, rather than temporal descriptions, resonates with recent biblical scholarship.[184] It is my own contention that, in his own time, and with his own theological vocabulary, Bonhoeffer tried to give voice to the same idea as Tanner does with the twin concepts of penultimate and ultimate. As we saw above, Bonhoeffer emphasized that the ultimate is not only temporary in nature, but also *qualitatively* different from the penultimate. And according to him, this qualitative difference not only reveals itself in the final consummation of the world, but already in the way in which it breaks into time in the moment of the justification by

180. It is important to stress that, in a subtle way, other theologians often carry out precisely what Tanner proposes, without, however, making the point as explicit as she does. This has been pointed out by Van de Beek, *God doet recht*, 21.

181. Barton, "New Testament Eschatology," 276.

182. Tanner, "Eschatology and Ethics," 46. It should be pointed out that, while Tanner uses the word "spatial," she does not, apparently, mean this in the physical sense of the word. "Spatial" should be understood metaphorically, in contrast with "temporal."

183. Barton, "New Testament Eschatology," 277.

184. See Levenson, *Resurrection and the Restoration of Israel*.

faith. Bonhoeffer does not, however, do away with the temporal dimension of Christian eschatology. In this respect he clearly differs from Tanner. How exactly we are to understand this temporal consummation of the world remains an open question, but it is essential for Christian theology to retain this element.

The Relevance of Bonhoeffer's Christological Threefold Partition for Environmental Ethics

In the section above I have described how Bonhoeffer's distinction between the ultimate and the penultimate has relevance for environmental ethics. It remains a question, however, of *how* exactly Christians should act in the penultimate. We saw how this question led Van 't Slot to turn for inspiration to Barth's theology. I argue, instead, that Bonhoeffer's description of the three moments in the relationship between Christ and the world takes on particular importance in this instance. We have seen earlier how Bonhoeffer understands the three moments of incarnation, crucifixion, and resurrection—all three being equal to each other—as the basic pattern according to which Christ relates to the world and, as a consequence, according to which Christian behavior must be formed. These three moments can also be applied to environmental ethics in particular.

The first to recognize this possibility was Nullens.[185] He interprets the incarnation as a sign of God's love for his creation, while Christ's crucifixion tells of God's judgment of the world, and the resurrection speaks of God's will for a new world. As we saw above, Bonhoeffer strongly warns against pulling these elements apart. Nullens echoes this point by warning against the development of an independent theology of creation, or of the cross, or the resurrection. Apart from this, Bonhoeffer's threefold partition has not yet been applied to environmental ethics. As such, in what follows, I would like to continue Nullens' work by indicating what the added value of Bonhoeffer's threefold partition is for environmental ethics. I will do so first by treating the three moments of incarnation, crucifixion and resurrection separately.

THE MOMENT OF INCARNATION IN RELATION TO ECOLOGY

I shall begin with the incarnation. In ecotheology, this moment has come to take on a great deal of significance—indeed, a great number of ecotheologians emphasize the importance of the incarnation. An example can be

185. Nullens, "Leven volgens Gaia's normen?," 199–206.

found in the work of Martha Kirkpatrick.[186] She takes her cue from John 3:16 and argues: "If 'world' may be understood not only as human society but as the entire cosmos, the Incarnation becomes a manifestation of God's necessity to be materially related to creation, to be immanent and fully present, that is, embodied, in all of life."[187] Similar proposals have been formulated by numerous other ecotheologians as well. There is nevertheless a significant deal of divergence over the question of how exactly Christ's incarnation is related to creation and environmental ethics. Douglas John Hall, for instance, interprets the incarnation primarily as an *example*: according to him, in the historical person of Christ, we find a model of stewardship, of life in the *imago Dei*.[188] For many other ecotheologians, this does not go far enough. Celia E. Deane-Drummond, for example, objects that this way of formulating the relation focuses too heavily on Jesus' exemplary function for human beings and too little on the real cosmic consequences of his incarnation. Instead, according to her, "it makes sense to see the incarnation as similarly being thoroughly identified with the earth as such—that is, a wider meaning than identification with humans alone, or even humans in companionship with animals, for example."[189] She works out precisely what such a revised incarnational ecology should look like by focusing on the cosmic Christology of the letters of Paul in particular.[190] Similar projects have been undertaken by Denis Edwards,[191] and John F. Dean.[192] Much more radical in nature is the work of Lisa Isherwood.[193] She offers a deconstructionist reading of the creation narrative, reconceptualizing Eve's eating of the tree of knowledge of good and evil, not as sin, but as a rich, appreciative attitude towards creation: a sensuous encounter with the tree's fruit, an openness to reality. This, for Isherwood, is what incarnation implies, and what forms the perspective from which it must be interpreted.

   This brief overview of the literature reveals both that Christ's incarnation is an important source of reflection for environmental ethics, and

---

186. Kirkpatrick, "'For God So Loved the World,'" 191–212.

187. Ibid., 203.

188. Hall, *Imaging God*.

189. Deane-Drummond, "Ecology and Christology," 100.

190. See also Deane-Drummond, "Deep Incarnation and Eco-Justice as Theo-drama," 193–206.

191. Edwards, "Deep Incarnation," 58–60.

192. Although it should be noted that his perspective is somewhat different: Dean explores poetry and describes how it relates to Christ and the incarnation, particularly insofar as ecology is concerned. See Dean, *The Works of Love*.

193. Isherwood, "The Tree, the Cross and Global Capitalism," 93–106.

at the same time, that it is interpreted in many different ways. Bonhoeffer can also contribute to the discussion because, although his treatment of the incarnation does not interpret the latter with regards to nature, we will see in chapter 3 that he strongly emphasizes a cosmic Christology—that is, he deliberately and consciously places Christ at the center of nature. It would therefore not be too great a stretch to give to his thoughts on the incarnation a specifically ecological interpretation. Doing so might prove to be quite helpful in balancing out the debate, in fact, especially in light of interpretations such as that of Lisa Isherwood. As we saw earlier in Bonhoeffer's entire, early theology, the moment of incarnation is a very critical one—it implies a judgment of the world as it is, just as we saw above, and it is only in Bonhoeffer's *Ethics* that this aspect retreats into the background. When interpreted in light of environmental ethics, what this means is that the incarnation cannot simply be used as a justification of the natural world as it is. Christ's becoming human is just as much a revelation of the world's evil, that is, the evil in the natural world, as it is an acceptance and "taking on" of that world. This helps provide the conceptual key necessary to criticize interpretations such as Isherwood's, which essentially deny any wrong within the natural world itself.

The Moments of Crucifixion and Resurrection in Relation to Ecology

There have also been attempts, albeit less frequent, to draw out the meaning of the crucifixion and the resurrection with regards to environmental ethics. An example from the Reformed tradition can be found in the work of Daniel L. Migliore.[194] Migliore recognizes and explores the possibilities of interpreting Christ's tripartite relationship to the world in light of environmental ethics. When writing about the hope for nature expressed in Rom 8:18–25, for instance, he says: "Implied in this biblical hope that is centered in the incarnate, crucified, and risen Christ are at least three insights about the destiny of nature."[195] It is nevertheless important to note that Migliore focuses somewhat less on the incarnation than on the question of how the moments of crucifixion and resurrection relate to the natural world, giving particular emphasis to the crucifixion, which he takes to be the most important of the three. He writes: "More than most doctrines of the saving significance of the death of Christ have acknowledged, the cross of Christ is the decisive event not only of God's redemption of human history but also

194. Migliore, "Eschatology and Ecology," 10–32.
195. Ibid., 28.

the decisive clue to suffering and redemption of natural history as well."[196] This leads directly, as Migliore argues, to a changed perspective on nature. He asserts in particular that Christians will, as a consequence, look upon nature, not as mere material that can be used in accordance with human desires, but, instead, "as a bearer of God's promises and as a fellow sufferer groaning for liberation and redemption."[197] Christians will accordingly come to show respect for the fragile web of life on this planet. With regards to the resurrection, Migliore notes that the same perspective helps us to conceive of nature as participating, together with humanity, in the hope of final transformation. In his own words: "The bodily resurrection of Christ is the ground of hope for all creation. It is the proleptic realization of cosmic transformation."[198] This hope for cosmic transformation is intrinsically bound up with personal hope, as Migliore argues, for human existence is a fundamentally embodied existence, and human bodies are an inextricable part of the material universe. As such, personal hope, of necessity, leads to a hope for the whole of creation. Hope for a new earth therefore expresses itself in a "cosmic solidarity," and leads to prayer and faithful action. Other theologians have also thought through the implications of the crucifixion and the resurrection on environmental ethics, but their number is limited.[199]

The work of Migliore displays a positive attitude towards nature and serves as a valuable contribution to environmental ethics from the Reformed tradition. It is conceivable, however, that his stress on the cross and the resurrection can easily lead to an undervaluation of the body, of nature and of *matter* in general. In other words, emphasizing the cross and the resurrection poses the threat of granting too much influence to Gnostic ideas. "Redemption" in this case comes to be understood as a "redemption *from*" the natural world—as a flight of the spirit *from* the body. This, of course, has been a great temptation for Christian theologians ever since the early days of the church. Although less apparent nowadays, at least in academic theology, Gnostic modes of thinking are still easily discernible in certain forms of Christian piety, influencing Christian attitudes to the natural world.[200]

196. Ibid.

197. Ibid.

198. Ibid., 29.

199. See Southgate, "Significance of the Cross and Resurrection," 75–77, as well as the popular, theological reflections of Brown, "The Gardener and the Groundling," 33–37. Work on these themes usually focuses on the question how to understand the crucifixion and the resurrection in relation to the natural sciences. See Gregersen, "The Cross of Christ in an Evolutionary World," 192–207, and Conradie, "Resurrection, Finitude, and Ecology," 277–96.

200. See Northcott, *The Environment*, 211–26.

Bonhoeffer's threefold partition can also help here by balancing the emphasis granted to the crucifixion and the resurrection with an equally strong emphasis on incarnation. In particular, his theology helps to alter the way in which the crucifixion and the resurrection are perceived, making clear they are not directed toward life's redemption in another world, or another dimension, but here on earth, for nature.

THE THREEPARTITION AS A WHOLE IN RELATION TO ECOLOGY

In terms of the general discussion of how the three moments bring Christ into relation with the world in general, the most important contribution that Bonhoeffer's theology can make is in stressing that the three moments must each be considered to bear an equal value, such that none is broken off from or given precedence over the others. The great advantage of Bonhoeffer's model in this regard is that, as Thomas notes, the three moments are not static in nature, but dynamic.[201] It is therefore possible to transpose this threefold, dynamic relationship into the various debates and discussions over environmental ethics, and, thereby, to alter their respective emphases as needed—while always keeping in mind that, for Bonhoeffer, the three moments each bear equal value.

One example of a nuanced treatment of the three moments can be found in the work of Northcott.[202] Northcott begins with the resurrection, which he takes as a foretaste of the eschatological Kingdom of God. What this means is that the resurrection is both a theological given as well as an ethical appeal, namely an appeal for restoration: "The resurrection [203] begins in history the work of restoration which is promised and draws the created order towards its goal of harmony and peace."[203] Northcott also brings Christ's crucifixion into connection with environmental ethics, offering a grand, cosmic interpretation of the latter. Citing Rom 8:18–19, he comments as follows: "Through this great event of redemptive suffering [viz. the crucifixion] the suffering and frustration of every living thing is drawn into the eternal purposes of God for the restoration of the cosmos."[204] Northcott does not limit himself to drawing on the crucifixion and the resurrection, however. He also works out how the incarnation applies to environmental ethics, stating: "The embodiment of God in the man Jesus Christ confirms the original goodness of created order, and substantial, material embodiment re-establishes the trajectory of this order towards God's good

201. Thomas, "Christus als Konnex," 352.
202. Northcott, *The Environment*, esp. 199–215.
203. Ibid., 202–203.
204. Ibid., 204.

purposes, and redeems that which is unredeemed in the embodied life of the cosmos."[205] Northcott's approach is rich, and biblically and theologically well-informed. It offers a good example of a possible contextualisation of Bonhoeffer's threefold partition with regards to environmental ethics.[206]

Bonhoeffer's Concept of the Natural in Relation to the Gaia Theory

In this section I shall work out how Bonhoeffer's nuanced concept of "the natural" can contribute both positively and critically to the current debate in environmental ethics, especially with regards to the Gaia Theory. This latter theory stresses that the individual ecosystems of the earth are all part of a larger superorganism. This superorganism regulates the interaction between the different ecosystems and actively optimalizes conditions for life. The founder of the Gaia Theory is James Loveslock, who developed it, together with Lynn Margulis, in the 1970s.[207] It is important to note that, according to Lovelock, the Gaia Theory is a *scientific* theory: in particular, it is based on the feedback mechanisms that are observed and described in Daisyworld, a mathematical program which describes how temperature regulation can arise from organisms interacting with their environment. Lovelock offers many different definitions of his theory. A widely accepted formulation is offered in the Amsterdam Declaration on Global Change, which asserts: "The Earth System behaves as a single, self-regulating system comprised of physical, chemical, biological and human components."[208]

After having been simply ignored at first, the theory was critizised by scientists such as Richard Dawkins and Stephen Jay Gould. It survived these criticisms, however, and gained a great deal of attention, undergoing constant revision, in the following decades.[209] The International Gaia Confer-

205. Ibid., 208.

206. The way that Northcott describes the incarnation, however, can be criticized from Bonhoeffer's perspective. Northcott sees the birth of Jesus Christ primarily as a confirmation of the goodness of the original creation. With Bonhoeffer, however, we saw how he also emphasizes the critical function of the incarnation. As will become clear later on, this links up with the criticism directed against Northcott's too uncritical alignment with the natural law tradition.

207. Lovelock developed the theory through various articles, which were collected and popularized in Lovelock, *Gaia*. Among his other publications are ibid., *The Revenge of Gaia*; and ibid., *The Vanishing Face of Gaia*.

208. "The Amsterdam Declaration on Global Change."

209. For an overview, see Joseph, *Gaia*. An example of a recent proposal for the theory's revision can be found in Kirchner, "The Gaia Hypothesis," 21–45.

ences can be seen as the official forum in which the theory has flourished, but it has been adopted by many other groups within the environmental movement as well.[210] Particularly interesting in this respect is the adaptation of the Gaia Theory by New Age adherents.[211] The Gaia Theory has also been espoused by many theologians, such as Rosemary Radford Ruether,[212] Berry Thomas,[213] Anne Primavesi,[214] and Bron Taylor.[215]

Instead of attempting to assess the scientific viability of the theory, I will correlate it with Bonhoeffer's conception of "the natural." No great stretch of the imagination is needed to perceive such a connection, as it were, in outline form: like the Gaia Theory, Bonhoeffer stresses that natural life seeks to restore an equilibrium that was upset through human organization. There are some important differences between the two accounts, however. The first difference is that, for Bonhoeffer, "the natural" is a theological concept, whereas for Lovelock et al., it is primarily a scientific one. Writing as a theologian, Bonhoeffer introduced the concept into German Protestant theology in order to describe how God orders the natural world vis-à-vis "the ultimate," that is, the revelation of Jesus Christ. Lovelock, in contrast, writes as a secular scientist, and uses the concept to account for the dynamic and evolving balance found in the earth's ecosystem as a whole. It is important not to lose sight of this crucial difference—equating one theory with the other would be a violation of the proper distinction between theology and biology. Another difference is that, for Bonhoeffer, the biological dimension of "the natural" hardly plays a role at all. As became clear earlier on, he takes it primarily as a cultural concept, whereas for Lovelock, it constitutes a theory within the realm of biology alone. A third difference is that Bonhoeffer's concept of "the natural" is a static one—the natural only fights against the unnatural, which, in the form of organization, comes up against the natural. Once the fight is over, however, the natural returns to its original form. Lovelock's Gaia Theory is quite different—not only does it seek to restore equilibrium, but it brings forth new life-forms as well: it is a dynamic, evolutionary concept through and through.

210. On the remarkable ability of "Gaia" to link science and religion with each other, and to help integrate political, social and ethical models and behavious, see Potts, "Imagining Gaia," 30–49.

211. An example of a New Age thinker who uses the Gaia Theory as a basis to call for environmental action is Starhawk, *Dreaming the Dark*. See also Letcher, "'Gaia Told Me to Do It,'" 61–84.

212. Ruether, *Gaia and God*.

213. Berry, "The Gaia Theory," 7–19.

214. Primavesi, *Sacred Gaia*; ibid., *Gaia's Gift*; and ibid., *Gaia and Climate Change*.

215. Taylor, *Dark Green Religion*.

Despite these differences, however, Bonhoeffer's concept of natural life can help to offer a positive theological assessment of the Gaia Theory. The first—and, as far as I know—only commentator to interpret Bonhoeffer's thoughts on natural life in this direction is Heinz-Eduard Tödt. He writes: "As we become aware of the ecological crisis, we are strongly motivated to take natural life seriously in its self-regulation and its own weight, and to accord to it a dignity and worth that transcends its usefulness for the human being."[216] While Tödt rightfully connects Bonhoeffer's concept of natural life with the self-regulatory process of nature, I do not agree with his conclusion that we are therefore obliged to accord it a dignity in itself. As we will see in chapter 4, Bonhoeffer himself developed an anthropocentric account of nature, and although he did so in *CF*, and has not restated his case since, his thoughts on the natural do not provide sufficient grounds to argue that he abandoned his earlier position in favor of an ecocentric approach. His thoughts on the relative independence of nature do fit together, however, with his assertion of the relative independence of nature vis-à-vis God, the Creator, and it is in this light that his thoughts should be interpreted, namely as an important nuance to his otherwise theocentric account of nature. They can be seen as a testimony to the way in which God regulates the biological life-process of the earth. This is also the way Northcott interprets the Gaia Theory. He connects it with the Bible and the Christian tradition, writing: "[T]he Gaia hypothesis resonates in some significant ways with the ecological account of the Hebrew and Christian ethical tradition . . . In particular the emphasis on the interactivity of all earth systems . . . and the relationality of these systems to human activity is also a fundamental feature of the cosmology of the Hebrew Bible."[217]

A theological appropriation of the Gaia theory can also help to relax, at least in part, the urgent apocalypticism present in so many pleas for environmental action, for the theory implies that life on the earth is not too heavily affected by anthropogenic destruction. Indeed, Lovelock even maintains that a nuclear war would not affect Gaia drastically.[218]

This latter statement, however, also points to the extreme ecocentrism inherent in the Gaia theory. On the theory's own terms, human beings have no primacy in the ecosystem. As Lovelock suggests, Gaia could dispose of the human race as a dangerous threat, and, in this way, go on to survive. As a biological theory, such a suggestion cannot be criticized by theology. It can be criticized, however, once it is transposed from the field of biology into that of ethics, that is, once it it taken as a guideline for ethical behavior.

216. Tödt, *Authentic Faith*, 147.

217. Northcott, *The Environment*, 111–12.

218. Lovelock, *Gaia*, 40–43.

This is what we see happening, for example, in the work of Primavesi. When asking about the significance of human life, Primavesi answers that human beings are not significant in themselves, but rather in relation to others and to the future.[219] In other words, for Primavesi, human beings fit within the great chain of being, and, as such, have no lasting significance in and of themselves. But this immediately begs the question: why even bother with environmental ethics? If Gaia is destined to survive in the end (at least, until the sun burns out, five billion years from now), it doesn't matter in the least what we human beings do to preserve the environment.[220] Northcott argues the same point, for according to him, the "extreme ecocentrim" of the Gaia theory "is clearly inconsistent with a Hebrew and Christian approach which regards human life as closest in form and purpose to the life of God, and which therefore places supreme moral value on human persons and communities."[221] This is the reason why in chapter 4 I will argue that a sound environmental ethics will need a (weak) anthropocentric outlook on nature, a good example of which we find in Bonhoeffer.

From the perspective of Bonhoeffer's theology, we must also oppose attempts to take Gaia literally (i.e., not simply as a theory, but as a goddess), as well as attempts to claim that there is something sacred or divine about nature, such as one finds in the New Age and deep ecology movements. Northcott makes the case that, precisely by stressing the world's oneness, or love for the world as a total concept, "this approach is in danger of erasing the particularity of place and ecosystem, the diversity of life, the distinctiveness of traditional human cultures and the moral and ecological life strategies such cultures have developed over time to preserve the land in balance with human needs."[222] This is indeed a serious danger, and it is therefore necessary to avoid absolutizing the theory. Instead, it should be perceived as an immanent, natural mechanism that God uses to structure life on earth. The theory should therefore be decentralized and should retain its "secularity."

219. In her own words: "Our lives are significant, ultimately, to every living being now and in the future. They do and will depend on Gaia's ability to self-regulate earth's temperatures within a range comfortable for human life. Just as the lives of those who have lived before us were significant contributors to our present comfort or discomfort." Primavesi, *Gaia's Gift*, 86.

220. This can be a dangerous consequence. As Scharper states: "By viewing humans as simply one life form among many, and a largely inessential one at that, Gaia woefully undervalues the human ability to destroy the life systems of the planet. Hence Gaia ultimately lacks a framework for critically assessing and challenging exploitative human activity." Scharper, "The Gaia Hypothesis," 218–19.

221. Northcott, *The Environment*, 112.

222. Ibid., 113. See also Nullens, "Leven volgens Gaia's Normen?," 112–30.

3

Nature in Relation to Christ

In chapter 2, I described how Bonhoeffer sees all of reality as existing in Christ. I also noted, at the same time, that his Christology underwent a steady and rather complicated development over time. In this chapter, I would specifically like to focus on the christological concentration of Bonhoeffer's middle period, especially in 1932 to 1933. These were the years in which he lecutred, at the University of Berlin, on Gen 1–3 (*CF*); during the same period, he also lectured, in closely related fashion, on Christology, placing Christ at the center of his understanding of nature, as well as of human existence, and of history. Together, these lectures contain the core of Bonhoeffer's theology of nature, and, in this chapter, I would like to delve into the implications that this has for environmental ethics. The chapter is divided into two parts: in the first part, I will give an account of Bonhoeffer's theology of nature, whereas in the second, I will transpose this aspect of his theology into the field of environmental ethics.

Christ at the Center of Nature

In the first part of this study, I shall lay out the main components of Bonhoeffer's christocentric theology of nature, treating each aspect in five separate sections. In the first section, I will describe how he saw Christ occupying the center of the original, good creation, prior to the Fall. The second part will then deal with the Fall and its effects on the natural world. Next, in the third section, I will deal with Bonhoeffer's view on Christ as the hidden center of fallen nature. Then, in the fourth section, I will describe Bonhoeffer's assertion of Christ as the redeemer of nature, focusing particularly on his sacramentology as the concrete outworking of this claim, while in the fifth and final section, I will explore Bonhoeffer's concept of the orders of preservation ("Erhaltungsordnungen") along with a description of his position in the debate surrounding natural theology.

Christ as the Center of the Original, Good Creation

In his lectures on Christology, Bonhoeffer asserts that Christ stands at the center of nature. While he focuses specifically on how Christ occupies the center of fallen creation, in *CF* it becomes clear that he saw Christ at the center of the original, good creation as well. The present section will explore the latter issue in particular.

Christology as The Key to Protology

Already on the first page of *CF*, Bonhoeffer asserts that no knowledge of the original creation is attainable if not through Christ. He defines Christ as the "end" and states: "Only the church, which knows of the end, knows also of the beginning."[1] The church believes this while being in the fallen, "old" world. In this situation, she believes in the "new" world, which he defines as both the world prior to the Fall, as well as the world in the eschaton, at the end of times. This belief, he says, is not grounded in anything but in Christ alone. Bonhoeffer's assertion that the beginning of the world can only be appropriated through Christ finds expression in the way he reads the biblical creation narrative. Since the Bible is the book of the church, he argues that therefore it should be read "in a way that begins with Christ and only then moves on toward him as its goal."[2] Concretely, this means that Bonhoeffer applies the method of kerygmatic exegesis to the text of Gen 1–3.

Not only do we only come to *know* about creation's beginning through Christ, but the beginning itself is only made *possible* by Christ. This point becomes clear in the commentary that Bonhoeffer offers on the biblical text. In commenting on Gen 1:1–2, for instance, he notes that the God of the creation is also the God of the resurrection: only because Christ has risen do we even know that God created the world *ex nihilo* in the first place. According to him, then, it is only by reading the creation narrative through the lens of Christ that the true meaning of the story is disclosed. While creation is not the stage on which the story of Christ is effectively played out, the fact of Christ's resurrection is, in retrospect, precisely what makes creation out of nothing possible in the first place.

---

1. DBWE 3:22.
2. DBWE 3:22.

Similarly, the goodness of the original creation is not to be understood as a goodness that creation has in itself. As Bonhoeffer asserts: "The goodness of the work consists precisely in its pointing emphatically away from itself to the Creator and to the Creator's word alone as that which is good— that is, in its pointing out that 'none is good but God alone'. It is in the sense of this word of Jesus that the first creation is 'good.'"[3] Thus the relation that Bonhoeffer asserts to exist between Christ and creation is certainly not reciprocal in nature. For him, "creation" does not exist independently over against God, not even before the Fall. As he claims, creation is a work of God's dominion, a display of his power. Indeed, this is a point that Bonhoeffer insists upon rather strongly—he stresses that there is nothing divine in nature itself. As he argues, "God is never the creation but always the Creator. God is not the substance [Substanz] of nature. There is no continuum that ties God to, or unites God with, God's work—except God's *word*."[4]

In this latter instance, Bonhoeffer does not specify just what exactly he means with this *Word* of God. As it stands for now, it does not explicitly refer to Christ. This leads John D. Godsey to make the claim that "God's word is not his nature or even his essence, but his commandment." According to Godsey, Bonhoeffer's assertion that God speaks "means he *freely* creates and remains free vis-à-vis his creation. God is in the world as word because he is the absolute Other beyond the world, and he is the absolute Other because he is *in the world!*"[5] Green arrives at essentially the same conclusion, arguing that, in Bonhoeffer's *CF*, "Word" refers specifically to God's command, and not to Christ. For this reason, he sees good cause to criticize the reference to the Word: "[I]t is noteworthy that nowhere in these lectures does Bonhoeffer use the *logos* doctrine with which classical theology had related Christology and creation. He does not take this opportunity which the combination of the biblical text and the tradition offered him."[6] As I would argue, both Green and Godsey are perhaps too hasty in arriving at this conclusion. On my read, it is much more likely that Bonhoeffer, while not specifically mentioning Christ, still has Christ very much in mind when referring to the Word of God. Indeed, his lectures on Christology are full of references to Christ as the Word (understood in Johannine fashion), as the section "Christ as Word" makes abundantly clear.[7]

3. DBWE 3:59. Bonhoeffer refers here to Mark 10:18b. According to Erich Klapproth, Bonhoeffer further said: "Jesus is good in that he points to God as good." DBWE 3:59, editorial footnote 8.

4. DBWE 3:40; italics original.

5. Godsey, *The Theology of Dietrich Bonhoeffer*, 121; italics original.

6. Green, *Bonhoeffer*, 190; italics original.

7. DBWE 12:315–18.

Another reason why it is likely that Bonhoeffer identified God's Word with Christ in *CF* has to do with the function that the Word has in these lectures. Bonhoeffer states that the relation between God and creation is defined by God's Word, which both brings forth and upholds creation. This, it should be noted, is how Bonhoeffer defends his account against the possible charge of Deism, with its understanding of the world as a clock that, after first being wound up, runs entirely on its own.[8] It is thus very likely that "Word" refers specifically to Christ, because it is he who connects Creator and creation, and thus sets the God of the Bible apart from the God of Deism. As such, it is possible to understand Bonhoeffer's reference to the Word of God in *CF* as a reference to Christ.[9]

In stating that creation is made possible by Christ and is upheld by Christ, Bonhoeffer establishes an intimate connection between the doctrines of Christology and creation.[10] This is an important turn. Although it is also clearly visible in later scholarship,[11] it appears that only since very recently has theology finally caught up with Bonhoeffer's proposal to see Christ as active in creation. McGrath notes that creation has often been seen as a work of the Father alone, but that there is no reason to do so. Christ, who is consubstantial with the Father, joins the Father in creating the world.[12] McGrath also observes that, "[i]n recent theological discussion, there has been a welcome and somewhat overdue realization of the need to return to a trinitarian understanding of creation, which recognizes the Christological dimensions of that doctrine and explores their implications."[13] The recognition of such a connection is important, because, as McGrath points out, this means that "there is a direct continuity between the study of the creator and of the redeemer . . . The study of the creation and of Jesus Christ are contiguous, not unrelated activities. Both creation and Christ bear witness to the one God, and the one divine rationality."[14]

---

8. DBWE 3:58–59.

9. See Feil, *The Theology of Dietrich Bonhoeffer*, 79.

10. A similar proposal has been formulated by Karl Barth: "[I]t is specifically in Christ, as the Father of Jesus Christ, that God is called our Creator." *CD* 1/1:389.

11. See Moltmann: "The starting point for a *Christian* doctrine of creation can only be an interpretation of the biblical creation narratives in the light of the gospel of Christ." Moltmann, *God in Creation*, 53–54; italics original.

12. McGrath, *Nature*, 186–91. See also Van de Beek, *Schepping*, 155–84.

13. McGrath, *Nature*, 188. An exploration of the relation between Christ and creation has been put forward by Gunton, *Christ and Creation*.

14. McGrath, *Nature*, 188–89.

THE RELATIVE INDEPENDENCE OF NATURE OVER AGAINST HUMANITY

For the benefit of the later discussion about the character of the Fall, it is equally important to establish that, according to Bonhoeffer, one important function of creation was to praise God. In his commentary on Gen 1:1–2, for instance, he asserts that even the "nothing" out of which the world was formed gives praise to God. In a related vein, concerning the darkness that lies on the face of the deep, he writes that this darkness gives glory to God as Creator.[15] Other examples can be mentioned as well of how, according to Bonhoeffer, already the unformed matter of nature worships the Lord.[16] As such, even though creation does not acquire an independent existence over against God, it surely does acquire value and worth, namely in that it brings about glory for God and points to him.[17]

As it stands now, the fact that creation praises God and is directed to God could be interpreted to mean that there is a certain continuum, or a certain analogy, between Creator and creation. Bonhoeffer also recognizes this possibility, but only to strongly oppose himself against it. In Barthian fashion, he asserts:

> It is not 'from' God's works, then, that we recognize the Creator—as though the substance, the nature, or the essence of the work were after all ultimately somehow identical with God's essence or as if there were some kind of continuum between them, such as that of cause and effect. On the contrary we believe that God is the Creator only because by this word God acknowledges these works as God's own, and we *believe* this word about these works. There is no via eminentiae, negationis, causalitatis![18]

With the final words of this quotation, Bonhoeffer opposes himself against the scholastic assertion that we can know about God through creation, in different ways.[19] This is an important point, for, in the debate over natural

15. DBWE 3:36.

16. See DBWE 3:36–39.

17. This beginning of a theocentric approach to nature should not be read in isolation from the rest of *CF*, where Bonhoeffer develops an anthropocentric approach to nature. This latter approach will be considered in chapter 4.

18. DBWE 3:41; italics original.

19. Bonhoeffer's mentioning of three ways probably goes back to Bernard Bartmann, who identified three ways of knowledge of God in scholastics. See DBWE 3:41, editorial footnote 5. Also Barth mentions the *via negationis, eminentiae,* and *causalitatis.* See *CD* 3/1:347.

theology, it places Bonhoeffer on the side of Barth. Later on in *CF*, and in other parts of his theology as well, he continued to maintain this position, but asserted that we can speak about certain orders of preservation, although only in relation to Christ. I will deal with this point in greater detail below.

The Fall: How "Creation" Became "Nature"

Bonhoeffer insists upon a fundamental distinction between the original, good creation, prior to the Fall, and fallen nature, after the Fall. Already in the Introduction to *CF*, for example, he states that between the original creation and the present world lies the same chasm as that between the present world and the world to come and that the relationship between the beginning and the present is that between life and death.[20] Further on, in his commentary on the biblical text, the character of the Fall becomes even clearer. The Fall, in this case, is seen as the result, as Bonhoeffer says, of the desire of human beings to be *sicut Deus*, that is, to be as God. This is a human desire to be in the middle, or, as Bonhoeffer puts it, to be its own limit. In acting upon that desire, Adam lost hold of his creatureliness, Bonhoeffer asserts: "Losing *the limit* Adam has lost *creatureliness*. Adam as limitless or boundless [Der grenzenlose Adam] can no longer be addressed with regard to Adam's creatureliness."[21]

The Effects of Humanity's Fall on the World

Bonhoeffer stresses the utter incomprehensibility of the Fall. With equal strength, he also asserts the devastating consequenes of humankind's Fall. It leads, first and foremost, to abusive, interhuman relationships.[22] But the Fall of humanity affects creation as a whole as well.[23] As Bonhoeffer makes clear, in God's creation, humankind's Fall is "both inconceivable and finally inexcusable,"[24] and therefore "the word *disobedience* fails to describe the situation adequately."[25] While non-human creation has not sinned itself, it

---

20. DBWE 3:22.

21. DBWE 3:115; italics original.

22. DBWE 3:122. For the consequences of the Fall for interhuman relations, see Visser, *Het zondebegrip*, esp. 82–89.

23. It is remarkable that Visser's study does not deal at all with the consequences of human sin for creation. When Visser speaks about Bonhoeffer's notion of the "fallen world," he sees this as a parable for the increase of human guilt. See Visser, *Het zondebegrip*, 86–87.

24. DBWE 3:120.

25. DBWE 3:120; italics original.

still suffers the consequences of humankind's first sin. Abromeit is therefore right when he summarizes Bonhoeffer's thoughts on the Fall's consequences for nature as follows: "[T]he history of nature depends on the history of humankind. Because of the failure of human beings, a 'curse' rests on nature. Nature has fallen because of humankind's Fall in sin."[26]

In spite of its innocence, creation suffers greatly from the Fall. Bonhoeffer uses the metaphor of a meteor, broken away from a larger object, blindly racing through space—this is the way in which fallen nature behaves itself, he says.[27] The language used is reminiscent of that of Friedrich Nietzsche[28] and depicts the devastating effecs of the Fall for nature. It leads to a grave loss of order. The loss of order is not the only effect to befall creation, morever. When commenting on Gen 3:14–19, where God proclaims his curse over nature, Bonhoeffer notes that nature, as an effect of the Fall, also becomes profoundly barren, no longer yielding her fruit to humankind. The original relation between humankind and nature is thus broken: nature comes, in a sense, to rebel against humanity, for, according to Bonhoeffer, the curse on nature leads to nature's "copying" of Adam's Fall—like Adam, it rises up against man, just as Adam himself rose up against God and was no longer obedient to him.[29]

Another significant consequence of God's curse upon nature, as a result of Adam's Fall, is that it no longer gives praise to its Creator as it did before—it no longer points to him as Creator. This consequence of humanity's Fall for nature is also mentioned in Bonhoeffer's Christology lectures. There he explains: "The fallen creation is no longer the creation of the first Word

---

26. "Geschichte der Natur [ist] von der Geschichte der Menschheit abhängig. Aufgrund der Verfehlung des Menschen lastet auf der Natur ein 'Fluch'. Die Natur ist mit der Sünde des Menschen gefallen." Abromeit, *Geheimnis Christi*, 279. Abromeit also establishes a parallel here to Rom 8:21vv, which I believe to be justified, even though Bonhoeffer doesn't mention the parallel himself. It can furthermore be noted that Bonhoeffer's thoughts resonate with what Moltmann says concerning the effects of the Fall: "Nature has fallen victim to transience and death. It has not fallen through its own sin, like human beings. To talk about 'a fallen nature' is therefore highly dubious." Moltmann, *God in Creation*, 68.

27. DBWE 3:120.

28. The editors of *CF* note that Bonhoeffer here paraphrases a passage from Nietzsche's *The Gay Science*. DBWE 3:120, editorial note 11. See Nietzsche, *The Portable Nietzsche*, 95–96.

29. DBWE 3:134. In this emphasis upon the curse of nature, one also finds a clear connection between Bonhoeffer and Luther, for Luther too stressed that nature as whole was cursed as a result of the Fall: "[T]he earth, which is innocent and committed no sin, is nevertheless compelled to endure a curse . . . [I]t will be freed from this on the Last Day, for which it is waiting." Luther, *Luther on the Creation*, 204.

... With that the continuity between Word and creature has been lost. That is why the natural world is no longer a transparent world. That is why the whole creation is no longer sacrament."[30] The loss of orderliness, mentioned earlier in *CF*, leads in this case to a profound unintelligibility—unlike before, the world no longer speaks of its creator. On this point, Green offers the following comment: "[I]n the world after the fall . . ., nature is mute and no longer speaks with unequivocal directness of its Creator."[31]

One final aspect of the Fall that is of particular interest here is that, according to Bonhoeffer, it also affects the capacity of human beings to know anything about God's original—and originally good—creation. According to him, this also counts for the biblical authors, which is the reason they speak of the original good creation in the way they do. There is thus no going back to the original, unambiguous, God-praising world before the Fall.[32] As Green summarizes: "In estrangement from God, neighbors, self, and nature, the sinful creature has no unmediated relationships to the primal creation nor any access to truth and liberation except through the revelation in Christ the Mediator."[33] Nor should human beings try, on their own, to win back such a relation, according to Bonhoeffer. As he claims, God accepts human beings in their fallen state and upholds them in the midst of fallen nature.[34]

Background and Criticism

Bonhoeffer's account of the Fall has deep roots within the broader, Christian tradition. On the one hand, I already indicated the clearly Lutheran background undergirding Bonhoeffer's understanding of nature's curse. In addition, the Augustinian character of his account of the Fall of nature can be noted.[35]

30. DBWE 12:318–19. This links up with what Moltmann says: "And yet a sadness lies over nature which is the expression of its tragic fate and its messianic yearning. It is enslaved and wishes to be free, for it is transitory." Moltmann, *God in Creation*, 68.

31. Green, *Bonhoeffer*, 218.

32. In this respect, Bonhoeffer's theology of sin is very reminiscent of Luther's. For a description of Luther's account of human sin, see Käfer, "Inkarnation und Schöpfung nach Martin Luther," 16–20.

33. Green, *Bonhoeffer*, 205.

34. DBWE 3:131.

35. This is noted by Schmidt. According to him, an Augustinian account of the Fall "presupposes the idea of a 'double historical process' (. . .), in which God's saving action had to appear as preserving action, whereas all changes had to be interpreted as perversions and destructions of the original, basic relations of social existence." Schmidt, "The Cross of Reality?," 222–23.

While Bonhoeffer's description of the Fall is clearly rich and multi-faceted, it is also open to criticism on certain points. We have already seen that Bonhoeffer is quite radical in the emphasis that he places on the depth of the Fall—according to him, nature as a whole completely and definitively lost the ability to praise God following the Fall. In asserting this, Bonhoeffer goes directly against both biblical testimony (Ps 148) as well as a large part of the Christian tradition.[36] This rather radical interpretation of the Fall very likely has to be understood against the backdrop of the historical period in which he lived, as well the influence that Karl Barth had on his thinking. Nevertheless, it still constitutes a rather formidable stumbling-block to recognizing the good that nature retains even after the Fall.

Christ, the Hidden Center of Nature

On account of the Fall, creation transforms into nature, and nature no longer points back to its Creator. And yet, Christ remains the Lord of fallen nature as well, if only in a more veiled way. Though this presence is certainly not fully and explicitly revealed as such, it is directly asserted in *CF*, in a paragraph at the end of Bonhoeffer's comments on Gen 4:1, where the biblical account narrates the birth of Cain, who murdered his brother Abel. In this instance, he says that the history of Cain ends with Christ as the murdered Son of God.[37] He refers to this event as the last, desperate grasping for the door of Paradise. Bonhoeffer then offers a christological re-interpretation of the tree of life in the following words:

> The trunk of the cross becomes the wood of life [zum Holze des Lebens], and now in the midst of the world, on the accursed ground itself, life is raised up anew. In the center of the world, from the wood of the cross, the fountain of life springs up. All who thirst for life are called to drink from this water, and whoever has eaten from the wood of this life shall never again hunger and thirst.[38]

As we see here, in the cross of Christ, the tree of life is placed back at the center of the world. It is, at the same time, a remarkably strange form of presence. Bonhoeffer asserts that "paradise" comes in the form of the hill of Golgotha, and that the tree of life is formed by the wood of the cross. This cross nevertheless comes to reoccupy the new middle-point of the fallen

---

36. On this theme, see in particular Schaefer, *Theological Foundations*, 103–20.

37. DBWE 3:145.

38. DBWE 3:146.

world: "The tree of life, the cross of Christ, the center of God's world that is fallen but upheld and preserved—that is what the end of the story about paradise is for us."[39]

CHRIST AS THE CRITICAL "MIDDLE" OF NATURE

In *CF*, Bonhoeffer does not spell out the full implications that his christo-logical interpretation of the tree of life bears for nature itself. Indeed, his language is much more poetic and moving than precise and analytical in nature. In his Christology lectures, however, he explicates just how he un-derstands the relation. He discusses it specifically under the title-heading "Christ as the Center of Nature."[40] With the assertion contained in this title, Bonhoeffer does not at all mean to say that Christ constitutes some kind of uncritical "middle-point" or center of the present, fallen nature. On the contrary, he opens this section of his lectures by defining Christ as the "new creation," arguing that by his occurrence all other creatures are defined as belonging to the "old creation."[41] In other words: for Bonhoeffer, Christ constitutes a critical occurrence in nature—he is there as the new creation, setting nature's fallenness in an even clearer light. Abromeit notes the pecu-liarity and uniqueness of Bonhoeffer's thoughts on this point: "Indeed, sur-prisingly, nature becomes an acting subject, just like history."[42] In particular, Abromeit situates this observation in the context of Bonhoeffer's lifelong resistance against Idealism.[43]

---

39. DBWE 3:146. Bonhoeffer's argument that Christ is the tree of life is, of course, not his own invention. It has biblical roots (see, for example, Rev 2:7) and throughout the centuries it has been a theme in both Christian theology as well as in the liturgy of the Christian churches. The Armenian churches, for example, have the ancient prac-tice called the "greening of the cross." Beyond Christianity, there is also a more general emphasis on trees as bearers of religious and spiritual symbolism—it can be found in many religions. See the panentheistic account of Kuikman, "Christ as Cosmic Tree," 141–54.

40. DBWE 12:327.

41. DBWE 12:327.

42. "Zwar wird erstaunlicherweise die Natur wie die Geschichte zum Handlungs-subjekt." Abromeit, *Geheimnis Christi*, 279.

43. Abromeit, *Geheimnis Christi*, 279. According to Abromeit, Bonhoeffer does not go so far as to state that nature itself has spirit ("Geist"), or freedom. He is referring in particular to Bonhoeffer's Christology lectures on this point. Factually, Abromeit is correct when he claims that nature does not have freedom, like humankind, even in the situation prior to the Fall. This should be established, however, in reference to *CF*—in particular, to those sections of the text where Bonhoeffer speaks of creation before the Fall.

As the *critical* center of nature, Christ also occupies nature's *hidden* center. As Bonhoeffer puts it, "Christ cannot be proved to be the redeeming creation within nature; he can only be preached as such."[44] This assertion reveals yet another aspect of Bonhoeffer's Lutheranism: when he asserts that, as a result of the Fall, we cannot "read" Christ in nature, he speaks as a theologian of the cross, just as Luther had done.[45] As H. Paul Santmire succinctly states: "Luther, on occasion, can speak powerfully of the immanence of God in nature, of the Creator's majestic presence 'in, with and under' all the creatures of the natural world. Luther can envision the whole creation 'as the mask of God' (. . .). This means, for Luther, that God is hidden there. But it also means that God is powerfully present there."[46] This very nicely sums up the precise point that Bonhoeffer sets out to establish in his Christology lectures concerning Christ as the hidden center of nature.[47]

DIFFERING CHRISTOCENTRIC COSMOLOGIES: COMPARING BONHOEFFER AND TEILHARD DE CHARDIN

In this regard, Bonhoeffer's theology of nature differs distinctively from that of his contemporary, the Catholic theologian, Pierre Teilhard de Chardin,[48] in spite of the fact both assert the cosmic scope of Christ's lordship, and in spite of the fact that both conceive of reality in christological terms.[49] This in itself led Heinrich Ott to address the proximity between the two thinkers in his work, "The Universal Christ in Dietrich Bonhoeffer and in Pierre Teilhard de Chardin."[50] In the latter text, Ott writes: "The perspective, 'Christ

44. DBWE 12:327. In light of this statement, it is unintelligible why Scott claims that "Bonhoeffer does not speak explicitly of Christ as hidden in nature." Scott, "Christ, Nature, Sociality," 423.

45. The assersion that Christ and creation are related can be traced back to the early church. See Edwards, "Eucharist and Ecology," 205. Yet it is likely that the direct influence on Bonhoeffer's christocentric theology of nature stems from Luther.

46. Santmire, "Martin Luther, the Word of God and Nature," 174.

47. The connection between Bonhoeffer and Luther on the point of Christ as the hidden center of the world, as an expression of the *theologia crucis*, has been brought to the fore by, among others, Prenter, "Bonhoeffer and the Young Luther," 161–81.

48. It should be noted at the outset that there is no evidence suggesting that the two theologians knew each other or each other's work—indeed, it appears to be highly unlikely that they did.

49. In the context of this chapter, it is noteworthy that Teilhard de Chardin is often cited as an important source in ecotheological studies. See, for example, Deane-Drummond, *Pierre Teilhard de Chardin on People and Planet*.

50. Ott, *Reality and Faith*, 374–87.

and Nature' is laid down in Bonhoeffer (cp. The lectures on Christology). Had it been worked out, something for which Bonhoeffer surely lacked not only the time but also the specific experience and the urge, it could well have taken a similar form to the vision which we do in fact find in Teilhard."[51] I am inclined to doubt Ott's assertion on this point. While he is right to draw attention to the remarkable convergence between Bonhoeffer and Teilhard de Chardin on the cosmic scope of Christ's work, there are also a number of important differences between the work of the two theologians. Bonhoeffer, for example, finds concretion of the cosmic Christ in the reality of the ethical decision, whereas Teilhard de Chardin finds concretion in matter itself.

The most significant difference, however, concerns the way that both theologians account for the meaning of the cross of Christ. For Teilhard de Chardin, "[i]n its highest and most general sense, the doctrine of the Cross is that to which all men adhere who believe that the vast movement and agitation of human life opens on to a road which leads somewhere, and that that road *climbs upward*."[52] In stark contrast with this vision, Bonhoeffer sees the cross standing for God's judgment over the world.[53] This makes Bonhoeffer's vision of Christ, as the hidden center of nature, more compatible with classical Protestantism.

THE SIGNIFICANCE OF BONHOEFFER'S CHRISTOCENTRIC THEOLOGY OF NATURE

Although a parallel can clearly be discerned between Bonhoeffer and Teilhard de Chardin, it should be noted that Bohoeffer's thoughts on Christ as the center of nature were unique in his time. As Abromeit remarks: "All in all, Bonhoeffer is, with these refections on nature, ahead of the theology of his time."[54] He argues that by doing so, Bonhoeffer opens up new possibilities for theology's engagement with nature. In the same connection, Abromeit also refers to Wolfgang Trilhaas, who speaks of Bonhoeffer as giving us "a new—and hitherto unsurpassed—view on nature."[55]

51. Ibid., 386–87.

52. Chardin, *The Divine Milieu*, 102; italics original.

53. See Bonhoeffer's *Ethics*, where he states: "The form of the crucified disarms all thinking aimed at success, for it is a denial of judgment." DBWE 6:90.

54. "Insgesamt ist Bonhoeffer mit einem solchen Nachdenken über die Natur der Theologie seiner Zeit voraus." Abromeit, *Geheimnis Christi*, 280.

55. "[E]ine neue—und bis heute noch nicht bewältigte—Sicht der Natur." Trilhaas, "Natur und Christentum," 1328. Cited in Abromeit, *Geheimnis Christi*, 280. Trilhaas claims here that Bonhoeffer was one of the first modern theologians to treat nature independently. He also mentions the work of Adolf Schlatter and comments on his, as

The uniqueness of Bonhoeffer's theology of creation comes out even more clearly when it is compared with that of Karl Barth, with whom he is closely associated. Like Bonhoeffer, Barth too defines his understanding of creation in relation to Christ. But unlike Bonhoeffer, he does not see nature as a relatively independent realm over which Christ is Lord. Instead, he famously describes creation as the "external basis of the covenant."[56] In other words, for Barth, creation exists for the sake of history alone. As he puts it, "Creation sets the stage for the covenant of grace. The story requires a stage corresponding to it; the existence of man and his whole world. Creation provides this."[57] Further on in *CD* 3/1, he says that creation is "the clear and necessary reflection of the covenant of grace."[58] Smedema, in a recent commentary on Barth's *CD* 3/1, points out that this does not necessarily entail a low view of creation.[59] And yet, in spite of the fact that Barth had a great deal more time and opportunity to work out his doctrine of creation (compare for instance the massive volumes of the *Church Dogmatics* with the much slimmer volumes of Bonhoeffer's collected lectures on this subject), he never worked out the relation between Christ and creation as strongly as Bonhoeffer did.[60]

Christ as the Redeemer of Nature

In his lectures on Christology, Bonhoeffer claims that Christ is not only nature's center, but also its Redeemer. He further specifies the character of this redemption by stating: "Nature will receive its freedom not through reconciliation but through redemption."[61] What this means, as Abromeit

---

well as Bonhoeffer's, theology of nature: "Such a theology of nature has direct practical consequences for preaching and pastoral care" ("Eine solche Theologie der Natur hätte dann unmittelbare praktische Wirkungen für Predigt und Seelsorge"). Trilhaas, "Natur und Christentum," 1328. It also has consequences for cosmology and ecology, as we will see further on.

56. This is the title of a major section in *CD* 3/1, "Creation as the External Basis of the Covenant," *CD* 3/1:94–228.

57. *CD* 3/1:44.

58. *CD* 3/1:318.

59. Smedema, *Grond onder de voeten*, esp. 125–26.

60. As Santmire notes: "[T]he great Karl Barth . . . refused to develop a theology of nature and, along the way, almost by default, set forth ideas about nature in instrumental terms that posed no real challenge to the ideas of rising above nature espoused by thinkers like Ritschl and Bultmann." Santmire, "Christianity (6c1)—Reformation Traditions," 342.

61. DBWE 12:327.

points out, is that nature still depends on the vicarious action of Christ—it is redeemed, albeit indirectly, by Christ's reconciliation of humankind. "A direct reconciliation of nature through the vicarious representative action of Christ is not possible," says Abromeit, "because nature does not have freedom. For Bonhoeffer, 'freedom' is one of the constitutive elements of vicarious representative action."[62] In this section, I would like to specify in detail how exactly Bonhoeffer develops and works out this understanding of Christ redeeming nature.

The Sacraments as a Prefigurement of the Redemption of Nature

Bonhoeffer indicates the specific way in which the redemption of creation is prefigured in Christian religious practice, namely in the sacraments. As he writes: "In the sacraments of the church, the old creation is set free from its servitude and obtains its new freedom . . . In this enslaved creation a sign is set up in which the elements of the old creation become the elements of the new creation."[63] Immediately Bonhoeffer asks the question of how exactly this is the case—*how* is the old creation set free in the sacraments? In answer to his own question, he writes: "To the extent that they are set free from their dumb condition, from their interpretation by humankind. These elements themselves speak and say what they are."[64] Here Bonhoeffer makes a bold and surprising assertion. The sacraments, as he sees them, do more than symbolize new life through death (the water of baptism) or through the broken body of Christ (the bread and wine of the Eucharist)—more than that, they also foreshadow the liberation of creation as a whole. Creation is fallen and no longer openly manifests Christ, or the divine *Logos*. But it does live in hope of redemption, as we saw earlier. In this case, Bonhoeffer speaks of the sacraments as a prefigure of this promised redemption. The sacraments thus form a sort of bridge between the original, good creation and the promised, new creation, and provide a foretaste of a redeemed natural world, which once again comes to manifest the reality of Christ.

Bonhoeffer's brief exposition on the sacraments ends with the following statement: "Only in the sacrament is Christ the center of nature, as the

---

62. "Eine direkte Versöhnung der Natur durch die Stellvertretung Christi ist nicht möglich, weil der Natur eben das Moment der Freiheit fehlt. Für Bonhoeffer gehört also Freiheit zu den Konstitutiva von Stellvertretung." Abromeit, *Geheimnis Christi*, 280.

63. DBWE 12:327.

64. DBWE 12:327.

mediator between nature and God."[65] Here Bonhoeffer rather abruptly cuts off the possibility of establishing a broader interpretation of the sacraments so as to include the created order. The reason for this is outlined earlier on in the Christology lectures, in the section entitled "Christ as Sacrament."[66] There Bonhoeffer points out that Christ's specific use of certain elements, as well as his hallowing of them, limits his presence to these sacramental elements alone. He asserts that not simply all natural elements are destined to be sacraments—only the preaching and the sacraments of the church speak of Jesus Christ, he says. This assertion is clearly positivistic in nature, and Bonhoeffer further confirms this point when he writes: "The number of sacraments in which Christ is present, and what is his will, still need no other grounds than their institution by the exalted Lord, thus purely positivist grounds. However, they are not symbols, but Word of God. They do not *mean* something—they *are* something."[67]

Bonhoeffer asserts that the sacrament is "wholly Word [ganz Wort],"[68] in the same sense that Christ is wholly Word—receiving the Eucharist is not simply an act, but a proclamation of the Gospel itself. It is Word, as he says, because "it proclaims the gospel, not as a wordless action, but as action that is made holy and given its meaning by the Word."[69] Because of this, Bonhoeffer also concludes that only he who believes in the Word that speaks in the sacrament effectively and wholly receives the sacrament as such.

However much the sacrament may serve as a form of the Word, it is important to point out, as Bonhoeffer insists, that is it "the Word *in bodily form*. The sacrament does not represent the "Word," for only that which is not present can be represented."[70] On the contrary, it is "the form of the Word that, because God speaks it, becomes sacrament."[71] The material form too is therefore equally important because "[t]he sacrament, in the form of nature, engages human beings in their nature."[72] One of the functions of this

65. DBWE 12:327.

66. DBWE 12:318–22.

67. DBWE 12:319; italics original.

68. DBWE 12:318.

69. DBWE 12:318.

70. DBWE 12:318; emphasis added.

71. DBWE 12:318.

72. DBWE 12:318. On this point, Feil offers the following comment: "Bonhoeffer did not wish to reduce the word . . . Because the word has its source in the incarnation of Jesus Christ (. . .) and because God's word entered into nature and history (. . .), the word alone is never adequate on its own for Bonhoeffer; it needs to be complemented by the materialization that the gathered congregation provides." Feil, *The Theology of Dietrich Bonhoeffer*, 49.

special bodily form of God's Word, of Christ, is thus to address human be-ings specifically in their *bodily* nature, that is, in their physical being, which is part and parcel of the created natural world of physical matter.

Bonhoeffer goes on to explain that, with the Fall, the continuity be-tween Word and creature was lost: "That is why the whole creation is no longer sacrament."[73] This is a crucial aspect of the original, good creation that Bonhoeffer did not mention before—namely that it was entirely and wholly *sacrament* due to its mediating function between human beings and God. This is a sacramental world, however, that was lost in the Fall. In the fallen world, as Bonhoeffer remarks, "Sacrament exists only where God, in the midst of the world of creatures, names an element, speaks to it, and hal-lows it with the particular word God has for it by giving it its name. Through God's speaking to it, this element becomes what it is."[74]

While the originally sacramental nature of the world was lost in the Fall, the loss was not definitive. On the contrary, the sacramentalizing of matter is precisely what takes place in the Lord's Supper, as Bonhoeffer asserts, through the Word of God, Jesus Christ.[75] From here, Bonhoeffer further links this line of reflection with the connection that he had already established in *CF* between Christology and the theology of creation: "As God spoke at the creation, 'Let there be light'. . ., so the Word addressed to the sacrament becomes [reality.]"[76]

The Development of Sacramentology in Bonhoeffer's Earlier Theology

Bonhoeffer's sacramentology was, it is important to note, already foreshad-owed in *CF*. In the context of writing about "The Human Being of Earth and Spirit,"[77] he first states that God desires to glorify himself in the body. He then writes that therefore, when the original body was broken through sin, God comes to restore this body in the elements of the sacrament. From here, Bonhoeffer next sketches out the effects and implications of Christ's

73. DBWE 12:318–19.

74. DBWE 12:319.

75. He says: "It is through Jesus Christ that the sacrament is hallowed and given its meaning. By his Word, God has bound himself to the sacrament, that is, Jesus Christ is one who is bound by the sacrament. The God-human Jesus Christ is wholly present in the sacrament." DBWE 12:319.

76. DBWE 12:319. The editors note that the sentence in the original text is in-complete. See DBWE 12:319, editorial footnote 46.

77. DBWE 3:74–79.

presence in the sacrament for nature: "Because he is the new creature in the bread and wine, therefore bread and wine are the new creation. Bread and wine are, by nature and *realiter*, the new food for the person who receives them in faith."[78] He explains that through Christ's presence in the sacraments, nature regains the purpose that it had prior to the Fall: it is again open towards human beings, and remains no longer locked in itself.[79] At the core of Bonhoeffer's theology of the sacraments, then, we see that nature is freed from its dumbness and rebellion, and again made free *for* human beings.[80] As Green explains: "[I]n the sacrament nature is restored to humanity by receiving the pro-me being of Christ . . . As by Christ's being-for-humanity, people are freed for one another, so Nature, too, is freed for humanity."[81]

BACKGROUND IN LUTHER: SIMILARITIES AND DISSIMILARITIES

Although Bonhoeffer's understanding that in the sacraments of the church, nature itself is set free, may appear to be a novel and fresh understanding, it is not his own invention. Rather, it has its background in Luther, whose theology saturates Bonhoeffer's in many ways.[82] This applies, for example, to Bonhoeffer's assertion that the sacraments signal the redemption of nature. Most clearly this is the case, however, with regards to Bonhoeffer's insistence on the sacraments as a form of God's word. In fact, he employs almost the same exact turn of phrase as Luther does in his Larger Catechism: "The Word must make the element a sacrament; otherwise it remains a mere element."[83] And according to the Augsburg Confession, which garnered Luther's approval, "[t]here are two parts to a sacrament, the sign and the Word. In the New Testament, the Word is the added promise of grace."[84] As Kenneth Craycraft comments, referring to Luther in particular: "The sacra-

78. DBWE 12:322; italics original.

79. DBWE 12:322.

80. In chapter 4, where I account for Bonhoeffer's anthropocentric approach to nature, it will become clear that Bonhoeffer understood nature as having being created *for* human beings. This is the same kind of language that Bonhoeffer uses to describe Jesus Christ: Christ took on flesh *for* others and, consequently, to redeem human sociality.

81. Green, *Bonhoeffer*, 218.

82. Bonhoeffer studied Luther's theology when he was a student (see DBWE 9:325–70), and his entire theology is saturated with phrases, quotations and hymns from Luther. Therefore, also in Bonhoeffer's discussion on the sacraments in the lectures on Christology Luther features prominently (see DBWE 12:318–23).

83. *The Book of Concord*, 448.

84. Ibid., 262.

ment is a form in which the Word comes to the believer. If the Word does not accompany the element, it is as any other element with no 'sacramental' meaning."[85] What this means is that, although the sacraments are a visible means of communication (in the sense that they are actions that are performed), Luther places a great deal of emphasis on hearing the sacraments, as opposed to simply seeing them—a view which Bonhoeffer shares.[86]

At the same time, it is important to point out that Bonhoeffer does not follow Luther's sacramentology slavishly. For example, in both *SC* and *AB*, he develops a novel understanding of the sociological meaning of the sacraments, for the most part without recourse to Luther.[87] More importantly, in his lectures on Christology he directly opposes himself against Luther's explanation of how Christ is made present in the sacraments. To be sure, as a Lutheran theologian, he asserts Christ's real presence in the sacraments, drawing attention in particular to Luther's position, which is expressed in the well-known formula *finitum capax infiniti*.[88] Yet Bonhoeffer also takes a certain distance from Luther in resisting the adoption of the formula.[89] When it comes to articulating Christ's presence in the sacraments, Bonhoeffer neither employs Luther's formula, *finitum capax infiniti*, nor the Calvinist *finitum non capax infiniti*, which Barth frequently and vigorously employed, and with which Bonhoeffer agreed during his days as a student.[90] Instead, he insists on coining his own variation, which runs as

85. Craycraft, "Sign and Word," 146.

86. Santmire points out that Luther did not invent this Word-focused view on the sacraments. Rather, "Luther took up, with a passion, the traditional Augustinian view that the sacraments are 'visible Words' . . . The Word is to the elements, he explained, as the soul is to the body." Santmire, "Martin Luther, the Word of God and Nature," 171.

87. In *SC* he does so in a section entitled "The Sociological Meaning of the Cultic Acts." DBWE 1:237–47. There he asserts that something "objective" happens in the administration of the sacraments, but that that objectivism consists of the faith of the gathered church in and by which the sacraments are administered. Bonhoeffer further explains this in *AB*. He there asserts that the sacrament is something that happens *extra nos*: "And I hear the gospel, join in the prayer, and know myself bound up in the word, sacrament, and prayer of Christ's community of faith, the new humanity, whether it is here or elsewhere. Bearing it, I am borne by it." DBWE 2:121.

88. This constitutes one of the defining characteristics of Lutheranism. See Brinkman, *Schepping en sacrament*, 59. Luther, of course, had originally employed the formula *finitum capax infiniti* in order to explain how Jesus could be truly God. See Huntemann, *Die dialektische Theologie*; and Schenk, "'Finitum est capax infiniti,'" 195–207.

89. This is *contra* Rasmussen, who implies that Bonhoeffer did in fact adopt Luther's formula. See Rasmussen, *Earth Community*, 272.

90. See Abromeit, *Geheimnis Christi*, 199.

follows: "Finitum capax infiniti non per se sed per infinitum."[91] The directionality at work in this formula is abundantly clear: Christ makes himself present (in the incarnation and in the sacraments) *from* God *to* the world. In other words, for Bonhoeffer, the finite is capable of bearing the infinite, not on account of its own nature, but on account of the infinite. In this sense, Bonhoeffer remains faithful to Barth's understanding. And yet, in asserting that the finite is capable of bearing the infinite, he remains faithful to Luther as well. As Burtness observes: "With Luther and against Calvin, Bonhoeffer insists that the finite (whether Jesus of Nazareth, or the bread and wine of the sacrament, or the here-and-now of a moral decision) is capable of bearing the infinite."[92] According to Rasmussen, Bonhoeffer crafted this formula in order to be able to assert "that God is amidst the living events of nature and history."[93]

The Relevance of Bonhoeffer's Sacramentology

It is important to note how Bonhoeffer's theology of the sacraments can be seen as an outworking of precisely what Paul Tillich has called for, namely a "new realism" with regards to the sacraments.[94] In a well-known article, which profoundly influenced contemporary environmental ethics,[95] Tillich stresses the need for Protestantism to rediscover the connection between nature and the Christian sacraments. Towards this end, he identifies four different ways of interpreting nature throughout history, and he then puts forward his own proposal: a realistic interpretation of nature, which will be able to provide the foundation of a new Protestant theory of the sacraments. With this interpretation, "natural objects can become bearers of transcendent power and meaning, they can become sacramental elements . . . Nature, by being brought into the context of the history of salvation, is liberated from its ambiguity. Its demonic quality is conquered in the new being in Christ."[96] As such, he continues, "nature is a bearer and an object of salvation. This is the basis for a Protestant rediscovery of the sacramental sphere."[97] Here we find a clear parallel between Tillich's proposal for a "new realistic interpretation" and the way that Bonhoeffer works out his own the-

---

91. DBWE 12:346.
92. Burtness, *Shaping the Future*, 33.
93. Rasmussen, *Earth Community*, 272.
94. Tillich, "Nature and Sacrament," 94–114.
95. Santmire, "Ecology, Justice, Liturgy," 270–71.
96. Tillich, "Nature and Sacrament," 102–3.
97. Ibid., 103.

ology of the sacraments. What is particularly important in this regard is the way that they both relate the sacraments to Christ. As Tillich says, "[W]e must remember that for a Christian the idea of a purely natural sacrament is unacceptable. Where nature is not related to the events of the history of salvation its status remains ambiguous."[98] Although there are certainly important differences between Tillich's and Bonhoeffer's theology of the sacraments,[99] they nevertheless stand in agreement on the idea that, in the sacraments, Christ really and truly proves himself to be the Transformer of creation.

In sum, Bonhoeffer's theology of the sacraments provides the answer to the question of how Christ is present as the redeeming creature within nature. In the sacraments, nature is set free once again both to proclaim its Creator and to serve humankind. The two Protestant sacraments are thus, for Bonhoeffer, the one—and only—place where the assertion of Christ as Redeemer of nature becomes real.

The Orders of Preservation and the Question of Natural Theology

One other important feature of Bonhoeffer's theology of nature is his concept of the orders of preservation ("Erhaltungsordnungen"), which features prominently in his theology of the period 1932 to 1933. According to his understanding, the orders of preservation are installed in the world by God in order to preserve it, as an anticipation of the world's redemption in Jesus Christ.[100]

Different Orders of Preservation in Bonhoeffer

In Bonhoeffer's theology, one finds at least two different kinds of orders of preservation. The first refers to the continual maintaining, or upholding, by God, of creation following its original coming into being. That becomes clear in Bonhoeffer's commentary on Gen 1:4a, for instance, where he recognizes "creating" and "upholding" as two sides of the one act of the Creator.[101] Traditionally, this activity of God has been understood in the

98. Ibid., 110.

99. Contrary to Bonhoeffer, Tillich does not limit Christ's presence to the two Protestant sacraments. He says: "No realm of such [i.e.: of natural] objects is, in principle, excluded from a sacramental consideration." Ibid., 106.

100. DBWE 12:362, editorial footnote 6.

101. DBWE 3:46.

sense of a *creatio continua*, but Bonhoeffer explicitly opposes himself to this interpretation: "There is an essential difference between creatio continua and upholding creation."[102] According to him, the concept of *creatio continua* robs God of his freedom as Creator. In addition, it relativizes the uniqueness and singular act of creation. Also, he argues that the concept doesn't take fully into account the fact that the world is fallen through sin.[103] Instead of *creatio continua*, Bonhoeffer speaks of preservation ("Erhaltung"). On his view, preservation and creation belong together from the very beginning: "*Creation* means wresting out of nonbeing [Nichtsein]; *upholding* means affirming being . . . Creation and upholding are at this point still one; they are related to the same object, God's original good work. Upholding is always *with reference to* creation, whereas creation is in itself."[104] Preservation *after* the Fall, as Bonhoeffer asserts, is something quite different, on the other hand. In this case, a second kind of order of preservation is introduced by Bonhoeffer, namely the specific forms of order that God gives to structure life after the Fall.

Bonhoeffer elaborates on this second variety of preservation in a number of different instances, but, interestingly enough, he focuses in particular, in *CF*, on Gen 3:21, where the biblical text narrates the account of how God made clothes for Adam and Eve. In this case he notes: "The Creator is now the preserver; the created world is now the fallen but *preserved world*."[105] At the same time, Bonhoeffer also draws attention to the fact that God does not leave the world, nor does he abandon human beings within it; instead, "God accepts human beings for what they are, as fallen creatures. God affirms them in their fallenness."[106] What this gift of clothes to human beings, who had only just discovered their nakedness, means for Bonhoeffer, is that God's action brings about a certain order, or restraint. What we see here is that this second kind of orders of preservation carries out a conserving function. As such, they are not eternal in nature, but only provisional.

The Orders of Preservation in Relation to Christ

As with the entire gamut of Bonhoeffer's theology of nature, so also here, the true meaning of the orders of preservation lies in their relation to Christ:

102. DBWE 3:46.

103. Just to be clear, this does not imply that, prior to the Fall, one could speak of a *creatio continua*, whereas afterwards, one would have something entirely different.

104. DBWE 3:47; italics original.

105. DBWE 3:139; italics original.

106. DBWE 3:139.

"[O]ur life is preserved only until it finds its end in—Christ. All orders of our fallen world are God's orders of preservation that uphold and preserve us for Christ. They are not orders of creation but orders of preservation. They have no value in themselves; instead they find their end and meaning only through Christ."[107] Once again, we see here just how central a role Jesus Christ plays in *CF*, and in Bonhoeffer's theology in general.

It is only insofar as the orders of preservation point to Christ that they have a function at all. As Larry Rasmussen comments, they "relocated all revelation in God in Jesus Christ, de-absolutized the orders of creation as autonomous spheres, and held their reality open to its eschatological fulfilment in Jesus Christ."[108] This point becomes particularly clear in the speech that Bonhoeffer delivered at the ecumenical youth peaceconference at Ciernohosrké Kúpele in 1932, entitled "On the Theological Foundation of the Work of the World Alliance."[109] There he notes how every order can be broken when it becomes introverted and hardened, and thus is no longer open for the possibility of new revelation.[110]

The Historical Context of Bonhoeffer's Use of the Orders of Preservation

Bonhoeffer's insistence on the use of the term "orders of preservation" has a clearly polemical function as well. In particular, it needs to be understood in the context of the 1930s, which, in Germany, were marked by great anxiety and uncertainty.[111] This context formed a fertile soil for the Nazi ideology of "Blut und Boden." Along very similar lines, theologians from the German Christian movement sought to bolster these Nazi ideals by appeal to the concept of the orders of creation ("Schöpfungsordnungen").[112] An ex-

107. DBWE 3:139–40.

108. Rasmussen, "Editor's Introduction to the English Edition." DBWE 12:37.

109. DBWE 11:356–69.

110. DBWE 11:363. The precise nature of these orders of preservation is outlined in Bonhoeffer's lecture "'Thy Kingdom Come!' The Prayer of the Church Community for God's Kingdom on Earth," DBWE 12:285–96. Here he mentions the state, marriage, family, and the nation as examples of such orders; see DBWE 12:293–95. He also expounds his concept of the orders of preservation in his seminar "Is There a Christian Ethic?," which he delivered in the summer semester of 1932; see DBWE 11:333–41. Similarly, the draft of the Bethel Confession presents a list of the following orders: "The orders that we have been given are those of gender, marriage, the family, the nation, property (work and the economy), profession, and government." DBWE 12:388. In the Bethel Confession, the orders bear the same function as in Bonhoeffer's theology.

111. See DBWE 3:148–49.

112. See Mayer, *Christuswirklichkeit*, 120.

ample of this trend can be found in the work of Paul Althaus, professor of theology at Erlangen, who published a pamphlet, arguing that the German people belonged to God's ordering of creation.[113] In his "On the Theological Foundation of the Work of the World Alliance," Bonhoeffer points out the danger of such an approach: "The danger of this argument is basically that everything can be justified on its basis. One need only portray something that exists as willed and created by God and then everything that exists is justified for eternity. . . ."[114] As concrete examples he mentions, among others, wars, the exploitation of the weak by the strong, and ruthless scientific competitiveness.[115]

Similarly, at the ecumenical youth peaceconference in April 1932, Bonhoeffer argues that the concept of creation orders "is a dangerous and treacherous foundation. Rather, in place of the order of creation, one should introduce the concept of the 'order of preservation' of God."[116] Again, these utterances, in order to be properly understood, need to be read in the context of their time, namely as a polemic against the *misuse* of the orders of creation.[117] This resistance was formally crysallized in the draft of the Bethel Confession, where the possibility of an independent knowledge of the orders of creation is explicitly rejected: "We reject the false doctrine that could consider any particular corporative order as belonging to God's orders of creation."[118]

However much Bonhoeffer's conception of the orders of preservation may have functioned as a reaction against the misappropriation of the concept of the orders of creation, it was certainly not limited to this function alone. As we saw above, Bonhoeffer directed the orders of preservation toward Christ, and it is primarily in relation to Bonhoeffer's Christology that

---

113. Althaus, *Theologie der Ordnungen*. For an extensive discussion of the various uses and understandings of "orders of creation" during this period, see Erickson, *Theologians under Hitler*, 98–104.

114. DBWE 11:363.

115. In his own words: "[T]he strife among the peoples of humanity, national struggle, war, class distinctions, the exploitation of the weak by the strong, economic competition as a matter of life and death." DBWE 11:363.

116. DBWE 11:353.

117. Clements points out that although Bonhoeffer rejects the concept of orders of creation altogether, the particular *sharpness* of his condemnation is directed first and foremost against the German nationalist theologians who "made a much freer and quite arbitrary use of the idea of 'orders of creation,' claiming above all that *the* supreme 'order of creation' is the people, race or nation to which one belongs and owes loyalty." Clements, "Ecumenical Witness for Peace," 163.

118. DBWE 12:391.

they need to be understood. As Feil notes: "The repudiation of the concept of orders of creation, which was under much discussion in those days and often hotly disputed, demonstrates that all of Bonhoeffer's theological arguments were grounded in christology, at least in the sense that there can be no theological argument independent of Christ."[119]

Nevertheless, it is the historical context that eventually led Bonhoeffer to abandon the term "order of preservation." Bethge notes that Bonhoeffer did so in 1933 on account of the fact that he saw it being abused as well, just as the term "order of creation" was before.[120] Later on in his *Ethics*, however, Bonhoeffer continued to use certain elements of his original concept in a new and transformed way, this time speaking of "divine mandates."[121] I will return to discuss this latter concept in detail in chapter 6.

THE ORDERS OF PRESERVATION AS A "THIRD WAY" BETWEEN BARTH AND BRUNNER

With his concept of the orders of preservation, Bonhoeffer placed himself in the middle of the heated debate over natural theology that was going on at the time. More often than not, he is seen as a supporter of Barth on the issue of natural theology.[122] According to Jordan Ballor, this is largely due to Barth's own interpretation and use of Bonhoeffer.[123] As will become clear, however, there are substantial differences between the respective positions that they adopted on the question. Those are reason enough for Ballor—and I agree with him—to see Bonhoeffer as occupying a third, middle position, with Barth on the one side, and Brunner on the other.

First of all, there is the difference with Barth. In stark contrast with Bonhoeffer, Barth's theology makes no use of a concept such as orders of preservation.[124] As a consequence, it proves to be very difficult for Barth

---

119. Feil, *The Theology of Dietrich Bonhoeffer*, 71–72.

120. Bethge, *Dietrich Bonhoeffer*, 459. This has led Mayer to conclude that Bonhoeffer used the term "Erhaltungsordnung" for two years at the most, namely from 1932 to 1933. See Mayer, *Christuswirklichkeit*, 123n115.

121. DBWE 6:388–408. See also Mayer, *Christuswirklichkeit*, 124.

122. See Benktson, *Christus und die Religion*, and Godsey, "Barth and Bonhoeffer," 9–27.

123. Ballor, "Christ in Creation," 14.

124. In his famous "No! An Answer to Emil Brunner," he writes: "We must go on to ask how far his 'preserving grace' is grace at all. We are ever and again allowed to exist under various conditions which at least moderate the worst abuses. Does that deserve to be called 'grace'? Taken by itself it might just as well be our condemnation to a kind of antechamber of hell!" Karl Barth, "No!," 84. Quoted in Ballor, "Christ in Creation," 10.

to provide a positive, theological account of the order found in nature and culture.[125] Bonhoeffer took note of this lacuna in Barth's theology and acted accordingly. As Pangritz rightly observes, Bonhoeffer's "discussion of the 'orders of preservation' is meant to fill in a gap in Barth's understanding precisely where the theological foundation ought to be for a binding proclamation of peace and social justice as concrete commandments."[126]

At the same time, Bonhoeffer does not seek an answer to the problem in the concept of the orders of creation, and in this respect, he differs from Brunner's position. Aside from this point, Brunner and Bonhoeffer stand in agreement with each other, by and large in that they both believe that God's primary relation to the world after the Fall is that of preservation. Brunner formulates this as follows: "The manner in which God is present to his fallen creature is in his *preserving grace*. Preserving grace does not abolish sin but abolishes the worst consequences of sin."[127] The only difference between Bonhoeffer and Brunner is that, after the Fall, Brunner finds *both* orders of preservation *and* orders of creation at work. A clear example on this point is found in marriage, which Brunner takes to be a creation ordinance, on account of the fact that it was established prior to the Fall. The state, in contrast, does *not* constitute an order of creation in Brunner's eyes, but solely an order of preservation intended to curb the worst effects of sin. As we see, then, for Brunner, orders of creation have a higher value, or a greater theological significance, than orders of preservation. Bonhoeffer, in contrast, does not see marriage as a creation order, even though, in the biblical account, it was clearly set in place before the Fall. Instead of defending this choice, however, he simply states it as a matter of fact. This has led Ballor to suggest that Bonhoeffer "might find that after the Fall marriage too is a preservation ordinance, since its inception was unrelated to sin, but it has, like the rest of creation, been affected and marred by sin, and therefore stands in need of preservation."[128]

125. See Ballor, "Christ in Creation," 10.

126. Pangritz, *Karl Barth in Dietrich Bonhoeffer*, 44. This difference with Barth is indicative of the general character of the relationship between Bonhoeffer and Barth at the time. As outlined by Bethge, the relationship between Barth and Bonhoeffer in the critical years 1932 and 1933 was in a phase characterized by the primacy of the practical over the theoretical and comprised of "theological differences, accompanied by a very close alliance in church politics." Bethge, *Dietrich Bonhoeffer*, 178. See also Van 't Slot, *Negativism of Revelation?*, 195–97.

127. Brunner, *Natural Theology*, 28; italics original. Cited in Ballor, "Christ in Creation," 8.

128. Ibid., 9.

It is not my aim in this section to give a detailed, theological evaluation of the various differences between Bonhoeffer, Brunner and Barth on the issue of the orders of preservation. Instead, I would simply like to draw attention to the fact that Bonhoeffer followed a sort of median path between his two counterparts. As Ballor concludes, echoing this point: "Bonhoeffer's doctrine of God's preservation allows him to affirm the radical nature of the Fall while maintaining some semblance of created value and goodness, however badly marred."[129]

The Significance of Bonhoeffer's Theology of Nature for Environmental Ethics

Here in the second part of this chapter, I shall transpose the key concepts of Bonhoeffer's christologically defined theology of nature, which we have just now explored, into the field of environmental ethics. I will divide the work up into five separate sections. In the first section, I will show how Bonhoeffer's assertion of Christ as the center of nature can help to overcome the subject-object division between nature and human beings. Next, in the second section, I will discuss the relevance of Bonhoeffer's concept of the Fall, though at the same time indicating its limits as well. The third section then applies Bonhoeffer's concept of Christ as the Redeemer of nature to environmental ethics, while the fourth does the same with respect to Bonhoeffer's theology of the sacraments. In the fifth and final section, I will show the relevance of Bonhoeffer's concept of the orders of preservation for environmental ethics.

Christ as the Center of Nature

In the first part of this chapter, we saw how Bonhoeffer took Christ to be the center both of the original, good creation and of fallen nature as well. What this implies is that nature as such has its own relation to God, and that this is also mediated by Christ, both before and apart from human beings, even though nature's primary goal, as Bonhoeffer maintains, is to serve human beings. We saw that, in asserting this, Bonhoeffer was one of the first modern theologians to treat nature in an independent fashion.

Bonhoeffer's claim that nature has to be perceived, or understood, christocentrically, has multiple implications for environmental ethics. First of all, it opens up an alternative to a "strong" anthropocentrism, which

129. Ibid., 10.

claims that nature only exists for the sake of human beings. (I will explore this point more fully in chapter 4.) Secondly, in claiming Christ to be the center of nature, Bonhoeffer's theology also provides a way to overcome the application of subject/object dualism to nature, in which nature is seen as nothing more than an object in relation to the human subject.

THE CARTESIAN OBJECT-SUBJECT DIVIDE AS A PROBLEM FOR ENVIRONMENTAL ETHICS

This Cartesian distinction between "nature" as object, on the one hand, and the human being as knowing and investigating subject, on the other, has played a fundamental role in the natural sciences. As Moltmann points out: "In natural science and technology, humans experience themselves as the ruling subjects of their world, not only the center and reference point of all things, but also the ontological foundation, the first and all-determining being."[130] Hence, nature is treated as an object by human beings, who dominate it through their work (both practically or theoretically).[131] As such, human beings alientate themselves from nature by standing over (or opposing themselves) against it, instead of being situated somewhere within it. Many have noted early on in the development of the field of environmental ethics that this alienation is a key reason, or determining factor, responsible for the current ecological crisis.[132]

Many attempts have been made to overcome this dualism between nature and human beings, even well before there was any awareness of the ecological crisis. Already in 1948, Paul Tillich sought to rediscover what he referred to as "the power of nature," proposing that "[t]he power of nature must be found in a sphere prior to the cleavage of our world into subjectivity and objectivity. Life originates on a level which is 'deeper' than the Cartesian duality of *cogitatio* and *extensio* ('thought' and 'extension')."[133] Also in the period before there was any awareness of the ecological crisis, the modern utopian Ernst Bloch took up the challenge of overcoming humankind's alienation from nature by turning to Schelling's nature philosophy.[134] In particular, he asserted a correspondence between humanity and nature: the

130. Moltmann, "Alienation and Liberation," 133. This essay by Moltmann has also been reprinted in ibid., *God in Creation*, 40–52.

131. Moltmann, "Alienation and Liberation," 133.

132. For just one example, see Santas, "Subject/Object Dualism and Environmental Degradation," 79–96.

133. Tillich, "Nature and Sacrament," 102; italics original.

134. Bloch, *The Principle of Hope*, 625–99.

human subject, as he claimed, exists in partnership with a corresponding nature subject. In other words, instead of seeing nature as a more or less passive object dependent upon a knowing, human subject, he insisted upon recognizing nature as standing on its own. As such, it can be perceived as its own subject, with its own history, independent of human beings. Once human beings learn to see and respect this independent subject and future of nature, "a community of nature [can] come about in which both can be at home."[135]

More recently, in the context of a growing awareness of the ecological crisis, many other endeavors have been made to overcome the subject-object division. An influential example in this regard is found in the work of J. Baird Callicott, who used the minimalistic Copenhagen Interpretation of quantum theory both to overturn the Cartesian partition and to develop a theory of inherent value in nature.[136] Many others then followed in Callicot's wake.[137] Another example can be found in the proposal to use Chaos theory as a way to overcome the Cartesian dualism present in environmental ethical thought.[138] Also historical studies are performed in the works of individual thinkers, looking for ways to overcome the dualistic approach.[139] Fighting against subject/object dualism in environmental ethics often forms a part of a larger political agenda, such as we see in the cases of ecofeminism[140] and the campaign for animal-rights.[141] The broader approach of these proposals most often aims, through their critique of subject/object dualism, at stimulating responsible human action towards the environment.[142]

Also in the field of Christian theology proper, the challenge of overcoming the subject-object divide, with particular regard to nature, has been widely recognized. Moltmann, for instance, to whom I have already referred, argues for a "naturalization of the human being," a term which assumes, as Moltmann says, "that, fundamentally speaking, the human being does not *confront* nature: he himself is nothing other than one of nature's products. Nature is the great subject which unremittingly brings forth new

---

135. Moltmann, "Alienation and Liberation," 135.

136. Callicott, "Intrinsic Value," 257–75.

137. For a critical yet sympathetic reception of Callicot's work, see Zimmerman, "Quantum Theory," 277–308.

138. Robinson, "The Relevance of *Chaos* to Environmental Ethics."

139. See Steiner-Aeschliman, "Immanent Dualism," 235–63.

140. See Adams, "'A Very Rare and Difficult Thing,'" 591–604; and Jackson, "Gender, Nature and Trouble with Anti-Dualism," 23–44.

141. Steiner, "Descartes, Christianity, and Contemporary Speciesism," 117–31.

142. A good example is Katz, *Nature as Subject*.

forms and manifestations of life, last of all the human being. The human being is therefore the object, since he is the product of productive nature."[143]

In contrast, Catholic theologian Peter F. Ryan argues in precisely the opposite direction by calling for what he refers to as a "humanizing" of nature, which he considers to be "subpersonal."[144] Though he starts out from a clearly anthropocentric position, he nevertheless emphasizes that "[o]ur dominion over nature is subject to moral norms that are available to reason even apart from revelation."[145] In particular, he claims that nature is intrinsically good, that is, a reflection of the goodness of the Creator, but that it can also be used to serve human goods. As he puts it: "If . . . one rightly judges that nature should be disturbed to meet human needs, then far from violating the inherent value of subpersonal reality, such use fulfils nature by humanizing and personalizing it, while also fulfilling human persons."[146] So according to Ryan, good and proper human dealings with nature unite "subpersonal" nature with human beings, and together they bring glory to God. The focus thus lies on modest, careful conduct with regard to nature, by which nature and humanity are connected.[147] These two examples serve to indicate the wide variety of theological proposals that have been put forward to overcome the subject-object divide.

Bonhoeffer's Christocentric Conception of Nature as an Alternative

Once we transpose some of Bonhoeffer's concepts, which I introduced above, into the language of the current debate, it becomes possible to add Bonhoeffer's own voice to the polyphony. Specifically, he manages to overcome the dualism between human beings, on the one hand, and non-human nature, on the other, by affirming Christ as the center both of human existence and of nature. In his person, Christ binds non-human and human nature together, redeeming both at the same time, or in the same move, as it were. Bonhoeffer's view of the oneness, in Christ, of nature and humanity, does not however lead him to reduce one term to the other. As will become clear further on, in chapter 4, Bonhoeffer clearly articulates crucial differences between human and non-human nature. He even sees non-human nature

143. Moltmann, "Alienation and Liberation," 133.

144. Ryan, "Secularist and Christian Views," 57–79.

145. Ibid.," 74.

146. Ibid., 75.

147. Ryan's position reflects, as one may have expected, Thomas Aquinas's position on the value of animals. See Wynn, "Thomas Aquinas," 154–65.

as primarily existing for the purpose of serving human needs (a fact which might *initially* seem to reiterate the same division between subject and object), even though nature also has its own independent value in Christ, apart from human beings. As such, in positing Jesus Christ as the center of and Mediator between human and non-human nature, his theology effectively overcomes the Cartesian divide.[148]

This application of Bonhoeffer's thoughts on Christ as the center of nature to ecology is similar to the way other authors transpose Bonhoeffer's christocentric conception of non-human nature to environmental ethics. Scott, for example, argues that in positing Christ as the center of nature, Bonhoeffer "proposes no separation between sociality and nature. Nature is not opposed to sociality but it is rather itself historical and social; likewise, sociality is historical and natural and, in its turn, history is social and natural."[149] Although Scott does not explicate the way Christ overcomes false separations between humanity and nature in the terms of object-subject divide, it can easily be noted that he nevertheless also proposes to use Bonhoeffer's conception of Christ as nature's center to overcome this separation.

The Viability of Confessing Christ as the Center of Nature

It can nevertheless be asked just how viable, or fruitful, the affirmation of Christ as the center of nature may actually be for the broader discussion. As a claim of faith, it is a response brought forth by God's revealing of himself, and is therefore not deducible from the facts of nature alone. But does this not lead to a sort of fideism? Is there any clear relation at all between the claim of faith and the sphere of natural science? Bonhoeffer does not offer much reflection on questions of this sort, though his theological mentor, Karl Barth, did.

As Barth explains, belief in God as Creator constitues an act of Christian *profession*. In the Introduction to *CD* 3/1, for instance, he states that faith in God the Creator, in the Apostolicum, is a confession and cannot

---

148. There is also another way in which Bonhoeffer manages to overcome the subject-object divide between human beings and non-human nature, namely, in the stress that he places on the fundamental bodily nature of human existence. Human beings, on his view, form an intrinsic part of the created natural world by virtue of their bodies. These assertions stand in very close proximity, incidentally, with Moltmann's insistence on the naturalization of humanity—more on this point in chapter 4.

149. Scott, "Christ, Nature, Sociality," 423.

be anything else—hence his use of the word *credo*.[150] Bromiley explicates Barth's intention. He argues that what comes first is not an engagement of the scientific community with apologetic arguments, or the offering of an overarching worldview. Rather, Christian faith "views the creature relative to the Creator, and its proper work concerns the Creator and his creative action considered in and of themselves."[151] In other words, Christian theology should start with drawing out the implications of the confession that God is Creator. What this entails is the belief that God does not exist on his own, but that created the world besides him, and, as a consequence, the world does not stand alone—on the contrary, it comes from God, and doesn't function in or out of itself. Another Barth-scholar, Smedema, explains how this is a mystery and therefore the object of faith. But, according to him, we would be wrong to accuse Barth of offering an inherently unprovable hypothesis, since Barth sees it, instead, as a confessing answer to God's self-revelation.[152]

This particular answer to the problem has concrete consequences for the way that Christians deal with and relate themselves to nature—a point which has been brought to the fore by Moltmann, for example. As he states: "Perceiving the world as creation . . . implies a particular attitude towards the world and a way of dealing with it which touches the existence of the perceiving person and draws him into a wider fellowship. Perpection of the world as creation confers felicity in existence. Offering the world to God in thanksgiving confers freedom in existence."[153] What this means is that, although seeing the world as creation clearly remains an act of faith, it is not an act of *blind* faith—on the contrary, it has direct and practical implictions.

The Fall of Nature

As we saw earlier on, Bonhoeffer asserts that nature itself, in spite of its innocence, suffered heavily as a result of the (human) Fall. Once demoted to its fallen condition, it no longer points back to God, or to Christ. While Christ remains the center of nature, he remains so only in a hidden way, that is, in a way accessible only through faith. Through humankind's Fall, nature too falls into a fundamental disarray, frantically seeking to deliver itself from its curse through natural disasters, as Bonhoeffer says.

150. As Barth claims: "To sum up, the statement concerning creation cannot be anything but an *articulus fidei.*" *CD* 3/1:22; italics original.

151. Bromiley, *Introduction to the Theology of Karl Barth*, 109.

152. Smedema, *Grond onder de voeten*, 118.

153. Moltmann, *God in Creation*, 70.

Ecological Criticisms of the Christian Doctrine of the Fall

Such accounts of the Fall have since come under sharp criticism from ecotheologians, in particular from proponents of deep ecology. As Nicole Roskos observes, "[r]ecent scholarship . . . critiques the cosmic fall for encouraging estrangement from Earth ecosystems [sic]. Some scholars reinterpret a distinctively human 'fall' from harmony with nature, others deconstruct the Fall altogether, so as to affirm natural forms of death and suffering as integral to the process of nature."[154] By way of example, I refer to the criticism of the Fall by Anne Primavesi, a long-time advocate of the Gaia hypothesis, which, as we recall, was originally developed by James Lovelock.[155] Louke van Wensveen summarizes the basic gist of Primavesi's—and others'—criticism of the Fall, noting that, according to her, "the concept is neither biblical nor consistent with an ecological appreciation for the necessary functions of disturbance, death, and decay."[156]

Bonhoeffer and the Remaining Relevance of Assering Nature's Fallenness

In spite of these criticisms, I remain convinced that, with Bonhoeffer, we need to keep reasserting the reality of the Fall—*especially* in light of the current ecological crisis, for this doctrine has great potential for uncovering structural evil both in nature and human society. What's problematic in Bonhoeffer's account of the Fall, however, is that he fails to address the question of how we ought to understand the Fall of nature with regard to the perspective of the natural sciences. As we saw, Bonhoeffer has little problem accepting Darwinian theory, and yet, at the same time, he doesn't give any indication of how we might go about reconciling evolutionary biology (according to which nature is "red in tooth and claw"[157]), with the classical Christian assertion of nature's original goodness (according to which death and decay only entered the world as ulterior effects of Adam's Fall). Though the question as such, as he says, doesn't concern him, it does concern many of those working in the field of ecotheology; and Bonhoeffer's claim that, due to the Fall, we cannot know anything about creation's situation prior the

154. Roskos, "Christian Theology and the Fall," 314.

155. See Primavesi, *From Apocalypse to Genesis*.

156. Wensveen, "Christianity (7a)—Theology and Ecology," 355.

157. Even though this expression is, of course, not from a biologist, but from Tennyson, *In Memoriam A. H. H.*, canto 56.

Fall, is unsatisfactory. This means that, in our attempt to understand the Fall in the context of natural science, we shall have to move beyond Bonhoeffer and to draw from other sources.[158]

I would also suggest that Bonhoeffer's conception of the effects of the Fall on nature are too radical in bearing. Indeed, he leaves no room for the possibility that, even after the Fall, nature remains (at least partially) capable of glorifying God as its Creator. As we saw, he asserts that, in the sacraments, nature is once again set free to give praise to God, but apart from these specific circumstances, he doesn't leave any room for a possible doxological capacity of fallen nature as such. In contrast, a more nuanced and ecologically sensitive conception of nature's doxological function is offered by Moltmann.[159]

Christ the Redeemer of Nature

Bonhoeffer's assertion that nature is redeemed in Christ is important for environmental ethics. As Northcott points out, "the recovery of an ecological ethic in the modern world requires the recovery of a doctrine of creation redeemed, and the worship of a creator who is also redeemer of creation."[160] Whereas Bonhoeffer only provides indications of what the relation between redemption and fallen creation involves, the task of explicating this relation in detail has been picked up, in recent years, by other theologians. One has, for instance, Moltmann's proposal to connect the two doctrines, which he states as follows: "If Christ is the ground of salvation for the whole creation, for sinful men and women, and for 'enslaved' non-human creatures, he is then also the ground for the existence of the whole creation, human beings and nature alike."[161] Similarly, Bouma-Prediger has treated the question how Christian soteriology relates to nature, arguing that redemption signals the restoration of nature, rather than its annihilation. According to him, "[s]oteriology (like eschatology) is earth-affirming."[162] In the study of Willis Jenkins mentioned earlier, *Ecologies of Grace*, Jenkins does not specifically

158. In recent years, groundbreaking work has been done in this regard by Mc-Grath, *Darwinism and the Divine*, 233–38.

159. Moltmann, *God in Creation*, 69–71.

160. Northcott, *The Environment*, 222.

161. Moltmann, *God in Creation*, 94. See Jenkin's summary of Moltmann's view on this point: "Jürgen Moltmann . . . develops his view of nature by appealing directly to that descriptive connection between soteriology and creation." Jenkins, *Ecologies of Grace*, 71–72.

162. Bouma-Prediger, *For the Beauty of the Earth*, 103.

indicate how redemption relates to creation; however, he "maps the way Christian environmental strategies draw from traditions of salvation as they engage the problems of environmental ethics."[163] In spite of these and other attempts to address the relation between redemption and creation, Ernst M. Conradie's conclusion is still justified: "Despite the extensive literature available on Christian ecotheology, comparatively little has been done on the theme of salvation."[164] Therein lies our task, the task at hand. Though Bonhoeffer's work does serve to point to this connection, or to signal its importance, he nevertheless does not give us enough direction on the theme in order to work out a fully Bonhoefferian vision on nature's redemption. He does, however, work on the theme of how the Christian sacraments are a preview of nature's redemption in Christ; by turning, in the following section, to consider this theme more closely, we should be able to get a better handle on the issue of nature's redemption.

The Sacraments as Preview of Nature's Redemption

We saw that, according to Bonhoeffer, the specific way in which Christ's redeeming presence is active in the world is through the sacraments. In the Word that is proclaimed over and in and through the elements of the sacraments, nature is set free from its dumbness and is once again made capable of giving expression, as a preview of its final liberation with the advent of Christ's kingdom, to its Creator. This way of defining the sacraments of the church was, as I already noted, unique in Protestant theology at the time; as such, it brims with promise for a Christian ecological ethics.

The potential of the Christian sacraments for articulating a properly Christian ecotheology has increasingly come to be recognized by scholars in recent decades.[165] When surveying the literature on the subject, it becomes clear that this potential has been developed in many different ways, depending in large part on the theological conception of nature that the author is working from. My present aim is not to give a general overview of this new and developing field, but rather to indicate how Bonhoeffer's account of the sacraments can be brought into connection with contemporary thought on the ecological implications of the sacraments, in addition to the critical function that it carries out.

163. From the back cover of Jenkins, *Ecologies of Grace.*

164. Conradie, "The Salvation of the Earth," 111. In chapter 1, I sketched the ongoing work to overcome this lacune, by Conradie and others.

165. See Oliver, "The Eucharist before Nature and Culture," 331–53; Ruether, "Ecological Theology," 226–34; and O'Malley, "Catholic Ecology and Eucharist," 68–78.

The Ecotheological Significance of Christ's "Real Presence" in the Sacraments

First and foremost, it is important to come to terms with Bonhoeffer's conception of the sacraments as "visible Words." Santmire makes the case that more often than not the concept of the sacraments as "visible Words" has—erroneously—come to mean that they were seen as pointers towards doctrinal truth, rather than as mediators of the Logos who came in the flesh. According to Santmire, this interpretation can be traced back as far as to the work of Melanchthon. "As a result," he says, "for some Christian traditions, the sacraments have tended to become illustrations of an idea, . . . rites that have been instituted by God for the sake of simple, even illiterate souls in order to teach them about what God has revealed more directly in the written or proclaimed Word."[166] For this reason, he asserts that it is necessary to retrieve the real character of sacraments as "visible Words." In this instance, Bonhoeffer's concept of the sacraments can help. We saw that, in the specific way that he asserted Christ's presence in the sacraments, he resisted Luther's formula, *finitum capax infiniti*, because he saw it as an answer to the "how" question, but not yet to the "who" question. Yet Bonhoeffer does affirm Christ's real presence in the sacraments, and, in this way, he provides an answer to the question of "who" it is that is present in the sacraments—namely Christ, the Humiliated One. This real presence of Christ has significant consequences for a theology of nature, and thus, by extension, for ecotheology, because it gives concrete theological expression to the value that the natural world has in Christ. For example, Kurt Hendel makes the case that Luther's love for nature and appreciation of its beauty, preserved by the Lutheran *finitum capax infiniti* formula, can provide a theological foundation of and inspiration for environmental action.[167] The same can be said of Bonhoeffer's theology as well.

Humans and Nature United in the Praise of God: Implications for Ecotheology

Secondly, Bonhoeffer's account powerfully brings human beings into connection with nature in the act of praising God. In the liturgy of the churches, Christians praise God as the creator, redeemer and sustainer of all life. This goes back to the Bible, to passages such as Ps 148, which depicts the realm of nature as a whole offering praise to God. Throughout the centuries, this

166. Santmire, *Nature Reborn*, 83.

167. Hendel, "*Finitum capax infiniti*," 420–33.

theme features as an ever-recurring motif in the Christian tradition, and figures most prominently in liturgical texts.[168] Yet on a theological level, sustained reflection on the praise that creation offers to God has been scarce. As Jame Schaefer points out: "Although the Bible and texts throughout the Christian tradition are replete with praises for God, reflections that affirm and call upon natural entities to praise God are scant."[169] Moreover, even in the work of Bonhoeffer, we do not find a fully developped account of how exactly nature gives praise to God. Although the idea may only be present in a dense, compacted form, it is undoubtedly present in his theology. And his assertion is an important one, for when, in the elements of the sacraments, nature is again set free to praise God, both it and human beings are united in their praise. In the act of praising God, both human beings and nature fulfill what they were originally intended to do, and human beings come to recognize that nature too, of itself, offers praise to God as well.[170] Timothy O'Malley picks up on this same theme, noting: "Praise, which is understood, requires that the Christian perceive the entire created universe as an arena for enacting praise, not simply in word but in action."[171] This leads O'Malley to urge for efforts on the part of the congregation to come to a better understanding of nature. In his own words: "Such a life of praise is not possible without a renewal of perception, taught through liturgical worship, whereby one begins to see the particularities of the created world as signs of God."[172] In this way, the Christian sacraments indeed offer an opportunity for believers to value the importance of non-human creation. In a closely related way, it can also serve as an opportunity for Christians to recognize the responsibility that they bear for the destruction of nature, and to admonish each other to adopt a lifestyle of modesty and care for the environment.

168. Edwards gives a description of certain aspects of this tradition, mentioning, by way of example, book 8 of the *Apostolic Constitutions* (fourth century), which features "a highly detailed celebration of creation." Edwards, "Eucharist and Ecology," 204–5.

169. Schaefer, *Theological Foundations*, 103.

170. The sacraments of the church offer a concrete case in point of how Bonhoeffer's Christ, as the center of nature, overcomes the subject-object division mentioned earlier. This possibility of employing, or understanding, the Eucharist in this way, is also noted by Oliver, "The Eucharist Before Nature and Culture," 350.

171. O'Malley, "Catholic Ecology and Eucharist," 73.

172. Ibid., 74.

The Need for Criticizing Universal Sacramentologies

Thirdly, one crucial feature of Bohoeffer's theology of the sacraments is his radical and explicit limitation of the sacraments to the two traditional, Protestant sacraments of baptism and eucharist. And yet a driving force in ecotheology seeks to extend the sacraments so as to include the whole created order, that is, to see nature itself as a sacrament.[173] As Philip Knights succinctly observes: "Much use of sacramentality in a Panentheist manner is a way of seeing the cosmos as a sacramental arena in which the things of the earth are not only signifiers of divine love but in some sense are active participants in the Divine."[174] Universal sacramentalism of this sort is particularly strong in Orthodox churches, and it is therefore hardly surprising that a great number of ecotheologians turn to this tradition in particular as a resource for ecotheology.[175] Also in the Catholic tradition, a wider sacramentalism is strongly present;[176] here too, connections between sacramentalism and ecotheology are firmly established.[177] With Protestantism, in contrast, there has been a strong tendency to limit the number of sacraments and, more broadly, to downplay sacramental theology.[178]

Bonhoeffer stands firmly in this latter tradition and asserts, as we saw, that the sacramental character of the world was lost in the Fall, and that it is only restored in the two specific, prostestant sacraments. Rather than seeing this as a drawback of his sacramental theology, I consider it to be a proper limitation, especially in light of the criticisms that have been leveled against the broader use of sacramental theology in ecotheology.

Rasmussen, for example, argues that the picture of society presented in many sacramentalist cosmologies is distorted. In particular, he takes

173. See Haught, "Catholicism," 201–2.

174. Knights, "'The Whole Earth My Altar,'" 60.

175. See Koyama, "The Eucharist," 80–90; George, "Towards a Eucharistic Ecology," 45–55; Gregorios, *The Human Presence*; Metropolitan John of Pergamum, "Preserving God's Creation," 76–85; and Ware, "Through the Creation to the Creator," 8–30. A helpful overview can be found in Chryssavgis, "The Earth as Sacrament," 92–114.

176. See Schaefer, *Theological Foundations*, 65.

177. See Hart, *Sacramental Commons*; Berry, *Evening Thoughts*; and ibid, *The Sacred Universe*.

178. Even in this (apparently somewhat more limited) tradition, one still finds many resources available for developing a more expansive view of the sacraments, which would include the natural world. In the Lutheran tradition, for instance, a tendency exists that leads towards a wider sacramentalism, which has been taken up in the work of H. Paul Santmire, as we saw earlier. Calvin too can arguably be said to have a sacramental theology of creation. See Hessel-Robinson, "Doctrine of the Lord's Supper," 182.

issue with the sacramentalist assumption of a harmony existing between social and natural interests. While many maintain that an organic and, as it were, symphonic harmony exists between the two spheres, according to him, "metaphors of organisms and symphonies don't expose the unequal and corrupted power relations of life among human beings, nor between humans and other creatures. They mask the fact that struggle and conflict so often *are* the status quo."[179] John Haught echoes the same criticism when he notes that the sacramentalist, lost in wonder before the whole created order, can all too easily become inclined to glory in what is—including its shortcomings.[180] For this reason, Rasmussen puts forward the suggestion of merging sacramental spirituality with the political agenda of liberation, especially as he sees the latter exemplified in the plight of indigenous peoples and in ecofeminism.[181] Conradie also voices criticism of sacramentalism, though he takes it in another direction. As he writes, "[t]he story of the universe is also a lengthy "saga" with vast epochs of redundancy and mere repetition, but, with great patience, also of continuous experimentation with novel forms of order. Nature itself is inherently restless, refusing to acquiesce in trivial forms of (sacramental) harmony."[182] Bonhoeffer's theology offers an alternative to sacramentalist cosmologies of this sort. While he asserts the real presence of Christ in the sacraments, he limits Christ's sacramental presence to these sacraments alone. He can thus be seen as an exponent of the "prophet" model of Rasmussen.[183]

In conclusion, we can see that Bonhoeffer's Lutheran theology of the sacraments opens a door onto rich and suprising connections with ecology. As Northcott indicates, referring to John Habgood, "[t]he enormous value of a sacramental approach . . . is that it makes of every Sunday Eucharist a powerful ecological parable of the capacity of matter itself to be redolent of the redemptive purposes of God for the creation and to mediate God's grace to the eucharistic participants."[184] This certainly holds true for Bonhoeffer's sacramental theology.

179. Rasmussen, *Earth Community*, 240; italics original.

180. Haught, *The Promise of Nature*, 110–12.

181. Rasmussen, *Earth Community*, 240–41.

182. Conradie, *An Ecological Christian Anthropology*, 139.

183. Rasmussen, *Earth Community*, 242–44.

184. Northcott, *The Environment*, 145. Northcott refers in particular to the work of Habgood, "A Sacramental Approach," 51.

The Orders of Preservation and The Possibility of Natural Theology

Just as in Bonhoeffer's time, so too today, a large part of the theological discussion surrounds the topic of the ordering of creation. With the aim of increasing the value of nature and of developing an ethics appropriate for the environment, many ecotheologians have turned their attention both to insights from the natural sciences concerning nature's ordering, as well as to the age-old Christian natural law ethic, which affirms the ordering of nature as well as the possibility of developing a natural theology. These theologians give particular emphasis to the harmony and beauty of the natural order, pointing to cooperation and mutuality between species, which together fosters and nurtures a complex, balanced planetary ecosystem in which everything is interrelated. They accordingly argue that it is the brutal and ignorant disturbance of this order that lies at the root of the ecological crisis; and in order to rectify this disturbance, they insist on carefully studying the natural world.

The Use of Natural Law Ethics by Ecotheologians

One theologian who develops such a natural law ethic is Northcott, in his influential book, *The Environment and Christian Ethics*. In the fifth chapter of his work, "The Order of Creation," he sets out to demonstrate "that the Hebrew Bible . . . presents the non-human world as a created order which is redolent of the purposes and providence of the creator God, though it is ontologically distinct from the being of God. The purposive order of the cosmos reflects the will and design of the creator."[185] He draws on the work of the anthropologist Robert Murray, who remarks on the reciprocal relationality between human and non-human life that characterizes primal cultures the world over. According to Northcott, we find the same relationality at work in the Hebrew Bible, in the form of the order of creation. Northcott contrasts this biblical ideal with the fact that "modern scientific myths of origin have been utilized to characterise the origins and nature of life, both nonhuman and human, as essentially violent, aggressive and competitive, 'red in tooth and claw.'"[186] He refers in this instance to biologists such as Richard Dawkins, who argues, in *The Selfish Gene*, that each individual animal, and even each gene itself, pursues its own interests, competing for

185. Northcott, *The Environment*, 164.
186. Ibid., 175.

power with other animals (or genes).[187] He contrasts this tooth-and-nail conception of nature's processes with the work of Mary Midgley,[188] and Eugene P. Odum, amongst others.[189]

In the sixth chapter of his book, "Creation, Redemption and Natural Law Ethics," Northcott opens up a discussion of natural law ethics in light of the New Testament and Christian tradition. Here he claims that because God manifests itself in the cosmos, it becomes a resource of "natural knowledge."[190] In this connection, he primarily refers to Aquinas' understanding of natural goodness. While he notes that Aquinas gave too little consideration to sin and its effects on the natural world, he nevertheless concludes that natural law ethics provides the strongest possible conceptual basis for the development of a Christian ecological ethics.[191] He then goes on to work out an ecological revision of natural law ethics, concluding that such a revision "presents from within the Christian tradition a moral valuation of natural order, and an account of relationality and the human self-in-relation, which arises from the objective reality of the biophysical world as well as from Hebrew and Christian revelation, and one that does not rely on human sentiment or on human reason alone."[192] Next, in his seventh chapter of his book, "Natural Law and Ecological Society," Northcott works out in concrete detail just what such a revised natural law ethics would look like. Despite the value that the non-human world bears, he follows Aquinas in identifying human beings as bearers of greater value than non-human beings. As such, he opposes himself against versions of deep ecology according to which conflicts between human and non-human goods should be resolved in favor of the integrity of whole ecosystems, rather than in favor of humans alone.[193]

Northcott's plea for the development of natural law ethics has been echoed by a cross-denominational collection of ecotheologians as well. Jenkins describes this current of ecotheology in terms of a strategy of eco-justice. The theology of Aquinas figures as the single most important source of inspiration for this line of thought.[194] This doesn't mean that ecological

---

187. Dawkins, *The Selfish Gene.*

188. Midgley, *The Ethical Primate.*

189. Odum and Odum, *Fundamentals of Ecology.*

190. Northcott, *The Environment*, 227.

191. Ibid., 232.

192. Ibid., 256.

193. Ibid., 266.

194. There have been many attempts to bring the work of Aquinas to bear in the field of ecotheology, see ibid., 226–33; Jenkins, *Ecologies of Grace*, 115–51; LeBlanc, "Eco-Thomism," 293–306; and Wynn, "Thomas Aquinas," 154–65.

use of natural law ethics is restricted to Catholics alone.[195] On the contrary, theologians such as Rasmussen,[196] and Moltmann,[197] both make room for natural law ethics in their respective accounts of ecotheology. Even the evangelical theologian Bouma-Prediger makes use of it.[198] For these reasons, Rebecca Gould arrives (correctly, I would argue) at the conclusion that, "[i]n contemporary ecological theologies today . . . the natural theology tradition is often being rehabilitated for ecological use."[199]

CRITICISMS OF THE USE OF NATURAL LAW ETHICS FROM A BIOLOGICAL STANDPOINT

In spite of these promising trends, the way in which ecotheologians frequently refer to the natural order has come under sharp criticism from Lisa Sideris.[200] Sideris has reviewed the works of McFague, Northcott, Ruether, Cobb, Moltmann, Birch, and Rasmussen, and in her view, each of these thinkers works from a view on nature that is far too positive in its bearing, giving preference to order over chaos, harmony over dissonance, and mutuality over competition. As such, they each resist a Darwinian account of nature—a point which, in Sideris' view, betrays their underlying romantic sensibilities. According to her, they "read" their own ideals of human communitarianism directly into nature: "My intention is . . . to illustrate how a scientifically inaccurate understanding of nature perpetuates ethical and theological imperatives that are inappropriate."[201] Jenkins summarizes Sideris' overall viewpoint quite well: "Whenever a theological ethicist privileges interdependence, balance, and cooperation in nature over evolution, predation, or death, she appears to let theological criteria determine her view of the natural world, in the face of credible scientific reports."[202]

195. Catholics also use this model as well, of course. See for example French, "Natural Law and Ecological Responsibility," 12–36; and Wynn, "Natural Theology In an Ecological Mode," 27–42.

196. Rasmussen, "The Moral Frame," in *Earth Community*, 344–48.

197. Moltmann, "The Knowledge of Creation," in *God in Creation*, 53–71.

198. He writes, for example: "[T]he universe is a place of order and structure, purposefully and lovingly designed by God . . . Everything has its place. Such a portrayal of cosmic fittingness evokes wonder . . . Where are we? In a world of wonders, wisely ordered by God." Bouma-Prediger, *For the Beauty of the Earth*, 88.

199. Gould, "Christianity (7h)—Natural Theology," 369. See also Nash, "Natural Law and Natural Rights," 1169–70.

200. Sideris, *Environmental Ethics*.

201. Ibid., 202.

202. Jenkins, *Ecologies of Grace*, 70–71.

One reason that Sideris sees for the flaws in these views of nature is their indebtedness to outmoded accounts of how ecosystems actually work. In this connection, the indication I made above concerning Northcott's reference to the work of Eugene Odum proves to be quite enlightening. Although Odum's account of ecosystems has been highly influential and has dominated the field for almost a decade, since the publication of his work, new hypotheses have arisen in biology that directly challenge his account, stressing the violent and selfish character of the biological world.[203]

Instead of arguing in favor of drawing from other theological sources for the development of an ecological ethics, Sideris sets out to develop an ethic that gives the violent and competitive character of nature (what she sees as) its proper due. In particular, she argues for a wilderness-ethic that respects the relations between predator and prey. As such, when it comes, in Jenkins' somewhat demeaning terms, to choosing between a wilderness ethic, "with its delight in predators and tolerance for blood," and, on the other hand, an ethic "liv[ing] out biblical peace by adopting pets, supporting zoos, and opposing the reintroduction of predators," she would clearly choose the former.[204] Sideris does not stand alone in her proposal either. Earlier on, wilderness ethicist Garrett Hardin pleaded on behalf of a preservation of wilderness that would go so far as not to allow a mountain rescue service helicopter to save a fallen climber.[205] As Northcott comments, in such a view, "[t]he preservation of the integrity of wilderness takes precedence over the threatened life of an individual fallen mountaineer."[206]

ECOTHEOLOGIANS RESPOND: CONTINUED, CRITICAL USE OF NATURAL LAW ETHICS

In response, Northcott blames Sideris for giving preference to empirical experience over against the Christian tradition. According to him, Christians have no need to deny the narratives of science when these have a firm, empirical basis. At the same time, he adds that "these narratives on their own cannot be sufficient guides to the meaning and purposes of the Triune God with regard to God's creatures."[207] This is a properly theological response, for, as Northcott points out, science alone, for a Christian theologian, is not

---

203. See Hagen, "Teaching Ecology," 704–23.

204. Jenkins, *Ecologies of Grace*, 71.

205. Hardin, "The Economics of Wilderness," 27. Cited in Northcott, *The Environment*, 107.

206. Northcott, *The Environment*, 107.

207. Northcott, Review of *Environmental Ethics*, 405.

yet enough to define truth—on the contrary, Christian narratives should be taken into account as well.

Even from the perspective of science, the account that Siders offers of natural selection can be called into question. Though not writing in direct response to Sideris *per se*, Mary Midgley, for example, resists the view that nature is actually as evil as many biologists would have us believe. Specifically, she takes issue with Herbert Spencer's evolutionary ethic, pointing out that "[e]volution is a much wider process which has produced sociality, generating love and altruism just as much as competition. If it had not done so (he could have said), there would never have been a human 'ethical process'. That process is every bit as much a product of evolution as its contrary is."[208] As Midgley observes, Spencer was not doing biology when he developed his view—as a political theorist, he was translating Darwinism, which he didn't understand all that well, into the realm of sociality and ethics, thereby leading to the development of Social Darwinism. Far from being a harmless theory, it gained concrete expression in fascist ideologies, most notably in that of Nazi Germany, where a strong conservationist ethic was coupled together with a xenophobic nationalism.[209] According to Midgley, then, one should not be too hasty in drawing ethical conclusions directly from biological accounts of nature. At the same time, it clearly cannot be denied that evil exists in nature, for example in predation.[210] It is this very fact that makes nature sufficiently ambiguous to be able to lead us towards radically different interpretations and understandings of it.[211]

Rasmussen also recognizes this moral ambiguity of nature, but instead of giving preference to one side or the other, he insists on bringing Christology into the discussion of natural order, referring in particular to Luther's Christology. As he has it, "[w]hat we can most reliably know of God's own way we know in the way of this Jesus, in his birth, ministry, crucifixion, and

208. Midgley, "Criticizing the Cosmos," 17.

209. See Biehl and Staudenmaier, *Ecofascism*, as well as Griffin, "Fascism," 639–44.

210. See Conradie, *An Ecological Christian Anthropology*, 44–51.

211. Drees seizes hold of this point: "Two contradictory interpretations of the world as we know it. Is reality hospitable to our existence, to be appreciated as something valuable? Or is the universe a vale of tears, optimized for generating bad luck, with the emergence of humans as nothing but a marvellous accident? These two different attitudes—praising and criticizing the cosmos—can be discerned in various responses to the natural sciences." Drees, "Introduction," 2. It should be noted that, with regards to the question of order, great differences exist between the sciences of physics and biology. As Rolston III observes: "Looking at nature systemically, we have discovered a 'fine-tuned' universe from astrophysics to nuclear physics, and a messy one from evolutionary and ecosystemic biology." Rolston III, "Naturalizing and Systematizing Evil," 67–68.

resurrection. God is like this Jesus."[212] When approaching the question from this angle, we can still recognize that "[p]redation . . . is an essential part of nature's cycles," all the while insisting that "[i]t is not a pattern of morality we praise and advocate . . . at least not on our better days."[213] In stark contrast with accounts like that of Hardin or Spencer, he notes how this is a course of conduct, or ethics, which, in effect, devours its own children, and is therefore to be "rejected here as a moral paradigm for sustainable community."[214] We cannot, as Rasmussen observes, rely on nature alone as our guide. Though it can be instructive and help to draw attention to nature, there needs to be a morality in addition to that. This morality is, at least in part, derived from the Christian tradition, and ultimately from Christ himself.

The Contribution Bonhoeffer's Concept of the Orders of Preservation Can Make

Though Bonhoeffer's theology cannot be seen as a major resource for the development of natural law ethics (on the contrary, reflection on natural law does not form a major component of his theology), his concept of the orders of preservation can be quite helpful here. Although the orders themselves primarily deal with *human* life, and not with non-human life, they can nevertheless serve as a paradigm for how we ought to perceive and make sense of the elements of order at work in nature. As Bonhoeffer emphasizes, the orders of preservation come from God, and yet, at the same time, there is a certain continuity in them which relates them primarily to observable phenomena in human social life. However, they serve as the orders of preservation only in their being derived from Christ, and not by themselves. Applied to natural law ethics, what this means is that we are free to recognize certain orders in nature, but only in relation to Christ, the Christ of the Gospels. It is only in and through Christ that the orders are normative—not in or of themselves. This makes it possible, for instance, to criticize a land ethics that encourages predation—in this case, the ethics could be criticized in reference to the *peace* of Christ. Similarly, a preservation ethics, which asserts the connectedness between the people and nature of a country, to the total exclusion and persecution of people from other races or countries (as in the case of Nazi ecology), can be criticized as well—in this case by the universality of Christ. Admittedly, I am only here providing an indication as

212. Rasmussen, *Earth Community*, 282.

213. Ibid., 347.

214. Ibid.

to how Bonhoeffer's Christologally defined concept of the orders of preservation could lead to a transformed, natural law ethics. The continual work of bringing biological "facts" into relation with Christology is nevertheless a fundamental aspect of any Christian ecotheology, at least so long it wishes to remain eco*theology*.

4

Human Beings as Distinctive Parts of Nature

IN CONTRAST TO THE TWO PRECEDING CHAPTERS, WHICH FOCUSED ON THE relationship between Christ and nature, I would specifically like to focus, both here and in chapter 5, on what Bonhoeffer has to say concerning the relationship between human beings and nature. For although Bonhoeffer understands all of reality in and through Christ, stressing that there are no relationships from which Christ is excluded, he nevertheless also has a great deal to say about the particular relationship between human beings and the earth.

In Bonhoeffer's view, though the relationship between human beings and nature is itself mediated through Christ, it nevertheless bears a distinctiveness of its own. His account of this relationship is indeed quite varied and multifaceted and can be summarized in view of four different perspectives. These perspectives are the following: 1) human life as *embodied* life, 2) human nature as distinct from non-human nature, 3) human beings as masters over non-human nature, and 4) the imperative for human beings to love nature. Although at first sight, some of these perspective may appear to contradict or work against each other in certain respects, it will become clear that, when properly understood, they complement each other and, when taken together, provide a full account of human life in relation to non-human nature. *CF* figures most prominently as the book in which Bonhoeffer works out each of these perspectives on the human/non-human relationship most fully. But, as it will become clear, they resonate throughout his entire theology as well, from his earlierst writings up until his writings from prison.

For practical purposes, I would like to divide up the discussion of these four perspectives into two separate chapters. Both here and in chapter 5, I will begin by giving a more general account of two perspectives in particular, only then bringing them to bear on the more specific question of environmental ethics.

Bonhoeffer's Description of the Relationship between Human Beings and Nature

I will begin by focusing on the first two perspectives on the human-nature relationship that Bonhoeffer develops, namely on human beings *both* as a part of nature and, at the same time, as qualitatively different from nature. I shall start out by exploring the first perspective.

Human Life as Embodied Existence

The first element of Bonhoeffer's theological anthropology that is relevant for the present discussion is his account of bodiliness, that is, of the fundamentally bodily nature of human existence. Already in his early theology, Bonhoeffer stresses that the human being is both body and spirit, and that both together form a fundamental unity. Later on in his work, this emphasis on bodiliness grows even stronger, a process which culminates in his *Ethics*. It is crucial to lay out his thoughts on this issue in some detail, for they are able to make an important contribution to ecotheology, as will become clear further on in this chapter. The theme is also important insofar as it forms the broader background of Bonhoeffer's anthropocentric approach to nature.

EMBODIED EXISTENCE AS A THEME IN BONHOEFFER'S EARLY THEOLOGY

The first remarks on human, embodied existence are offered by Bonhoeffer in *SC*. In particular, he describes the human being as being both nature ("Natur") and spirit ("Geist"). *Nature* refers in this case to the fundamental relatedness of human beings to the natural world, whereas *spirit* refers to the human capacity to relate both to God and to others. These two moments are not to be considered as separate aspects of the same reality, but rather as an integral whole. On account of the subject matter and the overall bearing of *SC*, Bonhoeffer focuses primarily on spirit, that is, on relationships between human beings, and between human beings and God. At the same time, he also acknowledges the fundamental importance of nature, or of bodily nature. In the context of a section entitled "Church and Eschatology," for instance, he writes: "Concrete community is possible only because human beings are equipped with a body. Thus we must think of the body as being essentially connected with the soul."[1] In this crucial passage, Bonhoeffer puts forward the body as a necessary foundation for the life of the spirit. As Clifford Green comments, "[a]ll the discussion about 'Geist' [in *SC*] should not lead us to ignore Natur as essential to human being. For human existence, Natur is especially, though not exclusively, the *body*."[2] Bonhoeffer bases this assertion on the New Testament teaching surrounding the bodily resurrection. In particular, he sees, in the doctrine of the new, resurrected body, the deepest layer of meaning at work in the Christian concepts of person and community. As he says, in a sentence following the preceding quotation from *SC*: "[I]n the resurrection, together with the soul, God will also create a new body, and . . . this new spiritual [pneumatisch] body will be the warrant and condition for the eternal community between personal spirits."[3]

However importantly the body may figure in Bonhoeffer's account, he nevertheless seems to imply that the body is only important insofar as it forms the *foundation* for the functioning of the spirit. This impression grows even stronger in light of an earlier statement that he makes in *SC*: "Nature . . . is the material that spirit forms and thus makes objectively and subjectively fruitful; the social intention of spirit, of course, is taken for granted. Spirit and nature are so closely connected that spirit is no longer conceivable without nature, nor human nature without social spirit."[4] Despite the fact that, in this passage, Bonhoeffer stresses the interrelatedness of nature and spirit, it nevertheless appears that nature is subjected to spirit as a necessary precondition, or foundation. This point has also been noted by Green, who observes: "The relations between Geist and Natur are reciprocal, though Geist has the priority."[5] This difference in priority, or value, doesn't appear everywhere, however. Towards the end of the third chapter of *SC*, for instance, Bonhoeffer speaks of body and spirit as being complementary to each other: "[T]he *spirit-form [Geistform], namely this love community, and the nature-form [Natur-form], i.e., the empirical community, are created to complement each other*; this allows one to draw conclusions about the nature of empirical community."[6] Citations such as these show that, in *SC*, Bonhoeffer's conception of human embodiment isn't fully consistent.

1. DBWE 1:286.
2. Green, *Bonhoeffer*, 46n62; italics original.
3. DBWE 1:286.
4. DBWE 1:69.
5. Green, *Bonhoeffer*, 46n62.
6. DBWE 1:105; italics original.

Bonhoeffer returns to the theme of human beings as both spirit and body in his Barcelona lectures on Christian ethics. In the second lecture of this series, for example, he introduces what he calls the sexual question, which he sees as one of the most burning questions of his time. In particular, he sees the reason for the question's heightened importance stemming from the growing importance attached to the body.[7] He also mentions sports in this regard.[8] As a consequence of this growing importance, he says that there is a mounting desire, in Western society, to attribute new rights to the body, which he takes as a positive sign. He states that just as spirit, so also nature originates in God, even more directly so than spirit.[9] Next, in the context of the lecture, he goes on to describe what this means as far as the problem of sexuality is concerned. In particular, he asserts that God created human beings as specifically gendered beings, that is, as man and woman, and that God desires human beings to embrace this fact, specifically insofar as the human body is the temple of the Holy Spirit. He argues that individual human beings have to decide how exactly they will conduct their lives, in the specificity of their being a man or a woman, in purity before God's eyes. In doing so, as he says, they are neither to go against their physical nature, nor against the spirit, but instead to allow God's Spirit to radiate through them.[10]

The Theme of Human Beings as Body and Spirit in CF

The theme of the human being as both body and spirit surfaces again in *CF*. These lectures in particular feature as a highpoint in Bonhoeffer's treatment of the issue during this period of his theological development. The first mention of the theme in *CF* emerges in Bonhoeffer's comments on Gen 1:26vv, which is of course the *locus classicus* of the doctrine of the *imago Dei*. In his discussion of this passage, he gives particular stress to the unique distinctiveness of human beings over against animals. At the same time, he also

7. He speak about "[t]he generally increasing value given to the physical—for example, in sports." DBWE 10:376.

8. It is indeed the case that sport received growing attention at the end of the nineteenth and the beginning of the twentieth century—the instalment of the modern Olympic Games in 1896 can be seen as just one of the fruits of this (international) process. Bonhoeffer apparently implied that this increased attention can be seen as the result of the increasing value attached to the human body in that time.

9. DBWE 10:376. Clifford Green, as one of the editors of the English edition, notes: "'Nature,' *Natur*, and 'spirit,' *Geist*, are two central and consistent categories in Bonhoeffer's theological anthropology." DBWE 10:369, editorial footnote 27; italics original.

10. DBWE 10:376.

fully accepts the intimate biological relationship between human beings and animals. As he says: "We in no way wish to deny humankind's connection with the animal world—on the contrary."[11] Similarly, a few lines earlier, he had implicitly accepted Darwinism, with its insistence on the development of the human body from those of animals. In spite of this, however, he still insists on stressing the peculiar distinctiveness of human beings: "This has nothing whatsoever to do with Darwin. Quite apart from that issue humankind remains in an unqualified way God's new, free work."[12]

Bonhoeffer reflects even more directly on human bodiliness in his commentary on Gen 1:28—2:4a, which he develops under the title "Blessing and Completion."[13] Concerning the blessing that God proclaims over human beings in this passage he says: "This blessing . . . affirms humankind wholly within the world of the living in which it is placed. It is humankind's whole empirical existence that is blessed here, its creatureliness, its worldliness, its earthliness."[14]

This particularly strong insistence on the earthiness of human beings is also worked out by Bonhoeffer in his comments on the second creation story (Gen 2:4bvv), specifically in his commentary on Gen 2:7, which is entitled "The Human Being of Earth and Spirit."[15] Concerning the passage according to which God formed the human being out of the dust of the earth, he notes that the text is very "earthy" and, as a consequence, a potential cause for offence.[16] Bonhoeffer also makes clear that, as a myth, the creation story is not intended to give us adequate information about the creation; at the same time, he insists that the story is, as the Word of God, *the* source of knowledge concerning the creation of human beings. In particular, the story makes two things clear on Bonhoeffer's view: first of all, it signifies the bodily proximity of the Creator to the creation. The fact that, according to the story, God forms the human being with his own hands, means "that it is really the Creator who makes me, the human being, with the Creator's own hands; it expresses the trouble the Creator takes, the Creator's thinking

11. DBWE 3:62.

12. DBWE 3:62. The editors note that Udo Kölner, one of the students attending the lectures, wrote: "Granting that Darwin was right, that humankind was descended from animals." DBWE 3:62, editorial footnote 9.

13. DBWE 3:68–70.

14. DBWE 3:68.

15. DBWE 3:74–79.

16. According to him, "The anthropomorphisms become more and more insupportable: God models or molds with clay, and the human being is fashioned like a vessel out of an earthen clod. Surely no one can gain any knowledge about the origin of humankind from this!" DBWE 3:75.

about me, the Creator's intention with me and nearness to me."[17] Secondly, the story signifies the divine power and authority of God, which Bonhoeffer describes as "fatherliness."[18] From here, Bonhoeffer focuses on the fact that the human being is taken from the earth. On his view, even Darwin and Feuerbach couldn't state the matter as strongly as the biblical text does.[19] As he says: "Humankind is derived from a piece of earth. Its bond with the earth belongs to its essential being. The 'earth is its mother'; it comes out of her womb."[20] This bodily existence is, on his view, absolutely essential to the human being.[21]

Bonhoeffer also illustrates his point through a brief discussion of Michelangelo's fresco of the creation of Adam in the Sistine Chapel. According to him, this fresco provides an excellent commentary on the biblical text insofar as it pictures Adam as a part of the earth out of which he was formed. As he observes: "[I]n this resting on the earth, in this deep sleep of creation, the human being now experiences life through being physically touched by the finger of God. It is the same hand that has made the human being that now, as though reaching from afar, tenderly touches and awakens the human being to life."[22] At the same time, Bonhoeffer also points out that, in Michelangelo's fresco, God's hand doesn't grab Adam or seizes hold of him, but rather sets him free. He then concludes by saying that the fresco reveals more about the creation of the human being than deep speculation is able to.

17. DBWE 3:76.

18. DBWE 3:76.

19. This is, of course, a reference to Darwin's theory that human life developed from non-human life. See Darwin, *On the Origin of Species*. Feuerbach is also mentioned in this connection due to his insistence on the earthiness of human beings. Elsewhere, Bonhoeffer characterizes Feuerbach's position on this point as follows: "[A human being is] not a transcendent being that only appears to exist but is *ens realissimum*." DBWE 11:186; italics original. See DBWE 3:76, editorial footnote 7.

20. DBWE 3:76. The phrase "earth is its mother" is a reference to Jesus Sirach, namely Sir 40:1b, which reads, in the English translation: "[T]hey [human beings] come forth from their mother's womb till the day they return to the mother of all." (RSV) As the editors of *CF* note, Bonhoeffer marked this verse in his copy of the Luther Bible. He also quotes it again later on—more properly cited this time—in his lecture entitled "Thy Kingdom Come." See DBWE 3:76, editorial footnote 8.

21. He states: "The body is not the prison, the shell, the exterior, of a human being; instead a human being is a human body. A human being does not 'have' a body or 'have' a soul; instead a human being 'is' body and soul." DBWE 3:76–77.

22. DBWE 3:78.

Bonhoeffer next focuses on the human being as spirit ("Geist").[23] As he observes, the human being alone was created by the Spirit of God being breathed into man's nostrils. In contrast, the other forms of life were the creation of God's Word alone. It is this peculiarity of the human being, namely that he lives as "Geist," which Bonhoeffer asserts. Yet again, however, he stresses the intricate interrelatedness between "spirit" and "nature" in the human being. As he says: "To live *as a human being* means to live as a body in the spirit. Flight from the body is as much flight from being human as is flight from the spirit. The body is the form in which the spirit exists, as the spirit is the form in which the body exists."[24] It is thus truly through the Spirit of God alone that the human body has life, and in this way, God is glorified in and through the human body. John Godsey summarizes Bonhoeffer's argument as follows: "The man who lives as a body in the Spirit is not differentiated from other life in his earthly origin, but he is unique in the fact that his body is the existence-form of God's Spirit on earth. God glorifies himself in this body."[25] Additionally, Bonhoeffer goes on to state that, when the human body, in its created being, is distorted by sin, it is later restored in the body of Jesus Christ, a reality witnessed to by the sacrament of the Lord's Supper.[26]

Also in the conclusion of his commentary on Gen 2:7, Bonhoeffer lays stress on the bodiliness of human beings. In particular, he asserts that it is precisely in being both nature and spirit that the human being exists as an image of God. Being made in the image of God is not something that takes place in spite of the human being's bodiliness ("Leiblichkeit"), but precisely because of it.[27]

23. Bonhoeffer's specific use of the word "Geist" in *CF* (to which I will turn in a moment) makes it clear that Green is right in pointing out that "the conceptual structure of 'spirit' and 'nature' [Bonhoeffer] developed in his first work remains consistent." DBWE 1:105–6, editorial footnote 145.

24. DBWE 3:78; italics original. The editors of *CF* point out that one of the students attending the lecture, Udo Köhler, wrote: "'The bodily is the end of God's ways.' So an older theologian once said." DBWE 3:78, editorial footnote 17. This is confirmed by the notes taken by Hilde Pfeifer and Ferenc Lehel. The theologian whom Bonhoeffer is drawing from here is Christoph Oetinger, and the citation that he quotes—and which he quotes again further on in *CF* as well—can be found in more than one place in Oetinger's work. See DBWE 3:121, editorial footnote 3.

25. Godsey, *The Theology of Dietrich Bonhoeffer*, 127.

26. As he says: "The body and blood of the Lord's Supper are the new realities of creation promised to fallen Adam. Because Adam is created as body, Adam is also redeemed as body [and God comes to Adam as body], in Jesus Christ and in the sacrament." DBWE 3:79.

27. He writes: "In their bodily existence human beings find their brothers and

Bonhoeffer again reflects on the relationship between human beings and non-human beings in his study of Gen 2:18–25. As this text lays bare, God formed the animals out of the ground and brought them to Adam to see how he would call, or name, them. Bonhoeffer notes that it was Adam's first experience of pain for him to realize that, among these "brothers" (as Bonhoeffer calls the animals), he could not find the equal partner that he was looking for. This inability stems from the animal's being subject to Adam, or subordinate to him, even in spite of the fact that the biblical text speaks very highly of the animals. Bonhoeffer stresses this last point, arguing that as far as he knows, no other religion speaks as highly of animals as the account of Genesis.[28] Bonhoeffer also notes, however, that Adam remains alone because what has come out of the ground, together with him, nevertheless remains alien to him. From here, Bonhoeffer then goes on to narrate and comment on the forming of Eve out of Adam's rib. For the moment, I would like to set this particular aspect of Bonhoeffer's commentary to the side, however; later on, I will return to discuss it in detail.

Though Bonhoeffer nuances and enriches his theological anthropology over the course of *CF*, he doesn't alter it at its core. This core, of course, is his double assertion of the human being as both body and spirit, which continues to echo throughout his theology. On occasion, however, he does modify his terminology a little bit. A case in point can be found in his *Discipleship*, where he states: "Body, soul, and spirit, that is, the form of being human in its totality, is to bear the image of God on earth."[29] Here a sudden and novel threefold partition seems to emerge in the place of his earlier double-headed assertion, but since he does not go on to explicate this further differentiation between "soul" and "spirit," either in *Discipleship* or elsewhere, it is more than likely an accidental formulation without any radical implications for the basic theme.

This double affirmation of human beings as both body and soul is by no means unique to Bonhoeffer. It has its background in the 19th century, when bodiliness ("Leiblichkeit") was an important theme in philosophy.[30]

---

sisters and find the earth. As such creatures human beings of earth and spirit are 'like' God, their Creator." DBWE 3:79.

28. As Bonhoeffer notes: "As far as I know, nowhere else in the history of religions have animals been spoken of in terms of such a significant relation. At the point where God wishes to create for the human being, in the form of another creature, the help that God is as God—this is where the animals are first created and named and set in their place." DBWE 3:97. It is without the boundaries of this book to determine whether or not this statement is true.

29. DBWE 4:283.

30. See Leonhard, *Leiblich lernen und lehren*, 45; and Rölli, "Philosophische Anthropologie im 19. Jahrhundert," 149–61.

The more direct context for Bonhoeffer's thoughts on bodiliness are the Christian anthropologies that other writers, in the movement of dialectical theology, had already developed. In particular, his insistence on the bodily nature of human existence restates what Emil Brunner had already said in a lecture entitled "Biblical Psychology."[31] In this lecture, Brunner had made the point that the human being was created as a "bodily" being and that this bodiliness belongs to its very existence. Later on, Karl Barth also accounted for the human being as body and spirit in a way very similar to that of both Brunner and Bonhoeffer.[32]

Bonhoeffer's second affirmation—namely, of the human being as spirit, or as soul—was most likely influenced by Wilhelm Vischer. In an article in *Zwischen den Zeiten*, Vischer writes: "[For the Hebrews] human beings don't *have* a soul; rather, they *are* a soul."[33] Furthermore, in Bonhoeffer's opposition against the Gnostic idea that the human being, coming from above, is trapped in the earthly world, he might also be drawing from his teacher, Reinhold Seeberg.[34]

The Theme of Human Bodiliness in Bonhoeffer's Ethics

It would of course seem perfectly natural for Bonhoeffer to continue developing his conception of human bodiliness in his lectures on Christology—indeed, his thoughts on Christ's humanity would have offered a great foundation for further developments—but he doesn't directly or explicitly mention the theme in these lectures. In spite of this fact, as Green points out, "[i]n the Christology lectures [,] there is an implicit foundation for a theology of bodily life. The suggestion is that the *one* Christ, who is the reconciler and liberator of 'human existence [which] is always both history [Geschichte] and nature [Natur],' re-establishes a proper interdependence of spirit and

31. Brunner, "Biblische Psychologie," 70–100. Bonhoeffer had read this work and underlined sections of it; see DBWE 3:76, editorial footnote 9.

32. In *CD* 3/1, for instance, he says: "Behind these prefigurative pictures . . . there stands the whole of Old Testament anthropology. Like the beast, man is formed of dust, animated by God and destined to return to dust and non-existence. But in contrast to the beast, he is animated by God directly and personally. Of all creatures he is chosen and called by Him directly." *CD* 3/1:238.

33. "[Für den Hebräer] *hat* nicht der Mensch eine Seele: er *ist* vielmehr eine Seele." Vischer, "Der Gott Abrahams," 285; italics original. This is pointed out by the editors of *CF*; see DBWE 3:77, editorial footnote 10.

34. This is also indicated by the editors of *CF*, who argue that Bonhoeffer might be drawing here from Seeberg, *Die Anfänge des Dogmas*, 297. See DBWE 3:77, editorial footnote 12.

body in an integrated person."[35] This is indeed the case, and the emphasis that Bonhoeffer places on Christ as center receives, as we saw in chapter 2, a new highpoint in *Ethics*, particularly in the way Bonhoeffer works out the concept of Christ-reality. We already saw how, in the manuscript "Ethics as Formation," Bonhoeffer identifies three basic relationships between Christ and reality, namely incarnation, crucifixion, and resurrection. With regards to the theme in the present chapter, the moment of incarnation is especially important, for it asserts Christ's "taking on" of human bodily life.

Although bodiliness does not figure in the manuscripts dealing with the relationship between Christ and the world, it is nevertheless an important theme in *Ethics*. In the manuscript "Natural Life," for instance, Bonhoeffer includes a section dealing with "The Right to Bodily Life."[36] In this instance, he asserts that the bodily life which human beings receive—and in a very real way, it is important to note, the body *takes precedence* over the human will—bears the right to be preserved. It "carries" the weight of natural rights—indeed, as Bonhoeffer claims, there wouldn't be natural rights if there were no human bodies. As such, for Bonhoeffer, the body must be preserved.[37]

The body, as Bonhoeffer says, is also that which distinguishes human beings from each other. Not even in marriage can anyone be as close to another as one is to him or herself. In this sense, the body creates a crucial spatial distinction from others, a distinction which forms the background of Bonhoeffer's assertion of the rights of bodily life. The first of these rights is the right to be protected from arbitrary killing, in which innocent life is intentionally destroyed. He works out the implications of this point in relation to military ethics and forced euthanasia in particular. This discussion, of course, must be understood against the historical backdrop of practices carried out in Nazi-Germany, with its policies of indiscriminate killing of civilians in conquered territories on the Eastern front, as well as its forced euthanasia of those who were not deemed fit for living.[38]

What's new and rather important here is Bonhoeffer's introduction of the category of "rights" in relation to bodily life. This can be seen in particular as a reaction against the adoption of Nazi laws. In light of these brutal

35. Green, *Bonhoeffer*, 233; italics original.

36. DBWE 6:185–96.

37. As he says, "The most primordial right of natural life is the protection of the body from intentional injury, violation, and killing." DBWE 6:185–86.

38. This historical context has been admirably described and detailed by Vosloo, who points out that, in Nazi Germany, the mechanical valuing of life as a mere means to an end inevitably led to the destruction of life which was deemed unfit. See Vosloo, "Body and Health," 23–37.

assaults on the value of human bodily life, it was necessary for Bonhoeffer to employ and develop a robust discourse of rights. As Rasmussen comments: "[T]he language turns to 'rights,' not least because Bonhoeffer had, through involvement in the conspiracy, learned of Hitler's grotesque violation of human beings."[39] As such, Bonhoeffer became the first modern German Protestant theologian to engage with "the natural," as was noted earlier on in chapter 2.[40] This can be seen as one of Bonhoeffer's most important contributions, as Green has pointed out: "His [Bonhoeffer's] later reflections on the natural, bodily life, pleasure, and sexuality are significant contributions to an aspect of Protestant theology which, as Bonhoeffer notes here, had long been neglected."[41]

In conclusion, throughout his theology, Bonhoeffer articulates a robust account of human embodied existence, he grounds it directly in Scripture, and he further strengthens it through his discussion of rights.

Bonhoeffer on Human Distinctiveness Vis-à-vis Non-Human Beings

The preceding discussion has shown just how strongly Bonhoeffer asserts the bond between human beings and the earth from which they were created. At the same time, he also stresses the uniqueness of human beings in that they alone, among all God's creatures, are imbued with spirit, or "Geist." Throughout his work, Bonhoeffer identifies and accounts for a number of different capacities that he sees as unique to human beings alone. One of these capacities in particular features predominantly throughout his work—namely, his assertion of the capacity for human sociality as unique. Since this is the first and most important distinction that Bonhoeffer makes in this respect—a distinction which also has the most relevance as far as environmental ethics is concerned—I will devote more sustained and detailed attention to it. The other, less important, distinctions that Bonhoeffer makes will be discussed only afterwards, and will receive much less attention.

Sociality as the Most Distinctively Human Feature

As I indicated already earlier on, Bonhoeffer describes the human capacity for sociality as the most important distinction between human and

39. Rasmussen, "Song of Songs," 308.

40. See also Rasmussen: "Bonhoeffer may in fact be the first German Protestant theologian to speak of 'rights.'" Rasmussen, "Song of Songs," 308.

41. Green, Bonhoeffer, 233.

non-human beings. The first instance in which he discusses this human characteristic is in *SC*. In a section entitled "Social Community as Community of Will,"[42] he begins by drawing attention to a pronounced continuity between animals and human beings regarding sociality. In a section deleted from the first published version (SC-A), for instance, he says: "Animal instincts connect the most primitive forms in which human beings coexist [Beieinandersein] with animal social life."[43] He specifically focuses on the experiences of hunger and sexual desire, in which he discerns two archetypes of social life.[44] He concludes that there are far-reaching parallels between human and animal sociality.[45]

To further flesh out this parallelism between man and animal, Bonhoeffer refers in a footnote to Alfred Espinas' influential work *Des Sociétés Animales*.[46] In the book, Espinas argues for a sociology that would be equally applicable to human beings and animals alike.[47] This reference, coupled together with the way that Bonhoeffer describes animal society, in his own words, signal to the reader that he sides with Espinas' position.[48] At the same time, in the lines immediately following this statement, Bonhoeffer asserts the existence of an important difference between human and animal forms of social life: "Human community per se is only present where conscious human spirit is at work, that is, where community rests upon purposeful acts of will."[49] On Bonhoeffer's view, then, the crucial difference resides in the fact that human sociality rests on acts of the will, or goal-directed behavior.[50] Whereas before, Bonhoeffer had echoed Espinas and seconded his

42. DBWE 1:80–86.

43. DBWE 1:80n63.

44. In hunger he recognizes the human desire to satisfy only one's own needs, either alone or with the help of others. This results in a model of cooperation amongst human beings that gives precedence to goal-attainment. Sexual desire is different, on his view. Instead of desiring some*thing* from another person, it desires the entire person. See DBWE 1:80n63.

45. In his own words: "The parallels between animal and human social drives are extensive. The sociality of animals is highly developed; the principle of solidarity is no less present than the formation of states, with division of labor, etc., which cannot be further elaborated here." DBWE 1:80n63.

46. Espinas, *Des Sociétés Animales*. Bonhoeffer employs the German translation of this work. See DBWE 1:80n63.

47. See Clough, "Interpreting Human Life," 57.

48. See also DBWE 1:80.

49. DBWE 1:81.

50. His point, however, is not that human sociality is created by acts of the will, but rather that acts of the will characterize human sociality in the first place. As he puts it, "Human community is essentially community of will, and only as such does it give meaning to its own natural form." DBWE 1:81–82.

view of animal and human sociality, with this statement, he directly opposes himself to the latter's account. The obvious tension that this creates is never laid to rest by him, though his later work does help to clarify his intention to continue building on this latter statement and to assert the distinctive nature of human sociality as based on acts of will.

One text that is particularly important in this respect is *CF*, where, again, Bonhoeffer writes about sociality as a distinctively human characteristic—indeed, this book contains Bonhoeffer's most elaborate treatment of the issue. In particular, he develops his line of thought in relation to his commentary on Gen 1:26–27, which narrates the creation of the first human beings, in a section entitled "The Image of God on Earth."[51] He begins by noting that, although God loves his creation (as a whole), he still fails to recognize himself in his work. Non-human creation is formed by God's command, and as such, it comes forth from the freedom of God, but does not itself share in that (or any) freedom—on the contrary, it is determined ("Bedingt").[52] Only in that which itself is free can the Creator recognize himself. Similarly, only that which itself is free can recognize God and praise him to the fullest.

At this point, as Bonhoeffer says, the story shifts focus to the creation of human beings. He argues that, in this case, the use of the Hebrew plural functions as a signifier of the event's importance. Also, the deliberation that takes places within the Godhead signals that God is doing something new, something qualitatively different than before. Bonhoeffer characterizes the human being who goes forth from God as "the last work," as "the new work," and as "the image of God."[53] According to him, this is the point where the continuity between human beings and animals breaks off. In the words of the passage cited earlier on, he says: "There is no transition from somewhere else here; here there is new creation. This has nothing whatsoever to do with Darwin. Quite apart from that issue humankind remains in an unqualified way God's new, free work."[54] Bonhoeffer appears to claim here that, in the creation of the human being, something new is taking place, which cannot be explained in terms of the evolutionary process itself. At the same time, he warns in particular against attempting to take a giant leap back into the world of the lost beginning and trying to rediscover human beings in their original, uncorrupted nature. What often happens as a result, he says, is that one reads one's own ideals into the text of the creation story. Real knowledge

51. DBWE 3:60–67.

52. DBWE 3:61.

53. DBWE 3:61–62.

54. DBWE 3:62. Bonhoeffer refers to Darwin, *The Descent of Man*.

of humankind's beginnings is not possible for human beings in their present (fallen) state; as such, nothing can be known of this lost world. It is only through Christ that we are able to discover what humankind was like in the beginning.[55] As we saw already in chapter 3, this is the same point that Bonhoeffer makes in relation to the primal state of the world as a whole.

Taking Christ as the central point of reference, Bonhoeffer argues that the image of God in humankind "means that humankind is like the Creator in that it is free."[56] This, it is important to note, is a freedom to worship the Creator, for, as Bonhoeffer says, in the language of the Bible, freedom is not something human beings have for themselves, but only for others: "No one is free 'in herself' or 'in himself' ['an sich']—free as it were in a vacuum or free in the same way that a person may be musical, intelligent, or blind in herself or in himself . . . Anyone who scrutinizes human beings in order to find freedom finds nothing of it."[57] The reason that Bonhoeffer gives for this is that freedom is a *relation*, and nothing more.[58]

Bonhoeffer then asks the critical question of how we effectively come to know this. Isn't this simply another way of speculating about humankind's beginning? "No," he insists. On the contrary, for Bonhoeffer, this is the message of the gospel itself, namely, the message declaring that, in Christ, God is free for human beings, and as a consequence, we too are made free for God.[59] Bonhoeffer recognizes the paradoxical nature of being created and yet being free at the same time, though according to him, the paradox needs to be further sharpened instead of being resolved. He states that human freedom is precisely this: *created* freedom. That is what defines human beings and sets them apart from the rest of creation, namely, their being created, as free, by a free God. At the same time, Bonhoeffer also introduces a second defining characteristic of human freedom, namely, their being free *for each other*.

Bonhoeffer develops this fundamentally social dimension of human freedom in his commentary on the phrase in Gen 1:27c, "male and female created he them" (KJV). There he claims that creatureliness ("Geschöpflichkeit") means that the human being is not alone, but, instead, that he or she

55. As Bonhoeffer puts it, "Only in the middle, as those who live from Christ, do we know about the beginning." DBWE 3:62.

56. DBWE 3:62.

57. DBWE 3:62–63.

58. In his own words: "Only by being in relation with the other am I free." And in the new paragraph directly following that line: "No one can think of freedom as a substance or as something individualistic. Freedom is . . . simply something that comes to happen, that takes place, that happens to me through the other." DBWE 3:63.

59. DBWE 3:63.

needs others.[60] Like freedom, this createdness too is not a quality that exists in itself, as Bonhoeffer claims—on the contrary, it can only be defined as "over-against-one-another, with-one-another, and in-dependence-upon-one-another."[61] In the same connection, Bonhoeffer opposes himself against the classic understanding of the *imago Dei* as an *analogia entis*, or more specifically, against the idea that there is a certain continuum at work between God's being and the human being. In contrast with this model of understanding, he argues in favor of an *analogia relationis* between God and human beings.

Just as God binds himself to human beings in complete freedom, so human beings are created in freedom both for God and for each other. Bonhoeffer further specifies the difference from an *analogia entis* in two ways. First of all, he again lays stress on the fact that the relation doesn't concern a quality, possibility, or structural element of human existence.[62] The relation is thus only a received relation, or a relation that is bestowed, and from this, the second point follows, namely, that, as *analogia relationis*, the image of God is not to be understood as something human beings have in their possession. On the contrary, it is only something that *refers* to the original prototype ("Urbild"), and only in this reference does it exist.[63]

This christological perspective on the meaning of being made in the image of God is developed more fully by Bonhoeffer later on, namely in the lectures on Christology that he delivered around the same time as his *CF*

---

60. DBWE 3:64. Bonhoeffer further works out his thoughts on the relation between, or amongst, human beings in his commentary on Gen 2:18–25, which narrates God's provision of a partner for Adam. See DBWE 3:94–102. He emphasizes that to Adam, Eve is not a source of pride or boasting, but of gratitude. Adam does not lay claim to Eve, as Bonhoeffer says, but sees himself intimately connected with her in an entirely new way. Bonhoeffer then emphasizes that the particular way in which a human being and his or her partner become one is not through a melting together of the two, or through the dissolving of their creatureliness into a single flesh—on the contrary, they remain distinct as persons. It is interesting to note, in this connection, that Bonhoeffer does not address Eve's submission to Adam, or woman's submission to man. Rather, the other (that is, Eve) forms a limit for Adam, in addition to the limit that God had already set in place in the command not to eat of the tree of knowledge of good and evil. See DBWE 3:99.

61. DBWE 3:64.

62. Rather, "it is a given relation, a relation in which human beings are set, a justitia passiva!" DBWE 3:65.

63. Bonhoeffer summarizes this point as follows: "Analogia relationis is therefore the relation which God has established, and it is analogia only in this relation which God has established. The relation of creature with creature is a relation established by God, because it consists of freedom and freedom comes from God." DBWE 3:65–66.

lectures.[64] In these lectures, he provides a christological basis for his theological anthropology by describing Christ as the one *pro me par excellence*. In particular, he argues that Christ is *pro me* in three forms, namely, in the Word, in the sacrament, and in the church. At the same time, Bonhoeffer asserts that Christ's *pro me* should not be understood as a pure function that emanates from Christ. Rather, it is in his being, as a person, that Christ is *pro me*. Bonhoeffer simultaneously stresses that Christ's personhood should not be interpreted ontically, but rather ontologically. To think of Christ in "ontic" terms means to think of him in his being "An-Sich," which constitutes an abstraction of personhood—a point that he also makes in *CF*. To think of Christ ontologically, in contrast, means to think of him in his relation to me, or to the human being.[65]

This christological basis is clearly visible in *Discipleship* as well. Towards the end of this book, Bonhoeffer opens up a section entitled "The Image of Christ,"[66] in which he begins by briefly recalling the point that he had made earlier on in *CF* concerning Adam both as a creature and as being "like God" at the same time. After recounting how this image of God was lost in the Fall, he notes that God wants to create his image on earth for a second time.[67] He argues that God takes on the image of humankind in the incarnation of Jesus Christ, when the image of God appears in Christ's life, in his teaching and in his action.[68] Yet it is not only in Christ's incarnation that the image of God is restored, but in his crucifixion and resurrection as well. In the context of further working out this point, he also makes clear that, although in Christ's incarnation, crucifixion, and resurrection, the image of God *is* restored (a point stated in the indicative),[69] it nevertheless

64. "Lectures on Christology (Student Notes)." DBWE 12:299–360.

65. As he says: "I can think of Christ only in existential relationship to him and, at the same time, only within the church-community. Christ is not in-himself and also in the church-community, but the Christ who is the only Christ is the one present in the church-community *pro-me*." DBWE 12:314; italics original.

66. DBWE 4:281–88.

67. DBWE 4:282–83.

68. As Bonhoeffer states: "In Jesus Christ, God's own image has come into our midst in the form of our lost human life, in the likeness of sinful flesh. God's own image becomes revealed in Jesus' teaching and in his deeds, in his life and in his death. In him God has created anew the divine image on earth." DBWE 4:284.

69. It is important to take note just how strongly Bonhoeffer stresses the indicative nature of the restoration of the *imago Dei* in humankind. As Feil comments: "God responds to our opposition to him in sin by restoring his image in us; he sets his image in Christ against the image of 'the god (we) have invented for (ourselves)' (. . .), the image of which is the falsification of the image God had intended. Because we cannot give ourselves what we have lost, God himself has become the image which we were meant to be." Feil, *The Theology of Dietrich Bonhoeffer*, 82.

indicates the presence of an imperative as well. In other words, human beings *must* be formed in this image, which is an appeal that Bonhoeffer bases in the New Testament. This threepartite relationship between Christ and the world—which functions as a cornerstone in Bonhoeffer's entire theology—has already been treated in detail in chapter 2.

In *CF*, Bonhoeffer strictly limits the possibility for sociality to human beings alone. There are also instances in his works, however, where he muses about the possibility of extending the *analogia relationis* to non-human beings as well. During his vicariate in Barcelona in 1928, for instance, he wrote a letter to Walter Dreß in which he recounted a pastoral encounter that he had had with a young boy in his congregation whose dog, Wolf, had died. In particular, he describes how the boy was totally devastated by his loss and asked whether or not he would one day see his dog again in heaven. Bonhoeffer then responded by saying: "Look, God created human beings and also animals, and I'm sure he also loves animals. And I believe that with God it is such that all who loved each other on earth—genuinely loved each other—will remain together with God, for to love is part of God. Just how that happens, though, we admittedly don't know."[70] According to David Clough, this suggests "that under pressure he might be prepared to countenance this kind of extension to the *analogia relationis* beyond the boundaries of the human."[71] This indeed seems to be the case, though he never established this extension formally; it can also be classified as a form of pastoral lenience. Surprisingly, Bonhoeffer also muses about this same possibility in prison, namely in the fictional fragments that he wrote during that time. In the first scene of the drama that he penned there, he wrote a conversation between "Little Brother" and his grandmother concerning a deer that had been shot by a hunter.[72] In the conversation, the little boy asked why the deer looked so quietly at the hunter while he was aiming at him and did not run away or show any fear. To this, his grandmother responds, at least at first, by suggesting that the deer perhaps didn't have any awareness of death. She then interrupts herself, however (or perhaps the boy interrupts her—on this point, the text isn't entirely clear) by asking why, given this fact, animals are so shy. His grandmother then answers as follows: "[M]aybe this wondrous beast knew its hunter and knew very well that it couldn't escape him. Maybe it sensed its hunter's great love, and that made it love its hunter a little, too, and look at him with such calm, fearless eyes. Maybe it knew death was near and yet wasn't afraid. Who knows,

70. DBWE 10:137, cited in Clough, "Interpreting Human Life," 66.

71. Ibid.; italics original.

· 72. "Drama, Scene 1." DBWE 7:26–37.

child?"[73] Although it remains unclear whether or not the deer really loved the hunter—leaving aside the obvious fact that the conversation was itself entirely fictional in nature—the story can nevertheless be seen as a modest opening toward a wider conception of sociality.

Background and Context

Bonhoeffer's thoughts on the *imago Dei* form a crucial part of his theological anthropology, and it is therefore necessary to indicate the historical context in which they arose. Not much work has been done on this background and, as a consequence, a number of important connections remain to be explored. One of these is the remarkable parallel between Bonhoeffer and Luther on this point—Bonhoeffer's *CF* has many parallels with Luther's lectures on Genesis, although it is not at all certain that he consulted this work either in his studies or for his teaching. Three of these parallels are particularly worthy of being noted. First of all, Luther too takes the "us" used in Gen 1:26a as a signifier of the importance of the event of humankind's creation.[74] Secondly, there is a certain degree of convergence between Luther and Bonhoeffer on the question of what exactly constitutes the *imago Dei.* Luther, for his part, makes mention of the Augustinian doctrine according to which this *imago* ought to be conceived of as an *imago trinitatis*—that is, as a reflection of the trinity in the human being's unity of mind, memory and will. At the same time, he also turns himself against this doctrine, for, according to him, it implies that Satan too was created in the image of God. In order to avoid this, Luther claims that the *imago Dei* is to be found in humankind's moral nature, which he defines, rather interestingly, in terms of freedom. Insofar as Adam is concerned, for instance, he writes that the latter "lived also a life truly divine; that is, free from the fear of death and of all dangers and happy in the favor of God."[75] With this, we see that the concept of freedom that Bonhoeffer uses to define the *imago Dei* was already present in Luther.[76] A third parallel between Luther and Bonhoeffer can be found in the way that they define the restoration of the image of God. Just as Bonhoeffer would do later, Luther points to Christ, in whom this image

---

73. DBWE 7:27.

74. In his own words, "this expression implies manifest deliberation and counsel; the like of which is found not in the creation of any former creatures. In those cases God says simply without any deliberation, counsel or particular design of mind . . . . But here where God wills to create man. he turns himself as it were to deep thought and enters into profound counsel and deliberation." Luther, *Genesis*, 107.

75. Ibid., 116.

76. It also appears later on in Luther's commentary: ibid., 118.

is restored. As he says, "[t]he divine object of the gospel is that we might be restored to that original and indeed better and higher image; an image, in which we are born again unto eternal life, or rather unto the hope of eternal life by faith, in order that we might live in God and with God and might be 'one' with him."[77]

There is also an important difference between Bonhoeffer and Luther concerning the *imago Dei*. Luther stresses that the restoration of the *imago Dei*, which is effected through Christ in the individual believer, is not fully perfected in this life, but will be perfected in the kingdom of God. He also stresses that, until this perfection is attained, it is not possible for Christians to understand what exactly the image of God, which was lost by Adam, effectively consisted in.[78] An excellent summary of Luther's position on this point is offered by Welz: "Luther espouses the idea that the imago Dei has been totally lost through sin (per peccatum amissa est) and that the mental faculties are corrupted and debilitated. Thus, the image of God needs to be repaired; yet, it cannot be made perfect in this life . . . The original re-semblance with God must first be regained, and this is a lifelong, even an eschatological, process."[79] The Holy Spirit plays an important role in this process, which is an aspect of Luther's thought of which Bonhoeffer was well aware. As a student, he wrote a research paper on Luther's doctrine of the Holy Spirit in which he specifically mentions how, according to Luther, the Holy Spirit restores humanity in the *imago Dei*.[80] And yet, in Bonhoeffer's own work on the *imago Dei*, this eschatological "not yet" is lacking.

In spite of these parallels on the question of the *imago Dei*, there is—yet again—no evidence suggesting that Bonhoeffer was directly influenced by Luther. The more direct source of influence, especially insofar as Bon-hoeffer's concept of the *analogia relationis* is concerned, is modernity. This has been pointed out by Christine Axt-Piscalar,[81] who makes the case that, in his definition of the *imago Dei*, Bonhoeffer was taking over a concept that had been central to modernity. This is indeed the case. Immanuel Kant, in his *Groundwork for the Metaphysic of Morals*, famously defined freedom as the necessary ability for human beings to be moral. According to him,

77. Ibid., 118–19.

78. "Until all this shall be fulfilled in us, we shall never be able fully to understand what that image of God was, which was lost by Adam in paradise." Luther, *Genesis*, 119.

79. Claudia Welz, "Imago Dei," 79.

80. "Seminar Paper on the Holy Spirit according to Luther," DBWE 9:325–70. In this paper, Bonhoeffer draws on Drews, *Disputationen Dr. Martin Luthers*.

81. Axt-Piscalar, "Das Bild Gottes auf Erden," 265.

"freedom must be shown to be a property of the will of all rational beings."[82] A bit further on, he formulates the same point even more precisely: "We must necessarily equip every rational being who has a will with the idea of freedom, this being an idea under which he must act."[83] Like Kant, Bonhoeffer insists upon understanding freedom in relation to *morality*. At the same time, however, he defines this freedom in relation to sociality, as opposed to the individual—for him, the self is only free in relation to others; freedom is not a "property" of the self. So while Bonhoeffer was undoubtedly influenced by the modern concept of freedom, he at the same time also redefined the concept as well.[84]

This redefinition must be understood against its historical background as well, namely, against that of the personalist movement. This has been noted by Scott, who writes that "[t]he neo-Kantian echoes are clearly audible in this [i.e.: Bonhoeffer's] personalist strategy."[85] The difference that sets Bonhoeffer's account apart from those of other personalist writers is that his conception of human freedom has a much more robust biblical content, particularly insofar as he relates it to the *imago Dei*.[86]

In addition, it must be noted that Bonhoeffer's insistence on establishing an *analogia relationis*, as opposed to an *analogia entis*, has to be understood in light of his criticism of the *analogia entis* in *AB*. In this instance, he treats the concept of *analogia entis* in the context of outlining an ontological solution to the Act-Being problem. He refers in particular to the work of Erich Przywara, who gives center stage to the *analogia entis*.[87] After briefly outlining Przywara's proposal, he criticizes it. According to him, the problem is that an *analogia entis* implies that human beings already possess, in themselves, the possibility of experiencing transcendence. As he says: "[H]uman existence is, once again, comprehensible through itself and also has access to God. This is the inevitable consequence of all systematic metaphysics."[88] And a bit further on, he argues: "[T]he Thomistic ontological concept of God cannot go beyond a metaphysics locked in the closed world. This is the

---

82. Kant, *Groundwork for the Metaphysic of Morals*, 42.

83. Ibid.

84. Green notes that, by defining freedom in this way, Bonhoeffer is able to overcome the individualism that permeates theological anthropologies that formulate the *imago Dei* in terms of a property. See Green, *Bonhoeffer*, 190–97. See also Axt-Piscater, "Das Bild Gottes auf Erden," 265.

85. Scott, "Postnatural Humanity? Bonhoeffer on Freedom and Order in Creation," 19.

86. See Abromeit, *Geheimnis Christi*, 239.

87. See Przywara, *Religionsphilosophie katholischer Theologie*.

88. DBWE 2:75.

case as long as it discovers in the existence of human beings possibilities to understand themselves and, therefore, God . . . this means that one cannot successfully make room for a revelation, that is, one cannot form theological concepts of being and act."[89]

It is important to stress that Bonhoeffer was the first to conceive of the *imago Dei* in terms of an *analogia relationis*. Although Karl Barth is often cited as the first proponent of this view, in actual fact, he was drawing from Bonhoeffer's theological invention. He himself accounts for this in *CD* 3/1, where he works out his own concept of the *imago Dei*.[90] After an exegetical survey in which he mentions the diverse opinions concerning the meaning of the *imago Dei*, he refers first of all to Wilhelm Vischer, who argued that God created a real counterpart for himself in humankind. Secondly, he draws upon Bonhoeffer's *CF*, especially in regards to what Bonhoeffer says concerning the *analogia relationis*. Barth makes use of these ideas as ingredients in his own conception of the *imago Dei*, which resembles Bonhoeffer's understanding of the term, but is nevertheless much more fully developed. In his theology, it plays a decisive role in the relationship between God and the world.[91] Though a detailed account of Barth's conception falls outside of the scope of the present monograph,[92] it is important to note that it is through this appropriation by Barth that Bonhoeffer's position first came to be be known.

CRITICISMS CONCERNING THE *IMAGO DEI* AS AN *ANALOGIA RELATIONIS*

Since the 1930s, many other theologians have begun to understand the *imago Dei* in terms of relationality, such that today, it has become the most popular view in systematic theology, at least in Protestant circles.[93] In spite of this popularity, critical questions can be raised concerning the relational conception of the *imago Dei*.

89. DBWE 2:76. Bonhoeffer's assessment of Przywara's position is shaped by his theological allegiance to Karl Barth, who turned himself against Przywara's formulation of the *analogia entis*.

90. *CD* 3/1:176–212.

91. See Van 't Slot, *Negativism of Revelation?*, esp. 186–88, and 241–60; and ibid., "Theonomy and Analogy in Ecclesiology," 45–58.

92. A great deal has been written on Barth's conception of the *imago Dei*. See the studies of Lee, "Barth's Use of Analogy," 129–51; Krause, "The Humanity of the Human Person," 159–76; and esp. Waap, "Gottebenbildlichkeit und Identität," 176–321.

93. See Middleton, *The Liberating Image*, 23.

The first such question concerns Bonhoeffer's and Barth's choice for an *analogia relationis* over against an *analogia entis*. As we have seen, Bonhoeffer argued that the image of God is not a property or a quality of the human being, but rather a relationship—a point later echoed by Barth. Yet this raises the question of whether or not what they have in mind is in fact another form of an *analogia entis* after all. Indeed, isn't the very capacity for being in relationship a form of substance (or a property) itself, albeit in a different form? Although Bonhoeffer never addressed this criticism, Barth recognized its validity and responded in kind. In reponse to a forum question posed at Princeton University, during his one and only visit to the United States in 1962, Barth said: "[S]ome of my critics said: 'Well, after all, an *analogia relationis* is also some kind of *analogia entis*'. And I couldn't deny it completely. I said: 'Well, after all, if *analogia entis* is interpreted as *analogia relationis* or analogy of faith, well, then I will no longer say nasty things about the *analogia entis*. But I understand it in *this* way.'"[94] In sum, understanding the *imago Dei* in human beings as an *analogia relationis* doesn't imply that it is entirely without substance. On the contrary, its substance consists precisely in the human capacity to relate to one another.

A second criticism aiming at the conception of the *imago Dei* as an *analogia relationis* concerns its relationship with biblical exegesis. The majority view among biblical scholars holds that the *imago Dei* in Gen 1:26 is not relational, but functional in nature—in particular, it asserts that human beings are representatives of God. According to the text of Genesis, human beings are living images of God, a statement which must be understood against the backdrop of Egyptian and Assyrian assertions that the king alone is the image of god on earth. As Middleton's review of the field of biblical studies on this theme concludes: "When the clues within the Genesis text are taken together with comparative studies of the ancient Near East, they lead to what we could call a functional—or even missional—interpretation of the image of God in Genesis 1:26–27 (in contradistinction to substantialistic or relational interpretations)."[95] Noting the contrast between this interpretation and the dominant interpretation of the *imago Dei* as consisting in relationality, Middleton argues for the abandonment of the relational

94. Barth, *Gespräche 1959–1962*, 499. Quoted in Johnson, *Karl Barth and the Analogia Entis*, 11–12; italics original.

95. Middleton, *The Liberating Image*, 27. This is the majority view in biblical studies, as Middleton makes clear earlier on when he writes: "[A] virtual consensus has been building since the beginning of the twentieth century among Old Testament scholars concerning the meaning of the imago Dei in Genesis, and this view is quite distinct from the typical proposals found among systematic theologians." Ibid., 25.

view in favor of the functional interpretation.[96] One could just as easily ask, however, if this position is too radical. Gijsbert van den Brink, who has also noted that biblical scholars commonly give a functionalist interpretation to the *imago Dei*, argues that "systematic theologians who take into account the entire canonical framework end up with a relational view (. . .)."[97] For this reason, he concludes that "[p]erhaps . . . the two of these are not as mutually exclusive as they are sometimes supposed to be."[98] This statement is too massive—not all theologians who take the canon as a whole into account end up with a relational view on the *imago Dei*.[99] Some do, however. One example is Abraham van de Beek, who stresses the unbreakable bound between human beings and God, as well as the utter dependence of human beings upon God, as that which defines the *imago Dei*.[100] Another example is Walter Brueggemann, who recognizes "representation" as one of the dimensions of the *imago Dei*, yet who nevertheless gives a mostly relational content to this concept.[101] What this means, then, is that although Bonhoeffer's conception of the *imago Dei* as an *analogia relationis* is inadequate insofar as his exegesis of Gen 1:26 is concerned, as a description of an important theme in biblical theology, it is adequate, if not uncontested.

A third criticism applies specifically to Bonhoeffer's outworking of the *analogia relationis*. Bonhoeffer asserts that it is in their being-free for each other that human beings are like God. This implies that for someone to be a person, there must be other human beings to whom he or she stands in a relationship. But if in this sense human beings are like God, doesn't this imply that God then also needs human beings to be fully God? This criticism has been raised by Christiane Tietz,[102] who also offers the rather obvious solution: to see human relationality as a mirror to the sociality that

96. In his own words: "[C]oncern for a theological reading of the *imago Dei* as rule [sic] does not justify imposing, in any heavy-handed fashion, categories or criteria from the Christian theological tradition (or even from the New Testament) on the Genesis *imago Dei* texts." Middleton, *The Liberating Image*, 32; italics original.

97. Van den Brink, "Evolutionary Theory."

98. Ibid.

99. An example of a systematic theologian with a functionalist interpretations of the *imago Dei* is, for example, Grudem, "Man in the Image of God," 442–44. Examples of biblical theologians who offer functionalist interpretations of the *imago Dei* are Zimmerli, *Old Testament Theology in Outline*, 36–37; and Anderson, "Made in the Image of God," 89–92.

100. Van de Beek, *Schepping*, 280–86, esp. 285.

101. See Brueggemann, *Theology of the Old Testament*, 451; and ibid., *Genesis*, 32.

102. Tietz-Steiding, *Bonhoeffers Kritik der verkrümmten Vernunft*, 306–9.

exists between the three Persons of the one Triune God.[103] This possibility has actually been recognized by Karl Barth, who argues: "The relationship between the summoning I in God's being and the summoned divine Thou is reflected both in the relationship of God to the man whom He has created, and also in the relationship between the I and the Thou, between male and female."[104]

The fourth criticism concerns the accuracy of Bonhoeffer's assertion that, in contrast to animal life, human sociality is based on acts of the will—or more specifically, his assertion that human beings alone possess consciousness.[105] This distinction, in spite of its seeming self-evidence, can be called into question in light of recent research. Most noteworthy in this respect is the work of Marian Stamp Dawkins,[106] which has shown, among other things, that a number of animal species do in fact possess a certain degree of consciousness. As a result of these and other findings, during the annual Francis Crick Memorial Conference of 2012, the Cambridge Declaration on Consciousness was drawn up, in which leading scientists declared that non-human animals possess consciousness.[107] Peculiarly, as we saw earlier on in this chapter, an early precursor of this proposal was Espinas, with whose work Bonhoeffer was well acquainted, but with whom he did not see completely eye-to-eye. There is indeed a difference between the sociality of humans and non-human beings, but this is a difference of *degree*, not of kind. This difference is nevertheless of such significance and importance that, as Polkinghorne insists, "the differences in degree . . . amount to differences in kind."[108] This still amounts to nothing more than a difference of degree, meaning that human beings are not the only ones that are "free for" each other. As such, non-human animals have that capacity as well—which is a point that, as we saw earlier, Bonhoeffer already mused over at various points in his work.

Further on in this chapter, I will argue that, in spite of its factual inaccuracy, Bonhoeffer's conception of the *imago Dei* as an *analogia relationis* still retains its value, particularly insofar as environmental ethics is concerned.

103. See also Holmes, "Bonhoeffer and Reformed Christology," 28–42.

104. *CD* 3/3:196. For commentary, see Tietz, *Bonhoeffers Kritik der verkrümmten Vernunft*, 307.

105. Earlier on in this chapter, we saw how Bonhoeffer argues in *SC* that self-consciousness is the prerequisite condition for acts of the will to happen.

106. Dawkins, *Through Our Eyes Only?*.

107. http://fcmconference.org/img/CambridgeDeclarationOnConsciousness.pdf (accessed July 21, 2016).

108. Polkinghorne, "Anthropology in an Evolutionary Context," 96. Cited in Van den Brink, "Evolutionary Theory."

Before doing so, however, it is both worthwhile and important to investigate the other distinctions that Bonhoeffer introduces in his work on the difference between human beings and animals, for although his discussion of the *imago Dei* figures as the most important distinction that Bonhoeffer makes, it is certainly not the only one.

Bonhoeffer's Other Distinctions Between Human and Non-Human Beings

The first place where Bonhoeffer discusses the difference between human beings and animals is in a sermon that he delivered in 1928.[109] In this text, he quotes Augustine's saying that the heart is restless until it finds rest in God. On his view, it is this restlessness in particular that differentiates human beings from animals.[110] In the same connection, he identifies this restlessness as the driving force behind human history and the creation of culture—while he sees it at the root of the yearning for immorality, he also finds in it the deepest motivations behind religious practice. This clearly implies that, according to Bonhoeffer, non-human animals have no morality. Although he never states this explicitly in his theological work, he does imply as much in his fictional fragment, "A Hot July Day,"[111] that he wrote in prison. Part of the storyline concerns a discussion between a child and his mother over a young bird that had been abandoned by its mother. In the story, the child, "Little Brother," asks: "Why did she do that?"[112] His mother then answers: "Probably because the baby bird was weak and sick."[113] This obsevation shocks the child, which leads him to ask his mother why the mother bird would have done such a thing. His mother then explains that, in the animal kingdom, only the strong and healthy can survive, adding that, with human beings, things are quite different. The boy objects to this, however, insisting that it is bad for the mother bird to kill her young in such a way; but the mother responds in kind: "No, Little Brother, it's not fair to say that. Animals are innocent; they don't know any other way to live."[114] Amusingly, on hearing this, Little Brother responds by saying that, if this is in fact the case with animals, he no longer wants to have a bird's

---

109. "Sermon on Romans 11:6." DBWE 10:480–85.

110. He says: "Restlessness is the characteristic feature distinguishing human beings from animals." DBWE 10:481.

111. DBWE 7:71–96.

112. DBWE 7:94.

113. DBWE 7:94.

114. DBWE 7:95.

house. While not directly or explicitly theological in nature, this fragment clearly reveals Bonhoeffer's conviction that the lives of non-human beings are bereft of morality.

Much like the first distinction, however, this one too has its own inadequacies. In particular, a great deal of research into animal life has suggested that basic forms of morality are indeed present in other animals as well, most notably in the higher apes, with whom human beings are so closely related.[115] As with sociality, here too there is a difference in degree between human beings and animals. Rasmussen draws this point out quite poignantly when he writes that "other animals are not moral in exactly the same way [as human beings]. Or, more precisely, they are not moral to the same extreme. They are not mad with morality."[116]

Another important distinction between human beings and animals emerges somewhat earlier on in *CF*, in Bonhoeffer's discussion of Gen 1:1–2, entitled "The Beginning."[117] Here he yet again develops his first distinction by asserting that animals have no awareness of past or future.[118] According to him, this explains why animals have no hatred or pride, in clear contrast with humans. These emotions in particular, he insists, are reserved for human beings alone. It is important to note, however, that this distinction is made rather offhandedly by Bonhoeffer; in addition, it can be criticized for its lack of accuracy, for the statement that animals have no memory goes directly against both popular belief ("having a memory like an elephant") as well as scientific study. Already in 1983, Endel Tulving wrote a book entitled *Elements of Episodic Memory*[119] in which he argued that non-human animals possess episodic memory as well. This thesis has gained increasing support from other scientific research,[120] and it calls into question the accuracy of Bonhoeffer's statement.

The issue of the distinction between humans and animals recurs throughout Bonhoeffer's later works as well. In his *Ethics*, for instance, he makes multiple distinctions between human beings and animals in the manuscript "Natural Life."[121] In a section of this manuscript, he writes about "The Right to Bodily Life,"[122] drawing particular attention to the rights sur-

---

115. See especially De Waal, *Good Natured*.
116. Rasmussen, *Earth-Honoring Faith*, 39.
117. DBWE 3:25–39.
118. DBWE 3:28.
119. Tulving, *Elements of Episodic Memory*.
120. See Clayton et al., "The Rationality of Animal Memory," 197–216.
121. DBWE 6:171–218.
122. DBWE 6:185–96.

rounding bodily pleasure. Here he asserts that, because the body constitutes an end in itself, it has a right to its enjoyment (or joy), which goes beyond the mere necessities of life. For support of this view, he cites verses from Ecclesiastes (9:7vv, 11:9, and 2:25) indicating that human beings are to enjoy food and the other pleasures of life on offer "under the sun." He also extends the same right to cover the issue of shelter and housing, stating that in contrast to animal shelters, which according to him only functions to provide shelter and a place to raise the young, a human house "is the space in which human beings may enjoy the pleasures of personal life in the security of their loved ones and their possessions."[123] He then goes on to make the case that clothing too does not merely serve to cover and protect the body, but to adorn it as well. In a similar way, he notes that bodily relaxation doesn't merely function as a means to strengthen the body, but also to bring rest and joy to a person. He mentions play as a particular example in this regard. Finally, he also makes mention of sexuality which, as he insists, yet again, is not only a means of procreation, but an expression of love between two people. Although he does not explicate the point in detail, he seems to imply that the enjoyment afforded by relaxation and sexuality is not experienced as such by animals. This distinction too, like the others, can easily be criticized for its lack of accuracy. Such critical work has been carried out by Clough, who was the first to assess the distinctions that Bonhoeffer makes in *Ethics* in light of current research. Concerning Bonhoeffer's assertions that human beings alone are capable of experiencing joy, for instance, Clough notes: "This opinion is easily invalidated by any dog owner."[124] At the same time, Clough also refers to research showing that animals do indeed experience joy.[125]

Bonhoeffer establishes yet another distinction between animals and humans in the manuscript on natural life, specifically in the section on "Self-Murder."[126] In this case, Bonhoeffer makes the point that, in contrast to human beings, animals are incapable of committing suicide,[127] a point he also made earlier on, in his lecture "The Right to Self-Assertion."[128] Like

123. DBWE 6:187.

124. Clough, "Bonhoeffer on Human Beings and Other Animals," 53.

125. In particular, Clough refers to the following reviews of scientific studies concerning this question: McMillan, "Do Animals Experience True Happiness?," 221–34; and Rollin, "Animal Happiness," 235–41. See Clough, "Bonhoeffer on Human Beings and Other Animals," 53n11.

126. DBWE 6:196–203.

127. DBWE 6:196.

128. DBWE 11:246–56, esp. 253.

the other distinctions, this one too is most likely inaccurate. Clough refers in particular to research showing that animals are likely capable of self-destructive behavior as well.[129]

A final distinction that Bonhoeffer makes between human and non-human beings in this *Ethics* manuscript is in the section on "Reproduction and Developing Life."[130] As the title of the section clearly indicates, the distinction between human beings and animals concerns the theme of sexual reproduction. Here Bonhoeffer argues that in contrast to animals, human acts of reproduction are conscious acts—presumably based on reasoned desire.[131] While the existence (and quantity!) of "unwanted births" among human beings certainly calls into question Bonhoeffer's latter assertion, a search of relevant research in the field of animal reproduction did not yield any answer to the question whether or not reproduction is a conscious act among non-human animals. Clough still insists on calling the distinction into question, particularly insofar as its theoretical consequences are concerned. On his view, the distinction relegates animals to what he refers to as "Cartesian instinct-machines,"[132] while it also idealizes human reproduction as a supposedly rational and conscious process. At the same time, Clough's own account can be called into question as well. Indeed, one could ask whether it really is the case that asserting the unconscious nature of animal reproduction necessarily leads to viewing animals as nothing more than instinctual machines. This certainly isn't the way in which the argument works for Bonhoeffer, at the very least. As far as Bonhoeffer is concerned, the fact that humans alone are conscious of reproduction does not at all imply a degraded status for animals; on the contrary, if he insisted on maintaining the distinction, this was, in large part, in order to oppose the marriage laws of Nazi Germany,[133] a fact which Clough is careful to note. It would seem, then, that the question depends on how one interprets the unconscious nature of animal reproduction—while some may see the assumption of the distinction leading to a degraded view of non-human, animal life, this need not necessarily be the case.

---

129. Clough refers to the work of Preti, "Suicide among Animals," 831–48; and Crawley et al., "Models of Self-Destructive Behavior," 299–310. See Clough, "Bonhoeffer on Human Beings and Other Animals," 54n15.

130. DBWE 6:203–14.

131. DBWE 6:203.

132. Clough, "Bonhoeffer on Human Beings and Other Animals," 56.

133. The Nuremberg laws, which defined distinctions between "Jews" and "Germans" prohibited marriages between these supposedly separated races. See DBWE 6:203, editorial footnote 112.

The Relevance of Bonhoeffer's Thoughts on the Relationship between Human Beings and Nature for Environmental Ethics

Here in the second part of the present chapter, I would like to indicate the possible contributions that the first two perspectives on the relationship between human and non-human nature, in Bonhoeffer's theology, can make to environmental ethics. On account of the fact that the two perspectives are quite different from each other (though they are also complementary in many respects as well), the contributions they can make to environmental ethics are diverse. As I will show, Bonhoeffer's thoughts on human bodiliness are relevant for a discussion that is markedly different from the discussion towards which his thoughts on human distinctiveness are oriented.

Bonhoeffer's Thoughts on Bodiliness in the Context of Environmental Ethics

In the present section, I will account for the relevance that Bonhoeffer's thoughts on human bodiliness bear insofar as environmental ethics is concerned.

THE THEME OF EMBODIMENT IN ENVIRONMENTAL ETHICS

In ecotheology, bodiliness features as a very important and prominent theme—the insight that a fundamental bond exists between human beings and the earth is seen as crucial for the development of an environmentally sensitive attitude towards the earth. In an essay entitled "The Alienation and Liberation of Nature,"[134] for instance, Moltmann draws attention to the importance of appropriating the newly discovered psychosomatic wholeness of the human person for ecology. As he argues, when individuals learn to accept their bodily nature, that is, their totality as body and soul, they take the first, crucial step in overcoming the ecological crisis, for they thereby begin to accept their interrelatedness with and dependence on the rest of nature. They become, as it were, truly "at home" on the earth.[135]

134. Moltmann, "Alienation and Liberation," 133–44.

135. Moltmann revives this point of view in his recent work. See Moltmann, *Ethics of Hope*, 153–54. There, he also adds a new element to the mix, namely the differentiation between males and females. He blames males in particular for perpetuating the notion that the body is something in need of control and mastery, and, similarly, that nature as a whole is something existing "outside" of (or apart from) human beings.

Other writers make similar appeals for the rediscovery of the body (or more specifically, of human bodiliness), though they do not develop their arguments along the same exact lines. Conradie provides a helpful overview of the various ways that it is understood.[136] In particular, he identifies five different perspectives. The first perspective is cosmological in bearing. It gives particular emphasis to the immense scale of the universe, both in time and space, which dwarfs both the place and history of human beings in it. It also emphasizes the radical interrelatedness of everything in the universe—a view that can be summed up in the popular idea that human beings are made out of stardust. In view of this, as well as of the universe's astounding complexity and fine-tuning, human beings are urged to adopt an attitude of humility in the way they view the world and themselves. As examples of writers working within this perspective, one has both Thomas Berry and Brian Swimme.[137]

The second perspective is that of evolutionary biology. This view too gives particular emphasis both to the lengthy periods of history that preceded the occurrence of human beings in the world, as well as to the intricate biological relatedness between human beings and other species. Many different authors have brought this perspective to bear on environmental ethics. A recent example of the trend is found in Larry Rasmussen, whose recent work on environmental ethics contains a section aptly entitled "The Zoo in you."[138] In this text, Rasmussen describes in detail how human bodies consist in a fascinating amalgam of organs and parts issuing originally from many different kinds of animals. He draws attention, for instance, both to the fact that our inner ear has a modified fish-head architecture, as well as to the fact that our eyes developed from the photoreceptor organs common to other animals. Every part of the human body, as he observes, is the result of the evolutionary interplay of environment and developing genes: "There is a 'zoo in you' and we're all a wondrous mess, the late, twisted offspring of weird and exotic forebears who had no idea whom they might become."[139]

Indigenous wisdom offers a third perspective in which the relatedness of human beings and the natural world is viewed and considered. Non-western, indigenous traditions from around the globe are characterized by a strong sense of the harmony and symbiotic integration existing between

---

Correlatively, he also insists that women are more much more naturally in tune with body and, as a consequence, with nature as a whole.

136. Conradie, *An Ecological Christian Anthropology*, 26–40.

137. Berry and Swimme, *The Universe Story*.

138. Rasmussen, *Earth-Honoring Faith*, 18–23.

139. Ibid., 19.

human beings and non-human nature. One of the chief proponents of this view, to which Conradie makes reference, is Tinker.[140]

The fourth perspective can be traced back to movements and historical figures in pre-modern Christian traditions, such as the Benedictine monastic order (with its emphasis on proper stewardship of the land), Francis of Assisi (who saw nature as a mirror of God's presence) and Hildegard of Bingen (who celebrated an organic unity with nature). Important work in retrieving these traditions in the context of ecotheology has been carried out by Matthew Fox,[141] and Jame Schaefer,[142] for example.

The fifth perspective is that of ecofeminism. In this case, the primary focus centers on the perceived link between partiarchalism and the domination of women by men, and, correlatively, on the domination of nature by (Western) male chauvinism. In opposition to this domination and its respective division of reality into dualisms (such as those between male and female, culture and nature, human and animal, etc.), ecofeminists erect the ideal of non-hierarchical, non-patriarchal relationships between human beings themselves, as well as between human beings and nature. An example of this perspective is offered in the work of Rosemary Radford Ruether.[143] In conclusion, Conradie notes that, together, these perspectives have greatly contributed to an awareness of the human relatedness to non-human nature.

Despite the positive effects that this understanding has had as a motivation for environmental action, theological questions can still be raised concerning the procedures and programs by which such action is carried out. This has been noted by Conradie, who writes: "In numerous ecological theologies such insights [into the interrelatedness of everything] are simply linked with Christian themes. Alternatively, Christian views have at times been integrated into a generalised discussion of the ecological wisdom which may be derived from the world's religious traditions, or simply from 'religion.'"[144] While Conradie stresses that theology can and should be informed by other disciplines and discourses, he also asks the critical question of whether or not borrowing such insights leads to an overly shallow form of natural theology.

It is here that Bonhoeffer's approach proves to be particularly helpful. As we saw in our discussion in the beginning of this chapter, Bonhoeffer

---

140. Tinker, "Creation as Kin," 144–53; and ibid., "An American Indian Response," 85–109.

141. Fox, *Illuminations of Hildegard of Bingen*.

142. Schaefer, *Theological Foundations*, 149–91.

143. Ruether, *Women Healing Earth*.

144. Conradie, *An Ecological Christian Anthropology*, 40.

gives a particularly strong emphasis to human earthiness, as well as to humanity's intimate relationships with other beings. Similarly, we saw that Bonhoeffer accepted Darwinism, specifically insofar as its understanding of human bodies developing, over time, from animal bodies, is concerned. Instead, however, of taking this Darwinistic insight as a foundation for his own understanding of the earthiness of human beings, he develops his argument from the perspective of the biblical texts themselves. More specifically, he articulates his thoughts on the interrelatedness of animal and human bodies by noting that, according to the Bible, human beings and animals are made from the same earth.

This difference in methodology gives a clear indication of the best way to move forward for a Christian ecological anthropology—namely, by starting out from the Bible's teaching concerning human beings, and by then interpreting this teaching within a framework influenced by scientific (and other) sources of knowledge that stress the interconnectedness between humans and nature. In this way, the specifically Christian character of ecotheology can be preserved, all the while avoiding the trap of playing the role of the handmaiden for the natural and social sciences. The biblical testimony concerning nature belongs to the *proprium* of ecotheology—a testimony that can and should then be brought into dialogue with findings and trends from other fields.[145]

In response to such a proposal, one could point out that the biblical texts in question are rather ambivalent in nature, and furthermore, that Bonhoeffer's comments themselves are not based on scholarly exegesis. Though these points are certainly valid, they do not, of themselves, diminish the importance of paying close attention to the biblical text. In addition, Bonhoeffer also offers an interpretive key to help in the deciphering of the biblical testimony, namely Christ, who came to the world and took on human flesh, and who, like all humans, was born *of* the earth. Although Bonhoeffer does not fully work out this—essentially Irenaean—insight, it nevertheless forms an important, hermeneutical lens through which to approach the biblical texts that attest to humankind's bodiliness.[146]

145. For a recent (and somewhat broader) insistence on the importance of concretely engaging with the biblical texts in Christian ethics—especially insofar as the Psalms are concerned—see Brock, *Singing the Ethos of God*.

146. This point has been developed, for example, by Conradie, *An Ecological Christian Anthropology*, 63–70.

The Contribution Bonhoeffer's Thoughts on Embodiment Can Make

Bonhoeffer's account of human bodiliness can also help to overcome a common shortcoming of approaches stressing the interrelatedness of human and animal bodies. Often in ecological theologies, the assertion of the intimate relation between humans and the non-human world is used to stress the importance of *all* forms of life—not just human life. While this is indeed a valuable insight, it is often pressed into the service of a broader ecocentrism seeking to deny the human being any special status within creation. An example of such an ecocentrist approach is offered in the work of Anne Primavesi, who notes the continuity between humans and other species: "This perception of our multilayered, multifaceted *SelfScape* can, and does change our perspective on ourselves. What am I, indeed, that God is mindful of me? What kind of God is mindful of me, such as I am? And over what time span, and through what changes, has God known me?"[147] These rhetorical questions lead Primavesi to radically reconsider the place of humanity vis-à-vis other species and to argue for a top-down revolution in which humanity loses hold its special status relative to the rest of nature.

Further on in this chapter, I shall develop a somewhat more detailed argument against ecocentric approaches of this sort. For the moment, all that I would like to draw attention to is the way in which Bonhoeffer's strong insistence on human earthiness succeeds in avoiding ecocentrism. As we saw earlier, Bonhoeffer insists that human beings are not only bodily related both to each other and to animals, but that their bodies are distinguished, or set apart, from others bodies, both human and non-human. It is not only by their spirit that human beings are set apart from other animals; on the contrary, the human body itself already bears the marks of personhood and individual distinctiveness just as clearly as those of kinship and interrelatedness. Granted that the bodies of human beings are intimately interrelated with countless other animal organisms (e.g. 10 percent of the human body's dry weight consists of bacteria), they nevertheless remain distinctively *human*—and they are addressed as such by God. This insistence, as we saw, makes it possible for Bonhoeffer to address the issue of the body's *rights*. In combination with his insistence on the body as an end in itself, as opposed to a mere means to an end, this language of rights helps provide a powerful incentive for environmental action (e.g. by recognizing that damaging the environment brings direct harm to people, especially in the Third World). The same point has also been raised by Rasmussen, who writes: "That which

147. Primavesi, *Sacred Gaia*, 17.

is necessary for bodily flourishing—and that certainly includes its protection against violation—merits a right secured by law. These rights are grounded in creation itself and belong to life's requirements for flourishing, since our bodiliness is our unbreakable bond with earth and all its creatures."[148]

The Relevance of Bonhoeffer's Anthropocentrism for Environmental Ethics

The guiding question of the present section concerns what Bonhoeffer's thoughts on human distinctiveness can contribute to the field of environmental ethics. Despite the fact that almost all of the distinctions that he introduces between human and non-human animals contain inaccuracies, the points that he makes, based on these distinctions, cannot and should not be dismissed as irrelevant. One point of his account that is particularly important for the articulation of a Christian environmental ethics is his concept of the *imago Dei* as an *analogia relationis*. Specifically, this concept is able to make two important contributions: 1) it upholds the special place of human beings vis-à-vis non-human beings, and 2) it helps address the social dimension of the ecological crisis. In this section I will describe these contributions.

The Debate over Anthropocentrism in Environmental Ethics

Earlier on, I indicated how biological research strongly suggests that sociality is not limited to human beings alone. For this reason, some authors have proposed that the scope of the doctrine of the *imago Dei* be broadened so as to include non-human animals as well. One such proposal has been made by David Cunningham, for instance. As Cunningham argues, the distinctions in kind that theologians often suppose to exist between human beings and animals are not firmly based on the facts. The real differences between human and non-human beings, as he maintains, are not differences in kind, but in degree. On this basis, he argues that "all flesh," and not only the flesh of humans bodies, is made in the image of God: "The primary focus of God's relational life ad extra is not only with human beings; it extends to all flesh, all living creatures."[149] On this basis, he argues for "moving away from a central focus on humanity as the image of God, and developing a

---

148. Rasmussen, "Song of Songs," 309.
149. Cunningham, "The Way of All Flesh," 114.

broader field of vision in which human beings take their place within the larger context of all flesh."[150] He also has other arguments to support his thesis, which I will not discuss here. While his motives for extending the *imago Dei* to non-human beings are certainly laudable, the project can (and should) be fundamentally called into question. Gijsbert van den Brink, for instance, calls the proposal "unconvincing" and argues that "we cannot escape the conclusion that, according to the biblical texts, the image of God is somehow uniquely present in the human species (in fact, Cunningham is probably one of the first interpreters who doubts this)."[151] Although Van den Brink goes on to admit that, in certain instanes, deeper theological reasons may exist for extending biblical notions of this sort, he does not see any good reason to do so with regards to a notion as theological fundamental as the *imago Dei*. While I agree with Van den Brink on this point, it is important to be clear and precise when addressing the various reasons for not extending the *imago Dei* to non-human beings.

This leads us to the important debate over anthropocentrism. Bonhoeffer's concept of the *imago Dei*, as unique to humans, is implicitly anthropocentric. That will become clear in the next chapter, which focuses on Bonhoeffer's explicit assertion that human beings ought to rule over nature as masters. Later on in *Ethics*, he states his position concisely: "It is through Christ that the world of things and values is given back its orientation toward human beings, as was originally intended in their creation."[152] Cunningham's position implies a radical break from this anthropocentric perspective—by extending the *imago Dei* to non-human animals, he seeks to expand the group of beings bearing intrinsic value to "all flesh"—not just human beings. In the respective positions of Bonhoeffer and Cunningham, then, we have two sides of a debate that, since its inception in the 1960s, has stood at the very heart of environmental ethics.

Anthropocentrism is most commonly understood as the view that human beings alone bear intrinsic value, while non-human aspects of nature possess only an instrumental value. This view of the relationship between human beings and nature can be traced back as far as antiquity, particularly to Aristotle.[153] This anthropocentric view has become the leading theme in much of Western thinking, a classic example of which can be found in

150. Ibid.

151. Van den Brink, "Evolutionary Theory, Human Uniqueness and the Image of God."

152. DBWE 6:260.

153. See Brennan and Lo, "Environmental Ethics." Other classical thinkers, such as Plato, and Stoic philosophers, also clearly work from anthropocentric assumptions. On this subject, see Nullens, "Leven volgens Gaia's Normen?," 220–27.

the philosophy of Immanuel Kant. Christianity too has been understood as advancing an anthropocentric position, a point which has been made, quite famously, by Lynn White Jr., who writes: "Especially in its Western form, Christianity is the most anthropocentric religion the world has seen."[154] For this reason, White insists on holding Christianity responsible, at least in part, for the present ecological crisis.

As a general trend in environmental ethics, anthropocentrism is thought to stand in need of being replaced by other, non-anthropocentric models, which see intrinsic value in human beings, in other species and in nature as a whole. A summary statement of this view has been offered by Tom Regan, who claims that the "presence of inherent value in a natural object is independent of any awareness, interest or appreciation of it by a conscious being."[155] Despite this general and rather widespread conviction, there is no current consensus on how exactly such a non-anthropocentric model should be worked out.

An early and very influential perspective on this issue has been formulated by Aldo Leopold. In his book *A Sand County Almanac*, he argues that ecosystems (in particular, the wilderness) possess intrinsic value. According to him, they represent communities of being, and, as such, human beings are under the obligation to preserve them. Famously, he coined the following ethical maxim: "A thing is right when it tends to preserve the integrity, stability, and beauty of the biotic community. It is wrong when it tends otherwise."[156] As we see here, the center of the ethical debate is shifted away from the human being to the community of the land as a whole. Leopold's proposal has been received in different ways. One important source in this respect is found in the work of J. Baird Callicott.[157] While Callicott had initially made the case that only the biotic community as a whole had intrinsic value (with the value of the individuals making up the whole being merely instrumental in nature), he later modified his position by claiming that individuals too possess intrinsic value.

As I already indicated earlier, the proposal to attribute intrinsic value to biotic communities (and to wilderness in particular) isn't the only non-anthropocentric theory available. Other theories, by way of contrast, insist that only living beings possess intrinsic value. One of the proponents of this view is Robin Attfield, who attributes intrinsic value to all individual life forms, regardless of whether or not they have consciousness. He stops

154. White, "The Historical Roots of our Ecologic Crisis," 1205.

155. Regan, *Deep Ecology*, 71. Cited in Brennan and Lo, "Environmental Ethics."

156. Leopold, *A Sand County Almanac*, 262.

157. Callicott, *In Defense of the Land Ethic*.

short, however, of attributing intrinsic value to ecosystems or to the biotic community as a whole: "[T]he class of things with moral standing does not extend beyond that of individual beings with a good of their own. Thus when species count it is because of their individual members, whether actual present ones or future ones which could live and flourish unless deprived in the present of the necessary ancestors."[158] Along the same lines, he also states: "Neither the preservation of ecosystems . . . nor diversity are of intrinsic value."[159]

A third perspective is that of animal rights theory, of which Tom Regan is a well-known advocate. Like Attfield, Regan argues that all mammals have inherent value, but the reason he gives for this is animals are sentient beings, meaning that they experience joy and pain, that they have a sense of identity, as well as a sense of historic and future time. He refers to this as the subject-of-a-life criterion: "Those who satisfy the subject-of-a-life criterion themselves have a distinctive kind of value—inherent value—and are not to be viewed or treated as mere receptacles."[160]

PROBLEMS WITH NON-ANTHROPOCENTRISM

By surveying these different views, we see that little to no consensus exists among philosophers concerning the ascription of intrinsic value to other-than-human beings or entities—a problem that has been widely noted.[161] Despite its popularity and broad acceptance, there are also a number of serious problems with these non-anthropocentric views, some of which I will discuss below.

The first problem concerns a contradiction emerging at the source of such value ascriptions. Although the stated goal of the proposal is to decentralize human beings, it nevertheless remains a human decision to ascribe intrinsic value. This point has actually been recognized by J. Baird Callicott, whom I mentioned above. As he writes, "there can be no value apart from an evaluator . . . all value is as it were in the eye of the beholder. The value that is attributed to the ecosystem, therefore, is humanly dependent or at least dependent upon some variety of morally and aesthetically sensitive consciousness."[162] The reason why Callicott still continues to speak of na-

---

158. Attfield, *The Ethics of Environmental Concern*, 156.

159. Ibid., 158.

160. Regan, *The Case for Animal Rights*, 243.

161. See Justus et al., "Buying Into Conservation," 187.

162. Callicott, *In Defense of the Land Ethic*, 27. See also Callicott, "On Norton and the Failure of Monistic Inheritism," 219–21, esp. 219.

ture as bearing an "intrinsic" value (as opposed to a merely instrumental one) is that he establishses a distinction between that which is valued for its human-centered uses and that which is valued for its own sake. Even then, the point still holds that, even in the case of intrinsic value, the value is being ascribed (and indeed, actively debated over) by human beings.

It is important to appreciate the inescapability of the above dilemma. When deep ecologists speak about the importance of maintaining the integrity of the ecological system, they are not basing themselves on the "objective," i.e. non-anthropocentric, value of nature, but on a thoroughly anthropocentric theory of value. Nature itself does not express any sort of preference for rich biodiversity—it is human beings who do that. This point has been noted by many philosophers.[163] By way of example, Colyvan, Linquist, et al. argue that "[t]he nonanthropocentric or ecocentric candidates for the basis of ecological value, such as biodiversity, do not tell us which biodiverse biotas we should prefer. To do that, we need anthropocentrism, which tells us that we should prefer the biodiverse biotas that are best for us."[164] Similarly, as Li argues: "[I]t is human beings who construct scientific disciplines, such as ecology, to articulate the 'objective' values of nature."[165] In sum, the inescapability of a human-centered perspective needs to be recognized and admitted, and not obfuscated.

Secondly, as the brief sketch of the different philosophical and theological accounts of non-anthropocentrism shows, large areas of disagreement exist among those who claim intrinsic value for other-than-human beings. While some only claim intrinsic value for sentient beings, others do the same for all living beings, while still others insist on extending intrinsic value to the whole of nature. This confusion reveals that the intrinsic value of non-human beings is not as self-evident as is often suggested. At the same time, it also raises the question of whether or not asserting the intrinsic value of other-than-human beings is actually helpful, from a theoretical point of view—given that it doesn't lead to unity among environmentalists, but rather to heated debate over academic propositions, then what is its value?[166]

Closely related to this is another problem, namely, that attributing intrinsic value to non-human nature does not lead to a consensus on how

163. See Grey, "Anthropocentrism and Deep Ecology," 463–75; and ibid., "Environmental Value and Anthropocentrism," 97–103.

164. Colyvan et al., "Philosophical Issues in Ecology."

165. Li, "On the Nature of Environmental Education," 258.

166. This pragmatic consideration has been voiced, rather famously, by Norton, to whose argument I will return later on. See Norton, "Environmental Ethics and Weak Anthropocentrism," 131–48.

human-nature relationships should be structured. This point is also made by Li: "[W]e might think that 'diversity' and 'stability,' as intrinsic and objective values of nature, are self-revealing and unequivocal . . . but it is human beings who need to ponder whether we want to make a deliberate effort to protect an endangered species or commit ourselves to non-intervention in face of a 'natural' fire in Yellowstone Park."[167] This becomes a particularly acute problem once the lives of human beings are involved in such a dilemma. When a mountaineer, for instance, takes a serious fall and injures him or herself in the wilderness, should a helicopter be sent to rescue him or her? Or should maintaining the integrity of the wilderness take precedence over the mountaineer's life? As we saw before, some, like Garrett Hardin, side with the latter option, while most other environmentalists—including most deep ecologists—prefer the former.[168]

Another problem with non-anthropocentrism lies in one of its core theses, namely, that "people who believe in the evaluative thesis of non-anthropocentrism are more likely to behave environmentally (i.e., behave in beneficial ways, or at least not in harmful ways, towards the environment) than those who do not."[169] Andrew Brennan and Yeuk-Sze Lo, from whose work the foregoing quotation is cited, have pointed out that, while a great deal of time and effort has been expended in analyzing and clarifying the claim that non-human beings and things also have intrinsic value, this "psycho-behavioural thesis" has gone largely unexplored.[170] Similarly, Colyvan, Linquist, Grey et al. point out that "nonanthropocentrism is not genuinely motivating. Deep ecology preaches to the choir, and even then, it does so only to that portion of the choir who are believers in intrinsic value."[171] It might even be the case that no unequivocal connection exists at all between ecologically responsible behavior and acceptance of non-anthropocentrism—a point that has been suggested by Northcott, who mentions the modern Japanese as an example: "Most modern Japanese hold to one or other variety of Shintoism, which has . . . a monistic perspective on nature, identifying the gods of Shinto belief with particular features of the natural order, and yet Japan as a nation is one of the most ecologically rapacious in the modern world."[172] What this reveals is that, in order to be able to say with more certainty how exactly non-anthropocentrism relates

167. Li, "On the Nature of Environmental Education," 258.
168. Hardin, "The Economics of Wilderness," 20–27.
169. Brennan and Lo, "Environmental Ethics."
170. Ibid.
171. Colyvan et al., "Philosophical Issues in Ecology," 21–22.
172. Northcott, The Environment, 161.

to actual ecological practice, the connection needs to be studied by means of the social sciences.

The Way Forward: Weak Anthropocentrism as an Alternative

Though this list of criticisms is not at all meant to be exhaustive, the problems listed do suffice, at the very least, to indicate that the position of non-anthropocentrism is plagued by a number of serious problems. This in no way is meant to imply, of course, that serious changes don't need to take place in humankind's relationship with nature. One way forward has been suggested by Brian Norton, who, in a famous 1984 article to which I have already referred, recognizes the need to challenge the human-nature relationship. Instead of developing a non-anthropocentric theory of value—which, as he notes, has logical problems—he establishes a distinction between strong anthropocentrism and weak anthropocentrism. Towards this end, he begins by distinguishing what he refers to as felt preferences versus considered preferences, which he defines as follows: "A *felt preference* is any desire or need of a human individual that can at least temporarily be sated by some specifiable experience of that individual. A *considered preference* is any desire or need that a human individual would express after careful deliberation, including a judgement that the desire or need is consistent with a rationally adopted worldview."[173]

From here, Norton goes on to define strong anthropocentrism as a position that allows felt preferences to determine what is of value. He defines weak anthropocentrism, in contrast, as a position that allows criticism (as well as encouragement) of these felt preferences—which means, in other words, that it only permits considered preferences to determine value. In weak anthropocentrism, then, "human behavior is limited by concerns other than those derivable from prohibitions against interfering with the satisfaction of human felt preferences."[174] As such, Norton says, weak anthropocentrism can help to address the most pressing problem for environmental ethics, namely, the individualism that forms the basis of most ethical systems (here he makes mention specifically of utilitarianism and deontology). As he says, "no successful environmental ethic can be derived from an individualistic basis, whether the individuals in question are human or nonhuman . . . an adequate environmental ethic is distinctive, not by

173. Norton, "Environmental Ethics and Weak Anthropocentrism," 328; italics original.

174. Ibid., 329.

being necessarily nonanthropocentric as many environmental ethicists have argued or assumed, but, rather, by being nonindividualistic."[175] As we see, then, although Norton recognizes that values are always ascribed by human beings, his distinction between felt and considered preferences reopens the possibility of criticizing humanity's dealings with nature. As he concludes, "weak anthropocentrism provides a framework adequate to criticize current destructive practices to incorporate concepts of human affinity to nature, and to account for the distinctive nature of environmental ethics."[176] In particular, he proposes, as a fundamental component of non-individualistic, environmental ethics, that one ought not to harm other human beings unjustifiably.[177] This component is relevant in light of the social dimension of the environmental crisis, explored in the next section.

By means of this brief discussion of the debate over anthropocentrism, I would simply like to show that there is no need for theologians to buy into non-anthropocentrism or, on that basis, to propose radical changes to Christian doctrine, such as that of the *imago Dei*.[178] There is, however, a great need for a genuine environmental ethic, and, as Norton rightly points out, this ethic needs to be genuinely non-individualistic in bearing. It is precisely in this respect that Bonhoeffer's relational understanding of the *imago Dei* can be of service, as I will argue further on.

The Social Dimension of the Ecological Crisis

Aside from the attention drawn to the debate over (non-)anthropocentrism, another key theme in environmental ethics concerns the exploration of the relationship between social injustice and ecological degradation—a theme which has strong ecclesial roots. As Willis Jenkins points out, for instance, "[t]hroughout the 1960s and 1970s, mainline churches discussed environmental issues within committees concerned for 'the responsible society' or 'the sustainable society.'"[179] By way of example, an early, influential study, carried out in the United States by the United Church of Christ Commission for Racial Justice, drew attention to the connection between racism and

175. Ibid., 330.

176. Ibid., 336.

177. Ibid., 333.

178. On account of the fact that the purpose of this subsection is to argue for the validity of an anthropocentric approach, I have not treated the specific theological alternative to both anthropocentrism and ecocentrism, namely theocentrism. For just one such theocentric proposal, see Van den Brom, "The Art of a 'Theo-Ecological' Interpretation," 298–313.

179. Jenkins, *Ecologies of Grace*, 62.

environmental degradation.[180] An important milestone in this context is the WCC covenant, "Justice, Peace and the Integrity of Creation," which represents the outcome of a process which started during the 1983 Vancouver assembly and came to fruition at the World Convocation in Seoul in 1990. On the topics of sociality and ecology, the covenant says: "The integrity of creation has a social aspect which we recognize as peace with justice, and an ecological aspect which we recognize in the self-renewing, sustainable character of natural eco-systems."[181]

Aside from official statements such as these, ecotheologians have formulated their own proposals to heal the rift in social and ecological life. Northcott, for example, makes the case that the relationality of God, human, and non-human life is central both to the Hebrew Bible and to the teachings of Jesus, and continues on in the Christian tradition as well. In particular, he contrasts biblical and subsequently Christian forms of relationality with modern, utilitarian individualism, arguing that human beings need to return to an understanding of the self "as traditionally constituted by the worship of God, and the correlative recognition of divine order in the cosmos and of divine intentionality in human society."[182] This nevertheless represents only one of many proposals put forward by Christian theologians working to bring the Bible and the Christian tradition to bear on the intersection of social and ecological problems.[183]

THE CONTRIBUTION BONHOEFFER'S CONCEPT OF THE IMAGO DEI AS AN ANALOGIA RELATIONIS CAN MAKE

The specific contribution that Bonhoeffer is able make to the discussion lies in his relational understanding of the *imago Dei*. As we saw, being made in God's image implies, according to Bonhoeffer, that human beings are both free from each other and free to take responsibility for each other. Since the doctrine of the *imago Dei* forms such a crucial cornerstone in Christian theology, a relational interpretation of this doctrine—which, as we saw, Bonhoeffer was the first to offer—can help form a strong foundation of an ethics of interpersonal responsibility. This potential of Bonhoeffer's *analogia relationis* has been recognized by others, whose work I will now explore in detail.

180. Commission for Racial Justice, "Toxic Wastes and Race in the United States."

181. World Council of Churches, "Entering into Covenant Solidarity," 174.

182. Nortcott, *The Environment and Christian Ethics*, 205.

183. See, among others, Jenkins, *Ecologies of Grace*, 61–76; and Rasmussen, *Earth-Honoring Faith*, 305–31.

The first to connect Bonhoeffer's doctrine of the *imago Dei* with environmental ethics was Peter Scott. As we will see in chapter 5, Scott considers Bonhoeffer's assertions of human mastery over nature as unhelpful—in particular, he takes issue with Bonhoeffer's sharp distinction between human beings as free *for* each other, but free *from* nature. In his opinion, it would be more ecologically friendly if Bonhoeffer's concepts of "freedom for" and "freedom from" were both to refer to the relationship between human beings and nature: "[M]ay it be argued that humanity is free *for* as well as free *from* nature?"[184] In order to answer this question, he investigates the structure of Bonhoeffer's use of analogy, which he identifies as an analogy of proportion: "[B]eing-free-for-others is related to relations between human beings."[185]

According to Scott, this makes it difficult to extend Bonhoeffer's analogy to non-human beings, for, in their being as non-human, they do not share the same sociality as humans do, and are therefore always and necessarily different. Taking this as a deficiency in Bonhoeffer's account,[186] he proposes that a different sort of analogy to be used, namely, an analogy of attribution. He refers in this case to Aristotle, who employed the analogy of attribution when stating "that all things, in so far as they are, enjoy the quiddity of substance."[187] By means of this second form of analogy, all things that exist (whether human or not) would be seen as "free"—the analogy would, as Scott argues, become "a transcendental category in which all being participates."[188] At the same time, Scott recognizes that reformulating Bonhoeffer's *analogia* in this way wouldn't leave much of his original position left over. First of all, it would be too close to an *analogia entis*, as he says—which Bonhoeffer, of course, specifically opposes. And secondly, he rightly remarks that the whole point of Bonhoeffer's *analogia relationis* was to identify that which is specifically human—*not* that which exists as such.

Scott does, however, recognize the ability of Bonhoeffer's conception of the *imago Dei* to deal with the social side of the ecological crisis. As he says, Bonhoeffer sees the reconciliation between nature and God as being

184. Scott, "Postnatural Humanity? Bonhoeffer on Freedom and Order in Creation," 17; italics original.

185. Ibid., 18.

186. This was also recognized by Scott in the first article he wrote on Bonhoeffer and ecology. Noting the anthropocentrism inherent in Bonhoeffer's theological anthropology, he says: "A breach in the wider community of life is evident here in Bonhoeffer's theology." Scott, "Christ, Nature, Sociality," 426.

187. Scott, "Postnatural Humanity? Bonhoeffer on Freedom and Order in Creation," 19.

188. Ibid.

mediated by human beings. As we saw in chapter 3, however, this is not quite adequate, for Bonhoeffer stresses that nature is not reconciled so much as it is redeemed. Nevertheless, Scott is right in observing that Bonhoeffer's conception of nature is anthropocentric in bearing, and he recognizes the value of this approach: "[T]his argument stresses human responsibility and—although Bonhoeffer does not say so—permits the identification of human injustices in human relationships with nature."[189] Furthermore, Scott recognizes that, in this way, Bonhoeffer closes off any supposedly direct and immediate access to nature as such, or nature in and for itself: "[B]y stressing that the way to nature is by God and human beings, Bonhoeffer makes difficult the transposing of natural categories into human affairs."[190] Although Scott's appeal to Bonhoeffer's theology of sociality is valuable, I would charge that he mars his *analogia relationis* beyond recognition. Whereas he sees Bonhoeffer's limitation of the *analogia* to human beings as a mere obstacle to be overcome, I would argue that it is precisely as such that it is valuable for environmental ethics.

Cloete also writes about Bonhoeffer's thoughts on the *imago Dei* in relation to environmental ethics. He argues that Bonhoeffer's stress on the fallenness of human beings means that their mandate to rule over the earth has been lost. In his own words: "They [humans] are fallen beings and therefore cannot claim the freedom and rights of humans in the image of God. Ultimately, Bonhoeffer is then indeed in agreement with contemporary scholars who believe that the notion of 'humans in the likeness of God' does not mandate the elevation of humankind above the rest of creation."[191] This is not an adequate presentation of Bonhoeffer's position, however—for although he indeed stresses that humanity is fallen, that does not, in his thought, negate humankind's exalted place over the rest of the world.

Also Burkholder writes about the ecological promise of Bonhoeffer's concept of the *analogia relationis*. He asserts that embodiment is essential to the *imago Dei*, in Bonhoeffer. That leads him to argue that, "since the *imago dei* [sic] requires embodiment, it also means that the *imago dei* entails being related to the rest of the natural world, or as he [Bonhoeffer] says, the earth. By extension, then, the freedom for others in the *imago dei* is not merely a freedom for others in the human community, but a freedom to serve the rest of the natural world."[192] Burkholder recognizes that Bonhoeffer differentiates "freedom from" creation and "freedom for" other human beings. Yet he as-

---

189. Ibid., 21.

190. Ibid.

191. Cloete, "Harmatology and Ecology," 158.

192. Burkholder, "Christological Foundations," 343; italics original.

serts that Bonhoeffer extends this "freedom for" others to non-human nature as well. For support of this claim he refers to his earlier assertion that for Bonhoeffer, human embodiment is central to the *imago Dei*.[193] This is a circular argument, for nowhere does Burkholder base his insistence that embodiment is part of the *imago Dei* in Bonhoeffer's works. And there lies the problem, for while it is true that embodiment is central to Bonhoeffer's theological anthropology, it is not part of his conception of the *imago Dei*, which, in its being an *analogia relationis*, is opposed to precisely this sort of an *analogia entis*.

Although inadequate with regards to Bonhoeffer, Scott and Burkholder are not alone with their proposals—rather, they join a wider stream of endeavors to recast the *imago Dei* doctrine so as to include non-human creation as well. I already referred to David Cunningham's proposal to allow the *imago Dei* to refer to "all flesh," instead of only to human beings. According to yet another, closely related strategy, we should continue to allow the *imago Dei* to apply to human beings alone, but then we should interpret it as a responsibility given to human beings vis-à-vis the rest of creation. An advocate of this view is Daniel K. Miller.[194] Noting that differences between animals and human beings are differences in degree, and not in kind, he argues that the *imago Dei* does not refer to a biological difference, but to a difference in teleology. Drawing from Barth and Brunner, whose conceptions of the *imago Dei* he compares, he argues that human beings are *responsible*—responsible for each other, for other animals and for the natural world as a whole: "Locating the *imago* in human responsible relationships . . . draws humans closer to other animals. Humans, in this way are defined not by the physiological or intellectual traits that separate them from other animals, but by the responsibility they have for being in relationship with animals."[195]

This is also the interpretation put forward by Douglas John Hall in his well-known book *Imaging God: Dominion as Stewardship*. Opposing himself against substantialist interpretations of the *imago Dei*, he too chooses a relational interpretation which—contrary to Bonhoeffer—is not limited to human beings, but extends to non-human creation as well: "[T]he whole intention of the relational conception of the image of God is to position the human creature responsibly in relation to the other creatures; not to demonstrate that this creature is higher, or more complex, or worthier, but to designate a specific function of this creature—a very positive function—in

193. See ibid., 343n20.

194. Miller, "Responsible Relationship," 323–37.

195. Ibid., 325; italics original.

relation to the others."[196] From here, Hall then goes on to develop a three-fold account of human relationality according to which human beings are in relation to God, to each other and to nature. The relation to nature in particular takes the form of "stewardship," which Hall sees as the true meaning of humanity's vocation to represent God on the earth.

One major problem with this interpretation—which has since become quite popular—is that stewardship is not an adequate term for describing how the Bible presents humanity's relationship with nature.[197] Another problem is that making the human-nature relationship the focus of the *imago Dei* runs the risk of losing sight of the importance of the human-to-human relationship. If this were to happen, a very convincing and accessible argument for environmental ethics would be lost, namely, that our dealings with the environment form an integral part of how we deal with other people, for abusing and destroying the environment hurts others, especially those who are most vulnerable. Roger Scruton recognizes this point in the following remarks: "Responsibility may embrace the whole of nature and the whole of time, but only by spreading to the point of transparency the solid stuff of person-to-person sympathy."[198] The importance of this social dimension at work the ecological crisis has been recognized by many others and many different proposals have been made to address it.[199] It is nevertheless not possible, on the basis of Bonhoeffer's relational concept of the *imago Dei* alone, to develop this dimension further. Such a development can only be carried out by means of his theology of responsibility and his concept of the divine mandates. For the time being, I would simply like to signal to the reader that Bonhoeffer's concept of the *imago Dei* as an *analogia relationis* forms a solid *foundation* for this dimension to be built upon.

196. Hall, *Imaging God*, 106–7.

197. This has been noted by Conradie, who writes: "[T]he terminology of stewardship is not directly used in the Bible and has been rarely used in the history of Christian theology to describe the relationship between humanity and the rest of creation." Conradie, *An Ecological Christian Anthropology*, 214.

198. Scruton, *Green Philosophy*, 208.

199. Nullens, "Leven volgens Gaia's normen?," 286–90; Northcott, *The Environment*, 257–327; and Rasmussen, *Earth-Honoring Faith*, 305–31.

5
Human Beings as Masters and Lovers of Nature

THIS CHAPTER CONTINUES THE EXPLORATION AND APPLICATION OF PER-spectives from Bonhoeffer's theological anthropology to environmental ethics. The two perspectives that are addressed here deal with Bonhoeffer's thoughts on human mastery over nature and the emphasis that he places on loyalty to the earth. In the chapter's first part, I will give a general description of both perspectives, whereas in the second part, I will apply them directly to the field of environmental ethics.

Bonhoeffer on Human Mastery over Nature and the Imperative to Love Nature

Here in the first part of the chapter, I will describe Bonhoeffer's views on human mastery over nature, as well as his call for human loyalty to the earth. Like the themes of human bodylines and distinctiveness set out in chapter 4, the themes treated in this chapter appear to be contradictory at first sight. However, a more thorough examination of the way Bonhoeffer develops them will show that, here too, instead of contradicting each other, the two perspectives complement each other.

Bonhoeffer on the Meaning of Human Mastery over Nature

In the present section, I shall focus on Bonhoeffer's thoughts concerning the relationship between human beings and nature, namely, that of *mastery*.

THE THEME OF HUMAN MASTERY IN BONHOEFFER'S CF

The theme of human mastery over nature is introduced in the same section of *CF* in which Bonhoeffer speaks about the freedom which human beings have for each other, that is, in the context of his commentary on Gen 1:26. There he states: "Humankind . . . in its likeness to God, is created within the world of the fixed and of the living. And whereas the freedom of human beings over against one another consisted in being free *for* one another, humankind's freedom over against the rest of the created world is to be free *from* it."[1]

What this citation makes clear is that Bonhoeffer does not extend human "freedom-for" to either animate or inanimate aspects of non-human nature. Rather, he introduces a sharp distinction between nature and human beings, claiming that human beings are free from nature. He immediately specifies what he means by stating, in the passage immediately following the preceding quotation: "That means that humankind is its lord; humankind has command over it, rules it. And that constitutes the other side of humankind's created likeness to God. Humankind is to rule—though it is to rule over God's creation and to rule as having been commissioned and empowered to rule by God."[2]

As will become clear further on in this chapter, the use of the term "mastery" ("Herrschaft," in German) in relation to nature is hotly contested in current debates surrounding environmental ethics. It is therefore imperative to have a firm understanding of what exactly Bonhoeffer means by this term. The first important thing to note is that Bonhoeffer, immediately following the quotation cited earlier, in which he describes human dominion over nature, states that the freedom from nature should not be perceived of as the freedom of the "spirit" one finds in Idealism. Rather, he says, the freedom to rule nature of necessity means being *bound* to nature.[3] Bonhoeffer thus re-emphasises what he had already asserted earlier on in *CF*, namely, that human life is essentially a *bodily* or *embodied* life. It is precisely insofar as human beings have bodies that they can, in their bodily existence, rule over other, non-human "bodies," both inanimate and animate. If human freedom from nature were defined as a spiritual freedom, in contrast, then human beings would not be called on to exercise dominion over nature—on the contrary, it would be more fitting to expect the Biblical text to demand that they flee from nature. Instead, Bonhoeffer places *equal* stress both on the fundamental earthiness of human beings and on their call to master nature and to subdue it. This twin emphasis also occurs further on in *CF*, where Bonhoeffer comments on Gen 1:28–31.[4] It is thus surely *not* Bonhoeffer's

1. DBWE 3:66; italics original.

2. DBWE 3:66.

3. Bonhoeffer speak about "the ideal of the spirit's being free from nature." DBWE 3:66.

4. DBWE 3:68.

intention to separate human beings from nature, but rather to show how they are related to one another. As Clifford Green comments, "[h]umanity's 'being-free-from-nature' is not some sort of Platonic or idealistic floating above the natural and bodily realm; ruling over nature is precisely the bond which involves the human creature intimately in the natural world."[5]

Having clearly articulated the ideal relationship between humanity and nature, Bonhoeffer is quick to point out that this picture of human beings simultaneously being a part of nature and, at the same time, ruling over it, is part of the world that mankind lost in the Fall. He uses the metaphor of the Walpurgis night, arguing that instead of *moving*, human beings are *being moved*.[6] Bonhoeffer unpacks this rather cryptic statement by explaining that human beings no longer rule over nature anymore, but, instead, are ruled by it—it is thus the world that rules over humankind, turning man into its slave, as it were: "Technology is the power with which the earth seizes hold of humankind and masters it."[7] In this passage, Bonhoeffer makes the point that, while human beings believe that, through technology, they rule over nature by liberating and harnessing nature's forces, they actually lose hold of their rule, or their power. In other words, for Bonhoeffer, human mastery over nature is *not* achieved by means of technological innovations. On the contrary, these technologies tend to make mankind ever more dependent on, and subordinate to, nature. On Bonhoeffer's view, then, it is precisely in adhering to the dominant, modern worldview, in which technology is seen as a salvific, liberating power, that mankind's *fallen nature* wins the battle for control over the earth *from human beings*.

According to Bonhoeffer, the effects of mankind's failure to effectively rule over the earth (which, again, is here understood in the precise sense of allowing *technology* to gain control) are disastrous: "And because we no longer rule, we lose the ground [Boden] so that the earth no longer remains *our* earth, and we become estranged from the earth."[8] The deeper reason that Bonhoeffer sees behind this failure to rule is the fact that we no longer recognize the world as God's creation, or as a gift from God. Closely related with this first failure is a second, namely, the failure to recognize God, and the other human beings, for whom the human being is "free for."[9] As we

5. Green, *Bonhoeffer*, 198.

6. In his own words: "This is said to us who, being in the middle, no longer know anything about all this and to whom it is all a pious myth or a lost world. We too think that we rule, but the same applies here as on Walpurgis Night: we think we are the one making the move, whereas instead we are being moved." DBWE 3:66–67.

7. DBWE 3:67.

8. DBWE 3:67; italics original.

9. He says: "There is no 'being-free-from' without a 'being-free-for'. There is no

see, then, Bonhoeffer makes clear that the *dominium terrae* is not to be understood as an independent exercise of power over nature in the way that one wants; on the contrary, the dominion can only be properly exercised in recognition of God and of other human beings.

The ruthless exploitation of nature by excessive dependence on technology is not the only way in which human beings fail to gain (or maintain) mastery over the earth. Bonhoeffer also takes a stand against the romantic eschewal of the exercise of lordship over creation.[10] Though Bonhoeffer does not work this point out in any further detail, the historical context in which he delivered the lecture makes clear that he was opposing himself against the romanticization of nature by the National Socialists.[11]

Between the ruthless and irresponsible exploitation of the earth, on the one hand, and the sentimental eschewal of lordship, on the other, Bonhoeffer sketches the contours of his own approach to nature, after the Fall, as follows: "God, the brother and sister, and the earth belong together. For those who have once lost the earth, however, for us human beings in the middle, there is no way back to the earth except via God and our brothers and sisters."[12] Human beings wishing to stand in a proper relationship to nature therefore need to come to God, and to each other, in recognition of their being "free for" God and for the other.[13] Here again we find Bonhoeffer pointing, if only implicitly, to sociality as the solution to the problem.

One final aspect of Bonhoeffer's account of human dominion over nature is that, according to him, it is *not* based on a supposed natural order but, instead, on God's word which grants human beings this authority.[14] With this, Bonhoeffer clearly closes off the possibility of maintaining a "natural" understanding of human mastery over nature.[15]

---

dominion without serving God; in losing the one humankind necessarily loses the other. Without God, without their brothers and sisters, human beings lose the earth." DBWE 3:67.

10. He says: "Already in sentimentally shying away from exercising dominion over the earth, however, human beings have forever lost God and their brothers and sisters." DBWE 3:67.

11. See Rasmussen, "Song of Songs," 299n16.

12. DBWE 3:67.

13. DBWE 3:67.

14. DBWE 3:66.

15. This is consistent with Bonhoeffer's resistance against natural theology found elsewhere in his work and his insistence, instead, on orders of preservation as the proper way of speaking how the order found in the world can be appropriated theologically.

Human Mastery and Technology in Bonhoeffer's Other Earlier Works

Although *CF* is the text in which Bonhoeffer develops his thoughts on human mastery and technology most fully, there are a number of other instances in his work from around the same time in which he gives voice to similar reflections. The fullest treatment of the subject from this period, aside from *CF*, is found in his lecture on "The Right to Self-Assertion,"[16] delivered on February 4, 1932 for the Technical University in Charlottenburg, where Bonhoeffer worked as a student pastor. In this lecture, he contrasts the Western approach to nature with the Eastern approach, which he sees exemplified in India. He first of all characterizes the Western approach—which encompasses both European and American societies—as typified by war and factory production. The history of the West, as he says, is a history of war. Both the machine and war are, in his view, typical Western phenomena—typical insofar as they represent attempts to overcome nature.[17] In contrast, Bonhoeffer sees Indian culture overcoming nature by understanding it and by vicariously suffering both with and for it. In stark opposition, the European man acts as the enemy of nature and, accordingly, is unable to love (or suffer with) it. More specifically, he sees demonic violence at work in nature and battles to overcome it. The Indian, in contrast, receives and accepts from nature what he or she needs, which is only possible because he or she loves nature and doesn't take up arms against it.[18] Bonhoeffer further elaborates his argument by asserting that the Western attitude towards nature spills over into the realm of inner-human relationships. The European not only has to fight against nature, but also against other human beings—an attitude which he sees horrifically exemplified in the Great War of 1914 to 1918.[19]

16. DBWE 11:246–56

17. In his own words: "[T]he machine and the war are the two forms of the Western solution to our problem." DBWE 11:251–52.

18. DBWE 11:252. Although the point remains to be read between the lines, as it were, Bonhoeffer's remarks on this contrast seem to imply that the generally harsher, natural conditions of Northern Europe helped bring about the Western attitude to nature. This point is made explicitly in Bonhoeffer's prison letters. In a letter to Bethge, dated June 30, 1944, Bonhoeffer writes: "The hot countries, from the Mediterranean to India to Central America, have really been essentially the intellectually creative countries. The colder countries have lived and been nourished by the intellectual [geistig] creativity of others, and their own original contribution, technology, basically serves the material needs of life and not the life of the spirit." DBWE 8:499.

19. DBWE 11:255. In pitting the Indian solution so strongly against the European one, Bonhoeffer exaggerates the features and the points of dissimilarity that

Aside from this lecture, Bonhoeffer also addresses the subject of human mastery over nature in other instances during the same period of his life. The first occasion can be found in a sermon on Luke 12:35–40, which he delivered in November 29, 1931 (first week of Advent), in which he writes about the huge changes that have taken place in the world. According to him, technology and science have become independent powers, bent on the destruction of humanity. The language he uses is almost apocalyptic: "Technology and the economy have become automatic powers that threaten to destroy human beings. They set themselves up on high, and their demons have become the gods of our time. Involvement in great conflicts between nations [Völker] drives nations to their downfall, and yet no one seems to be powerful enough to prevent this fate."[20] Just as in *CF* and the lecture on "The Right to Self-Assertion," the tone here is decidedly negative in nature—the human being is placed in juxtaposition with the broader, historical movements of the times, of which technology and science form an important part.

This negative tone is also discernable in Bonhoeffer's radio speech "The Führer and the Individual in the Younger Generation,"[21] delivered almost exactly one year after his lecture on "The Right to Self-Assertion," namely, on February 1, 1933. Here again he mentions the theme of technology, this time in connection with an observation concerning the younger generation as a whole, namely, that they will need to try to cope with a world that is characterised by novel historical realities. As the first of these, Bonhoeffer mentions the experience of technology triumphing over the human world.[22] As before, so here too, he judges the great scientific and technological developments of his day in starkly negative terms. We can

---

distinguish the one from the other, and therefore gives a somewhat distorted image (or caricature) of either culture. As Rasmussen observes, in regards to Indian culture, "Bonhoeffer romanticizes India here. Gender and caste analysis never enter his appraisal, and his address slides too easily into an unqualified affirmation of sacrifice for the larger community." Rasmussen, "Song of Songs," 314. It is nevertheless important to note that Bonhoeffer doesn't reduce the Western approach to nature, on the one hand, to a purely animalistic or instinctive solution, while elevating the other, Indian approach, to some sort of humanistic ideal. On the contrary, he judges such an appraisal as superficial. It is not that the one is active and the other passive, nor that the one is destructive and the other productive; no, both the Western and the Eastern solutions are reflective and deliberative solutions—not just instinctive ones. They are the result of deliberative human attempts to grapple with nature.

20. DBWE 11:410.

21. "The Führer and the Individual in the Younger Generation." DBWE 12:268–82.

22. He says: "Technology, which was intended to master nature, had been turned against defenseless humans and thus robbed of its essential meaning!" DBWE 12:271.

conclude that technology was indeed an important theme for Bonhoeffer during this period and that he viewed it very negatively.[23]

THE THEME OF HUMAN MASTERY IN BONHOEFFER'S ETHICS

Bonhoeffer addresses the themes of mastery and technology in his *Ethics* as well. In the manuscript "Heritage and Decay," for instance, he writes that, in the time of the Enlightenment, humankind's liberated *ratio* led to significant growth of technological power—a fundamentally novel event in world history. Throughout most of world history, as he argues, technology served the needs of religion, of royalty, of culture and of people, a fact which he sees exemplified in the great architectural feats of the world, such as the Egyptian pyramids and the cathedrals of the Middle Ages. Modern technology, in contrast, freed itself from its service to humanity. The spirit that produced this historical change is the spirit of violent domination, in which technology becomes an end in itself. According to Bonhoeffer, "Technology has become an end in itself. It has its own soul; its symbol is the machine, the embodiment of violation and exploitation of nature."[24]

Next Bonhoeffer notes how faith protests against modern technology insofar it senses that technology is driven by human hubris, that is, by the desire to create a world running counter to the one God created. In this context, he says: "The benefits of technology pale beside its demonic powers."[25] But the faith that resists technology is nevertheless a naïve faith, on Bonhoeffer's view, as he points out that it cannot be denied that technology grew precisely in "Western soil," on which Christianity had such a formative influence.[26] Insofar as Eastern countries are concerned, technology takes on a different role, as Bonhoeffer observes. In this case, instead of being an end in itself, it finds its place again in the service of God. In this connection, Bonhoeffer cites a journalistic report on king Ibn Saud, the founder of Saudi-Arabia, who had reportedly said that he wanted machines from Europe, but not the irreligiosity connected with it.[27]

23. Bonhoeffer also lectured on the specific theme of "Technology and Religion" during the winter semester of 1932 and 1933, in which he delivered his *CF* lectures. See DBWE 12:118–20, esp. 119.

24. DBWE 6:116.

25. DBWE 6:116.

26. He says: "We cannot overlook that technology has flourished only in Western soil, and that means in the world determined by Christianity, especially by the Reformation." DBWE 6:116.

27. Bonhoeffer reports Ibn Saud as having said: "I have procured machines from Europe, but I do not want its irreligiosity. The Muslim peoples must awaken from their

The issue of technology as an expression of human mastery over nature also plays a role in the *Ethics* manuscript "Natural Life." In the introduction to this manuscript, Bonhoeffer sketches out the contours of his own approach as a path between vitalism and mechanism. Whereas vitalism absolutizes life, and therefore ends in nihilism, so mechanism also absolutizes life, but only as a means to an end, leading to the same nihilism as vitalism. Technology is mentioned further on in the manuscript. The context is Bonhoeffer's discussion of the problem of birth control, which he links to the growth of human, technological mastery over nature. He sees birth control as something negative, an evil to be avoided. At the same time, he acknowledges how technological applications have reduced the evil of childdeaths and increased the average life span.[28] A realization such as this helps to temper Bonhoeffer's criticism of technology somewhat. As he notes, when one sets out to blame technology for rendering people unwilling to make the sacrifice of having a large family, one should not overlook the fact that it was precisely these technological innovations that made the population growth possible in the first place.[29] Like in his lecture on "Self-Assertion," Bonhoeffer here recognizes that technology is not something standing "outside" of or at a distance from human society—on the contrary, it already forms the very context in which our deliberations take place.

Bonhoeffer's Thoughts on Technology in his Writings from Prison

This realization—of which I have only sketched the basic outline, or form— grows even stronger in Bonhoeffer's prison writings, where he returns to the theme of human, technological mastery over nature for the last time. The most notable mention of the theme is in the outline of a book that Bonhoeffer planned to write while in prison.[30] The theme of the book concerned the question of how the church should go about coping with, or relating to a world "come of age," and to the reality of growing non-religiousness. The planned book would have had three chapters, the first of which bore

---

long dream. They need weapons, but the strongest weapon is faith in God, humble obedience to the divine laws." DBWE 6:117. The editors of the *Ethics* point out that Bonhoeffer's quotation probably derives from Donkan, *Die Auferstehung Arabiens*. See DBWE 6:117, editorial footnote 65.

28. DBWE 6:208.

29. DBWE 6:208.

30. "Outline for a Book." DBWE 8:499–504.

the preliminary title "Taking Stock of Christianity,"[31] which would have offered a description of the (then) current state of affairs. In summarizing the planned contents of this chapter, Bonhoeffer observes that one sign of the coming of age of humanity consists in the desire to be independent of nature through insurance, "against 'accidents,' 'blows of fate'; if it is impossible to eliminate them, then at least the reduction of danger."[32] Just as he had done before, so too here Bonhoeffer notes how, in the period of modernity, the West conquered nature through technical organization, as opposed to spiritual means, such as had been used in the time before modernity (Bonhoeffer does not specify these "spiritual means," but arguably he is referring to the Christian religion as a worldview through which people made sense of the world). In this Outline, however, he takes it a step further, insisting that, as a consequence of this technical domination, "What is unmediated for us, what is given, is no longer nature but organization."[33]

Bonhoeffer's use of the word "organization" to refer to humanity's use of technology signals an important departure from his earlier writings. This has been noted by De Lange, who makes the case that Bonhoeffer no longer understood technology as a means of manipulation and control. On the contrary, as he says, Bonhoeffer came to the realization that technology, as organization, could be seen as a form of language. According to De Lange, "Language and technology have the same purpose: they constitute a network of meaning and thus create human, inhabitable order in a chaotic universe."[34] In a similar vein, he claims that "together . . . technological resources constitute an *environment*: a single technological universe. A unity of meaning, independent of nature."[35] According to this new understanding, then, technology now forms the most immediate environment of human beings, instead of nature. And rather than referring disapprovingly to technology, as he had done in his earlier writings, Bonhoeffer accepts this state of affairs as a part of the world created by a humanity come of age. De Lange points this out as well. As he argues, Bonhoeffer's "Outline" should not be read *prescriptively*, that is, from the perspective of a humanist cultural critic, but rather *descriptively*, as a cultural-historical explication of where humanity stands at that point—humanity has come of age.[36] De Lange concludes,

31. DBWE 8:499.

32. DBWE 8:500.

33. DBWE 8:500.

34. De Lange, "'The Spiritual Force Is Lacking.'"

35. Ibid.; italics original.

36. Ibid.

then, that, "[i]n the first section of 'Outline for a Book[,]' coming of age and technology are *intrinsically* connected to each other."[37]

The fact that Bonhoeffer's understanding of technology shifts in this way does not mean that he no longer sees technology presenting any problems. On the contrary, while he recognizes that technical organization was instrumental in taming the dangers of nature, he also notes the emergence of a new danger to humanity, namely, of organization itself. At this point, as Bonhoeffer says, humanity no longer has the spiritual power to battle its own technological organization: "The question is: What will protect us from the menace of organization? The human being is thrown back on his own resources. He has learned to cope with everything except himself. He can insure himself against everything but other human beings. In the end it all comes down to the human being."[38] This quotation is reminiscent of Bonhoeffer's observation, in *CF*, that, in the illusion of control offered by technology, human beings lose hold of God, of their fellow human beings and of the earth itself. Yet while in *CF*—and, further on, in his other writings—his implicit conclusion was that human beings needed to refrain from being mastered by their fallen nature, through the use of technology, he here accepts technological organization as a part of the world in which humanity has come of age.

De Lange points out that, in this light, Bonhoeffer's assertion—namely, that mankind doesn't possess sufficient spiritual force to confront technology's organization—should be understood as a description of the problem that modern human beings have become for themselves. His statement that, in the end, everything comes back to focus yet again on the human being, is an indication that the problem has to be overcome, not by taking a step back, but by realizing it as a problem and by taking responsibility for it— only a path such as this befits human beings who have come of age.[39] The same point has also been brought out by Treier, who writes: "Bonhoeffer's account of modernity rightly says yes to this coming of age whereby false

37. Ibid.; italics original. This goes against Burkholder, who does not perceive of a break between Bonhoeffer's "Outline" and his earlier thoughts on technology in *CF*. According to him, Bonhoeffer, in his "Outline," "believed the desire to be free of the capricious aspects of nature had actually enslaved human beings within their own organisational structures, leaving humans with no 'power of the soul' to face the vicissitudes of life." Burkholder, "Christological Foundations," 344.

38. DBWE 8:500.

39. In his own words: "This is what Bonhoeffer apparently means with 'being of age': not a factual or ideal autonomy, no optimism with regard to the possibilities of humanity, no blind faith in the progress of technology, but insight into the moral situation with which a technological culture confronts us: being radically responsible for the continuation of the world." De Lange, "'The Spiritual Force is Lacking.'"

religion is overcome in the name of human freedom, while also saying no to the hubris that turns such apparent freedom into new forms of God-denying and others-dominating necessity."[40]

The foregoing overview of the theme of human mastery over nature reveals both the consistency and the development of Bonhoeffer's thinking on the question. What remains consistent throughout his work is the idea that human beings are called to master nature. In most of his work, Bonhoeffer argues that humanity fell short of this calling precisely insofar as it relied on technology, thereby failing not only in the mastery of nature, but also in the loss of relationship with God and with their fellow human beings. With his *Ethics*, and even more directly with his writings from prison, however, Bonhoeffer comes to see technology as an ontological dimension of life that cannot be escaped and that has to be taken seriously as part and parcel of humanity's "coming of age." As such, rather than restoring relationships with God and fellow human beings by shying away from technology, Bonhoeffer argues that human beings need to focus on the question of how, in modernity's technological environment, faith in God, and taking responsibility for others, should be lived out.

BACKGROUND AND PARALLELS OF BONHOEFFER'S THOUGHTS ON HUMAN MASTERY

As with the concepts studied in chapter 4, Bonhoeffer does not provide us with the background against which he developed his thoughts on human mastery and technology. However, we are able to detect a few of the sources and parallels that gave shape to his views.

First of all, it can be noted that, just as we saw with the *imago Dei*, Bonhoeffer's assertions about the relationship between human beings and the natural world closely resemble those of Luther. There are a number of interesting parallels between Bonhoeffer's CF and Luther's commentary on Genesis, for instance. The first concerns the deep rift that they both draw attention to between the original relationship between humanity and nature and the one set in place after the Fall. Prior to the Fall, there was no enmity between human beings and animals, as Luther asserts. He pictures Adam as "a naked man without arms, without walls, nay, without any vestiture of his own body, but standing alone in his own naked flesh, [who] finds himself lord over all birds, all wild beasts and all fishes, etc."[41] Dominion for Adam was a joyful matter, according to Luther—in particular, he writes about the

---

40. Treier, "Modernity's Machine," 109.

41. Luther, *Genesis*, 121.

joy and pleasure that Adam must have felt when he was set before the entire animal kingdom. His dominion, again according to Luther, consisted in *understanding* the animals: Adam and Eve "understood all the affections, the senses, the feelings and the powers of all the animals of the creation."[42]

Remarkably, a second point of convergence between Bonhoeffer and Luther concerns the character of human mastery over nature after the Fall. Just as Bonhoeffer would assert later on, Luther insists that, following the Fall, humanity lost its original relation of dominion over nature; instead of ruling nature through understanding it, humanity came to rule it by means of technology. As examples, Luther mentions how human beings seize birds and fish by means of capture, a practice which leads, according to him, to some "appearance of dominion over the other creatures. This dominion however is very trifling indeed, and far, very far, beneath the original dominion. For under that there was no need of art or stratagem, to give man influence over the beast."[43] In a similar way, we saw already how Bonhoeffer identifies technology as the means by which fallen humanity tries to retain its position as nature's master, but ultimately fails. The only difference is that for Luther, technology consists of manual instruments, each crafted individually, whereas for Bonhoeffer, technology becomes much more pervasive in nature—on the foundations of modernity, it becomes mechanized and grows to become so all-encompassing that it forms an ontological dimension of life.

An important difference between Luther and Bonhoeffer concerns—again—the expectance of eschatological restoration. As Luther believed in the "literal" Fall of humanity, he also expected the future restoration of human mastery over nature. Concerning humanity's original dominion over nature, he says that "it is good for us to know and to think upon this state of things, that we may sigh after that day which shall come in which shall be restored unto us all things we lost by the sin of Adam in paradise."[44] Yet the eschaton, for Luther, does not simply consist in the restoration of Adam's original dominion over the natural world. Instead, he speaks about "that life which Adam also ever held in expectation,"[45] namely, a life made possible by the cross of Christ, as Luther asserts. For Bonhoeffer, in contrast, the eschaton does not contain such an expectance for a renewed human domination over the natural world.

42. Ibid.
43. Ibid., 123.
44. Ibid.
45. Ibid.

Apart from these parallels with Luther's theology, there are readily observable parallels between Bonhoeffer's negative assessment of technology (which he started changing around the time that he wrote his *Ethics*) and the cultural "milieu" of his time—during the *interbellum*, prominent thinkers across continental Europe made their condemnation of the modern world public. Examples are the works of the German philosopher Oswald Spengler,[46] the Dutch historian Johan Huizinga,[47] and the Spanish philosopher José Ortega y Gasset.[48]

The change that came about in Bonhoeffer's assessment of the modern world and of technology in particular—and which occurred most noticeably during his time in prison—has to be understood in the context of his view on the history of modernity, which was strongly influenced by his reading (in prison) of W.A. Dilthey's *Weltanschauung und Analyse des Menschen seit Renaissance und Reformation.*[49] De Lange has drawn attention this connection, but he also notes that "in the draft of the book that he was about to write based on his new insights . . . little of this reading shows up in a direct way."[50] As he points out, in Bonhoeffer's assessment of the modern experience of Christianity, it is "not the rationality of the individual subject but technology as a social environment [that] supplies the primary explanatory framework for the coming of age of humankind (and—as a corollary of this—its religiouslessness)."[51] De Lange therefore does not see Dilthey having a direct influence on Bonhoeffer's thought. Instead, he draws a connection between Bonhoeffer's work in prison and the views on technology put forward by Dutch novelist Harry Mulisch, who summarizes his own understanding of technology in the following dictum: "God is dead and technology is his corpse."[52] As De Lange comments, "[o]ne can say that Bonhoeffer moves away from Dilthey—who hardly speaks about technology at all—and ends up close to Harry Mulisch."[53]

Another important parallel, or comparison, can be drawn between Bonhoeffer's thoughts on technology and those of Jacques Ellul (1912 to

46. Spengler, *Der Untergang des Abendlandes.*

47. Huizinga, *In de schaduwen van morgen.*

48. Ortega y Gasset, *La rebelión de las masas.*

49. Dilthey, *Weltanschauung und Analyse des Menschen.* Bonhoeffer also read Weizsäcker, *Zum Weltbild der Physik.* On this influence, see Holder, "Science and Religion in Bonhoeffer," 115–32.

50. De Lange, "'The Spiritual Force Is Lacking.'"

51. Ibid.

52. Ibid. De Lange refers in particular to Mulisch, *Voer voor psychologen*, 130–40.

53. De Lange, "'The Spiritual Force is Lacking.'"

1994), who was roughly Bonhoeffer's contemporary. Reflection on technology forms an important component of Ellul's work.[54] The similarity between the two on the theme of technology has been noted by Treier, who writes: "Ellul is worth mentioning because he was able to pursue concerns over the technological spirit far more thoroughly than Bonhoeffer while being intriguingly similar: a dialectical thinker, influenced by Kierkegaard and Barth; an opponent of 'metaphysics' and 'religion'; and an author of a large-scale ethics focused on freedom."[55] In particular, according to Treier, both writers assert the significance of Christ for Western culture, and both criticize the misuse of technology for teleological purposes. Because Ellul was able to develop a more sophisticated and detailed case for his views on technology and modernity, he was also able, on Treier's view, to see more clearly than Bonhoeffer that technology doesn't simply consist in the use of value-neutral objects towards a good end, but also in a broader, socio-cultural phenomenon. At the same time, Treier also insists that Bonhoeffer's thoughts on the subject remains distinctive, "for he does not lose the good and focus only on the bad. Ellul's acknowledgement of our using technology seems always and only to concede the inevitable. Rather than seeing human hubris as the tragic side of a more providentially blessed phenomenon, Ellul insists that technology is evil in an important, even fundamental sense."[56] For this reason, as Treier remarks, Ellul loses hold his dialectical point of view and ends up painting technology in excessively sombre, melancholy colors, thereby underestimating technology's positive potential.[57]

CRITICISM AND APPROPRIATION OF BONHOEFFER'S THOUGHTS ON HUMAN MASTERY AND TECHNOLOGY

Quite surprisingly, little attention has been given to Bonhoeffer's thinking on human mastery and technology. The only exception is Clifford Green, who criticizes Bonhoeffer's thoughts on human mastery over nature. He starts off positive, arguing that "[w]hile Bonhoeffer gives no explicit critique here of the ruthless and wanton exploitation of nature which has characterized the technology and capitalist economies of the modern industrial era, he alludes to this."[58] At the same time, Green also calls Bonhoeffer's criti-

---

54. Ellul wrote three major monographs on technology: Ellul, *La Technique, ou l'Enjeu du siècle*; ibid., *Le Système technician*, and ibid., *Le bluff technologique*.

55. Treier, "Modernity's Machine," 106.

56. Ibid., 108.

57. Ibid., 109.

58. Green, *Bonhoeffer*, 197.

cism of technology into question. In a footnote, he voices the suspicion that "[t]here could . . . be some romantic, anti-technical bias here which would need rethinking in light of the affirmation of reason, science and technology which emerges in the prison letters."[59] As has become clear, there is indeed an "anti-technical bias" in Bonhoeffer's work, although this changes in his later writings, as we saw. Green also wonders, "in the context of the present environmental crisis, whether the terms 'lord' and 'lordship' are the most suitable to interpret the 'dominion' of Genesis 1:26."[60] Although this criticism is somewhat anachronistic, it will nevertheless be addressed later on. In any case, what Green draws attention to is the fact that Bonhoeffer bars himself, in principle, from this criticism by distinguishing between "dominion" proper and "exploitative dominion."[61]

Apart from Green's criticism, and the interpretative essays on Bonhoeffer and technology from De Lange and Treier mentioned above, very little sustained reflection has been devoted to this aspect of Bonhoeffer's thought.[62] One rather peculiar result of this state of affairs is that the writers who do draw on his theology as a resource for their own theological reflection on technology often do so without directly referring to his thoughts on the matter. One case in point can be found in Brian Brock's recent book *Christian Ethics in a Technological Age*.[63] In describing Christ's "concrete claim" on human life today, he draws extensively on Bonhoeffer's theology, specifically from his *Ethics*.[64] Nowhere, however, does he specifically engage with Bonhoeffer's thinking on technology as such. The same goes for George Pattison's *Thinking about God in an Age of Technology*. While Pattison draws explicitly from Bonhoeffer in his description of the challenge of speaking about God in a modern world come of age,[65] he doesn't devote any attention to the specific implications that Bonhoeffer drew, from this historical process, for a theological assessment of technology.

The challenge of engaging with Bonhoeffer's thinking on human mastery and technology is thus still very much an open, unanswered one. In the second part of this chapter, I shall attempt to carry out just such an

---

59. Ibid., n30.

60. Ibid.

61. Green, *Bonhoeffer*, 197n30.

62. For another brief engagement with Bonhoeffer's thoughts on the issue, see Rasmussen, "Ethics of Responsible Action," 210–11.

63. Brock, *Christian Ethics in a Technological Age*.

64. See, in particular, ibid., 167–90.

65. Pattison, *Thinking About God*, 18–22.

engagement—albeit a modest one—by asking how Bonhoeffer's thinking on the matter could potentially contribute to environmental ethics.

Bonhoeffer's Imperative to be Loyal to the Earth

The second theme of this chapter (and the fourth and final dimension of Bonhoeffer's theological understanding of the relationship between human beings and the earth) concerns his insistence that Christians are to *love* the earth of which they are a part, and over which they are appointed as masters. This forms an important theme that can be found throughout Bonhoeffer's entire corpus, and it is particularly relevant for environmental ethics, as will become clear. This theme is closely related to a number of other themes in Bonhoeffer's theology. Yet this concept has a substance of its own, and thus, in order to establish the relation between the two, I would first like to trace its development in Bonhoeffer's thinking in the following section.

The Theme of Loyalty to the Earth in Bonhoeffer's Early Theology

The theme of loyalty appeared powerfully for the first time during Bonhoeffer's vicariate in Barcelona, a period during which he spoke, on many occasions, concerning the "earthiness" of the Christian faith. This is most clearly the case in his lectures on "Basic Questions of a Christian Ethic," which he delivered at the time.[66] As a guiding statement of these lectures, Bonhoeffer asserts that ethics is a matter of earth and blood—a point which he formulates into a sort of program from the very opening of the lectures: "Ethics is a matter of blood and a matter of history. It did not simply descend to earth from heaven. Rather, it is a child of the earth, and for that reason its face changes with history as well as with the renewal of blood, with the transition between generations."[67] The same assertion then returns towards the end of his lectures as well, where, in summarizing his argument, he notes: "Ethics is a matter of earth and blood, but also of God, who made them both."[68]

Sandwiched in between these statements is a passionate appeal for what could be called a sort of "earthly spirituality." In clearly Nietzschean fashion, Bonhoeffer urges his audience to show fidelity to the earth, which he presents as the only viable attitude for Christians to adopt: "It is only through the depths of the earth, only through the storms of a human

66. "Basic Questions of a Christian Ethic." DBWE 10:359–78.

67. DBWE 10:360.

68. DBWE 10:376.

conscience, that the window to eternity opens itself up to us."[69] In order to bolster his point, Bonhoeffer turns to the Greek myth of the half-giant Antaeus, the son of Poseidon and Gaia, who could not be defeated by anyone as long as he kept his feet planted on the earth. One day, however, during a fight, one of his adversaries (Heracles) managed to lift him from the earth. At that very moment, Antaeus lost his supernatural power, which had come to him through his contact with the earth, his mother.[70] The application that Bonhoeffer draws from this story is that the human being who leaves the earth and its tribulations at the same time loses the power that still upholds him or her in the world.[71] Bonhoeffer identifies the earth as our mother, just as God is our father, and "only those who remain true to the mother are placed by her into the father's arms. Earth and its distress—that is the Christian's Song of Songs."[72]

Later on during his time in Barcelona, Bonhoeffer returns to reconsider the same myth. In a sermon that he delivered on Rom 12:11c (translated by Bonhoeffer as "Serve the time"[73]), for instance, he emphasizes that all time is immediately present before God: "'Every moment is in direct relationship with God."[74] This leads him to urge his listeners truly to be who they are, here and now. Addressing himself specifically to children and teenagers, for instance, he urges the youth to fulfill the essence of the particular phase of their lives, for if they do so, they please God and their lives are, in a sense, saturated with eternity.[75] In other words, it is precisely in their being children of the earth that God loves human beings; they can only live out who they truly are when they stay true to their mother, earth, and when they live in solidarity with their brothers (or fellow human beings). It is at this point that Bonhoeffer recounts the myth of Antaeus, stressing again its rich significance for proper, Christian living.[76]

As the editors of DBWE 10 conclude, the theme of loyalty to the earth enters Bonhoeffer's theology with the introduction of the myth of Antaeus.

69. DBWE 10:377.

70. DBWE 10:377–78.

71. DBWE 10:377–78.

72. DBWE 10:378.

73. This is clearly a faulty translation of the Greek.

74. DBWE 10:528. This is a reference to Ranke, *Über die Epochen der neueren Geschichte*, 17. (This reference is pointed out by the editors. See DBWE 10:528, editorial footnote 7.)

75. In his own words: "[T]hen God will be pleased with you and you will have penetrated from time to eternity." DBWE 10:530.

76. DBWE 10:531.

From this point forward, the myth is there to stay: "The symbol of Antaeus will accompany Bonhoeffer even into his very last conversations concerning the ethics of this-worldly responsibility."[77] At the same time, some have observed that Bonhoeffer didn't fully integrate the myth into the rest of his theology at this point in time.[78] This latter point links up with the more general observation that, during Bonhoeffer's time in Barcelona, his theology was not yet fully integrated. On the contrary, one can detect the presence of contrasting themes that have yet to be resolved. With regards to the theme under consideration, it can be shown that, while on several occasions (such as the ones mentioned above), Bonhoeffer's conception of the world is decidedly positive in nature—thereby leading him to urge his public to remain loyal to the earth—on other occasions, his conception takes on a much more negative tone.[79] In spite of this lack of integration, it remains the case that, in Barcelona, the theme of loyalty to the earth was first introduced into Bonhoeffer's work.[80]

The Theme of Loyalty to the Earth in the Lecture "Thy Kingdom Come!"

An important development in Bonhoeffer's thought on loving and remaining faithful to the earth can be observed in a lecture that he delivered in Berlin on November 19, 1933, entitled "Thy Kingdom Come! The Prayer of the Church-Community for God's Kingdom on Earth."[81] Indeed, this lecture could be seen as a highpoint insofar as the theme under consideration is concerned.[82] As the title itself indicates, the theme of the lecture centers

77. DBWE 10:628.

78. As Feil notes, for instance, "The picture of Antaeus, the giant, remains pagan; it has the appearance of Titanism and is open in its form here to an interpretation much more in the sense of Albert Camus's *The Myth of Sisyphus* than in the form of Christian faith." Feil, *The Theology of Dietrich Bonhoeffer*, 113; italics original.

79. This shows itself, for example, in a sermon that Bonhoeffer delivered in August of 1928, on 1 John 2:17. DBWE 10:516–21.

80. This runs directly against the assertion of Terrence Reynolds, who, in his treatment of faithfulness to the earth in Bonhoeffer's prison writings, argues that "[t]his somewhat surprising defense of earthly affection or human love in relative independence from Christ, [is] absent from all of Bonhoeffer's work before 1939 and yet predominant in his work in prison." Reynolds, "Dietrich Bonhoeffer's Encouragement of Human Love," 55.

81. DBWE 12:285–97.

82. Feil entitles the section in which he treats this lecture: "Bonhoeffer's 1932 Discussion of the World: First Summit," in ibid., *The Theology of Dietrich Bonhoeffer*, 114.

on the character of the Kingdom of God. Bonhoeffer opens by stating that Christians choose either to be otherworldly or secularists, in which case their faith in the Kingdom of God loses its substance. He first addresses Christian otherworldliness, however, characterizing it as a desire for something better than the earth. Bonhoeffer claims that this attitude first presented itself as an option when human beings discovered the "trick" to being religious, even "Christian," at the expense of the earth. Otherworldliness constitutes, for Bonhoeffer, a form of despising the earth, and a church that is otherworldly in this sense of the term can be sure to attract all kinds of weak, foolish, and idealistic people, whom Bonhoeffer refers to as "disloyal children of the Earth."[83] While he recognizes that the weak do indeed need help, which is offered by Christ, he nevertheless insists that Christ does not help people by comforting them, but by making them strong: "Christ does not lead him into the otherworldliness of religious escapism. Rather, Christ returns him to the Earth as its true son."[84]

From here, Bonhoeffer goes on to address the other failure that he sees in the way Christians relate to belief in the Kingdom of God, namely, secularism. To begin, he clarifies his point by indicating just what he understands by *Christian* secularism—a turn of phrase which is likely to appear somewhat contradictory at first sight. On his view, in Christian secularism, the character of the Kingdom of God as being "not yet" is lost, and the church transforms into nothing more than an instrument for religious-moral action. A church that is characterized by this form of secularism does not attract weak people, as Bonhoeffer says, but strong people, that is, faithful sons of the earth. The problem is that, in this case, the church loses sight of God, who is henceforth seen as pleading his own case, as electing people out of his own free will, and as having no need for human beings to help him—God thus becomes one who "intends to be Lord on Earth."[85] With this, Bonhoeffer concludes that otherworldliness and secularism are in fact two sides of the same coin, or more precisely, of the same lack of belief in God's heavenly Kingdom.[86] Whoever tries to flee the world does not find God, but only his or her own dream of a better world. And the same goes for the person who tries to change and refashion the earth without God.

Bonhoeffer tries to navigate between these two, disappointing alternatives, by arguing—as he did in *CF* (for which, see chapter 3)—that human

83. DBWE 12:266.
84. DBWE 12:286.
85. DBWE 12:288.
86. DBWE 12:288.

beings live on an earth that is both blessed and cursed by God.[87] To deal with the complexity implied in this multidimensional conception of earth, Bonhoeffer refers—again, as in *CF*—to Christ: "Christ has entered into this cursed Earth; the flesh Christ bore was taken from this ground. On this ground the tree of the curse stood, and this . . . establishes the kingdom of Christ as God's kingdom on this cursed ground. This is why the kingdom of Christ is a kingdom that has been lowered into the cursed ground from above."[88] The curse that rests on the earth is not made manifest in the thorns and thistles that it brings forth, as Bonhoeffer says, but in the way that it veils God's face from us. This doesn't give us an excuse to flee the earth, however. On the contrary, one cannot properly pray for the coming of the Kingdom of God when one does not first step into the reality of the sorrow that one and others experience.[89] As Bonhoeffer says: "The hour in which we pray today for God's kingdom is the hour of the most profound solidarity with the world."[90]

Later on in his lecture, Bonhoeffer also brings the theme of Christ's resurrection into the discussion. In the resurrection, as he says, the curse that God laid on nature is broken and the Kingdom of God breaks through on the earth. *This* event, he continues, is the reason why we ought to love the earth and be faithful to it. In other words, it is only because God broke the curse on the earth that can we are able to take it seriously, or to love it. This doesn't mean that the earth is completely freed from the curse, however, for until the completion of Christ's (second) coming in the last days, the world

---

87. DBWE 12:288.

88. DBWE 12:288–89. In this citation, Bonhoeffer does not strictly differentiate between Christ's incarnation and his crucifixion—on the contrary, both events are mentioned together in the same sentence. His account of Christ's threefold relationship to nature (incarnation, crucifixion, and resurrection) as developed in his *Ethics* (see chapter 2) helps to clarify this ambiguity.

89. Bonhoeffer switches here from the curse that rests on the earth to the reality of sorrow among human beings. Presumably, Bonhoeffer implies that human beings suffer through the Fall of nature and their suffering matters primarily (though on basis of his thoughts on Christ as the Redeemer of nature one would say: not exclusively) and asks for our care.

90. DBWE 12:289. In this context, Bonhoeffer also quotes—yet again—Sir 40:1, which speaks about the earth as the mother of us all. As we saw in chapter 4, Bonhoeffer also drew from this text in *CF*. There is a crucial difference in context, however, for in *CF*, he uses the quotation to stress the fundamental bodily nature of human beings, whereas in the present lecture, he stresses the imperative for human beings to love the earth.

stands under a twofold sign: under the sign of the curse, on the one hand, and under the sign of the Kingdom of the Resurrection, on the other.[91]

This lecture figures as a highpoint in Bonhoeffer's thinking on loving the earth and, as such, it merits a more detailed, extensive examination. When one compares the lecture with the earlier writings from Barcelona, what one sees, first and foremost, is Bonhoeffer's continued stress on the importance of loyalty to the earth. By introducing his dialectic of "this-worldliness" versus "otherworldliness," he even strengthens his case for this loyalty.[92] Unlike the Barcelona lectures, the case that Bonhoeffer's later lecture presents for fidelity to the earth is more solidly integrated with other elements of his theology. Feil notes in particular how the present world comes ever more clearly into focus.[93] As one case in point in this regard, consider the relation that Bonhoeffer draws between the world and the cross of Christ. Earlier on, we saw how, in the Barcelona lectures, he formulated the event of the crucifixion in individualistic terms—if anything, it wasn't (yet) fully and truly related to the world at all. This changes, as we see, in the Berlin address. As Feil notes, "Bonhoeffer . . . saw this kingdom of God as having been really sunk down into the cursed ground. Even though it is eschatologically hidden, God's kingdom, being Christ's kingdom, is truly in the world, and not somehow above it."[94] At the same time, Feil also notes how, in "'Thy Kingdom Come!,'" the resurrection figures prominently, whereas it was lacking in the Barcelona lecutres.

91. In the remainder of the lecture, Bonhoeffer works out two different forms in which this—at present only partially visible—kingdom of the resurrection manifests itself in the world, namely, in the body of the church, and the institution of the state. In both of these forms, as he argues, the kingdom of God is present "among us," that is, in the midst of our earthbound lives. From here, he then concludes the lecture by making reference to the new heaven and earth to come, insisting that it is well and truly a new *earth* that God will make—see DBWE 12:295. It does not become clear how Bonhoeffer did perceive of the new earth—whether he believed in a renewal of this present earth, or in the creation of an entirely new earth. This lack of clarity is also noted by Burkholder, who nevertheless believes that Bonhoeffer would choose the first option. See Burkholder, "Christological Foundations," 349.

92. See Moltmann, "Theologie mit Dietrich Bonhoeffer," 21.

93. As he says: "The issue for Bonhoeffer . . . was no longer the departing of the world but the coming of God's kingdom to the earth." Feil, *The Theology of Dietrich Bonhoeffer*, 114.

94. Feil, *The Theology of Dietrich Bonhoeffer*, 119. Feil also notes the difference between this understanding of God's kingdom and that of Karl Barth, where, as we saw in chapter 3, the earth remains "external" as "External Basis of the Covenant." *CD* 3/1:94–228.

THE RETREAT OF THE THEME OF THIS-WORLDLINESS IN
BONHOEFFER'S MIDDLE PERIOD

Following the "'Thy Kingdom Come!'" lecture, the theme of this-worldliness, as well as the plea for loyalty to the earth, retreats into the background
of Bonhoeffer's work. Feil notes that, as early as *CF*, it no longer figures as an
important theme. This is indeed the case—although Bonhoeffer intensely
engages with nature in these lectures, he doesn't draw many consequences
out concerning the subsequent attitude that humans should adopt with regard to nature.

The theme of worldliness retreats even further in *Discipleship*, where
Bonhoeffer posits an almost complete separation between Christians and
the world. Feil brings this point out quite clearly in the title that he affixes
to his discussion of the theme of the world in Bonhoeffer's work during this
period, namely, "The Detached View of the World of the Middle Period."[95]
As he observes, "It seems that the negative thread of the understanding of
the world which Bonhoeffer had developed in Barcelona was being taken up
again, a thread which existed without relation to a positive one."[96]

In spite of this gradual retreat of the theme of worldliness, it is important to point out that Bonhoeffer never recounted it, even when he came
under considerable pressure to do so. During the dangerous period of time
in which he worked as director of the training of illegal seminarians, for
instance, he composed an (unfinished) meditation on Ps 119. Concerning
Ps 119:19 ("I am a stranger in the earth: hide not thy commandments from
me." [KJV]) he writes: "I am a guest on earth—with this I confess that I
cannot remain here, that my time here is short. Neither am I entitled to
possessions and a house here."[97] A passage such as this would admittedly
seem to point in the direction of an otherworldliness, but Bonhoeffer
doesn't bring his meditation on the verse to a close with this thought alone.
On the contrary, he continues by recognizing the fact that the earth feeds
him and that it has a right to his work and strength.[98] Similarly, Bonhoeffer recognizes the temptation of an ungodly homesickness ("Heimweh") for
another world, which he sharply condemns. Though being a guest on earth,

95. Feil, "The Detached View of the World of the Middle Period," in ibid., *The
Theology of Dietrich Bonhoeffer*, 125–38.

96. Ibid., 137.

97. DBWE 15:522.

98. He says: "It is not my prerogative to despise the earth that sustains my life.
I owe it faithfulness and thanksgiving. I may not evade my destiny to be a guest and
a stranger, and thereby God's call into this sojourner status, by dreaming away my
earthly life with thoughts about heaven." DBWE 15:522.

to borrow from the language of Ps 119:19, would seem to imply a sense of not really belonging there, or of being lost in foreign territory, what it means for Bonhoeffer, in contrast, is that human beings are to partake of the work, the suffering and the joys of the earth. It thus does not mean that humans are to dream away their lives in waiting for God's promise to be fulfilled. The object of God's promise—which Bonhoeffer also identifies as "homeland" ("Heimat")[99]—, is not specified in this verse, as Bonhoeffer notes. He does observe, however, that we know that it can't refer to the earth. In this instance, then, the negative conception of the world as temporal and fleeting still continues to dominates. At the same time, the way in which Bonhoeffer qualifies human life on the earth still retains some of his earlier appeal for genuine this-worldliness.[100]

While loyalty to and love for the earth are not explicit themes in *Ethics*, the theme of the world undergoes significant developments in these manuscripts. Concepts such as Christ-reality, Christ's threefold relationship to the world and the distinction between the ultimate and the penultimate all form part of a theology seeking to embrace the whole of reality. More directly related to the theme presently under investigation is the pathway that Bonhoeffer traced, in the manuscript "Natural Life," between mechanism and vitalism. There, he makes the argument that life is always *formed* in some sense or another.[101] Vitalism negates this idea, as he says, for it always presents life as an end in itself, which, as a consequence, destroys itself.[102] Life is thus an abyss, a movement without an end or a goal; as absolute, it collapses in on itself. This isn't to neglect the fact that a kernel of truth hides tucked away in the view of life as an end in itself. As Bonhoeffer observes, "It arises from the false absolutizing of an insight that is essentially correct, that

99. DBWE 15:522.

100. As Feil comments: "The reference to a homesickness for the other world that is quite godless relates this text very profoundly to Bonhoeffer's consistent warnings against a false eschatology, which is expressed in a particularly clear fashion in the prison letters." Feil, *The Theology of Dietrich Bonhoeffer*, 140.

101. See esp. DBWE 6:178–81.

102. He says: "Life that makes itself absolute, that makes itself its own goal, destroys itself. Vitalism ends inevitably in nihilism, in the destruction of all that is natural." DBWE 6:178. Bonhoeffer formulates this point in a different way in the manuscript "Heritage and Decay." In the latter instance, he warns against a divinization of human beings, the roots of which he sees in Luther's discovery of the freedom of the Christian individual and the Catholic doctrine of the essential goodness of humans. Together, on his view, these doctrines end up divinizing humanity, which he firmly opposes: "But deifying humanity is, properly understood, the proclamation of nihilism . . . An unbridled vitalism arises, absorbing all values into itself and only finding peace in self-destruction, in nothingness [Nichts]." DBWE 6:123–24.

life, both individual and communal, is not only a means to an end but also an end in itself."[103] In this way, we see Bonhoeffer taking a certain distance from a mechanistic view of life—while he criticises certain aspects of vitalism, he nevertheless recognizes the necessity of seeing life, at least in part, as an end in itself.

The Flourishing of the Theme of Love for the Earth in Bonhoeffer's Prison Writings

The theme of love for the earth returns in force in Bonhoeffer's prison writings—indeed, it figures as a recurring topic of discussion in the many letters and papers that he wrote, particularly to his friend, Eberhard Bethge, and to his fiancée, Maria von Wedemeyer. The reason for Bonhoeffer's persistent return to this theme is at least partly biographical in nature. In the period of time during which he awaited his trial, for instance, we find a letter in which he writes to Bethge about the difficulties he had been encountering in his attempts to cope with being locked up—especially when waking up in the morning. In particular, he writes about how he often prayed to be free again. He then juxtaposes his unrest and desire for freedom with what he calls "a false serenity that is not at all Christian."[104] From here, he goes on to say: "We need feel no shame as Christians about a measure of impatience, longing, protest against what is unnatural, and a strong measure of desire for freedom and earthly happiness and the capacity to effect change."[105] Instead of retreating inwardly into a passive acceptance of his imprisonment, we see how Bonhoeffer's outlook was one of bold, daily resistance ("Widerstand"[106])—in recognition of the importance of his earthly life, he manifested a resilient will to fight. A few lines further on in the letter to Bethge, Bonhoeffer explicitly criticizes the flight inwards in the following terms: "I hope you don't think that I will emerge from here as a man of the "inner line," now much less than ever! And in the same way I believe this of you."[107] Bonhoeffer rejects this attitude outright; indeed, his focus is on the present situation, the "here and now."

103. DBWE 6:178.

104. DBWE 8:184.

105. DBWE 8:184.

106. I draw this term from the title of the earlier, influential publication of Bonhoeffer's prison letters, see Bonhoeffer, *Widerstand und Ergebung*.

107. DBWE 8:184. As the editors of DBWE 8 note, the term "innere Linie" was used widely in the Bekennende Kirche as the designation of a group of believers who thought that the church should focus on its own spiritual life, and who viewed the

It appears, then, that this affirmation of earthly, natural life formed a decisive part of the personal attitude through which Bonhoeffer coped with the experiences of prison life. He also reflected on it theologically, however, as many of his letters, which have since become quite famous, bear out. One of the most poignant of these is a letter that he wrote to Bethge on July 21, 1944, just one day after the failed attempt to carry out a military coup.[108] In the letter, Bonhoeffer describes to his friend how, in the previous few years, he increasingly discovered "the profound this-worldliness of Christianity."[109] The Christian faith, as he says, is not about being a *homo religiosus*, but about being a real human being in the way that Jesus Christ was a real human being. Further on in his letter, Bonhoeffer narrates how, while traveling in the US thirteen years earlier, he had a conversation with a young French pastor.[110] While discussing what they wanted to do with their lives, the pastor said that he desired to become a saint. Concerning this comment, Bonhoeffer writes: "This impressed me very much at the time. Nevertheless, I disagreed with him, saying something like: I want to learn to have faith."[111] He then goes on to say, however, that for a long time he had thought that he could learn to have faith by attempting to live a holy life. He identifies his work in *Discipleship* as the end of this particular road. At the same time, he also says that, later on, he had learned "that one only learns to have faith by living in the full this-worldliness of life."[112] Only when one ceases to try to make something of oneself—be it a saint, or simply a just and pious person—and truly lives a "this-worldly" life, taking seriously all its tasks, questions, experiences and challenges, does one become a Christian: "[T]hen one takes seriously no longer one's own sufferings but rather the suffering of God in the world. Then one stays awake with Christ in Gethsemane. And I think this is faith; this is μετάνοια. And this is how one becomes a human being, a Christian. (Cf. Jer. 45!)."[113] This "earthly dimension" also figures as

---

world in starkly apocalyptic terms. See DBWE 8:184, editorial footnote 32. The editors also note the linguistic proximity between the movement's name and the strategy of the "inner emigration," which was a term used to describe the path often taken by German intellectuals during the years of the Nazi regime.

108. DBWE 8:485–87.

109. DBWE 8:485.

110. The French pastor in question is Jean Lasserre, with whom Bonhoeffer traveled on a cross-country trip through the US during his postdoctoral year at Union Seminary.

111. DBWE 8:486.

112. DBWE 8:486.

113. DBWE 8:486.

a central theme in many of the other letters that Bonhoeffer wrote during his time in prison.[114]

In Bonhoeffer's renewed focus on the theme of this-worldliness, he revisits and redefines a number of his earlier concepts, such as his distinction between the ultimate and the penultimate.[115] Apart from familiair concepts such as these, Bonhoeffer also introduces new concepts, and it is on those that I will specifically focus here. Particularly two concepts are important: 1) Bonhoeffer's stress on the importance of the Old Testament; and 2) his twin concepts of *cantus firmus* and counterpoint ("Kontrapunkt") as manifestations of the "polyphony of life."

First of all, a new element that appears in the prison letters concerns the emphasis that Bonhoeffer places on the importance of the Old Testament. On November 18, 1943, for instance, he wrote to Bethge that, during his time in prison, he had read through the Old Testament two-and-a-half times.[116] This reading (and re-reading) undoubtedly had an influence on what he wrote two weeks later, in a letter to Bethge, dated December 5, 1943. In this instance, he informs Bethge that his thinking and feeling has become "in line with the Old Testament."[117] He comments on this as follows: "Only when one knows that the name of God may not be uttered may one sometimes speak the name of Jesus Christ. Only when one loves life and the earth so much that with it everything seems to be lost and at its end may one believe in the resurrection of the dead and a new world."[118] In this context he warns against taking a shortcut to the New Testament: "Whoever wishes to be and perceive things too quickly and too directly in New Testament ways is to my mind no Christian."[119]

114. Another famous example can be found in the wedding sermon that he wrote for his friend Bethge. See DBWE 8:82–87.

115. See, for example, DBWE 8:213.

116. DBWE 8:181.

117. DBWE 8:213.

118. DBWE 8:213.

119. DBWE 8:213. Also in other letters Bonhoeffer emphasizes the distinctive "earthiness" of the Old Testament, thereby criticizing both metaphysical and individualist theologies. In a letter he wrote to Bethge, dated May 5, 1944, for example, he makes the point that the biblical message does not have to do with some sort of elusive, heavenly otherworldliness, but with *the present* world. See DBWE 8:371–74. And in a letter written on June 27, 1944, also to Bethge, he argues that, in contrast with oriental religions, the text of the Old Testament does *not* give body to a religion of redemption ("Erlösungsreligion"). In particular, he insists that it is a huge mistake to divorce Christ from the Old Testament and to interpret the gospel narrative in the context of Eastern religions of redemption. The difference between these religions and the Old Testament, according to him, is that the Old Testament views redemption historically.

The importance of the Old Testament for Bonhoeffer in prison has been noted by a number of scholars, who offer clues that can contribute to the understanding of this change of emphasis. Wendel, for example, points out that despite the strength by which it appears, it would nevertheless be incorrect to see Bonhoeffer's turn to the Old Testament as an entirely new development in his thinking.[120] At the same time, Wendel also notes certain discontinuities between Bonhoeffer's earlier work and his prison writings. In total, he lists four such discontinuities, the most important one, at least as far as our present discussion is concerned, being the fact that, in Bonhoeffer's writings from prison, he abandoned his earlier christological interpretation of the Old Testament.[121]

The second new element in Bonhoeffer's work on "this-worldliness" in his prison writings is found in the twin concepts of *cantus firmus* and counterpoint, both of which are introduced in a letter dated May 20, 1944. In this letter, Bonhoeffer addresses a tension which he senses in his friend Bethge, namely, a tension between celebrating faithfulness to the earth and loving God and his Kingdom. Bonhoeffer understands, or is able to appreciate, this tension, and points to the danger of losing hold what he calls the "polyphony of life".[122] As he explains, "What I mean is that God, the Eternal, wants to be loved with our whole heart, not to the detriment of earthly love or to diminish it, but as a sort of cantus firmus to which the other voices of life resound in counterpoint."[123] Bonhoeffer here is clearly introducing a musical metaphor, namely the counterpoint, which stands in relation to the *cantus firmus*.[124] While the *cantus firmus* is understood as faith in God and his Kingdom, the counterpoint is always related to this *cantus firmus*. One counterpoint, Bonhoeffer claims, is the theme of faithfulness to the earth, as the Bible itself already indicates: "Even in the Bible there is the Song of Solomon, and you really can't imagine a hotter, more sensual, and glowing love than the one spoken of here (cf. 7:6!). It's really good that this is in the Bible,

---

The religions of redemption, in contrast, are decidedly unhistorical in nature insofar as they are concerned exclusively with eternity and the afterlife. See DBWE 8:447.

120. Wendel, *Studien zur Homiletik*, 102–9.

121. Ibid., 104. This has also been noted by Moltmann, "Theologie mit Dietrich Bonhoeffer," 21. For more commentary on Bonhoeffer's emphasis on the Old Testament, see Mayer, *Christuswirklichkeit*, 249–50.

122. DBWE 8:393–94.

123. DBWE 8:394.

124. The Latin phrase *cantus firmus* and the German word "Kontrapunkt" are both musical terms. *Cantus firmus*, literally "fixed song," refers to the melody that forms the basis of a composition. "Kontrapunkt" comes from the Latin *punctus contra punctum* and describes, in musical theory, the counter voice, based on the *cantus firmus*.

contradicting all those who think being Christian is about tempering one's passions (where is there any such tempering in the Old Testament?)."[125] As long as the *cantus firmus* is clear, the counterpoint can be developed as fully as possible, Bonhoeffer argues. He refers in particular to the Chalcedonian formula and the way in which it articulates the relation between Christ's divine and human natures, just as in the musical polyphony, the *cantus firmus* and counterpoint harmonize with (or against) each other. This he sees as an apt metaphor for the Christian life, which brings him to advise Bethge in the following terms: "I wanted to ask you to let the cantus firmus be heard clearly in your being together; only then will it sound complete and full, and the counterpoint will always know that it is being carried and can't get out of tune or be cut adrift, while remaining itself and complete in itself."[126]

In letters such as these, we see how Bonhoeffer's thoughts on "this-worldliness" are far from being purely and simply theoretical in nature—on the contrary, they take the form of Christian counsel offered in private to his best friend. Bonhoeffer's prison letters are not limited to letters of advice, moreover, for he also wrote many love letters to Maria von Wedemeyer, his fiancé. In this case too, the "this-worldliness" of the Christian faith figures as an important theme. In a letter dated August 12, 1943, for instance, he writes about the hardship that has befallen them both, as well as their relationship, due to his imprisonment. He sees these circumstances in a positive light, however—namely, as a clear sign of God's grace, for it calls them both to persevere in their faith. Concerning this faith, he has this to say: "[M]ay God grant it to us daily. I don't mean the faith which flees the world, but the faith that endures in the world and loves and remains true to that world in spite of all the hardships it brings us."[127] Here we find Bonhoeffer's plea to love the earth, which he first voiced in Barcelona, reiterated, only this time it has lost any possible trace of naiveté. On the contrary, by this point in time, it had clearly come to form an integral part of Bonhoeffer's outlook on life, as well as of his vision of the future with Maria as his prospective wife, as the lines following the previous quotation make clear: "Our marriage must be a 'yes' to God's earth. It must strengthen our resolve to do and accomplish something on earth."[128] In this affirmation of God's earth, Bonhoeffer sees the true way of the Christian. As he concludes: "I fear that Christians who

---

125. DBWE 8:394.

126. DBWE 8:394.

127. Bonhoeffer and Von Wedemeyer, *Love Letters from Cell 92*, 64.

128. Ibid.

venture to stand on earth on only one leg will stand in heaven on only one leg too."[129]

These lines, in and of themselves, form a fitting conclusion of our presentation of the theme of love for the earth in Bonhoeffer's writings. Our overview of the development of the theme throughout the course of Bonhoeffer's theological career is perhaps best summed up by Rasmussen's conclusion that "both the younger and older Bonhoeffer profess an indefatigable love and embrace of earth, its distress included."[130]

Background and Influences

Though the pure and simple presence of the theme of love and faithfulness to the earth can be firmly established in Bonhoeffer's work and personal writings, it is much more difficult to account for the philosophical and theological background underpinning it as a theme.

The most direct influence is that of the philosophy of life. When Bonhoeffer took up residence in Barcelona in the 1920s, this new philosophy had taken hold of the German elite. As De Lange observes, "the German intelligentsia had . . . exchanged its nineteenth-century idealism for a philosophy of life, a hymn on the irrationality of the lived life, which proceeds and transcends reflection."[131] This attitude, which was exemplified in Nietzsche's "Übermensch," influenced Bonhoeffer's description of Christian life during his time in Barcelona, as De Lange says. Other scholars of Bonhoeffer also agree.[132]

Apart from this more general influence of the philosophy of life, a more direct influence can be found in Bonhoeffer's own reading of Nietzsche. As Feil notes, Bonhoeffer had read Nietzsche in his youth, which directly influenced the course of his thinking in Barcelona.[133] As we saw earlier on in our discussion of the lectures on Christian ethics, Bonhoeffer urged his public to remain loyal to their "mother," earth.[134] This, incidentally, is a paraphrase of Nietzsche's famous dictum in *Thus Spoke Zarathustra*: "I conjure you, my brothers: *remain true to the earth* and don't believe those who speak to you of superterrestrial hopes! They are poisoners, whether they know it

129. Ibid.

130. Rasmussen, "Song of Songs," 298.

131. De Lange, "Aristocratic Christendom," 77.

132. See, for example, Moltmann, "Theologie mit Dietrich Bonhoeffer," 23.

133. Feil, *The Theology of Dietrich Bonhoeffer*, 113. Nietzsche's influence on Bonhoeffer is not limited to this period only; it is, in fact, discernable in his entire oeuvre.

134. DBWE 10:378.

or not."[135] It is thus clear that Bonhoeffer strove to appropriate Nietzsche's thought into his own theological understanding of the relationship between human beings and the earth.[136]

Apart from the influence of the philosophy of life and of Nietzsche, it is difficult to take stock of other influences at work in Bonhoeffer's thinking on worldliness and fidelity to the earth. Instead of searching for further sources of influence, it would be much more accurate to see the gradual development of this theme as the result of his own thought, or more specifically, as the result of his enduring quest to answer the question "who is Christ actually for us today?"[137] Bonhoeffer became increasingly aware that, in order to discover who Christ is, one needs much more than prayer and thought—indeed, the quest engages the whole of a human life. As such, a genuine Christian life is a life lived in unreserved fidelity to this very earth on which Christ lived, for which he died, and from which he was raised again.

Moltmann makes the case that a theological parallel to Bonhoeffer's thoughts on the theme of love and fidelity to the earth can be found in the work of Christoph Blumhardt. Noting the striking parallel between Bonhoeffer and Blumhardt, Moltmann calls the two "bothers in the same spirit."[138] The only difference, as he notes, is one of context: "Whereas Christoph Blumhardt spoke out against the neo-pietistic individualist interpretation of salvation, Bonhoeffer protested against the liberal distortion of Christianity into a gnostic 'religion of redemption.'"[139] Whereas the theme of loving the earth has, quite naturally, permeated Christian theology from its very beginnings,[140] there is undoubtedly a great deal of truth to Moltmann's statement that, in the modern, Western context, Bonhoeffer and Blumhardt offer the most radical appeals for this love for the earth.

135. Nietzsche, *Thus Spoke Zarathustra*, 30; italics original.

136. The most thorough treatment of the relationship between Bonhoeffer and Nietzsche to date is offered by Capozza, *Im Namen der Treue zur Erde*.

137. DBWE 8:362.

138. "Brüder im gleichen Geist." Moltmann, "Theologie mit Dietrich Bonhoeffer," 22.

139. Moltmann, *Ethics of Hope*, 119.

140. See Schaefer, *Theological Foundations*, 255–66.

The Ecological Relevance of Human Mastery over Nature and Loyalty to the Earth

In this second part of the chapter I shall apply the two themes investigated above—namely, Bonhoeffer's assertion of human mastery over nature and his appeal for loyalty to the earth—to environmental ethics, seeking to determine what sort of contribution they could make to the discussion. I will begin by addressing the theme of mastery, and then shift over to the theme of loyalty.

The Relevance of Bonhoeffer's Thoughts on Human Mastery over Nature

In this section I shall assess the ways in which Bonhoeffer's thoughts on technology and human mastery over nature can be brought to bear on environmental ethics. In total, I see at least two possible contributions that he can make.

BONHOEFFER'S CONTRIBUTION TOWARDS RETAINING THE RELEVANCE OF THE DOMINIUM TERRAE

Firstly, Bonhoeffer's work on human mastery over nature can help to restore credibility to—not to mention a proper understanding of—the biblical understanding of the *dominium terrae*. By and large, the idea of human mastery over nature has come under sharp criticism, especially in light of the ecological crisis—indeed, environmental ethicists almost universally reject it, together with anthropocentrism, with which it is closely linked.[141] As scholars frequently argue, the Judeo-Christian tradition bears a significant part of the responsibility for bringing about the ecological crisis. This, at the very least, is the argument put forward by White in his famous article "The Historical Roots of our Ecologic Crisis." As White alledges, the exploitative relationship between human beings and nature is intrinsically connected with the Judeo-Christian heritage. By overcoming animism, nature as a whole underwent what White refers to as a process of thoroughgoing disenchantment, which, in turn, eroded many of the inhabitations that had held people back from seeking to gain control and mastery over nature: "By destroying pagan animism, Christianity made it possible to exploit nature

---

141. See Jason Brennan, who argues, rather succinctly, that "[s]omething is wrong with the desire to dominate nature." Brennan, "Dominating Nature," 514.

in a mood of indifference to the feelings of natural objects."[142] In spite of the fact that White recognizes the danger of formulating broad generalizations of this sort, he undoubtedly oversimplifies matters in making this claim—indeed, numerous studies which have been written since, often (at least in part) in reaction to his highly influential article, have given voice to this very criticism. Although these critical studies address the issue from a wide variety of perspectives, the majority of them identify *modernity*—not Christianity—as having paved the way for nature's ruthless exploitation, as well as the resultant ecological crisis.[143]

The majority of theologians accept critical theses such as White's. In turn, they often respond by reinterpreting the relevant biblical texts in a supposedly ecological-friendly way. As Conradie observes, "[m]ost ecological reinterpretations of Genesis 1:28 attempt to move away from an understanding of dominion as domination. Instead, the meaning of dominion is interpreted in terms of the metaphor of stewardship."[144] An example of such a reinterpretation is offered by Walter Brueggemann, who interprets dominion through the metaphor of a caring shepherd who guides and protects his flock.[145] Many other such examples could be listed as well, but for our present purposes, we have no need of a detailed analysis of them.[146]

142. White, "The Historical Roots of our Ecologic Crisis," 1205.

143. This point has already been noted by Nullens, "Leven volgens Gaia's Normen?," 209–48. Nullens lays the blame on the shoulders of the Enlightenment, which he qualifies as utopian, arrogant and Pelagian. A similar, more fully developed case has been made by Rappel, *"Macht euch die Erde untertan."* For a more concise statement of the point, see Bryant, "The Modern Myth of Mastery and the Christian Doctrine of Creation," 56–68. Together, these authors are right to criticize White and others for overstating their case when they argue that Christianity has been the most important—or even sole—factor responsible for fostering an exploitative mindset with regards to nature. At the same time, it is undoubtedly true that Christianity—Protestant Christianity in particular—has helped bring about the modern mindset. As we saw earlier in chapter 5, Bonhoeffer himself recognized this. A brief—though comprehensive and nuanced—view on the factors responsible for shaping Europe's mindset of ruthless dominaton has been put forth by Pattberg, "Conquest, Domination and Control," 1–9. According to Pattberg, the "ideology of domination and control[,]" which first took shape in Europe between 1450 and 1750, is composed of four core elements: "[F]irst, the emerging early modern state; second, the legacy of the Judaeo-Christian tradition; third, the Scientific Revolution of the 17th century; and finally the rise of early capitalism." Ibid., 5.

144. Conradie, *Christianity and Ecological Theology*, 77–81.

145. Brueggemann, *Genesis*, 32–33. Also mentioned in Conradie, *Christianity and Ecological Theology*, 78.

146. Boersema identifies Claus Westermann as the first scholar to propose, with a certain degree of caution, an ecofriendly reading of Gen 1:28. He refers to

There are two major problems with this reinterpretation that I would like to highlight in particular. First of all, it fails to do justice to the Genesis texts pertaining to the notion of the *dominium terrae*. A strong majority view exists among biblical scholars that maintains that the Hebrew verbs used to describe humanity's relationship with animals (and, by extension, nature as a whole) possess a "strong," or even violent connotation. Ruether, for example, writes that "we should acknowledge that the language used in the bestowal upon humans of dominion over the earth in Genesis 1 is one of dominating power and sovereignty. The words translated 'subdue' and 'have dominion' are those of militarist trampling down and subduing of a foe."[147] In a review of the broader scholarly discussion, Conradie arrives at the following conclusion: "Despite . . . attractive efforts to offer ecological reinterpretations of Genesis 1:27–8, the exegesis of this text remains deeply problematic. The Hebrew words *kabash* ('subdue') and *radah* ('have dominion') cannot be completely 'pacified.'"[148]

The second problem with the ecological reinterpretation of the *dominium terrae* is that it presupposes a particularly rosy, romantic and unproblematic view of nature. It is remarkably easy, especially for Westerners, whose most immediate environment is often kept at a significant distance from nature, either to forget or neglect nature's dangerous and horrific sides. For many people living in the developing world, in contrast, the violence and cruelty of nature is still very much a reality. Indeed, nature is very often quite cruel, harsh and inhospitable, and the language of caring, nurturing and stewardship fails to adequately reflect this. This is a point that, as we already saw in chapter 3, has been made by Lisa Sideris, who has evaluated the incorporation of biology into the work of ecotheologians. As we saw earlier with regards to Bonhoeffer's thoughts on Christ's threefold relationship to nature, nature is both beautiful and cruel, and the moments of the incarnation, the crucifixion, and the resurrection can help provide an adequate and nuanced paradigm through which Christians can understand these contrasting aspects of nature. Bonhoeffer's thoughts on humanity's calling to master nature can help to further specify how this paradigm can be applied.

Before exploring this contribution, however, I would first like to engage with the one and—up until now—only attempt to transpose Bonhoeffer's

---

Westermann, *Genesis 1–11*, 219–20. See Boersema, *Thora en Stoa over mens en natuur*, 70n64. Boersema also makes mention of other exegetes who propose similar readings. A recent example is Wöhrle, "*Dominium terrae*," 171–88.

147. Ruether, "Ecological Theology," 226.

148. Conradie, *Christianity and Ecological Theology*, 78. The same point has been made by other scholars as well. See Boersema, *Thora en Stoa over mens en natuur*, 67–75; and Nullens, "Leven volgens Gaia's normen?," 280–95.

conception of mastery into the field of environmental ethics. I am thinking here in particular of Peter Scott, whose article I discussed already in
chapter 4.[149] In this article, Scott analyses Bonhoeffer's distinction between
human beings' freedom *from* nature, and their freedom *for* each other. In
particular, he draws attention to a number of this position's strengths, most
notably its affirmation of human responsibility. According to him, however,
"it seems odd to address ecological dependencies only in terms of a structure of responsibility, that is, without attention to the natural reality that is
being responded to."[150] On his view, the nature that humans are called to
master is—unbeknownst to them—not "pure" nature, but a nature that has
already been prepared for mastery. In other words, it is already a *formed*
nature, or a nature that has been shaped and worked over in advance. Scott
then compares Bonhoeffer's advocacy for human mastery over nature with
the approach of Reiner Grundmann, a Marxist philosopher who, in Scott's
words, "calls for the further mastery of nature on the grounds that in the
perfection of such 'mastery' lies deliverance from ecological terrors."[151] The
image to which Grundmann makes appeal is that of a violinist practicing
the violin. When a violinist's performance is deficient in one way or another,
these deficiencies are attributed to his or her lack of mastery of the instrument—not to the instrument itself. Along the same lines, Grundmann argues (according to Scott) that "any deficiencies in ecological performance
must be addressed by attention to the further mastery of nature and not by
calling into question the 'true' human vocation to master nature."[152]

From here, Scott identifies a difficulty with such an argument (an argument which, incidentally, he attributes to Bonhoeffer as well), namely,
that it presupposes a decision about nature "as already shaped in advanced
ways for human purposes and ends."[153] The metaphor of the musician in
relation to his or her musical instrument matches point for point with the
relationship between a farmer and the—already cultivated—farmland that
he works over, as Scott says. He calls this reading of the text of Genesis into
question, arguing that what the creation narrative presents us with, instead
of something previously formed, is "a sequence of creaturely forms that
ends in the human, indicating only a habitat of the human and the need

149. Scott, "Postnatural Humanity? Bonhoeffer on Freedom and Order in Creation," esp. 16–17.

150. Ibid., 16.

151. Ibid. Scott does not offer a reference to Grundmann's work, but he appears to
be drawing from Grundmann, *Marxism and Ecology*.

152. Scott, "Postnatural Humanity? Bonhoeffer on Freedom and Order in Creation," 17.

153. Ibid.

for humanity to transform its habitat."[154] He therefore sees Bonhoeffer's distinction (between human beings' freedom for each other and their freedom from nature) "as being an interpretation more conclusive than can be established from a reading of the text *simpliciter*."[155]

There are two points in Scott's interpretation and evaluation of Bonhoeffer's position that I would like to call into question. First of all, the comparison that he draws between Bonhoeffer's understanding of human mastery of nature, on the one hand, and those of Grundmann, on the other, is not a valid one. After identifying their positions as compatible, he attacks Grundmann's violin metaphor, and while his criticism may be adequate in the case of Grundmann, it is not in the case of Bonhoeffer. On the contrary, Bonhoeffer's view on human mastery of nature does not presuppose a view of nature as having already been pre-formed. Indeed, it is exactly the other way around. In *CF*, for instance, Bonhoeffer describes the relation of human beings to an uncultivated, or "wild" nature that has not yet been mastered by human beings. Secondly, Scott's argument that Bonhoeffer reads too much into the biblical text can also be challenged. As we saw above, a broad consensus exists among biblical scholars concerning the fact that the Hebrew verbs used in Gen 1:26 and 1:28 do, in fact, mean "to rule."[156] While we have seen that this assertion has often been attacked by ecologists—with subsequent proposals for reinterpretation—, it is not at all clear how a "*simpliciter*" reading could possibly suggest otherwise.

In light of these observations, it appears that a much more fruitful way to appropriate Bonhoeffer's thoughts on the human mastery of nature is to take them as they stand. His assertion that humans are called to master nature accords both with the biblical mandate of Gen 1 and with the deeply ambiguous reality of nature itself. In its fallen form, creation, or nature, needs to be mastered, that is, to be put in the service of humanity. Only when this is achieved is nature restored to its original purpose.

In the earlier discussion, at the beginning of this chapter, of Bonhoeffer's interpretation of the biblical mandate, we noted how Bonhoeffer did not see the mandate as a warrant for using, against nature, all of the powers and technologies that modernity has developed—on the contrary, such an allowance would be reckless, irresponsible and dangerous on Bonhoeffer's view. As we saw, Bonhoeffer's understanding of the mandate was qualified by two important nuances. Firstly, there was his negative evaluation

154. Ibid., 21.

155. Ibid.; italics original.

156. For a comprehensive account of the discussion, see Boersema, *Thora en Stoa over mens en natuur*, 67–75.

of technology, to which I shall return in a moment. Secondly, we saw how he closed off the path leading to a natural understanding of human mastery over nature. This is an important point to note in light of the criticism often levelled against the form of secularized "natural theology." According to Bonhoeffer, true mastery over nature can only be achieved when it is exercised in recognition of the divine mandate to master nature. What this means is that lordship over nature can only be exercised in recognition of the rights and interests of our fellow human beings—a point that Bonhoeffer makes explicitly in his discussion of technology. This clearly sets Bonhoeffer's understanding of human mastery over nature apart from that of the Enlightenment worldview, as exemplified in Francis Bacon, who saw human mastery of nature as an expression of man's superiority. Such a view can rightfully be criticized, to borrow from Nullens, as both Pelagian and arrogant.[157]

The Contribution of Bonhoeffer's Theology for an Appropriation of Technology

The second contribution that Bonhoeffer's thoughts on human mastery over nature can make to environmental ethics lies in his evaluation of technology. In ecological writings—that is, both in ecotheology and, more broadly, in environmental ethics—one is able to note a widespread consensus on the important role that technology has played in bringing about the ecological crisis. This has been recognized by White, who has identified the marriage of science and technology as the direct cause of the ecological crisis: "Western Europe and North America arranged a marriage between science and technology, a union of the theoretical and empirical approaches to our natural environment."[158] What this statement implies, as Anna Case Winters points out, is that "[s]cience *might* have been oriented toward *scientia*, knowing and understanding the world, but once wedded to technology . . . knowledge is ordered toward control."[159] Since the publication of White's influential work, many others have also pointed to the dangers of technology.

One such scholar is Scruton, who, drawing from Martin Heidegger's important criticism of technology, notes how, "[a]ccording to Heidegger[,] technology has ceased to be a way of relating to the natural world and has

---

157. See Nullens, "Leven volgens Gaia's Normen?," 242–48.

158. White, "The Historical Roots of our Ecologic Crisis," 1203. White places the blame on the shoulders of Christianity: "Our science and technology have grown out of Christian attitudes toward man's relation to nature." Ibid., 1206.

159. Winters, *Reconstructing a Christian Theology of Nature*, 70; italics original.

instead become a *challenge* to nature."[160] Scruton appreciates Heidegger's criticism, asserting that "it corresponds to a widely held intuition, that the human psyche has changed under the impact of its own discoveries. The myth of Prometheus suggests that human beings have never been wholly at ease with their technological competence and have always suspected it to be an offence against the gods."[161] In particular, Scruton draws attention to the social divisiveness that has resulted from technology's development, as well as the alienation, the instrumentalization and the fracturing of the world in unconnected realms.

Similar analyses have been made by many ecotheologians as well. Northcott, for example, identifies the ecological havoc brought about by alienation and consumerism as the result of technology: "Technology, and the economy of money which is its supreme manifestation, achieves an autonomy from divine command, from human community and from natural order, eliminating moral value and spiritual significance along with natural necessity."[162] Northcott's assertions are shared by Conradie, who refers to technology as a "particular manifestation of structural evil."[163] While Conradie recognizes and acknowledges certain benefits that technology has brought about, he focuses much more attention on the negative effects that it has had on the planet and society. On his view, "the exercise of knowledge and power can and has been contaminated by the pervasiveness of the predicament of evil, often manifested in colonialist arrogance and capitalist greed."[164] The ambiguous nature of technology, as he argues, is a direct consequence of the broader framework of which it is a part, namely, the drive towards progress.[165] Both Northcott and Conradie draw on Bonhoeffer's negative assessment of technology in their work.[166]

While it's true that Bonhoeffer focused on the more negative aspects of technology for most of his life, we saw how he gradually changed his views and eventually came to accept technology as an integral component of the modern world. This features as an important nuance in his thinking,

160. Scruton, *Green Philosophy*, 232; italics original.

161. Ibid., 243.

162. Northcott, *The Environment*, 257.

163. Conradie, *An Ecological Christian Anthropology*, 187.

164. Ibid., 188.

165. Ibid.

166. Conradie quotes Bonhoeffer's statement in *Ethics* that technology's benefits pale in comparison with its demonic consequences. Ibid. Northcott, for his part, quotes the passage from *CF* in which Bonhoeffer describes technology as the power by which fallen nature grabs hold of human beings, instead of the other way around. See Northcott, *The Environment*, 222.

for it means that his theology cannot be used one-sidedly in order to condemn technology. On the contrary, his later thoughts on technology invite theologians to take seriously the fact that technology has, in fact, become part of the very structure of human life. As Donald MacKenzie and Judy Wajcman observe, "[t]echnology is a vitally important aspect of the human condition."[167] What this means, at least for someone like De Lange, is that, in the context of assessing Bonhoeffer's potential contribution to the debate on technology, "[t]heologians that radically criticize technology are like passengers in an airplane that instruct air control to shoot down their plane."[168]

We saw earlier how Bonhoeffer, in observing the fact that technological organization has become humanity's most immediate environment, instead of nature, stressed the importance of developing a robust, human-centered ethic of responsibility, which would be capable of providing guidelines for dealing with this novel, technological environment. This is surely a valuable contribution, for although there has been sustained theological reflection on matters such as biotechnology and genetic engineering,[169] there is still a significant lack of theological reflection on technology as such,[170] even though a number of recent publications on the issue could be seen as signs of a turning tide.[171] Bonhoeffer's emphasis on the need for a human-centered ethic of responsibility can help to further stimulate critical, theological engagement with technology and, at the same time, to raise awareness of technology as a basic, ontological dimension of the contemporary experience of human life.[172]

167. MacKenzie and Wajcman, "Introductory Essay," 1.

168. De Lange, "'The Spiritual Force is Lacking.'" In the same light, it is difficult to ignore the irony of the fact that those directly opposing modern technology often write their books on computers, publish their blogs on the Internet and travel all around the world on modern forms of transportation in order to attend congresses on environmental ethics. Just to avoid any potential misunderstanding, I am not making this observation as an *ad hominem* argument, but rather as a reflection on just how intertwined technology has become with modern life.

169. See Deane-Drummond, *Theology and Biotechnology*; Gregersen and Drees, *Human Person in Science and Theology*; and Drees, *Technology, Trust, and Religion*.

170. See George Pattison: "[T]echnology as such has rarely been thematized as the matter of theological reflection." Pattison, *Thinking about God in an Age of Technology*, 1.

171. Apart from the works already referred to above, see Waters, *From Human to Posthuman*.

172. An important examination made in this direction has been carried out by Ledger, "Towards a Theology of Technology," 124–29. Drawing on Bergmann and Heidegger, Ledger resists what she refers to as a "technological culture" of instrumentalism, rationality and control. She provides a theological critique as well, arguing

Love for the Earth as a Motive for Environmental Ethics

In this section, I will assess the value of Bonhoeffer's thoughts on this-worldliness, as well as his subsequent imperative to love the earth, as far as environmental ethics are concerned.

Bonhoeffer's Appeal to Love the Earth as an Antidote to Otherworldliness

First of all, Bonhoeffer's plea to remain loyal to the earth can be seen as a further outworking of his argument that Christians are able to fully participate in every aspect of worldly existence. As we saw in chapter 2, recognizing worldly reality as a whole as Christ-reality allows Christians to see the value and importance of regaining and maintaining a sustainable environment. Bonhoeffer's appeal to love the earth goes beyond a mere granting of permission, moreover—as we saw, he suggested that Christians stand with both legs planted firmly on the earth, and although he made this suggestion in a private letter to his fiancée, it could be taken as an apt summary of what he said and wrote at other times as well.

This appeal offers an important antidote against otherworldliness. As we saw in chapter 2, Bonhoeffer's distinction between the ultimate and the penultimate can function as a means to counter one particularly powerful form of otherworldliness in particular, namely, the flight into a literalist, eschatological vision, or "rapture culture," which stresses the immanent coming of Christ and subsequently disavows the importance of caring for the earth in its present form. Otherworldliness has other—often closely related—articulations as well, however. While Christians espousing a literalist eschatology, especially in North America, are often politically active—if only on a limited number of issues, such as supporting the State of Israel—, many other Christians, who may or may not have a literalist eschatology, shy away from engagement with "the world" altogether. This attitude can materialize in pietistic movements, as well as in the liberal understanding of Christianity as a religion of redemption.[173]

"that instrumentalism and the idolising of human technological capacities do not take proper account of the relatedness of God's creation." Ibid., 127. As a counterproposal, she makes use of the metaphor of the world as a house, "a home where people dwell in relation to God, themselves and the world around them." Ibid. This "theology of technology" as she calls it, addresses us in our capacity for relationality, instead of our capacity for command and control.

173. Though this is, of course, not to say that all liberal theology is "otherworldly"—see the many different liberation theologies, for example, which are intensely focused on salvation in the "here and now."

The tendency to detach and disengage from the world is certainly deepseated within Christian theology. Even Northcott, in his nuanced and rich description of the contribution that Christian theology is able to make to environmental ethics, refers to "[t]he ultimate teleological directedness of human life towards salvation and heaven."[174] He makes use of this teleology in order to critizice the impetus of materialism in Western culture, arguing instead for "the development of the practices of prayer and meditation, and of those virtues, such as justice and prudence, which not only make for whole persons and the wiser use of natural resources but are also said to prepare the person for the life of heaven."[175] While Northcott's criticism of materialism is certainly valuable and worthy of note, his appeal to heaven as the ultimate telos of human life backfires—indeed, one could easily argue that, by casting heaven as the Christian's ultimate destination, the task of caring for the earth necessarily loses its importance, or *raison d'être*. Though this is undoubtedly far afield from the point that Northcott was trying to get across, the fact that his somewhat vague—and perhaps offhanded—reference to heaven is able to lead to such a conclusion reveals the deeply problematic nature of the Christian understanding of heaven.

Bonhoeffer's strong resistance against this kind of attitude—which, as we saw, he combatted in the form of the "innere Linie" in the Confessing Church—can be an important resource in challenging Christian disengagement from the world. A number of scholars have drawn attention to this point. Moltmann, for example, uses Bonhoeffer's resistance against otherworldliness, as well as his insistence on remaining loyal to the earth, in order to counter what he calls "[t]he traditional Christian hope."[176] which, on his view, amounts to a religion of redemption. According to him, this religious otherworldliness is directly responsible for ecological disasters and for the changing climate. In order to help save humanity from ecological havoc, as he argues, what we need is an appeal to remain loyal to the earth, such as Bonhoeffer voices.

A similar application of Bonhoeffer's thoughts on this theme has been carried out by Larry Rasmussen. In "The Whole of Earthly Life," for instance, he writes the following: "I find Bonhoeffer fruitful for a world in which Christian faith must express love of God as fidelity to Earth if Christianity is to contribute to sustainability in a humanly dominated and jeopardized biosphere."[177] From here, Rasmussen then goes on to mention some

174. Northcott, *The Environment*, 325.

175. Ibid.

176. "Die traditionelle christliche Hoffnung." Moltmann, "Theologie mit Dietrich Bonhoeffer," 25.

177. Rasmussen, "The Whole of Earthly Life," 68.

of Bonhoeffer's texts which I treated earlier in this chapter. Concerning the thoughts that Bonhoeffer voiced in Barcelona on fidelity to "mother Earth," for example, he writes that "Christianity is judged by its contribution to Earth's care and redemption. If Christianity is not, in its practices, an Earth-honoring, Earth-positive faith in which the whole Community of Life . . . has moral standing, then it is not truly faithful."[178] In other essays of his, Rasmussen has also made other, similar uses of Bonhoeffer's thoughts on loyalty to the earth in the context of environmental ethics.[179]

Also Burkholder applies Bonhoeffer's plea for loyalty to the earth to ecology. He summarizes Bonhoeffer's thoughts on the matter as follows: "The end goal of soteriology is . . . not deification or any kind of extraction into a future world, but fully embracing life on earth as a creature of God."[180]

It should thus be quite clear that, in Bonhoeffer's appeal for genuine this-worldliness and fidelity to the earth, we find a rich potential resource for a Christian ecological ethic.[181]

THE CRITICAL FUNCTION OF BONHOEFFER'S APPEAL TO LOVE THE EARTH VIS-À-VIS CURRENTS OF EARTH SPIRITUALITY

His work can fulfill an important critical function as well, particularly insofar as deep ecology is concerned. Like Bonhoeffer, many contemporary ecologists speak of "turning to earth," or even of experiencing a sort of earth-focused "conversion." A clear example of this trend can be found in the work of F. Marina Schauffler, who combines both terms in the title of her book *Turning to Earth: Stories of Ecological Conversion.*[182] As she argues in this text, in order for environmental degradation to stop, human beings must first have what she calls a "change of heart": "Restoring the health of *outer ecology*—the collective web of life and elemental matter in which we participate—depends on a renewal of *inner ecology*, the spiritual beliefs and ethical values that guide our actions."[183] Schauffler's stated aim is clearly holistic in nature, for on her view, environmental action needs to be complemented with a conversion on the level of feelings and beliefs. Indeed, she goes so far as to argue that it is this inner ecology that, at the moment, requires the

178. Ibid., 70.

179. See Rasmussen, "Bonhoeffer's Song of Songs," 186–93; and ibid., "Introduction," 1–22.

180. Burkholder, "Christological Foundations," 348.

181. For a further outworking of this theme, see Marshall, *Heaven Is Not My Home.*

182. Schauffler, *Turning to Earth.*

183. Ibid., 3; italics original.

most attention. In order to foster and draw her reader's attention to this sort of inner change of heart, she sets about describing what she refers to as "ecological conversions" in American nature writers, analysing how the experiences took place and what sort of stages they progressed through.

Similar appeals for inner transformation are often echoed by Christian theologians, such as Sallie McFague. In her book *Super, Natural Christians*, for instance, McFague contrasts what she calls "the arrogant eye" and "the loving eye." She identifies the arrogant eye as a view of the world in which nature is seen as an object by distant, disembodied observers, or more specifically, by the masculine, patriarchal gaze. The loving eye, in contrast, is not so much opposed to its arrogant counterpart, as McFague insists, but instead "suggests something novel in Western ways of knowing: acknowledgement of and respect for the other as *subject*."[184] What is particularly important for McFague in this way of knowing is the sensory experience of nature, and most particularly the sense of touch. "Touch[,]" as she writes, "gives us an immediate sense of our bodies as existing in a world composed of other resistant bodies—other people, other animals, other things."[185] Other-than-human nature is thus seen to belong, on her view, to the "Thou" of Martin Buber's "I-Thou" distinction, which, again according to McFague, should be used in relation to nature in the place of Buber's similar "I-It" distinction.[186] In this light, McFague makes an appeal for closer and more intimate encounters between human beings and nature, citing writers such as John Muir as examples, just as Schauffler does in her book.

Another example of the Christian appropriation of deep ecology can be found in Thomas Berry's proposal for "earth spirituality."[187] As Berry argues, in light of the ecological havoc caused by human beings, what we need is a new spirituality of the earth: "[W]e must pass on to give some indication of the new attitude that needs to be adopted toward the earth. This involves a new spiritual and even mystical communion with the earth, a true aesthetic of the earth, a sensitivity to earth needs [sic], a valid economy of the earth . . . In spirituality, especially, we need to recognize the numinous qualities of the earth."[188] Berry's particular formulation is quite stark, moreover, for he argues that spirituality itself should no longer be conceived in terms of the relation between human beings and God alone, but also between humans and the earth: "A spirituality is a mode of being in which not only the divine

184. McFague, *Super, Natural Christians*, 34; italics original.
185. Ibid., 93.
186. Ibid., 100–103.
187. Berry, "Earthly Spirituality," 64–68.
188. Ibid., 66–67.

and the human commune with each other, but we discover ourselves in the universe and the universe discovers itself in us."[189]

Appeals such as these have brought Roger Scruton to address what he calls the "salvationist" character of deep ecology, as well as the "cult of Gaia," which he sees as being reminiscent of the great salvific religions which presented themselves as a remedy to a great sense of despair.[190] Elsewhere in his work, he identifies parallels between the ecocentric literature and the literature of religious conversion.[191] While Scruton's generalization may perhaps go too far—there is indeed a considerable diversity of viewpoints among deep ecologists—, he rightly points out that certain forms of deep ecology take the form of a religion of redemption—be it a religion aimed not at gaining eternity in heaven, but on earth in the here and now.[192]

The problem with such a quasi-religious view is not only that it fails to provide a motive for "common people" to care for the environment (as argues Scruton), but also that, in the language of Christian theology, it comes dangerously close to divinizing the earth. While loving the earth is undoubtedly important, it needs to have certain checks and boundaries in place in order to avoid devolving into a pseudo-religion. It is my own contention that Bonhoeffer provides just these sorts of necessary checks and boundaries. We saw, for instance, how his appeal to love the earth was grounded in Christ's affirmation of the earth; similarly, we saw how love for Christ formed the *cantus firmus* in relation to which the counterpoint of loving the earth could fully (and properly) be developed. These rich thoughts of Bonhoeffer's help to defend against an earthly spirituality that would seek to bypass Christ, even while, at the same time, they continue to assert the importance of remaining faithful to the earth. As such, they constitute a powerful and compelling Christian alternative to current attempts to divinize the earth.

189. Ibid., 67.

190. Scruton, *Green Philosophy*, 85–86.

191. As Scruton writes, "The literature here in vast; much of it is also tortured, and in a peculiar way private, like the literature of religious conversion, which tells the reader that the 'scales have fallen' from the writer's eyes." Ibid., 195.

192. This point is also made by Zimmerman, who admits that "[s]ome deep ecologists . . . view self-realization as involving a sudden conversion experience." Zimmerman resists this form of deep ecology, for in his view, it "may further the efforts of critics to describe deep ecology as irrationalist and also potentially ecofascist." Zimmerman, *Contesting Earth's Future*, 108.

6

Bonhoeffer's Theology of Responsibility and the Social Dimension of Environmental Ethics

In this chapter I focus on another theme that runs like a thread throughout much of Bonhoeffer's works and personal life, and which plays a fundamental role in his ethical theology, namely, the theme of responsibility, or of free, vicarious action carried out on behalf of others. In particular, I would like to focus on two distinct concepts that fit under the heading of this broader, more general theme: vicarious representation ("Stellvertretung") and the divine mandates. While in the first half of the chapter I will outline the meaning that these concepts have in Bonhoeffer's thought, in the second, I shall address the question of their potential relevance for environmental ethics.

Two Concepts from Bonhoeffer's Theology of Responsibility

Here in this first part of the chapter, I will begin by focusing on the theme of responsibility in Bonhoeffer's ethics. As will become clear in the following pages, this theme bears an intimate connection with many other concepts in Bonhoeffer's theology, even though it changes and develops over the course of his career. It is also closely bound up with Bonhoeffer's personal biography insofar as it played the role of a powerful motivation—and rationale—for his resistance against the Nazi regime, which ultimately culminated in his participation in plans to assassinate Hitler. Bonhoeffer's most structured and elaborate discussion of responsibility can be found in the *Ethics* manuscripts. In these texts, Bonhoeffer develops what could be called a sort of matrix of responsibility, which features four distinct, yet closely related elements. In *Ethics*, he also addresses the concept of the divine mandates with which, or through which, he attempted to develop a blueprint for post-war society.

In what follows, I will focus specifically on Bonhoeffer's concept of vicarious representation, which figures as an integral part of his matrix of responsibility (which will be shortly described below), as well as on his concept of the divine mandates. Since Bonhoeffer developed his theology of responsibility most fully in his *Ethics*, this work will once more be taken as the starting point of the discussion. Within the perspective of the *Ethics*, I will address both the earlier and later developments of the theme. I will first focus on the concept of vicarious representation, before taking up the theme of the divine mandates.

Responsibility as Vicarious Representative Action

Bonhoeffer outlines the structure of the responsible life in two manuscripts of *Ethics*, namely, "History and Good [1],"[1] and "History and Good [2]."[2] As the second manuscript is somewhat more systematic than the first, my discussion will focus primarily on it.

Following an introduction in which many of the manuscript's core ideas are presented in embryonic form, as it were, Bonhoeffer provides a detailed look into the structure of the responsible life in a section bearing that title.[3] At the beginning of this section, he starts out by making two distinctions. Firstly, he distinguishes between *bondage* (i.e., being bound to other human beings and to God) and *freedom* (i.e., the freedom of the individual life). Within this distinction, another twofold structure can also be discerned. While bondage, on the one hand, takes the form either of vicarious representative action ("Stellvertretung") or accordance with reality ("Wirklichkeitsgemäßheit"), individual freedom manifests itself either in individual accountability ("Selbstzurechnung") or in the bold venture of concrete decision ("Wagnis"). Together, these four elements form the matrix of the responsible life. In what follows, I shall focus in particular on the first moment, namely, that of vicarious representation, for it has the greatest potential as far as environmental ethics are concerned.

First and foremost, I would like to begin by accounting for the concept itself, both in terms of its content and its development throughout the course of Bonhoeffer's thought. Then, in the second section, I will address the background and historical context out of which it arose. In the third and

1. DBWE 6:219–45.
2. DBWE 6:246–98.
3. "The Structure of Responsible Life." DBWE 6:257–89.

final section, I will engage with some of the criticisms that have been leveled against it.

BONHOEFFER'S CONCEPT OF VICARIOUS REPRESENTATION

As indicated above, vicarious representation figures as the first form of bondage that Bonhoeffer outlines in his matrix of responsibility. He argues that vicarious respresentative action takes place in relationships in which a person acts on behalf of others. As simple, everyday examples, he offers the figures of the father, the statesman, and the instructor of an apprentice. He goes on to note, however, that even those who do not stand in such obvious, socially well-defined relationships are able to bear responsibility for others; indeed, he insists that even unmarried people are capable of living lives of vicarious responsibility.[4] In the latter case, the individual is able to carry out vicarious, responsible action in a rather special way, namely, on his or her *own* behalf, *as human beings*—as such, they live vicariously for humanity as a whole. While such an example may seem to be somewhat odd or out of the ordinary, this certainly cannot be so, for Bonhoeffer invokes the example of Jesus himself in this case.[5] He then takes a further step, arguing that, through Jesus, all human life, in its essence, is vicarious representation: "Jesus . . . the Son of God who became human, lived as our vicarious representative. Through him, therefore, all human life is in its essence vicarious representation . . . His entire living, acting, and suffering was vicarious representative action [Stellvertretung]. All that human beings were supposed to live, do, and suffer was fulfilled in him."[6] At the same time, Bonhoeffer also insists on the absoluteness of responsible living: only those who are selfless live responsibly, that is, only those who completely devote their lives to others. However, he also warns against turning the other into an absolute, in which case one can only but ignore one's other responsibilities, or one's responsibilities to other persons. In this case, as Bonhoeffer argues, one's action would be completely arbitrary and would lack genuine responsibility.

---

4. Clearly, Bonhoeffer means to say that unmarried, independent adults are not part of the structure of vicarious responsibility found in families—they can, of course, be part of such structures in their jobs (as statesmen and instructors, for example).

5. He also points out that Jesus didn't have to bear the particular responsibilities involved in marriage, in caring and providing for a family, or even in following a vocation. Yet, precisely for this reason, as Bonhoeffer notes, Jesus' responsibility and vicarious, representative action for all humanity comes out in even greater relief. See DBWE 6:258.

6. DBWE 6:258.

Bonhoeffer observes that vicarious representative action extends beyond the realm of human relationships as well: "There is also a responsibility for things, conditions, and values, but only by strictly keeping in mind that the origin, essence, and goal of all things, conditions, and values is determined by Christ (John 1:4), the God who became human. It is through Christ that the world of things and values is given back its orientation toward human beings, as was originally intended in their creation."[7] In this passage, Bonhoeffer stresses the christological orientation of acting responsibly on behalf things and values in order to criticize the common understanding of standing up and acting on behalf of *causes*. In particular, he points out that the values of the true, the good, the right, and the beautiful can, in certain instances, be elevated to the position of false idols, in which case what might have been responsible action devolves to the level of an obsession that destroys human beings. For Bonhoeffer, it is always and necessarily on behalf of human beings that responsible action is carried out—responsibility for a cause is only allowed if it is directed towards them.[8]

The *Ethics* manuscripts are not the first instance where Bonhoeffer develops this line of thought on (Christ's) vicarious representation as the foundation of responsibility—on the contrary, they figure as a relatively late and significantly more developed expression of his thought. The first appearance of the concept of vicarious representation can be found in *SC*. In a section of the text entitled "The Concept of God and Social Basic-Relations in Terms of the I-You-Relation,"[9] he clearly situates responsibility in the context of his theology of sociality. In this context, he points out that responsibility is a fundamentally social concept, and not an individual one: "The I comes into being only in relation to the You; only in response to a demand does *responsibility* arise."[10] The uniqueness and singularity of the other person as a "You" is fundamental for Bonhoeffer, for, as he insists, the

7. DBWE 6:259–60. Here again we see the strong anthropocentric orientation of Bonhoeffer's theology. As Clifford Green points out, "Bonhoeffer had made this point in his Christology lectures when treating Christ as the mediator of God and nature." DBWE 6:260, editorial footnote 51.

8. Bonhoeffer further elaborates on this point when referring to Paul's letter to the Romans: "For all of creation . . . waits with longing for the revelation of the glory of the children of God; indeed, creation itself will be freed from the bondage of its transience (which also consists of its false self-deification) to participate in the glorious freedom of the children of God (Rom. 8:19, 21)." DBWE 6:260. This is another instance of Bonhoeffer's anthropocentric point of view, such as I described earlier in chapter 4. It also links up with his thoughts on the redemption of nature, as I described in chapter 3.

9. DBWE 1:54–57.

10. DBWE 1:54; italics original.

other cannot simply be ignored or set to the side by the individual, nor can any form of social unity negate the plurality of the persons involved. It is only in recognizing the other as a "You," or as a person, that the individual him- or herself becomes a person, that is, an I.[11] The appeal that the other makes on the individual is total, absolute. It is thus not the individual person who makes him- or herself into an "I," or who recognizes the other as a person. On the contrary, *"God or the Holy Spirit joins the concrete You; only through God's active working does the other become a You to me from whom my I arises. In other words, every human You is an image of the divine You."*[12] Bonhoeffer here makes clear that the "You" character of the other, instead of simply being an attribute that is borrowed from God, is created by the divine You, and, like the divine You, it too is real, absolute, and holy.[13] This of course does not mean that the other person is holy in him- or herself, however—only God is holy, and it is he alone who makes the other into a "You."

In *SC*, Bonhoeffer explicitly grounds his thoughts on the I-You relationship, along with the responsibility arising thereby, in Christ. As he writes, *"It is not an ethical possibility or standard, but solely the reality of the divine love for the church-community; it is not an ethical, but a theological concept."*[14] It is the principle of vicarious representative action that, in turn, also makes relationships between Christians into something unique, Bonhoeffer asserts—instead of being limited to the individual's relationship with Christ, it spills over into the relationships between Christians as well. This is possible only in the church community, which itself, as a whole, rests on the principle of vicarious representation.[15]

11. By expressing his thought in this way, Bonhoeffer criticizes the idealistic conception of personhood. He voices the same criticism more directly and explicitly in a footnote where he contrasts his proposal with idealism, and more specifically, with the work of Kierkegaard and Fichte. In particular, he calls into question the way in which Kierkegaard speaks about the origin of the ethical person: "Kierkegaard's ethical person, too, exists only in the concrete situation, but his is not in any necessary relation to a concrete You. His person is self-established rather than being established by the You." DBWE 1:56n12. In this way, as Bonhoeffer says, Kierkegaard remains bound to the idealist position and lays the foundation for an extreme individualism in which the other is only relative to the individual, and no longer absolute.

12. DBWE 1:54–55; italics original.

13. In this context, Bonhoeffer also mentions the *imago Dei*. As we saw in chapter 4, *CF* is a work in which Bonhoeffer develops this grounding of human sociality in the *imago Dei* more fully.

14. DBWE 1:156; italics original.

15. Bonhoeffer specifies this point in the section of his text entitled "The Church Established in and through Christ—Its Realization." DBWE 1:145–57. In particular,

Bonhoeffer does not further develop the theme of "Stellvertretung" in *AB*. In *CF*, however, it figures yet again as an important theme, as we saw in chapter 4. In this instance, Bonhoeffer develops his thoughts on human distinctiveness in terms of being free-for each other. And while he furthers this line of thought in his Christology lectures, his understanding of vicarious representation does not come to the fore. One place where he does reflect further on the theme, however, is in his lectures on "The Nature of the Church."[16] Here he puts it forward as an organizing principle in the life of the church, particularly insofar as intercession and prayer are concerned in the church community.[17] As Friederike Barth observes, texts such as these indicate how the concept had come to form a "structural principle" ("Strukturprinzip") in Bonhoeffer's theology of Christian life.[18]

The structural role of vicarious representation also comes to the fore in *Discipleship*. In this case, Bonhoeffer once again focuses on Christ as the one who lived and died vicariously for the whole world, thereby overcoming the world's suffering. He asserts in particular that this vicarious action is thoroughly unique: only Christ's suffering was able to redeem the world. At the same time, he also asserts that the church is called to bear the suffering of the world: "[T]he church-community itself knows now that the world's suffering seeks a bearer. So in following Christ, this suffering falls upon it, and it bears the suffering while being borne by Christ. The community of Jesus Christ vicariously represents the world before God by following Christ under the cross."[19] Moreover, it is not only the church that is called to bear the world's suffering, but individual believers as well. As Bonhoeffer says, "disciples are called to bear what is put on them. Bearing constitutes being a Christian. Just as Christ maintains his communion with the Father by bearing according to the Father's will, so the disciples' bearing constitutes their community with Christ."[20]

---

he describes how the church is established by Christ's vicarious, representative action and becomes the form of his presence in this world. On his view, this action "contains profound implications for social philosophy." DBWE 1:156.

16. "Lecture Course: The Nature of the Church (Student Notes)." DBWE 11:269–332.

17. In Bonhoeffer's own words: "Intercession [is] vicarious representative action." DBWE 11:323. A bit further on, he continues: "In this way the brotherhood of vicarious representation for all happens. There only intercessory prayer is possible." DBWE 11:324.

18. Barth, *Die Wirklichkeit des Guten*, 248.

19. DBWE 4:90.

20. DBWE 4:90–91. Yet, as Bonhoeffer notes, the follower of Christ does not only suffer on behalf of Christ, but also on behalf of the church: "What is clear, however,

The concept of vicarious representation that emerges from these earlier writings is one in which Christ's life is seen as singular and unique—his life and death alone are truly salvific in nature. And yet, at the same time, Bonhoeffer also insists that Christ's life and death serve not only as an example for his followers; more than that, they become the only true way of life, both for individual believers and for the church as a whole. As we saw a moment ago, in the *Ethics*, Bonhoeffer broadens his perspective and presents "Stellvertretung" as a structural principle of human life as such. Rasmussen says that "Bonhoeffer has shifted the emphasis from the qualitative difference between Christ's deputyship and a man's doing good for his neighbour to the daily Christian *and* non-Christian life as a life that intimately partakes of Christ's deputyship at every turn and in a multitude of even unavoidable ways."[21]

Bonhoeffer continues to develop this line of thought in his later writings. In *Letters and Papers from Prison*, for instance, he sums up his thoughts on Christ's vicarious representation in a famous, key passage, asserting "that Jesus only 'is there for others.'"[22] In these letters that he wrote from prison, he also succinctly articulates the church's role, much along the same lines, in an equally famous passage: "The church is church only when it is there for others."[23] Here we note an important, though subtle, change in terminology: instead of using the word "Stellvertretung," Bonhoeffer speaks of "being-there-for-others." This change in terminology does not signal a radical change in his understanding of the concept of vicarious representation, however; on the contrary, Bonhoeffer is simply expressing essentially the same idea in a new way. A significant conceptual shift from his earlier work is nevertheless clearly delineated here as well, as also Friederike Barth observes.[24] She points out that in this further development of Bonhoeffer's thinking, the church has not simply become unnecessary; on the contrary, as the body of Christ in the world, it must be understood as the empirical and spiritual center of the movement involved in being-for-others, that is, this movement from inside to outside, or from church to world: "It is

---

is that those suffering in the power of the body of Christ suffer in a vicariously representative [stellvertretend] action 'for' the church-community, 'for' the body of Christ. They are permitted to bear what others are spared." DBWE 4:222. Further on, he continues to develop the same thought: "Such vicariously representative action and suffering, which is carried out by the members of the body of Christ, is itself the very life of Christ who seeks to take shape in his members (Gal. 4:19)." DBWE 4:222.

21. Rasmussen, *Dietrich Bonhoeffer*, 40; italics original.

22. DBWE 8:501.

23. DBWE 8:503.

24. Barth, *Die Wirklichkeit des Guten*, 248.

this movement from church to world that is now central in the thought of Bonhoeffer, after the early and middle phases of his theology had served the development of ecclesiology."[25]

Having given this short overview of the development of the theme of vicarious representation in Bonhoeffer, it is important to stress that the core of the concept remains the same throughout all Bonhoeffer's works. That core is that for Bonhoeffer, it is primarily a christological concept: it describes first and foremost the life and mission of Jesus Christ, who suffered and died vicariously, on behalf of all humanity. Bonhoeffer's particular point is, however, that Jesus' vicarious representation is not *exclusive* but *inclusive* in nature, insofar as it invites Christians to mirror Christ's example.[26]

In this sense, the concept of vicarious representation is very much like that of Christ-reality. As we saw earlier, Bonhoeffer understands Christ's advent in the world through the moments of the incarnation, the crucifixion and the resurrection, each of which constitutes a fundamental reshaping of reality; henceforth, authentic human living can only be lived out in relation to the same threefold relationship to reality. The concept of vicarious representation—which can and should be seen in connection with the more overarching concept of Christ-reality—follows along similar lines by making clear how Christ's life of vicarious responsibility is both unique and singular, even if, at the same time, it forms the pattern of all true, human living. As—again—Friederike Barth observes, "the suffering and death of Christ at the cross [is] really penal suffering, but as vicarious penal suffering, taken on out of love, it also that what Albrecht Ritschl calls the fulfilment of his 'professional obedience,' in continuation of his active obedience of the true and real fulfilment of the commandment."[27] Inter-human vicarious representation is thus not merely an "ethical" or "social" concept bereft of theological content. On the contrary, as Abromeit makes clear, "[t]he personal vicarious representation, accomplished by Christ, creates between all persons who live because of Christ, a personal community. All these people receive their self-understanding from him."[28]

---

25. "Auf diese Bewegung von der Kirche zur Welt hin kommt es nun im Denken Bonheoffers an, nachdem die frühe und die mittlere Phase seiner Theologie der Entwicklung einer Ekklesiologie." Ibid., 249.

26. Ibid., 252.

27. "[A]ls Leiden und der Tod Christi am Kreuz [ist] wirklich Strafleiden, aber als stellvertretendes Strafleiden aus Liebe zugleich auch das, was Albrecht Ritschl die Erfüllung des Berufsgehorsams nennt, also in Fortsetzung seines aktiven Gehorsams die wahrhafte und wirkliche Erfüllung des Gebots." Barth, *Die Wirklichkeit des Guten*, 252.

28. "Die personale Stellvertretung, die Christus leistet, schafft zwischen allen

The Future as a Dimension of Bonhoeffer's Theology of Responsibility

Although no element of his concept of vicarious representation, for the benefit of the later discussion it is important to clarify that Bonhoeffer also sees the future as an essential dimension of his theology of responsibility, even if he does not explicitly include it within the matrix of responsibility that he develops in his "History and Good" manuscripts. The most well-known description of this dimension can be found in his essay "After Ten Years,"[29] in which he writes: "The ultimately responsible question is not how I extricate myself heroically from a situation but [how] a coming genera-tion is to go on living."[30] This is, moreover, neither the first nor the only in-stance in which Bonhoeffer articulates the concept of vicarious in relation to eschatology. On the contrary, he already drew this connection in another manuscript of his *Ethics*, namely, "Heritage and Decay."[31] Towards the close of this text, he writes about the situation in the West, which he describes as "hostile" towards Christ. As he observes, the world has turned itself away from the ordering power, or *katechoon*, which Paul speaks about in 2 Thess 2:7. In line with traditional, Reformation thinking, he identifies this *kat-echoon* as the ordering power of the state, which rules by the power of the sword. Though the church is commanded to support this power of the state, which must of course be distinguished from that of God himself, Bonhoef-fer argues that the *corpus Christianum* is crumbling and that the church of Christ stands in an increasingly hostile world. The church's task remains a lofty, future-oriented one, however: "As bearer of a historical heritage, the church, while waiting for Judgment Day, has an obligation to the historical future."[32] From here, Bonhoeffer immediately explains why the prospect of the "youngest day" does (or should) not lead the church to an attitude of passivity: "Its vision of the end of all things must not paralyze its historical

---

Personen, die ihr Leben Christus verdanken, eine personale Gemeinschaft. Alle diese Menschen beziehen ihr Selbstverständnis aus ihm." Abromeit, *Geheimnis Christi*, 271.

29. "An Account at the Turn of the Year 1942–1943: After Ten Years." DBWE 8:35–52.

30. DBWE 8:42. Immediately following this passage, Bonhoeffer continues: "Only from such a historically responsible question will fruitful solutions arise, how-ever humiliating they may be for the moment. In short, it is much easier to see a situation through on the basis of principle than in concrete responsibility. The younger generation will always have the surest sense whether an action is done merely in terms of principle or from living responsibly, for it is their future that is at stake." DBWE 8:42.

31. DBWE 6:103–33.

32. DBWE 6:132.

responsibility. The church must leave the end to God as well as the possibility that history will continue. Both remain its concern."[33] As these instances make clear, Bonhoeffer does indeed see the future as a constitutive element of responsibility.

Background and Context of Bonhoeffer's Concept of Vicarious Representation

While the foregoing discussion has shown how the concept of vicarious representation developed throughout Bonhoeffer's work, it is important to note that these developments did not take place in total, theoretical isolation—in spite of the concept's originality and distinctiveness, it only came to take shape in Bonhoeffer's thought as an answer to the ecclesial-political realities of the times; in addition, its formation was also heavily influenced by the contemporary philosophy of the period. Two particular sources of influence are noteworthy in this regard, namely, the movement of personalism, and the school of responsibility in political theory.

Insofar as personalism is concerned, recent scholarship has shown that the movement played a crucial role in Bonhoeffer's formation of the concept of vicarious representation. As Friederike Barth has pointed out, for instance, Bonhoeffer's concept must be read against the background of the work of Friedrich Gogarten, of Emil Brunner, and, most notably, of Eberhard Grisebach.[34] Recognition of this connection is long overdue, especially in light of the fact that many scholars have claimed that Bonhoeffer was not directly influenced by personalist writers at all,[35] nor, in particular, by Friedrich Gogarten.[36] What Bonhoeffer drew in particular from personalism is the idea that the I-You relationship forms a fundamental part of

---

33. DBWE 6:132.

34. Barth, *Die Wirklichkeit des Guten*, 195–230. See Bonhoeffer's own comments on Grisebach in "Thesis Fragment about M. Heidegger and E. Grisebach." DBWE 11:244–46.

35. Floyd argues that the movement of personalism appears to have had little or no influence on Bonhoeffer. Referring to the work of thinkers such as Martin Buber, Eugen Rosenstock-Huessy, Gabriel Marcel, Hans Ehrenberg, Ferdinand Ebner, and Franz Rosenzweig, he writes: "Bonhoeffer . . . appears to have been writing Sanctorum Communio with little or no knowledge of their similar work. Thus as Michael Theunissen has noted concerning the personalist movement in general, Bonhoeffer was evidently quite typical in working out his position in relative independence of these others." Floyd, *Theology and the Dialectics of Otherness*, 118.

36. See Axt-Piscalar, "Das Bild Gottes auf Erden," 267n6. She refers to Gogarten, "Das Problem einer theologischen Anthropologie," 493–511.

what it means to be human. It is nevertheless important to keep in mind that he didn't simply adopt personalist themes uncritically; instead, he reworked and refashioned them christologically. We already saw this in *SC*, where Bonhoeffer grounded interhuman relationships in Christ—a line of thought that he continued to develop in his other works as well. This christological specificity of his concept has been widely recognized by Bonhoeffer scholars. As Mayer notes, for example, "Bonhoeffer's concept of vicarious representation is Christological through and through."[37]

A second important source of influence for Bonhoeffer's thinking on vicarious representation can be found in the philosophical discussion of responsibility that was being held at the time. While the discussion may have been quite novel, the word itself had of course been around for quite some time, deriving originally from the Latin verb *responde*.[38] Though the term originated in a juridical context, at the beginning of the twentieth century, its meaning was significantly broadened and applied to other fields as well. In the famous text of "Politik als Beruf," for instance, Max Weber introduced the concept into the domain of political science.[39] In his reflections on the reality of the state and political life, he argued that, by itself, a deontological ethic ("Gesinnungsethik") did not suffice to address the complexities of modern political life—what was needed, in addition, was an ethic of responsibility ("Verantwortungsethik"). On his view, a politician should not only advocate on behalf of certain (deontological) ideals, but, at the same time, should also be able both to calculate political costs and to negotiate for the sake of the goals to be attained. In this way, his thinking wedded deontology and consequentialism. While he was keenly aware of the stark differences between deontological and consequentialist approaches to political life, he never came out explicitly in favor of one or the other. Instead, he argued that they were complementary to each other and that they had to be held together.[40]

37. "Stellvertretung ist bei Bonhoeffer ein durch und durch christologischer Begriff." Mayer, *Christuswirklichkeit*, 182–83. The same observation has been made by Feil, who writes, "Because Jesus Christ is the sole mediator he alone also establishes the new community." Feil, *The Theology of Dietrich Bonhoeffer*, 80. And Rasmussen argues that, "[l]ike all of Bonhoeffer's themes, responsibility has a christological foundation. It is grounded in Jesus Christ's being as being-for-others." Rasmussen, *Dietrich Bonhoeffer*, 38.

38. See Bayertz, "Eine kurze Geschichte," 3–71.

39. Weber, "Politik als Beruf," 396–450.

40. See Kim, "Max Weber"; and Verstraeten, "The Tension between 'Gesinnungsethik' and 'Verantwortungsethik,'" 180–87.

Bonhoeffer had already begun to engage with Weber's work as early as in *SC*, but at that point in time, he focused primarily on the themes of sociology and the church. In *Ethics*, on the other hand, we find him referring, albeit indirectly, to Weber's work on responsibility. In particular, he mentions both Weber and Otto von Bismarck, making the point that they both use the word "responsibility" in a highly developed, ethical sense.[41] He then contrasts their use of the term with his own conception of responsibility, which is defined along christological lines, arguing that, in the biblical sense of the word, "responsibility" means bearing witness before others (or giving an account) of Christ. (He refers in particular to the following biblical passages: 1 Tim 4:16, 1 Pet 3:15, and Phil 1:7; 17.) While Bonhoeffer takes his cue in large part from the biblical text itself, he also expands upon it, making the case that Christians not only bear witness before other human beings concerning Christ, but also the other way around, namely, *before* God *on behalf of* other human beings: "Being accountable [Verantwortung] *for* Jesus Christ before human beings at the same time means being accountable for human beings before Christ; only thus can I take responsibility for myself before God and before human beings."[42] On this basis, Friederike Barth rightly concludes that, in Bonhoeffer's thinking, the concept of responsibility receives a "foundational Christological focus."[43]

Some Key Criticisms of the Concept of Vicarious Representation

The concept of vicarious representation is often regarded as one of the most decisive and innovative aspects of Bonhoeffer's theology.[44] It is also one of the most well-known concepts. As William Schweiker observes, for example, "[t]he meaning of responsibility as representative action, acting for others, was especially emphasized in Christian ethics by Dietrich Bonhoeffer."[45] Many scholars have written on the theme (some of whom have already been

41. DBWE 6:255. For further literature on Weber's and Bismarck's positions, see DBWE 6:255, editorial footnote 31.

42. DBWE 6:256; italics original.

43. ". . . grundlegende christologische Zuspitzung." Barth, *Die Wirklichkeit des Guten*, 234.

44. Abromeit, *Geheimnis Christi*, 268.

45. Schweiker, *Respsonsibility and Christian Ethics*, 57. In addition, see Brian Gregor, who writes that, "[f]rom the perspective of contemporary philosophy, one of the most interesting aspects of Bonhoeffer's thought is his claim that the self is constituted in ethical responsibility for the other person [*Andere*]." Gregor, "Bonhoeffer's 'Christian Social Philosophy,'" 201; italics original.

mentioned),[46] and although the concept is generally well received, it has nevertheless received a significant deal of criticism as well. As Ann Nickson notes, "this concept of vicarious action or deputyship in Bonhoeffer's ethics . . . has been subjected to the most vehement criticism."[47]

Oswald Bayer, to give an example, is quite pointed and sharp in his criticism, describing Bonhoeffer's conception of "Stellvertretung" as a "post-Christian natural theology, with which he remains in the grip of Hegel's philosophy of religion."[48] On his view, Christ's vicarious, representative action is transformed by Bonhoeffer into an *abstractum*. Along similar lines, he also charges that Bonhoeffer's Christology is based on his anthropology—*not* the other way around. Friederike Barth has challenged this criticism, however. According to her, Bayer's interpretation can be classified as an *ad malam partem*, for it focuses exclusively on the text of *Ethics* and doesn't make the necessary effort to situate the concept in its proper context, which, on her read, is necessary for a proper understanding of what Bonhoeffer effectively had in mind.[49] Barth also challenges the suggestion that Bonhoeffer was following Hegel in developing his account of vicarious representation. According to her, a pure and simple adoption, or copying, of Hegel's concept would be very much out of character for Bonhoeffer and would represent a significant lapse in scholarly rigor which, itself, would require further explanation.

This nevertheless does not yet fully dispose of Bayer's criticism that Bonhoeffer's conception of vicarious representation is based on anthropology, and not on Christology. Bayer is not alone in this criticism, moreover. Eberhard Jüngel has also draw attention to the problem.[50] As he argues, Bonhoeffer only interprets the being of Christ on the basis of a deeper, anthropological foundation, or way of thinking.[51] The proper move, he insists, should be the other way around: "It is not from the perspective of an anthropologically identifiable structure of vicarious representation that the mystery of Christ becomes fathomable, but precisely the other way around:

46. In addition to the sources already mentioned, see Daub, *Die Stellvertretung Jesu Christi*; Menke, *Stellvertretung*, 207–19; Glenthøj, "Der Gedanke der Stellvertretung," 48–61; and Kang, "Von der 'Nachfolge' zur 'Ethik der Verantwortung,'" 150–52.

47. Nickson, "Freedom and Responsibility," 132.

48. "[N]achchristliche natürliche Theologie, mit der er im Banne der Religionsphilosophie Hegels steht." Bayer, "Christus als Mitte," 273; italics original.

49. Barth, *Die Wirklichkeit des Guten*, 250–51.

50. Jüngel, "Das Geheimnis der Stellvertretung," 243–60.

51. Ibid., 253.

'The mystery of human existence is revealed in the encounter with Jesus Christ.'[52]

This is surely a very serious criticism, but if one properly overviews the concept of vicarious representation in Bonhoeffer's work, it quickly becomes clear that it is based on a misunderstanding. As we saw earlier in the discussion, Bonhoeffer bases his understanding of this concept on the life of Christ—indeed, Christ's vicarious representation forms the foundation on which Bonhoeffer develops his thought on inter-human "Stellvertretung." The primacy of Christology is very clearly set out in Bonhoeffer's writings on the matter, as the majority of scholars recognize. In addressing the criticism made by Jüngel, for example, Ann Nickson makes the point that "Bonhoeffer's theology and ethics are always grounded christologically; it is Christ the incarnate Son of God who defines true humanity, never vice versa."[53] As she rightfully argues, in Bonhoeffer's theology, humanity's shared participation in Christ's ministry always comes in second place, that is, in response to his own vicarious representation.

This primacy of Christology in Bonhoeffer's concept nevertheless leads to other criticisms. Doronthee Sölle, for example, puts forward an argument leading in precisely the opposite direction, complaining that Bonhoeffer's concept is limited by Christian theology, or more specifically, by biblical revelation.[54] According to her, this is only part of the problem, for she also thinks that the concept is too closely bound up with the notion of responsibility ("Verantwortung") and that it overlooks the specific connection with a broader, religious problem, namely, of Jesus Christ as vicarious representative. The core of Sölle's criticism maintains that Bonhoeffer's concept attempts to combine elements that do not properly belong together, like water and oil. Though running along slightly different lines, essentially the same criticism has been voiced by Klaus Kodalle, who argues that, "[i]f Jesus is the fulfilment of history, when in Christ alone the responsibility for human beings has been fulfilled, then why must inevitably 'all life destined for vicarious representation."[55]

This latter criticism can be countered by paying sustained attention to the inner structure of Bonhoeffer's concept. Indeed, he does not simply

52. "Nicht von einer anthropologisch identifizierbaren Stellvertretungsstruktur her wird das Geheimnis Christi begreifbar, sondern ungekehrt gilt: 'Das Geheimnis der menschlichen Existenz wird in der Begegnung mit Jesus Christus offenbar.'" Ibid.

53. Nickson, *Bonhoeffer and Freedom*, 135.

54. Sölle, "Die Dialektik von Angewiesenheit und Verantwortung," 121–29.

55. "Wenn Jesus die Erfüllung der Geschichte wäre, wenn sich in Christus allein die Verantwortung für den Menschen erfüllt hätte, dann müsste doch nicht zwangsläufig, 'alles Leben zur Stellvertretung bestimmt' sein." Kodalle, *Dietrich Bonhoeffer*, 103.

combine two different understandings of the concept (one being social-eth-ical in bearing, while the other being properly Christian) into a superficial unity, or synthesis, such as Sölle would have us believe. On the contrary, the social-ethical dimension of vicarious representation should be seen as a nat-ural consequence of Christ's vicarious representation. This is pointed out by Abromeit, among others, who argues that the concept is both christological and anthropological at the same time. The anthropological dimension, as he insists, is a direct consequence of the christological one: "[I]n Bonhoeffer, everything is aimed at the continuation of the movement, started in God, among human beings."[56] This is indeed an apt summary of Bonhoeffer's overall aim, for it sees Jesus' vicarious representation as fundamental and as qualitatively different from inter-human "Stellvertretung."

Sölle also formulates a second criticism of Bonhoeffer's concept of vi-carious representation. In particular, she argues that it lacks a clear, eschato-logical dimension, as a result of which the moment of the "now" is given too much weight.[57] Sölle's observation is correct: in Bonhoeffer's theology, re-sponsibility is directed on the present moment—and on the rights of future generations as well, as we saw earlier—and there is no orientation towards a literal eschaton. Yet Sölle's conclusion that therefore the present moment is overemphasised does not automatically follow. In Bonhoeffer's theology, the individual life is not overburdened with messianic expectations. The "History and Good" manuscripts stand in the context of Bonhoeffer's other *Ethics* manuscripts, such as "Ultimate and Penultimate Things," in which he criticizes precisely such a radicalism.

Friederike Barth, who takes great pains to refute a number of the criticisms aimed at Bonhoeffer's concept of vicarious representation, also formulates a criticism of her own, namely, of his idea that single people also live lives of vicariously responsibility by being responsible for themselves as human beings. On her view, the problem with this idea is that it advances, as if out of the blue, a very general conception of being human that is no longer rooted in concrete, social relationships. In addition, as she argues, it runs against Bonhoeffer's firm grounding of his anthropology in Christol-ogy; in other words, it contradicts his understanding of Christ as the only "Stellvertreter," the only one who acts on behalf of all humanity.[58] On this point, Barth's criticism is certainly justified—in his desire to do justice to the lives of single people, Bonhoeffer appears to have overstepped the bounds of

56. ". . . alles läuft bei Bonhoeffer darauf hinaus, daß die Bewegung, die in Gott angefangen hat, unter den Menschen weitergeht." Abromeit, *Geheimnis Christi*, 281.

57. Sölle, "Die Dialektik von Angewiesenheit und Verantwortung," 127–28.

58. Barth, *Die Wirklichkeit des Guten*, 249.

his own line of thought. It should nevertheless be noted that this criticism is a relatively minor one and does not, by itself, call the concept of vicarious representation into question.

Bonhoeffer's Concept of the Divine Mandates

In his *Ethics*, Bonhoeffer does more than indicate the need for responsible action and describe the structure of the responsible life—he also provides a framework in which this responsibility is to be carried out, namely, in accordance with the *divine mandates*. He describes this framework in two different *Ethics* manuscripts: firstly, in "Christ, Reality, and Good,"[59] and secondly, in the last, fragmentary, manuscript of *Ethics*, "The Concrete Commandment and the Divine Mandates."[60] There are also other instances, both in Bonhoeffer's earlier and later work, in which the concept of the divine mandates features prominently, both with or without explicit mentioning. These texts will be examined here as well.

THE CONCEPT OF THE DIVINE MANDATES IN BONHOEFFER'S ETHICS

In the first of the *Ethics* manuscripts in which Bonhoeffer mentions the concept of the divine mandates, "Christ, Reality, and Good," he describes the context in which the mandates are to be understood. As we saw in chapter 2, it is here that he introduces his fundamental concept of Christ-reality, that is, his assertion that "God" and "world" are not separated, but fundamentally one in Christ. It is in the very body of Jesus Christ, he says, that we find God and world together: "The body of Jesus Christ, especially as it is presented to us on the cross, makes visible to faith both the world in its sin and in its being loved by God, and the church-community as the company of those who recognize their sin and gratefully submit to the love of God."[61] Bonhoeffer immediately stresses, however, that this togetherness, in Christ, of God and the world, does not negate the possibility of articulating relative distinctions within this one, selfsame reality. We saw this already in chapter 2, where I drew attention to the room that Bonhoeffer left open for a two-kingdom theory in light of the larger concept of Christ-reality, and also in the distinction that he made, in the same context, between the ultimate and the penultimate. Here again, he introduces yet another distinction, namely,

59. DBWE 6:47–75, esp. 68–74.
60. DBWE 6:388–408.
61. DBWE 6:68.

between the following four mandates: work ("Arbeit"), marriage ("Ehe"), government ("Obrigkeit"), and church ("Kirche"). As he argues, making an appeal both to John 1:10 and Col 1:16, all these mandates are rooted and grounded in Christ. He makes clear that his doctrine of the mandates is yet another way to try to overcome the disctinction between the "worldly" and "spiritual" realms: "There can be no retreat . . . from a 'worldly' into a 'spiritual' 'realm'. The practice of the Christian life can be learned only under these four mandates of God."[62] Bonhoeffer insists that all four mandates, which he grounds directly in the Bible, and directs to Christ, are "divine," not just the church.[63]

Bonhoeffer next proceeds to a more detailed investigation of each of the divine mandates. Concerning work ("Arbeit"), he writes: "Through the divine mandate of work, a world should emerge that—knowingly or un-knowingly—expects Christ, is directed toward Christ, is open for Christ, and serves and glorifies Christ."[64] Through the divine mandate of work, the world is directed, and made open to Christ, as Bonhoeffer asserts. At the same time, it is important to point out that he is not at all naive in his view of how this is effectively worked out in reality, as the following passage makes clear: "That the descendants of Cain should fulfill this mandate casts a deep shadow over all human work."[65] What is true for work is also true for marriage: it is meant to honour Christ and to further his kingdom. And like work, it is also creative, for, in marriage, new human beings are brought into existence.[66] In addition, the same shadow that falls over work falls over mar-

---

62. DBWE 6:69.

63. What is more, Bonhoeffer claims that the mandates offer an analogy between earthly and heavenly realities. Concerning "Arbeit," for instance, he notes that work, in the form of both gathering and working over raw materials, partly functions in order to glorify earthly houses, "like the heavenly city that shines with gold and precious stones." DBWE 6:71. Similarly, insofar as the analogy of marriage is concerned, in which human beings become one before God, we see the unity of Christ with his church. He refers in particular to Eph 5:31vv in this respect. The church, with its mission extending to all people and mandates, finds its analogy in God, for whom all reality is one in the incarnated Son, Jesus Christ. Government is the only mandate for which Bonhoeffer does not provide an analogy. His attempt to draw out these analogies between heavenly and earthly realities is indicative of his tendency to use the method of correlation, to which Mayer has drawn attention: Mayer, *Christuswirklichkeit*, 180.

64. DBWE 6:71.

65. DBWE 6:71.

66. Bonhoeffer does not explain how this would apply to a marriage that, for whatever reason, did not result in bringing forth children. As we shall see in a moment, this problem is addressed later on when he widens the mandate to include both marriage ("Ehe") and family ("Familie").

riage as well: as the Genesis account reveals, the first son that was created through human marriage (namely, Cain) was born outside of paradise and soon became the murderer of his brother. The third mandate, namely, that of government, differs from the former two in that it does not bring forth value or life of itself; instead of being creative itself, it depends on the former two mandates. More specifically, it is entrusted with the protection and ensurance of work and marriage both by performing wedding ceremonies and by setting the proper limits to work and the economy.[67] Like the first two mandates, however, it too is directed to Jesus Christ: "By establishing justice, and by the power of the sword, government preserves the world for the reality of Jesus Christ."[68] The fourth mandate, namely, that of the church, differs from the first three insofar as it stretches itself over them, ensuring that they do not lay claim to the human being entirely, and forbidding the separation of human life into separate spheres. As Bonhoeffer says, "Human beings as whole persons stand before the whole earthly and eternal reality that God in Jesus Christ has prepared for them."[69] The overall intention of the divine mandates, as Bonhoeffer asserts, is to properly situate human beings vis-à-vis "reality [which] in all its manifold aspects is ultimately *one* in God who became human, Jesus Christ."[70]

In the second *Ethics* manuscript in which the theme of the divine mandates appears, "The Concrete Commandment and the Divine Mandates," Bonhoeffer approaches the mandates within the perspective of their foundation in Christ. In particular, he stresses that they are the different forms in which we encounter Christ's commandment.[71] In the same context, he also mentions the concept of Christ-reality again, arguing that the mandates are "organizing structures—'orders'—of the reality of Christ, that is, of the reality of God's love for the world and for human beings that has

67. This restrained view on the state is remarkably similar to O'Donovan's position on the task of the state, as outlined in his book *The Ways of Judgment*.

68. DBWE 6:72–73.

69. DBWE 6:73. This emphasis on the church as one of the mandates shows that the concept clearly presupposes that the people falling under the mandate are already Christians. On a more fundamental level, the whole concept implies that, if a person wants to experience order in the world, he or she must be first be a Christian. See De Lange, *Grond onder de voeten*, 267.

70. DBWE 6:73; italics original.

71. Bonhoeffer wrestles with the word "Mandate" and even considers using other, closely related terms, such as "Stände" and "Amtes." He rejects both these possibilities, however, and, for lack of a more viable alternative, rests content with "Mandate," stating that, in elaborating the concept, he will incorporate the proper meaning and content of both rejected alternatives.

been revealed in Jesus Christ."[72] Within this new perspective, Bonhoeffer sets out accounting for each of the four mandates and introduces some changes along the way. This time, not only the sequence of the mandates has changed, but some are given different names as well: marriage ("Ehe"), for instance, is transformed into marriage and family ("Ehe und Familie"), and work ("Arbeit") is recast, much more broadly, as culture ("Kultur"). In the manuscript, Bonhoeffer also explains why the divine mandates are limited to just these four. As he says, only these four constitute a form of God's authorization: "God's commandment is to be found not wherever there are historical forces, strong ideals, or convincing insights, but only where there are divine mandates [Mandate] which are grounded in the revelation of Christ."[73] Bonhoeffer gives particular emphasis to this point, asserting that not every order necessarily constitutes a divine mandate. To directly equate the two would, in his view, lead all too easily to a sanctioning of any exisiting order, "and thus to a romantic conservatism that no longer has anything to do with the Christian doctrine of the four mandates."[74] This gives the impression that the concept of the divine mandates is strongly positivistic—an impression that is confirmed when Bonhoeffer asserts that the mandates do not come from below but from above. As he says, the mandates are directly implanted in the world as organizing structures, which clearly refutes the idea that they are an outgrowth of history.[75]

Taken on such terms, Bonhoeffer's conception of the divine mandates could be seen as coming dangerously close to the notion that all earthly power-relations, however abusive, are sanctified by God. In order to defend against such an interpretation, he goes on to give three important qualifications, or limiting restrictions, to the concept. First of all, he stresses that the divine mandates are not identical with earthly power relations: "Under no circumstances may the more powerful simply invoke the divine mandate

72. DBWE 6:390.

73. DBWE 6:388. Brock sums up this point quite nicely in the following remark: "The mandates are thus not properly understood as metaphysical axioms, ethical blueprints, or programs; they are Christologically keyed signposts indicating the features of reality that allow us to encounter Christ." Brock, "Reading as Meditation," 90. The point could (and should) even be stated more strongly than this: as the editors of *Ethics* point out, for Bonhoeffer, the mandates form a "real presence" of Christ in the same sense in which Luther spoke of the Lord's Supper. See DBWE 6:401, editorial footnote 44; and also Nissen, "Responding to Human Reality," 210.

74. DBWE 6:389.

75. In order to understand why Bonhoeffer stresses the order coming from "above," one must again look to the historical context. In National Socialism he recognized a revolt coming from "undernearth," that is, from the masses, a revolt direct against the cultured elite and devastating in its effects.

in their dealings with the weaker."[76] Secondly, he emphasizes that the mandates also *create* the (world) below, adding that the above and the below belong intrinsically and inseperably together in a mutually delimiting relationship. Thirdly, he makes the point that the relations between people who are "above" and "below" are relativized by the relation that all human beings have to God, who is the Master of both master and servant. When this insight is lost and being "above" others is exploited, or being "below" is challenged through rebellion, the relationship of those who stand above and those who stand below is transformed into enmity, mistrust and deceit.[77] According to Bonhoeffer, it is only faith in the commission of authentic order from above that can banish the demonic power that arises from below: "When this faith breaks down, then the entire arrangement that has been implanted in the world from above collapses like a house of cards."[78]

Bonhoeffer next makes an important point about the relationship of these mandates to each other. In a key citation, he writes the following: "Only in their being with-one-another [Miteinander], for-one-another [Füreinander], and over-against-one-another [Gegeneinander] do the divine mandates of church, marriage and family, culture, and government communicate the commandment of God as it is revealed in Jesus Christ."[79] What this means is that none of the mandates can exist for or by itself alone, nor can any one of them take the place of any of the others. Although Bonhoeffer doesn't explicitly state it, his conception of the mandates could be seen as bearing a personal structure: just like human beings, the mandates exist *for* each other.[80] In this way, as Bonhoeffer asserts, God safeguards the exercise of every mandate, making sure that one mandate doesn't take precedence over the others. Moltmann, who praises this particular aspect of Bonhoeffer's conception of the divine mandates,[81] perceptively discerns how Bonhoeffer limits each mandate in two ways: "[B]y the eschatological reign of Christ, so far as its existence and function is concerned, and by the

76. DBWE 6:391.

77. Bonhoeffer speaks about "the forces of rebellion." DBWE 6:392. The editors point out that this language is reminiscent of the language used in CF to describe nature in its being out-of-joint as a result of human sin. See DBWE 6:392, editorial footnote 14.

78. DBWE 6:393.

79. DBWE 6:393.

80. This point has also been noted by Scott, "Postnatural Humanity? Bonhoeffer, Creaturely Freedom, and the Mystery of Reconciliation in Creation," 126.

81. He writes: "This coordination of the mandates strikes me as a specially felicitous thought of Bonhoeffer's." Moltmann, "The Lordship of Christ and Human Society," 88.

other mandates in regard to its limits."[82] Another consequence of Bonhoeffer's conception is that it overcomes the privatization of Christian ethics. As Martin Honecker observes, "The concept of the Mandates also challenges a reductionist understanding of Christian ethics, that only concerns itself with a purely individualistic conception of the human being, by drawing the social dimension in again."[83]

From here, Bonhoeffer sets out to describe each of the four mandates, beginning with that of the church. It is the church's task, as he asserts, to proclaim God's revelation in Jesus Christ. He describes this proclamation of the church in a twofold way: 1) as being a means to an end, namely, as a means oriented toward the effective proclamation of Christ to the whole world, and 2) as an end in itself, in the sense that the church-community's act of proclaiming Christ is the very fulfillment of the church's mission. In this context, Bonhoeffer mentions yet again the concept of vicarious, representative action, which, according to him, defines this dual relationship of means and end most clearly. As he says, "The Christian community stands in the place in which the whole world should stand. In this respect it serves the world as vicarious representative; it is there for the world's sake. On the other hand, the place where the church-community stands is the place where the world fulfills its own destiny."[84] In this way, the church follows its Lord, who himself came for-the-world and not for himself, proclaiming the Kingdom of God. Following this discussion of the task of the church, Bonhoeffer's manuscript unexpectedly and abruptly breaks off, thereby leaving his description of the other mandates unfinished.

BACKGROUND AND FURTHER DEVELOPMENTS OF THE CONCEPT OF THE DIVINE MANDATES

It is important to note that, although the *Ethics* manuscripts contain the fullest expression of Bonhoeffer's concept of the divine mandates, the first traces of it can be found in two earlier essays that he wrote on the relationship between church and state. Though he does not yet explicitly define either church or state in relation to divine mandates, the concept as such is clearly present in both texts. In the first essay, "The Church and the Jewish

---

82. Ibid.

83. "Auch überwindet der Mandatsbegriff eine Reduktion der christlichen Ethik auf den Bezug zur rein privatistisch verstandenen Persönlichkeit des Menschen und bezieht die Sozialität mit ein." Honecker, "Christologie und Ethik," 155.

84. DBWE 6:404–5.

Question,"[85] written in 1933, he asks the question of how the church should respond to the racial laws introduced by the Nazi government. He asserts that it is normally not the task of the church to speak to the state concerning specific political actions or decisions. Rather, "The church has neither to praise nor to censure the laws of the state. Instead, it has to affirm the state as God's order of preservation [Erhaltungsordnung] in this godless world."[86] At the same time, he insists that the church *can* ask whether or not the state is acting legitimately, "that is, [asking if it performs] actions that create law and order, not lack of rights and disorder."[87] So, just as the church cannot interfere in the state, so the state may not act outside its proper limits. If it does, that is, if it tries to impose itself on the other orders (in this case, by enforcing racial laws not only on the German nation but also on the church), the church has to react. Bonhoeffer outlines this reaction in three steps: firstly, it asks the state whether it is acting legitimately; secondly, it helps the victims of the state's action; and thirdly, if the state continues to deny its task and to transgress its limits, it may take direct action, such as active resistance, in order to stop the state from doing so.[88]

Bonhoeffer further develops his criticism of the Nazi state in his essay "A Theological Position Paper on State and Church,"[89] or more specifically, in a section of the text entitled "Government and the Divine Orders in the World."[90] In this text, he begins by noting that the task of the state, like that of the church, is rooted in Christ: "Government has the divine task of preserving the world with its God-given orders in reference to Christ."[91] This rather radical task, which clearly prefigures Bonhoeffer's later notion of the state's divine mandate, is further explained in the section "Government and Church."[92] Here Bonhoeffer writes: "Government is established for the sake of Christ. It serves Christ, and thereby it also serves his church. The reign of Christ over all government certainly in no way implies the reign of the church over government. But the same Lord whom government serves

85. DBWE 12:361–70.

86. DBWE 12:362.

87. DBWE 12:364.

88. This program for the church's resistance against a state that oversteps the limits of its task has been commented on widely. See esp. Mayer, "Die Bedeutung von Bonhoeffers Mandatenlehre," 58–80; and ibid., "Zuviel Staat oder zowenig Staat?," 126–58.

89. DBWE 16:502–28. This essay was included in the earlier collection of *Ethics* manuscripts by Eberhard Bethge. See Bonhoeffer, *Ethik*, 353–75.

90. DBWE 16:518–21.

91. DBWE 16:518.

92. DBWE 16:521–26.

is the head of the church-community, the Lord of the church."[93] The government may thus demand obedience from the church, but it cannot interfere with the spiritual office ("Amt") of the church.[94] The church has a task as well, namely, to call the whole world (which clearly includes the state) under the lordship of Christ. As such, it reminds the state that Christ is Lord of both church and government, and it calls both government personnel and civil servants to belief in Christ. And not only that: "It knows that in obedience to Jesus Christ the task of government is properly executed."[95]

As we saw already in our discussion of *Ethics*, Bonhoeffer's thoughts on the relationship between church and state are taken up and developed further into a much broader and more developed conception. It is important to note that, in these earlier essays, the context is clearly that of resistance agains the all-pervasive Nazi state. In the *Ethics* manuscripts, in contrast, this context shifts into the background—the issue in this case has to do with the construction of a post-war society.[96]

The *Ethics* manuscripts, although clearly figuring as a highpoint in Bonhoeffer's thought, are far from being his final word on the matter—indeed, the concept of the divine mandates reappears in a prison-letter that he wrote to Renate and Eberhard Bethge, dated January 23, 1944.[97] In this letter, he makes reference to what Bethge had written to him about friendship in their previous correspondence. As the context makes clear, Bethge had made the point that friendship differs from marriage and kinship in that it doesn't have generally recognized rights; instead, it "depends entirely on its own inherent quality."[98] In response, Bonhoeffer comments that it is no easy task to classify friendship sociologically: "It probably must be understood as a concept subsumed within culture and education [Bildung], whereas brotherhood falls within the concept of church and comradeship within the concepts of work and politics."[99] After going on to note that marriage and family, work, state and church each have their concrete divine mandate, he

93. DBWE 16:521.

94. Rasmussen recognizes the conservative nature of this limited function of the state in Bonhoeffer: "Bonhoeffer's was a conservative argument . . . His answer was a law-and-order answer about the duties of a limited state, limited in its reach by rights it cannot abrogate . . . Here was a conservative argument for bold resistance under circumstances of manifest injustice and the failure to be a proper constitutional state." Rasmussen, "Life Worthy of Life," 64.

95. DBWE 16:522.

96. See De Lange, "'Miteinander, Füreinander, Gegeneinander.'"

97. DBWE 8:264–71.

98. DBWE 8:267.

99. DBWE 8:267.

asks: "[B]ut what about culture and education?"[100] In response to his own question, he relates that he is not at all satisfied by subordinating culture or education to the mandate of work, because they do not belong to the realm of obedience, but rather to the playground of *freedom*, which surrounds the divine mandates. As he says, "Someone who doesn't know anything of this sphere of freedom can be a good parent, citizen, and worker, and probably also a Christian, but whether such a person is a full human being (and thus also a Christian in the fullest sense) is questionable to me."[101] He then adds, in a more critical note, that the Protestant-Prussian world has been so strongly defined by the four mandates that this "playground of freedom" has entirely retreated. From here, in order to open up a space for his personal friendship with Bethge, which had been so important to him during his time in prison, he opens the door to include friendship in the somewhat more ambiguous realm of "culture and education." The letter also clearly brings out an aspect of Bonhoeffer's intention with regard to the concept of the divine mandates that we didn't see before, namely, the theme of *freedom*, which clearly supplements something that had been lacking in his understanding of the just relations between the different spheres of life. What we find here, in other words, is not only a call to acknowledge the proper limits of the spheres of life, but a call to live life in all its *fullness*. As Moltmann says, "what Bonhoeffer is aiming at in his idea of the mandates is a comprehensive view of life as a whole. He wants to find out what life really means to be. He is utterly opposed to any systematization or one-sidedness . . . Only by a comprehensive embodiment of all these aspects, each complementing the others, is a sociology under the sign of reconciliation in Christ meaningful or productive."[102] Here, in sum, the concept of the mandates transforms into truly a *positive* concept that affirms the fullness of earthly existence.

We can see, then, that the concept of the divine mandates is of great importance to Bonhoeffer, and also that, over the years, it continually grew in importance. As De Lange has it, "Bonhoeffer's doctrine of the divine mandates, [which] initially was just one chapter among others of his social ethics, . . . eventually [gained] a fundamental meaning for his entire ethics."[103]

100. DBWE 6:268.

101. DBWE 6:268.

102. Moltmann, "The Lordship of Christ and Human Society," 60.

103. "Bonhoeffer's Mandatenlehre, [der] anfangs vielleicht nicht mehr als nur ein Kapitel unter andere in der Sozialethik war, . . . [kann] zuletzt aber eine grundlegende Bedeutung für Bonhoeffers Ethik-Entwurf insgesamt zugemessen werden." Lange, "'Miteinander, Füreinander, Gegeneinander.'"

Relation to The Concept of the Orders of Preservation

On the basis of the foregoing discussion, we are able to note a number of crucial differences between the divine mandates and Bonhoeffer's earlier conception of the orders of preservation. As we saw in chapter 3, during the years 1932 to 1933, Bonhoeffer made use of the latter concept in order to speak about the ordering of natural life, which he contrasted, in a critical way, with the concept of the orders of creation ("Schöpfungsordnungen") that had been misused by the German Christians. When he noticed that the concept of the orders of preservation ("Erhaltungsordnungen") began to be misused in a similar way, he gave up using the concept altogether. In the language of the mandates, however, he is clearly seeking, yet again, to speak about the divine ordering of the world. With this shift, it is not only the name, but the concept itself, that is transformed. Like the orders of preservation, the divine mandates are tied exclusively to Christ, but they clearly differ from the former insofar as they are divine *commandments*, which demand obedience, instead of *structures* that can be discerned. As a consequence, the concept takes on a much more dynamic nature, even though Bonhoeffer speaks of it in rather static terms. As Martin Honecker notes, "[t]he concept of the divine mandates, with his emphasis on 'divine commission,' doubtlessly adds a dynamic elements, which can break open the static nature of an unhistorically understood conception of order."[104] This dynamic element, in stark contrast with the idea of fixed and established orders, makes it possible to apply Bonhoeffer's theology of the divine mandates to new fields, and, at the same time, to adjust it in light of new challenges, as I will show further on.

What's also new in comparison with the earlier concept of orders of preservation is the addition of an eschatological dimension—the concept of the divine mandates must be seen, as Moltmann has pointed out, as something that Bonhoeffer consciously situates in the difference between the ultimate and the penultimate. On the subject of the penultimate, for instance, Moltmann writes the following: "Standing in this time and in this space are the mandates—including the church—provisional in an eschatological sense. Under this earthly physical covering of the ultimate, a world is to arise which is waiting for Christ, receptive to him and so serving him and glorifying him."[105] This is clearly an important observation, for it places

---

104. "Der Mandatsbegriff bringt mit der Hervorgebung des 'göttlichen Auftrags' zweifellos ein dynamischen Element, welches die Statik eines ungeschichtlich verstandenen Ordnungsdenkens aufzubrechen vermag." Honecker, "Christologie und Ethik," 155. This change is also noted by Wolf, "Bonhoeffers Begriff der Mandate," 171.

105. Moltmann, "The Lordship of Christ and Human Society," 81.

Bonhoeffer's concept of the divine mandates in a completely different light. As Moltmann observes, "the mandates are positive, godly institutions, bulwarks against chaos, but at the same time processes of integration, open to the coming of Christ."[106]

One final difference has to do with the fact that Bonhoeffer's concept of the divine mandates is more open to empirical reality than his earlier concept was. As Mayer points out, "[c]ontrary to the doctrine of the orders of preservation . . . the concept of the divine mandates takes up in itself the earthly form of the structures of the command in an act of correlating the will of God with empirical reality in the concept of the Christ-reality."[107] This growing openness to empirical reality is characteristic of Bonhoeffer's theology in general. As a consequence, his doctrine of the divine mandates becomes much more concrete than his earlier concept had been, the function of which was more polemical in nature.[108] We already saw this growing openness to empirical reality above, in the letter written to Bethge, where Bonhoeffer exhibited a certain readiness to make room for friendship in the mandate of "Kultur"—which, in turn, is a reformulation of the mandate of "Arbeit."[109] This focus on reality "as it is," including its fallenness, also means that the mandates do not describe the "perfect" ordering of society—indeed, it is not without reason that the mandates are said to be posed over-against-each-other ("gegeneinander"). The mandates are, as was already prefigured in the concept of "Erhaltungsordnungen," orders for maintaining a relative peace in the fallen creation.[110]

---

106. Ibid.

107. "Im Unterschied zu der Lehre von den Erhaltungsordnungen . . . nimmt der Mandatsbegriff die irdische Gestalt des Sollens-strukturen im Akt der Korrelation von Gotteswillen und Empirie in die Christuswirklichkeit auf." Mayer, *Christuswirklichkeit*, 181.

108. Despite Bonhoeffer's wish for the mandates to describe reality as it is, the concept of course remains at the level of an interpretation of that reality. See Abromeit, *Geheimnis Christi*, 134.

109. The editors of the German edition of Bonhoeffer's prison letters comment on this point in the following terms: "Bonhoeffer's letters from Tegel contained theological reflections from the very outset. Their special feature was that they referred immediately and directly to the concrete life situation of imprisonment . . . The possibility of conflict between marriage and friendship prompted a theological reconsideration of the doctrine of mandates." DBWE 8:584–85.

110. See Rasmussen, "The Ethics of Responsible Action," 206–25; Moltmann, "Die Wirklichkeit der Welt," 63; and Mayer, "Die Bedeutung von Bonhoeffers Mandatenlehre," 65.

Theological Influences on The Concept of the Divine Mandates

Apart from the relation to Bonhoeffer's earlier theology, it is also important to draw attention to the theological background of Bonhoeffer's doctrine of the divine mandates. First of all, it should be noted that the concept is closely related to Luther's doctrine of the estates ("Stände"), which is a term that, as we saw already, Bonhoeffer considered using instead of mandates ("Mandate").[111] In his own work, Luther identified three such estates, namely, *ecclesia*, *oeconomia*, and *politia*.[112] *Oeconomia* refers in this case both to family life and to work, which is understandable, given the feudal context of the Late Middle Ages during which Luther was writing. In Bonhoeffer's time, family life and work had grown apart from each other to such an extent that Bonhoeffer felt the need to come up with a separate, independent mandate for the latter. Apart from the introduction of this new mandate, however, Bonhoeffer doesn't alter Luther's original doctrine. This has been noted by various scholars.[113] Finally, it is important to note a clear parallel between Luther and Bonhoeffer regarding the limits of the power of the state,[114] though it is true that Bonhoeffer developed his doctrine in a radically different context than Luther did, and also that, even more clearly than Luther, he grounds the power of the state directly and explicitly in Christ.[115]

One also finds a relation to Karl Barth's theology here as well. Bonhoeffer was well aware of Barth's *CD* 2/2 at the time of writing the *Ethics*, and

111. Mayer shows, however, that Luther himself also spoke about "mandates." See Mayer, "Die Bedeutung von Bonhoeffers Mandatenlehre," 63.

112. A classic study on Luther's doctrine of the mandates remains that of Wingren, *Luthers Lehre von Beruf*. See also Schwarz, "Luthers Lehre von den drei Ständen," 15–34; and Bayer, "Natur und Institution," 116–46.

113. As Moltmann says concerning Luther's doctrine of the Stände: "This is precisely the teaching which Bonhoeffer endeavors to refurbish. And it is so much better expressed in his doctrine of the mandates than in any theology of the orders." Moltmann, "The Lordship of Christ and Human Society," 74. See also Trowitzsch, "Luther und Bonhoeffer Zugleich," 185–206; and Duchrow, "Dem Rad in die Speichen fallen," 34.

114. Moltmann draws this point out through a quotation of Luther: "Omnes status huc tendunt, ut aliis serviant. Mater custodit puerum; ipsa non indiget, sed puer. Vir cogitur surgere: posset dormire, sed quia uxorem et pureos nutrire cogitur, ideo surgendum. Nos omnia invertimus." Quoted in Moltmann, "The Lordship of Christ," 88–89. This is indeed remarkably similar to what Bonhoeffer writes about the function of the state as servant.

115. See Körtner, *Evangelische Sozialethik*, 51.

it is quite likely that this work influenced him.[116] In particular, this can be seen in the stress that Bonhoeffer places both on the mandates as concrete *commandments* of God and on life in the mandates as a form of obedience. As Moltmann notes: "In this idea of the mandates as 'the place where God secures obedience to himself' Bonhoeffer comes very close to the special ethics of Karl Barth."[117] There is, however, also an important difference between the ways in which Bonhoeffer and Barth conceive of the mandates. Though Barth clearly acknowledges the mandates, he places much more emphasis on the in-breaking character of God's word giving concrete guidance in specific situations. According to him, the mandate only comes in existence "in the power of the divine command itself, in the ethical event."[118] Van 't Slot comments on this as follows: "So here again, Barth prefers a more 'actualist' or 'eschatological' approach than Bonhoeffer in his ongoing quest for permanence in an ethics of God's commandment."[119] This is also noted by Abromeit, who argues that Bonhoeffer maintains a middle-position between Barth's actualistic position and the Roman Catholic position, which gives much greater emphasis to the role of reason.[120] One can also locate other influences on Bonhoeffer in this regard.[121] Apart from these sources of influence, there are also parallels between Bonhoeffer's concept of the divine mandates and the work of other theologians.[122]

116. Bonhoeffer read *CD* 2/2 in galley proofs at the Lake of Geneva on May 13, 1942. See DBWE 16:276–77.

117. Moltmann, "The Lordship of Christ and Human Society," 73.

118. *CD* 3/4:22.

119. Van 't Slot, *Negativism of Revelation?*, 206.

120. Abromeit, *Geheimnis Christi*, 135.

121. Krause claims that Bonhoeffer adopted the concept of the divine mandates via Vilmar. See Krause, "Bonhoeffer," 62. Krause is referring in particular to Vilmar, *Dogmatik*; as well as ibid., *Die Lehre vom geistlichen Amt*.

122. It is interesting to note that Brunner developed thoughts closely related to those of Bonhoeffer. See Brunner, *Die politische Verantwortung des Christen*, 12–13. On the pages, however, a difference between the two theologians also becomes clear: Brunner sees the divine order of the state as less important than the divine order of family, because the latter institution pre-dates the Fall, whereas Bonhoeffer sees both orders as equally important. We already noted this difference earlier on as well, in chapter 3. Furthermore, West has drawn attention to a parallel between Bonhoeffer and Calvin concerning the purposes and activities of civil government, such as protecting public worship, encouraging civil righteousness, and promoting general peace and tranquility. West, "Ground under our Feet," 235–73, esp. 263. This is mentioned in DBWE 6:393, editorial footnote 16. The proximity between Bonhoeffer and Calvin can perhaps best be explained by Bonhoeffer's appropriation of Barth, whose account of the divine commandment is reminiscent of that of Calvin.

SOME KEY CRITICISMS OF BONHOEFFER'S CONCEPT OF THE DIVINE MANDATES

Bonhoeffer's concept of the divine mandates has received a great deal of attention, both negative and positive in nature. Instead of going into some of the positive criticisms, some of which have already been mentioned above, I would like to deal in particular with two of the more well-known negative criticisms.

The most prevalent criticism put forward against Bonhoeffer's concept maintains that it bears the marks of patriarchalism. More specifically, the stress that Bonhoeffer places on the "above" and the "below," as set in place by God's commandments in the form of the divine mandates, has been seen as supportive of a hierarchical society. In *CD* 3/4, for instance, Barth, quite famously, asks the rhetorical question if, "[i]n Bonhoeffer's doctrine of the mandates, . . . there [is] not just a suggestion of North German patriarchalism?"[123] This rather condensed, elliptical criticism has been drawn out and explicated by others in greater detail.[124] At the same time, however, it is important to note that, with his concept, Bonhoeffer is not explicitly arguing for the maintenance of authoritarian power structures. On the contrary, the basis for authority within the sphere of the mandates is vicarious, representative action, that is, responsibility. As Moltmann notes, "it should be noted that Bonhoeffer is not talking of a purely external authority derived from an official position, but an authority which is existential and personal, resting upon self-sacrifice and vicarious action for others."[125] The mandates are not derived from Platonic ideas, Moltmann asserts, but form an answer to reality, an answer of life lived in obedience and in Christ's discipleship. As such, "The imperative structure of the mandates . . . rests upon the indicative structure of deputyship, whether the latter is already present or still to be achieved."[126] Moreover, we saw already that Bonhoeffer

123. *CD* 3/4:22. Later on, Barth made this point yet again in a letter to Landes-superintendent Herrenbrück: "And how was it with the 'Mandates' of his *Ethics*, with which I tussled when I wrote [*Dogmatics*] III/4?" Barth, "From a Letter of Karl Barth," 90; italics original. It should be noted, at the same time, that Barth values Bonhoeffer's emphasis on the divine origin of the mandates and joins him in emphasizing that the madates originate from above, rather than from below. Also, more generally, Barth recognizes the proximity of Bonhoeffer's *Ethics* to his own ethics, writing: "[T]he same attitude to the link with dogmatics is a commendable feature of the brilliant *Ethik* of Dietrich Bonhoeffer [. . .], which unfortunately exists only in a fragmentary and provisionary form." *CD* 3/4:4; italics original.

124. See, for instance, De Lange, *Grond onder de voeten*, 268.

125. Moltmann, "The Lordship of Christ and Human Society," 86.

126. Ibid.

emphasized the point that every "above" is itself relativized by God, who stands above everything on earth that is "superior" and "inferior," and to whom all are responsible.

A second criticism holds that, in *Ethics*, Bonhoeffer limits the number of mandates too severely, and that he does not defend his delineation of the mandates sufficently. Take for instance the following question posed by Karl Barth: "Why . . . are there only four (or five) mandates and no others?"[127] Not only is Barth unconvinced by Bonhoeffer's attempts to biblically defend his choice for just four mandates, but he would like to leave room open for other potential mandates as well. Moltmann raises a criticism running along similar lines. Although he supports Bonhoeffer's emphasis on the divine origin of the mandates, he argues that Bonhoeffer's way of going about conceiving of them is indicative of a typically Western way of thinking, adding that the concept is not as firmly grounded in the biblical text as Bonhoeffer implies.[128] While this line of criticism is undoubtedly justified to a certain extent, a number of finer, more nuanced observations could help situate Bonhoeffer's line of thought within its proper context. First of all, it is important to note that Bonhoeffer's intention with the divine mandates was not to impose an idealistic scheme on reality, but rather to serve as an explication of reality "as it is." Even though his overall account may not prove as successful or all-inclusive as he might have hoped, in its focus on phenomenologically accessible reality, it has considerable potential to criticize false and misleading construals of reality. As we saw earlier, Bonhoeffer himself already started to do just this somewhat later on: while in prison, he found himself confronted more than ever with the value of friendship, which led him to consider making room for the experience in the context of the mandate of Kultur. A second nuance of this sort is suggested by Moltmann. As he points out, precisely in their status as commandments issued by the living God, there is the possibility for change within the mandates. In his own words: "The negative rigidity which has been the object of complaint might be removed by integrating them into the living history of God. And then, finally, we shall see the law in the hand of the Lawgiver and the mandate in the hand of the God who commissions men to his service."[129]

Moltmann bases this observation on the striking connection that Bonhoeffer draws, in prison, between the divine mandates and the concept

127. *CD* 3/4:22.

128. Moltmann, "Die Wirklichkeit der Welt und Gottes konkretes Gebot nach Dietrich Bonhoeffer," 63. Others have posed similar objections. See Wolf, "Bonhoeffers Begriff der Mandate," 171; and Honecker, "Christologie und Ethik," 156.

129. Moltmann, "The Lordship of Christ and Human Society," 94.

of *freedom*, insisting that this very connection supplies the theological justification needed to argue for possible alterations in the conception of the divine mandates. This is certainly a rather speculative move on Moltmann's part, for there would appear to be little ground in the prison letter itself to support such a reading—indeed, it is based on associative thinking, not on "exegesis" of the letter itself. And yet Moltmann is undoubtedly right to insist that the focus on the commandment-character of the mandates has the potential for change and adjustment. The mandates, in other words, are not institutions in themselves, but forms of God's commandment.[130] This accordingly makes it possible to adjust and change both the number and function of the mandates over time. It also marks an important difference from the arguably more fixed form of the "Erhaltungsordnungen," such as we saw earlier.

Responsibility and Environmental Ethics

In this section I return to the social dimension of the environmental crisis, which I dealt with already, however briefly, in chapter 4. As I indicated in that section, Bonhoeffer's thoughts on human relationality as the content of the *imago Dei* can function as a foundation for addressing this social dimension. The concepts of vicarious representation and of the divine mandates are able to add even more substantial contributions to the discussion, namely, by specifying this human relationality in terms of responsibility, and by furnishing a structure in which this responsibility can be carried out in public life. Here in the present section, I shall focus, first of all, on describing the contributions that Bonhoeffer's concept of vicarious representation can make to environmental ethics; secondly, I shall focus on the applications that can be made from his understanding of the divine mandates.

The Relevance of Bonhoeffer's Concept of Vicarious Representation for Environmental Ethics

Since its introduction into political philosophy by Weber in 1919, the concept of responsibility has come to play an important role in practical philosophy—indeed, it has been applied to many different fields of study, environmental ethics being one of them. By way of example, in 1979, Hans Jonas wrote his famous book, *The Imperative of Responsibility*, which has been foundational in the formation of the ecological movement in Germany.

130. See Dumas, *Dietrich Bonhoeffer*, 170.

In this book, Jonas describes ecology as a new dimension of responsibility: "Nature as a human responsibility is surely a novum to be pondered in ethical theory."[131] Since the publication of this text, the concept of human responsibility for the environment has become very widespread indeed. It has found expresssion in corporate culture, for instance, in the form of the popular phrase that companies bear responsibility for people, profit and planet.[132]

Bonhoeffer's concept of vicarious representation is able to make at least two important contributions to this discussion of responsibility in environmental ethics. First of all, it can provide responsibility with a strong, christological basis, yet in such as way that makes it accessible to non-Christians as well. Secondly, it is able to include care for nature in the concept of responsibility. In what follows, I will elaborate on these contributions in detail, describing each of them separately.

VICARIOUS REPRESENTATION AS AN ALTERNATIVE TO RESPONSIBILITY FOR FUTURE GENERATIONS

In *The Imperative of Responsibility*, Jonas not only introduces responsibility as an important concept, specifically for the field of ecology—he also introduces a specific incentive for responsibility, namely, the rights of future generations.[133] In other words, for Jonas, acting responsibly simply means that actions and decisions made in the present require that the interests of future generations be considered alongside those of people currently living. To focus exclusively on the concerns and needs of the present is, in Jonas' view, to act irresponsibly.

Since the publication of Jonas' work, the concept of human responbility towards future generations has grown significantly in popularity—many philosophers have worked at explicating it and further developing it.[134] It

131. Jonas, *The Imperative of Responsibility*, 7.

132. This threefold formulation of responsibility was first coined by Elkington, *Cannibals with Forks*.

133. See the chapter of Jonas' book entitled "The Horizon of the Future," in *The Imperative of Responsibility*, 110–18. Jonas goes on to outline the political consequences of this responsibility in the following chapter: "How Far Does Political Responsibility Extend into the Future?," in ibid., 119–24.

134. See Laslett and Fishkin, *Justice between Age Groups and Generations*; Auerbach, *Unto the Thousandth Generation*; Kim and Harrison, *Self and Future Generations*; and Visser 't Hooft, *Justice to Future Generations and the Environment*. For a succinct defense of ascribing rights to future generations, see Gosseries, "On Future Generations' Future Rights," 446–74.

has also been picked up by scholars working in the field of international politics.[135] Indeed, the rights of future generations have even come to be included in the constitutions of countries such as Japan, Norway and Bolivia.[136]

The notion of the future forming a constitutive aspect of responsibility has been developed in a different direction by Georg Picht.[137] In his description of the concept's history, Picht draws particular attention to the way it was used in a certain juridical context. In particular, he argues that the concept was originally formed in a fundamental relation to Christian eschatology; more specifically, he insists that it was the expectation of the final judgment that formed the basis of bearing responsibility, or acting responsibly, in the present. In his own words: "Only the Final Judgment could give rise to the idea that life as a whole must serve to prepare one for this Final Responsibility. As a moral concept, responsibility is therefore of Christian provenance. To put it more precisely: it is an eschatological idea."[138] This explains why, on Picht's view, the concept of responsibility can only be rightly understood once its anchoring in Christian theology is fully and properly acknowledged. Whether this is true or not, it is a fact that a great deal of theological discussion has been stirred up on this topic as well—many theologians have identified the biblical and theological roots of the concept and put it to use in the context of environmental ethics.[139]

This proposal for orienting responsibility in relation to future generations has attracted a number of philosophical criticisms, however. First of all, future generations, because they do not yet exist, are incapable of reciprocating the care taken on their behalf.[140] Secondly, it is far from being clear what the needs of future generations effectively consist in—indeed, per-

---

135. In the context of the UN, for example, environmental ethics are often outlined in the form of tasks to be fulfilled in responbility to future generation. See for example the well-known declaration from the General Conference of UNESCO, "Declaration on the Responsibilities of the Present Generation towards Future Generations."

136. See Gosseries, "On Future Generations' Future Rights," 448.

137. In this section, I am taking my cue from Picht, "The Concept of Responsibility," 185–203. Picht's primary work on the subject is ibid., *Wahrheit, Vernunft, Verantwortung*.

138. Picht, "The Concept of Responsibility," 190. Barth makes exactly the same point. He too points to the eschatological context of the concept of responsibility, and concludes: "The idea of responsibility, rightly understood, is known only to Christian ethics." *CD* 2/2:642.

139. See Würthwein and Merk, *Verantwortung*; Römelt, "Natur als Gegenstand menschlicher Verantwortung," 77–96; Muers, *Living for the Future*; and Körtner, "Schöpfungsglaube und Verantwortungsethik," 101–15.

140. See Parfit, "Future Generations," 113–72.

haps they are very different from what we presently imagine them to be.[141] Thirdly, it can be asked to what extent, or in what sense, "possible" (i.e. not yet existing) persons can be said to have rights.[142] Each of these objections—which I shall only allude to here—are quite serious in nature; taken together, they pose serious problems for those seeking to account for environmental responsibility solely in relation to the rights of future generations.

There is another problem as well: as Scruton has pointed out, emphasizing the rights of future generations fails to provide a convincing argument for why ordinary people should be concerned about the environment. As he argues, developing and showing concern for future generations is only possible on the basis of concrete attachments of one sort or another—for example, the attachment between parents and their children. In the following, key citation, Scruton notes that "[r]esponsibility may embrace the whole of nature and the whole of time, but only by spreading to the point of transparency the solid stuff of person-to-person sympathy."[143]

It is here in particular that Bonhoeffer's concept of vicarious representation is able to help. Earlier on, I showed that future generations are, in fact, part of Bonhoeffer's concept of responsibility.[144] At the core of his concept, however, is a focus on the "Other," in the here and now, who claims the responsibility of the "I." This way of grounding responsibility in the here and now, as well as Bonhoeffer's focus on concrete persons, constitutes a much more immediate and direct impetus for environmental responsibility than considerations bearing on future generations. In chapter 4, where I referred to the social dimension of the ecological crisis, I made the case that one of the strongest motives to get involved in environmental care is the fact the ecological crisis affects human beings—often in dreadful ways. Bonhoeffer, of course, grounds this appeal in his Christology, but as we saw, he developed his concept in such a way that it also included the non-religious,

141. This point is also made by Nullens and Michener, who write: "On the one hand, Jonas emphasized the unpredictability of the future and the open-endedness of life in general. On the other hand, he wished to take the future as his starting point for developing a universal ethic. This ambivalence permeates his entire ethical model and, in our view, presents a problem difficult to resolve." Nullens and Michener, *The Matrix of Christian Ethics*, 91.

142. See De George, "The Environment, Rights and Future Generations," 93–105.

143. Scruton, *Green Philosophy*, 208.

144. This is noted by Burkholder, who applies it to environmental ethics. After first describing how concern for future generations motivated Bonhoeffer in his activities in the resistance, he argues that it leads to "a sustainable lifestyle, which attempts to satisfy the present needs of the human community while ensuring that the needs of future generations will also be met." Burkholder, "Christological Foundations," 352.

vicarious responsibility of secular people. As such, his concept is fit to motivate both Christians *and* a more general, secular public, thereby making it
an example of public theology *avant la lettre*. This potential of Bonhoeffer's
understanding of vicarious representation has been recognized by William
Schweiker, who argues that "Bonhoeffer's point holds even if we bracket his
ecclesial and Christological claims."[145]

Including Ecological Concern in the Concept of Resonsibility

Although the concept of responsibility is predominantly employed in relation to God and human beings, it has also, or more recently, been introduced
in relation to nature. One example of such an application can be found in
the work of Jürgen Hübner.[146] In the context of an explication of Western
anthropocentrism, Hübner makes the point that, although human beings
have an exalted position within the created order, this does not allow them
to abuse nature, "but obliges them to maintain and promote the foundation of the life conferred to each creature, so much so that their lives are
interconnected with those of human beings."[147] The basis of this obligation
is not so much concern with other human beings as it is with nature itself.
In short, for Hübner, human beings need to be responsible to nature as well,
and not just to each other. Such a responsibility should, according to him, be
enacted in the form of a partnership, and not in an arbitrary spirit of dominion. Human beings should come to realize that, in large part, they are now
responsible for how evolutionary history will develop. This huge responsibility calls for a joint, or combined ethical approach, in which individual
ethics is combined with social ethics.[148] Here we see how a responsibility for
nature comes to form a part of a concept of responsibility that essentially
remains anthropocentric in nature: human beings ought to care for nature
because—or precisely insofar as—they themselves are a part of it.

Many theologians have come to agree with this view, and as a consequence, they have begun to argue for a similar broadening of the concept
of responsibility.[149] As Sallie McFague writes, for instance, "[w]hat is be-

145. Schweiker, *Responsibility and Christian Ethics*, 57.

146. Hübner, "Ökologische Verantwortung," 203–51.

147. "[S]ondern verpflichtet ihn zur Erhaltung und Förderung der Grundlagen
des jedem Geschöpf verliehenen Lebens, so sehr dies fortan ein mit dem Menschen
verbundenes Leben sein wird." Ibid., 233.

148. Ibid., 234.

149. Also in official church documents on the ecological crisis the concept of
responsibility plays an important role. See John Paul II, "The Ecological Crisis."

coming increasingly clear is that the way we must reflect God is to accept responsibility for planetary well-being."[150] Certain evangelical theologians have also come to recognize the need to redefine the concept of responsibility in relation to ecology. In a discussion of Job 38:1—42:6, for instance, Bouma-Prediger makes the point that the imagery used in these biblical texts "generates an ethic of proper place and appropriate limit. In short, the moral order envisioned by this text is an ethic of ecological hospitality and responsibility."[151] Equally important in this regard is the "Evangelical Declaration on the Care of Creation,"[152] in which the double-sided nature of Christian responsibility is described in terms very similar to those used Bonhoeffer (albeit with an explicit inclusion of the term "ecology"). As the first point of the declaration states, "[m]en, women, and children, have a unique responsibility to the Creator."[153] For anyone even casually familiar with the Bible and Christian doctrine, this statement will likely sound very familiar and unoriginal. The second point, in contrast, introduces something quite novel and striking: "Men, women, and children, created in God's image, also have a unique responsibility for creation. Our actions should both sustain creation's fruitfulness and preserve creation's powerful testimony to its Creator."[154] The book in which this Declaration is printed contains a collection of essays written by Christian theologians (as well as by scholars from other disciplines), the aim of which is to explain this second dimension of responsibility in greater detail.

In the essay of I. Howard Marshall, for example, the author uses the analogy of social concern to explain why Christians should be engaged in ecological action.[155] He describes how social concern has often been understood in opposition to the call to evangelise, the latter being seen as much more important than the former. According to him, this view has come to be supplanted, or at the very least, emended, through the devotion of sustained attention to the Old Testament prophetic speeches, which saw social life and religious life as being closely interconnected with each other. In a similar way, he says, responsibility for the welfare of other human beings implies a need for ecological action. In another essay from the same collection, Moltmann makes a similar point in language very clearly reminiscent

150. McFague, *A New Climate for Theology*, 167.

151. Bouma-Prediger, *For the Beauty of the Earth*, 97.

152. Evangelical Environmental Network, "An Evangelical Declaration on the Care of Creation," 17–22.

153. Ibid., 20.

154. Ibid.

155. Marshall, "Commitment to Creation," 94–98.

of that of Bonhoeffer.[156] He points to the second dimension of responsibility mentioned in the Declaration, namely, responsibility before God. This, on his view, has immediate consequences for ecology: "If we realize that it is God, Creator of heaven and Earth, who is making us responsible to himself, the extent of the things for which we are responsible to him and the extent of the things for which we ourselves are responsible also become clear: we are responsible for that part of God's creation over which we human beings can rule."[157] Slightly further down the page, he continues his thought: "Before God we are responsible for the Earth and its creatures to 'protect and heal' as much as we can."[158]

Bonhoeffer's understanding of responsibility can assist in this adaptation, or broadening, of the concept of responsibility to include care for nature. Although he may not have explicitly included the realm of nature in his account, he did, at the very least, open up very real, theoretical possibilities for doing so. As we saw earlier, according to Bonhoeffer, responsibility takes place in relation to God and human beings, or more specifically, in the double movement of responsibility of God vis-à-vis human beings, and of human beings before God. We also saw that, on his view, human beings can bear responsibility for things and states of affairs. Because responsibility takes places between persons, these things and states of affairs can never motivate responsibility in or by themselves: human beings are not responsible *to* things. However, part of their responsibility to other human beings and to God can include responsibility *for* things. It is of course only a small step to apply this way of thinking to ecology: nature can be seen as a "state of affairs' for which human beings are responsible, for, as Hübner rightly points out, ecological integrity decisively influences human integrity as well. People suffer on account of the decreased quality of water, air and soil, as well as on account of other evils resulting from the current ecological crisis. Since, according to Bonhoeffer, Christians are responsible to Christ for these suffering human beings, there is a strong appeal for them to address the crisis.[159]

156. Moltmann, "God's Covenant and our Responsibility," 107–13.

157. Ibid., 109.

158. Ibid.

159. Also Burkholder recognizes the fact that Bonhoeffer opens up the possibility to place nature within the reach of human responsibility Burkholder, "Christological Foundations," 352. Oddly enough, however, he does not base himself on the "History and Good [2]" manuscript, but on the first manuscript of *Ethics*, namely, "Christ, Reality, and Good." He draws attention to the fact that, in this manuscript, Bonhoeffer's concept of the good includes the non-human creation that surrounds human beings; see DBWE 6:53. This is certainly the case—Bonhoeffer's concept of Christ-reality

An Ecological Application of Bonhoeffer's Divine Mandates

In this section I would like to return to Bonhoeffer's doctrine of the divine mandates, with the aim of applying it to the field of contemporary environmental ethics. In a similar vein, in chapter 3, we saw how his concept of the orders of preservation could be applied to environmental ethics. As we saw there, that concept was used specifically by Bonhoeffer in order to oppose the kind of natural theology that was bolstering the German Christians, who supported the Nazis. Because of this, I chose to transpose that concept into the debate over the notion of Gaia and, in particular, to put it to use in criticizing an all too facile, theological justification of the Gaia theory. Bonhoeffer's concept of the divine mandates can make a similar contribution, albeit in a different discussion—although it can be seen as a further development of his concept of the orders of preservation, we saw that it differs distinctively from that concept. It also has a very different sort of function, namely, as a blueprint for a post-war society. It is therefore warranted to bring Bonhoeffer's concept of the mandates to bear on the discussion of environmental ethics.

Before considering this contribution in detail, I would first like to indicate some of the specific challenges that this process of theoretical transpostion faces. This will figure as the theme of the next subsection. In the following subsection, I will then account for the contribution that Bonhoeffer's concept of the mandates can make in the current context of neoliberalization, focusing in particular on how it can help to expose certain injustices and to stimulate self-regulating activities within the mandate of the economy. In the third subsection, I shall focus specifically on the mandate of the state and explore in detail how it could be applied in the context of globalization. Fourthly, and finally, I shall describe how Bonhoeffer's thoughts on the mandate of the church can help strengthen the church's environmental action as a civic community.

---

overcomes false distinctions and perceives the natural world and humanity as being one in Christ. This was described in chapter 2, where I argued that this concept is a powerful motivation for taking care for creation. Yet when it comes to arguing for human *responsibility* for the natural world, it provides only an indirect foundation. The way Bonhoeffer speaks about responsibility for "things" and "states of affairs" in the "History and Good [2]" manuscript provides a much more immediate and logical foundation for such a broader conception of responsibility.

The Abiding Relevance of Bonhoeffer's Concept of the Divine Mandates

Translating Bonhoeffer's concept of the divine mandates into the world of today must be carried out with a certain degree of caution and circumspection: the criticisms listed earlier require that any appropriation of his concept of the divine mandates will need to be critical in nature. One other factor also needs to be taken into account, namely, the social and cultural differences between Bonhoeffer's time and our own. Some of these differences have been formulated quite pointedly by De Lange, already in 1985. In particular, he points to the apologetic tendency of the *Ethics*, to the strong difference between 'Oben' and 'Unten,' to the concept's inherent conservatism, as well as to Bonhoeffer's intention to unite a Christian "Abendland."[160]

Although De Lange is certainly right to draw attention to these differences between Bonhoeffer's time and our own, I would argue that he goes too far in concluding that the relevance of Bonhoeffer's work for us today is reduced to a bare minimum. Indeed, De Lange himself admits as much at a later point. In a 1996 article, he calls for a rethinking of institutional ethics, in which he believes that Bonhoeffer's doctrine of the mandates can help.[161] In particular, he sees Bonhoeffer's work contributing in the following two ways. First of all, he argues that Bonhoeffer can help to bridge the historical gap between present-day politico-philosophical accounts of institutions and the early-modern socio-ethical tradition of the Reformation (mentioning Luther specifically in this regard). Secondly, he believes that Bonhoeffer can make a theological contribution as well, namely, in helping to recognize, in the form of institutions, the active presence of God in his creation, thereby helping ethics to regain a certain "objectivity": by insisting on God as the source and criterium of the good, Bonhoeffer's work could act as a counterbalance against contemporary trends of subjectivism and moral relativity.

---

160. De Lange, *Grond onder de voeten*, 271. De Lange's assessment differs markedly from that of Huntemann, who in 1989 wrote that Bonhoeffer's concept of the mandates "was developed . . . against a spirit that is not only similar to the spirit of our time, but can also be thought of as something like a penultimate that preceded the ultimate that is our time." Huntemann, *The Other Bonhoeffer*, 254. Huntemann notes that the importance of responsibility ethics has only grown in the meantime, which leads him to the following conclusion: "Thus, Bonhoeffer's ethics of order is all the more significant precisely for the present day." Ibid. In my own estimation, Huntemann's judgment here is inadequate—the "spirit of our time" has undergone marked and irreversible changes, making a direct, uncritical application of Bonhoeffer's concept of the divine mandates simply impossible.

161. De Lange, "'Miteinander, Füreinander, Gegeneinander.'"

At the same time, De Lange notes, Bonhoeffer's recognition of plurality in creation, brought forth by God himself in the form of institutions, keeps him from falling back into metaphysical monism: "Through Bonhoeffer's concept of the divine mandates, ethics receives a theocentric basis, yet at the same time every theocratic aspiration is rooted out."[162] A third and final reason why Bonhoeffer's concept of the divine mandates is relevant today is provided by Ernst Wolf. As Wolf indicates, Bonhoeffer's concept provides a bridge between "responsibility" and concrete social institutions.[163]

For these reasons the concept continues to be discussed and employed in current debates among Christian ethicists. Wolfgang Huber, for example, provides a liberal reading of Bonhoeffer's theory of the mandates, emphasizing that the institutions provide spaces in which people have freedom to take responsible action.[164] Another example is Hans G. Ulrich. In his impressive attempt to revive the Lutheran theology of orders in the context of contemporary discussions on social and governmental institutions, he makes extensive use of Bonhoeffer's concept of the divine mandates.[165] In what follows, I shall indicate what contribution the concept can make to environmental ethics in particular.

The Mandates as Unmasking Structures of God's Revelation

In order to transpose Bonhoeffer's concept of the divine mandates into the field of environmental ethics, it is necessary to reflect on the ways in which the socio-political and economical landscape has changed, for it is against this background that the ecological crisis is in need of being addressed.

In the time in which Bonhoeffer wrote and thought, Bonhoeffer took up opposition against the Nazi regime, which perverted the government so as to rule over the other spheres of life. Such states still exist today, and it is noteworthy that, in strongly state-controlled societies, environmental care is often seen as being of little importance—indeed, in such conditions, the environment is often further endangered, and natural resources are

162. "Mit Bonhoeffers Mandatenlehre empfängt die Ethik eine theozentrische Basis, zugleich aber ist jede theokratische Aspiration mit der Wurzel ausgerissen." Ibid.

163. Wolf, "Bonhoeffers Begriff der Mandate," 171.

164. Huber, "Freiheit und Institution," 113–27. It should be noted, however, that, in general—and in contrast to Bonhoeffer's theology of responsibility—the concept of the divine mandates has not been very influential; despite Bonhoeffer's best intentions, it hardly played any role in the post-war debates concerning the construction of a new society. See Dinger, "Mandate und Institutionen," 244–53.

165. Ulrich, *Wie Geschöpfe leben*, 78, 114, 138, etc.

deliberately and thoughtlessly plundered.[166] However, the greatest challenge for ecology today is not found in the threat of "big government," as De Lange observes, but in that of "big business," that is, in the dominion of the economy over all other spheres of life. In listing off the ethical challenges faced in modern times, De Lange draws attention to the dominance of the economy in particular.[167] Other scholars have also put forward similar charges against the threat of big business.[168]

Many have argued that addressing the domination of the economy, as well as the related (but different) process of globalization, is an important task for environmental ethics.[169] In this context, Bonhoeffer's concept of the divine mandates can function as a powerful theological resource. Although he offers no concrete answers to questions about how the economy should be ordered, his account of the different spheres of life can contribute to a proper discernment of the problem and, as such, can help provide an answer.[170] In particular, it can help to address the veiled nature of the domination of the economy over almost every sphere of life. In a discussion of neoliberalism, for instance, Hansen makes the following observation: "Its force lies in the ability to penetrate the interstices and fissures of societies undergoing serious economic, political and cultural crises. This is why many find it difficult to analyze something which appears so fluid, flexible, elastic, but which nonetheless keeps undermining cultures and traditional political institutions."[171] Neoliberal globalization, as Hansen says, poses a more indirect threat: "What is affected are the world, and the human capacity to develop cultural and political strategies of resistance and change."[172]

---

166. This has been illustrated most strikingly in the former Soviet Union. See, for example, Weiner, *Models of Nature*.

167. De Lange, "'Miteinander, Füreinander, Gegeneinander.'"

168. See Duggan, *The Twilight of Equality*; and Brown, "American Nightmare," 690–714. More dispassionate overviews of how neoliberalism undermines the traditional nation-state are offered by Leys, *Market-driven Politics*; and Harvey, *A Brief History of Neoliberalism*.

169. For just one example, see Hansen, "Neoliberal Globalization," 185–203.

170. In what follows, I focus in particular on the contribution that Bonhoeffer's concept of the mandates can make to current discussion concerning the economy and neoliberalism. A discussion of Bonhoeffer's thoughts on the economy itself lies outside the scope of the present book. On that topic, see Duchrow, "Dem Rad in die Speichen fallen," 16–58; Frick, "Bonhoeffer's Theology and Economic Humanism," 49–68; Falcke, "Ansätze für eine Wirtschaftsethik," 376–95; and Pangritz, "Dietrich Bonhoeffers Kapitalismuskritik," 5–12.

171. Hansen, "Neoliberal Globalization," 170.

172. Ibid., 172.

The contribution that Bonhoeffer can make to the debate over neo-liberalism is outlined by Markus Franz,[173] even though Franz focuses not simply on neoliberalism but on society as a whole. He draws in particular from Foucault's conception of discursive practices ("dispositifs") that function as "mechanisms of managerial power."[174] According to him, the concept encompasses "a thoroughly heterogeneous ensemble, consisting of discourses, institutions, architectural forms, regulatory decisions, laws, administrative measures, scientific statements, philosophical, moral and philanthropic propositions—in short, the said as much as the unsaid."[175] The specific point made by Foucault is not just that these social structures are, in fact, manifestations of power, used for oppression, but that they are also meant to thoroughly *obfuscate* their oppression. As Franz summarizes, "it is possible that human persons within such networks are formed to perceive themselves as free and sovereign while they are actually being subjected to specific but hidden power relations."[176] Franz also dwells on the work of Italian philosopher Giorgio Agamben, who further develops Foucault's concept by detailing the extent to which both public and individual life are ever increasingly governed by modern discursive practices. Agamben describes these dispositifs as representing an "extreme phase of capitalist development in which we live."[177] This citation clarifies the fact that the "dispositifs" in question are not only (veiled) manifestations of political and social power, but also of economic power-relations. Agamben introduces religion and relgious practices as possible means to reclaim human freedom in light of the oppression of such dispositifs.

From here, Franz goes on to develop his own proposal, which consists in bringing Bonhoeffer's concept of the divine mandates to bear on the discussion of discursive practices. With great insight, he makes the case that the mandates, in their character as commandments of God, constitute forms of *revelation*—in other words, they aim at publicity.[178] According to him, "Bonhoeffer is able to 'convert' and reclaim elements of power and

---

173. Franz, "The Conversion of Social Life," 133–49.

174. Ibid., 134.

175. Ibid., 136. Franz draws here from Foucault, "The Confession of the Flesh," 194.

176. Franz, "The Conversion of Social Life," 136.

177. Agamben, *What Is an Aparatus?*, 15, cited in Franz, "The Conversion of Social Life," 140.

178. Ibid., 146. Further on Franz writes: "Drawing on the divine commission, immanent authority likewise has to take on the open character of publicity, if it wants to claim legitimacy." Ibid.

authority Foucault and Agamben find ineliminably problematic."[179] The way in which Bonhoeffer's concept of the mandates—as well as, more broadly, the Lutheran understanding of orders—does this, as Franz says, is by constituting "certain recognizable sites as *res publica*—public and concrete places where human beings act together and where they can understand and experience their action as cooperation with God in the light of the promises of God."[180] Here Franz draws a close parallel between the current subjugation of all spheres of life and the Nazi ideology against which Bonhoeffer took up arms—according to him, the trespassing of all spheres of life that was committed through the Nazi ideology is comparable to the way in which life is managed by the dispostifs unearthed by Foucault. As he argues, it is this connection in particular that promotes Bonhoeffer's concept of the divine mandates to the position of a powerful theological resource for resistance.

In total, Franz discerns three specific contributions that Bonhoeffer can make in this regard. First of all, he further elaborates his assertion that the mandates publicize their influence over people: "In theological terminology, God's commandment, which continually forms the mandates as discursive practices, has the character of a revelation, a self-disclosure."[181] In their character as revelations, they also retain a critical distance over against the very orders to which they give shape—in other words, instead of simply justifying the imposition of orders which would be immanent unto themselves, the mandates, as commandments, give shape to a set social structures that are "open" and directed towards God. Franz further specifies this point by drawing attention to what he sees as the second contribution that Bonhoeffer's concept of the mandates is able to make. As God's commandments, the mandates are incapable of becoming independent. The "ultimate authority," as Franz puts it, "remains in the hands of God, who never legitimizes any order nor relinquishes the power of governance itself to an economic technique, but continues to rule through his own Word and promises."[182] Thirdly and finally, Franz argues that Bonhoeffer's stress on the mandates as forms of God's commandment makes a simultaneous appeal to human freedom. The reason for this is that people only have the ability to respond to the commandment in obedience when they are first recognized as free subjects. In other words, even though the mandates come in the form of commands, they presuppose freedom, just as the obedience that they demand is an act born out of a free decision. In conclusion, Franz identifies

179. Ibid., 143.
180. Ibid.; italics original.
181. Ibid., 146.
182. Ibid., 147.

Bonhoeffer's mandates as a theological conception of social life that forms a genuine alternative to the obfuscation and repression of life by the power of modern dispositifs: "[B]y encouraging theology to reclaim its distinctiveness as a careful attention to God's commandment, Bonhoeffer significantly enables a public speech and action not easily absorbed into the dominating discourses of our time."[183]

Franz's account of the way in which the mandates, in their function as God's commandment, uncover and reveal power-structures, is quite insightful and very helpful. Moreover, it falls right in line with Bonhoeffer's original intention for them, for, as we have already seen, Bonhoeffer meant for the mandates to keep each other in check. Laying bare just how pervasive and powerful the mandate of work has become, for example, is one of their important functions. In this way, an open discussion of the mandate can be facilitated, that is, a discussion that does not concern itself with trying to abolish any and every form of power, but only with allocating and managing this power responsibly. According to Bonhoeffer's formulation of the mandates, this discussion can take place outside of the mandate of work itself—in other words, the economy can be discussed within the framework of the other mandates, namely, in politics, in the family, in the church and in other civil communities.[184] The main function of Bonhoeffer's mandates is, however, to stimulate critical discussion in the mandate itself, or to put it more precisely, in the field governed by the mandate. Precisely because it is a distinct mandate, the extent to which other mandates can influence it is limited. A new and improved formulation of the function of the economy must therefore be worked out by the theorists and scholars working on the mandate of the economy itself.[185]

This necessity is recognized by Scruton, who, while acknowledging free-market capitalism as the cause of numerous environmental problems, argues that it can also help to contribute to (at least part of) a solution.[186] In particular, he offers a number of examples of how people throughout the world have set up systems of property rights in order to manage valuable resources. He points, for example, to certain Native Americans tribes who have

183. Ibid., 149.

184. These discussions are, however, often hindered by a lack of knowledge concerning the mandate of the economy.

185. This point is also made by Lovin, who argues: "Those who actually have experienced responsibility for business or law, for example, must be assumed to know what these institutions require better than those who want to impose an alien leadership structure on them, or use them to serve other purposes." Lovin, "The Mandates in an Age of Globalization," 24.

186. Scruton, *Green Philosophy*, 137–82.

developed just such a system of rights for salmon-fishing on the Columbia River. Another example can be found in the Lofoten fishery in Norway, where "[r]egulation was entirely in the hands of the fishermen themselves, who operated a system of voluntary restraint and conflict resolution for over a hundred years."[187] The system has since disappeared, however, as a result of the Common Fisheries Policy set in place by the European Union, in which—as the name indicates—control of Europe's fisheries is carried out centrally. As Scruton argues, the success of practices and institutions like these reveal that allowing the free market to do its job need not result in ruthless competition or environmental degradation; on the contrary, they should rather be seen as the best way to express "the rational self-interest of essentially co-operative people."[188] Scruton goes on to make the rather convincing case that the use of feedback-mechanisms at work in the free market can be a very effective means for restoring an equilibrium between the planet and people's economic interests. At the same time, he also remains somewhat cautious and insists on differentiating between "little" business and "big" businesss. He argues that big businesses and corporations can "pay off" the negative effects of their activities (by hiring a Corporate Social Responsibility consultant, for example). He takes issue in particular with joint-stock companies. According to him, "[b]y separating ownership from control, and insulating both the shareholder and the director from the full costs of their mistakes, these legal devices encourage risk-taking beyond anything that the market would otherwise allow."[189] In short, for Scruton, in order to prevent excesses and environmental harm, what is needed first and foremost are systems of feedback and an allocation of responsibility.

Fortunately, these mechanisms do indeed function within the mandate of the economy. While it is true that the activities of certain multinationals are tangled up in egregious structural injustices (such as corruption, child labor, and dangerous working conditions), the public outcry that has occurred concerning some of these injustices has been so great that many companies now take steps in order to ensure, for example, that their supply chains are ethical and sustainable. A case in point is the scandal that arose surrounding Nike in the 1990s once it became clear that the companies to which it outsourced the production of its shoes made use of child labor and compulsory overtime. Nike's initial refusal to accept responsibility led to a public relations nightmare, which, in turn, eventually compelled the

187. Ibid., 142.
188. Ibid., 144.
189. Ibid., 179.

company to take steps in order to ensure that their contractors abided by their ethical standards.[190]

Instances such as these have given rise to widespread efforts among companies to ensure that their supply chains are both sustainable and free from involvement in social injustice.[191] One examplary case in this regard is that of Sedex,[192] a company specializing in providing ways for its clients (namely, other companies) to distribute and share ethical data amongst themselves. At present, over thirty thousand companies are committed in this undertaking. By using self-regulatory services such as these, companies can help to ensure that their supply chain abides by a set of ethical guidelines. Bonhoeffer's doctrine of the mandates can help to strengthen these self-regulatory activities within the mandate of work.

EXTENDING THE MANDATES AS GLOBAL PRACTICES

Despite the clear potential for self-regulation within the mandate of the economy itself, it is still necessary to provide external limitations and boundaries capable of countering the excesses of neoliberalization. One of the main reasons why these excesses are so elusive and difficult to address (or actively resist) is their global character. This takes shape, for example, in the economic power of vast, multinational corporations. These companies are able—if they wish—to circumnavigate the strict regulations and controls of law abiding states and to transfer their polluting (and otherwise unethical) activities to states with weaker regulations, states that are often sensitive to corruption. This has been noted, for example, by Rasmussen, who writes that "the economy has gone global and . . . outgrown the forms of political community. Economic supply lines and structures of power, technology, finance, and information all spill over national boundaries, and populations find themselves without democratic authority to regulate this global economy."[193]

In this context, Bonhoeffer's concept of the mandates can, paradoxically, be used to argue for a strengthening of the *state*. As we noted above, Bonhoeffer struggled against a state that, in his day, had grown obscenely

190. This story has been aptly described by Beder, "Putting the Boot In," 24–28, 66–67.

191. For a relatively recent overview of such developments, see Seuring and Müller, "Sustainable Supply Chain Management," 1699–1710.

192. http://www.sedexglobal.com/about-sedex/what-we-do/ (accessed July 21, 2016).

193. Rasmussen, *Earth-Honoring Faith*, 180. For a thorough analysis of this proces, see Held et al., *Global Transformations*.

and perversely powerful. Very much in spite of this, he nevertheless continued to acknowledge the necessity of the state as such, or more specifically,
the particular task that the state is called to carry out. Just as he warned
against too *strong* a state, he also warned against the state being too *weak*.[194]
This emphasis on the importance of the state, as one of the divine mandates,
can be quite helpful in the present context, but in order to put the concept
to work, it must first be refashioned in order to address current economic
and political conditions.

Some work has already been carried out on this front since the recognition, by a number of scholars, of the potential of Bonhoeffer's theology
for addressing the issue of globalization. One recent example is found in the
work of Joerg Rieger, who notes that, in his experience as a member of the
resistance against the Nazis, Bonhoeffer learned to look to the underside of
human experience—the point of view of the socially disadvantaged. In this
context, Rieger notes that "Bonhoeffer . . . not only offered critical views of
globalization from above but also supported and helped shape what must be
considered movements of alternative globalization."[195] In particular, Rieger
identifies the Confessing Church and the resistance against Hitler as examples of such movements. This move is somewhat problematic, however,
for the term "alternative globalization" hardly applies to the movements
of the Confessing Church or to the resistance. In addition, while Rieger's
insistence on resistance against global injustices is certainly valuable, it is
rather difficult to imagine what sort of model Bonhoeffer's participation in
an attempted tyrannicide could offer for contemporary movements against
global injustice.

Running along slightly different lines, Cornel W. du Toit writes on
Bonhoeffer's concept of responsibility in the context of globalization and
weak nation-states. Specifically, he puts Bonhoeffer's thoughts in prison
about living *etsi Deus non daretur* to use, claiming that when, for example,
weak states are coerced into accepting unfavorable trade agreements, which
would have negative effects on their citizens, "then those citizens should act
as if government is not a given."[196] What this means in concrete terms, according to him, is that citizens should make appeal to international powers
and authorities capable of safeguarding national and local interests. As he
argues, this move—namely, the creation of a global civil society—represents

194. See Mayer, "Zuviel Staat oder zuwenig Staat?," 126–58.

195. Rieger, *Globalization and Theology*, 25.

196. Du Toit, "Etsi Deus Non Daretur?," 63; italics original. As the title of the article itself clearly indicates, this is a reference to the famous dictum *etsi Deus non daretur*. It is remarkable that Du Toit fails to mention Bonhoeffer's concept of the divine
mandates as a concrete framework for social responsibility.

the *only* way forward in (what he refers to as) a postdemocratic world. As an example of such a transnational civil body, he refers in particular to the NEPAD.[197] He then combines this idea together with the plea of Hans Küng and others for a "world ethics," or for a "universalisation of values in an ecumenical context," as he calls it.[198]

While I agree with Rieger and Du Toit that Bonhoeffer's theology can and should be used to empower citizens to act responsibly, which implies and necessitates the creation of structures of governance on a global level, I nevertheless find it hard to understand why, in turning to Bonhoeffer, they ignore, or sidestep, the concept of the divine mandates. As we have seen, the concept deals directly and explicitly with state governance, and applying it to the challenges posed by globalization make it unnecessary to take such giant leaps in drawing connections between these challenges, on the one hand, and, on the other, Bonhoeffer's experience of the underside of society, or his thoughts on living *etsi Deus non daretur*.

One scholar who *does* recognize the potential of Bonhoeffer's doctrine of the mandates for the globalization debate is Scott, who draws particular attention to the possible application to the field of environmental ethics.[199] In particular, Scott argues for an ecological revision of the concept of the mandates, indicating five specific ways in which it should be reframed. First of all, he asserts that "a reference to the ecological is an essential precondition for interpreting the mandates—human living must be understood by comprehensive and consistent reference to the biosphere."[200] Secondly, he points out that the mandates must be understood as activities, rather than structures. He sides here with Karl Barth's criticism of the rigidness of Bonhoeffer's conception. Focusing on the mandates as structures leads us, as he argues, *away* from the challenges of present-day reality: "What would require theological scrutiny are global *activities* that are always carried through in specific places, that is, with both economic and ecological components."[201]

---

197. New Partnership for Africa's Development, http://www.nepad.org/ (accessed July 21, 2016).

198. Du Toit, "Etsi Deus Non Daretur?," 63.

199. Scott, "Postnatural Humanity? Bonhoeffer, Creaturely Freedom, and the Mystery of Reconciliation in Creation." At the beginning of this essay, Scott indicates that his discovery of the possibility for ecological application of Bonhoeffer's doctrine of the divine mandates is rather recent; as such, it is not reflected in his earlier essay on the value of Bonhoeffer's theology for environmental ethics. See Scott, "Christ, Nature, Sociality."

200. Scott, "Postnatural Humanity? Bonhoeffer, Creaturely Freedom, and the Mystery of Reconciliation in Creation," 126.

201. Ibid., 127; italics original.

In this connection, Scott mentions global trade as a key theme. On his view, attention should focus on the exploration of just economic relationships between people, and these relationships should themselves form part of a response to a broader global imperative towards dialogue between different people-groups. Thirdly, the mandates need to be extended to a global level, as Scott insists. He argues here for a global construal of the mandate of government. Mentioning the heated discussion over the legality of the 2003 US-UK invasion of Iraq, he raises the question of the level at which the government should be involved in such decisions: should these decisions be made nationally and unilaterally, or should they be restricted to cases in which broader international agreement and discussion are involved? He himself indicates a clear preference for the latter option.

Fourthly, Scott argues that each mandate has a counterpart: "[F]or work, it is non-work and non-paid work, including care of children, the elderly and the infirm; for marriage, it is alternative parenting and sexual arrangements (. . .); for government, it is self-government, as suggested by anarchism; for church, it is other religions."[202] Scott sees these counterparts to the mandates as being secured by the mandates themselves, or as companions to them. As an example, he refers to the legal recognition of homosexual relationships as a counterpart to the mandate of marriage. As a result of this balancing, or equilibrium, "[t]he mandate normalizes and thereby does not exclude this 'broken middle'; instead, through such normalizing, the mandates stabilize activities of the 'broken middle,' granting dignity to them. Through such a conferral what is excluded are injustices in the counterparts and what is permitted is ordination of the good."[203] Concretely, this means that dignified homosexual relationships may call into question heterosexual relationships that, although under the mandate, are not lived in freedom and justice. Fifthly and finally, Scott also proposes to use the ecological revision of the concept of the divine mandates as a check against the hierarchical tendencies at work in Bonhoeffer's concept. He perceives these tendencies also elsewhere in Bonhoeffer's work, for example in his emphasis on the strong difference between human and non-human life—an emphasis Scott challenges. Due to the limited scope of his essay, Scott does not venture to revise each and every mandate in detail. But he does indicate the general direction that such revisions would need to take, asking in particular if it is possible to develop an ecologically concrete and, at the same time, more provisional theological ethic than Bonhoeffer's account of the mandates originally offered. He mentions the emphasis that Bonhoeffer

202. Ibid.
203. Ibid., 128.

places on the concreteness of the command of God as opening up a promising way forward in this regard.

Scott's intention to use Bonhoeffer's concept of the divine mandates constructively in creating an ecological theology is to be praised, but a critical assessment of his proposals for revision is necessary. His first proposal—namely, his idea that the mandates should be interpreted with reference to the ecological—is a good and indeed mandatory step for an ecological revision of the concept. Also his second proposal—to view the mandates less as fixed institutions than as activities—has merit. It is nevertheless somewhat strange that Scott doesn't seem to be aware of the potential for such a revision already at work in the concept itself—for Bonhoeffer, as we saw, does indeed see the mandates as commandments of the living God, which clearly endows them with a certain dynamic element. Apart from that, it also appears that Scott doesn't sufficiently recognize the fact that, although Bonhoeffer stresses that the divine mandates are commandments, these commandments take the form of *structures*, or of institutions, such as that of church and the government. An ecological appropriation of the mandates would clearly need to recognize this. Scott's third proposal—to extend the mandates to a global level—is a very valuable one and I will come back to it later.

Firstly, however, it is necessary to dwell, however briefly, on Scott's fourth and fifth proposals. His fourth proposal, as we saw, was to recognize the counterpart of each mandate and to see those counterparts as belonging to the mandates themselves. The first problem with this suggestion is Scott's apparently limited understanding of the content of Bonhoeffer's mandates. Concerning marriage, for example, it is true that Bonhoeffer's account at first seems to imply that only procreative relationships belong to the mandate, but we saw earlier how Bonhoeffer later broadened it, renaming it "Familie," so as to include other relationships of love and care as well. The same is true for the mandate of "Arbeit," which Bonhoeffer also chose to rename later on. As "Kultur," it clearly includes much more than the day-jobs which people submit themselves to in order to make money. Volunteer work, study and other unpaid activities falling under the heading of "Bildung" are certainly part of it as well, which makes Scott's proposal for the creation of a "counterpart" quite unnecessary. The second problem is that, in his proposal for recognizing the good in the counterpart of the divine mandates, Scott goes against some of Bonhoeffer's explicit intentions with the divine mandates. When he proposes that "government" (a mandate which Bonhoeffer, significantly, does *not* rename) finds its counterpart in anarchism, thereby implying that Christians should recognize the good in a movement championing the lack and destruction of order, he is clearly not only departing from but undermining the understanding of government that Bonhoeffer had in mind. Bonhoeffer held a firm belief in the "Rechtstaat" and had a cautious approach to democracy. As we saw, he asserted that the mandates create a clear and well-defined "Oben" and "Unten." Apart from the issue of how one judges these aspects of Bonhoeffer's original conception, it must be asked whether the adjustments of the kind that Scott proposes do not in fact maim the concept beyond recognition. In the end, Scott is undoubtedly right to assert that a revision must take place in order to make Bonhoeffer's concept more ecologically sensitive, and, at the very least, his first three proposals ought to be valued for calling attention to this need.

By proposing a reconstruction of the mandates as global practices, Scott clearly makes a decisive choice. He could just as easily have chosen to be critical of the process of globalization altogether, asserting instead the importance of strengthening individual nation-states; indeed, such a decision would have been more in line with Bonhoeffer's explicit definition of the mandate of the state. While asking what Bonhoeffer may or may not have preferred (as a possible application or emendation of his account) doesn't get us any further than the presuppositions of the interpreter, I do believe that Scott makes the right choice in accepting the process of globalization as inevitable. This is also in line with Bonhoeffer's own thoughts on acceptance of the world as it is, and about acting in accordance with reality. It is clear that the process of globalization has both advantages and disadvantages and that debate over which of these outweighs the other will no doubt continue. But the process itself is unstoppable and irreversible, as was the creation of the modern nation-state in the nineteenth century. By accepting this state of affairs, it becomes possible to consider how to set more powerful structures of accountability and responsibility into place on the global level. We saw how, within the mandate of the economy, this effort has already been undertaken by certain corporations and multi-nationals. Yet it isn't sufficient to rely on the self-regulatory power of the economy itself; in order for life to flourish, the economy must be confronted with "hard" limits set by the state in order to protect people and goods in situations where there is no economic interest to do so.

How governance can and should take form on a global level is one of the great challenges confronted by both theorists and policy makers alike. While there exist multiple platforms of global governance, such as the ILO, the WHO and UNCTAD, they each suffer from a lack of power to assert their authority. As Scruton observes, "a general weakness in international treaties . . . is that they rarely create the motive for obeying them when it is in the interest of one of the parties to defect."[204] In contrast, international bodies that do possess real authority, such as the EU, suffer from another major problem, namely, overregulation. This is also pointed out by Scruton, who draws attention both to the alarming growth of the EU's bureaucratic apparatus and to its top-down organization, which, in his estimation, shows little respect for national differences: "The EU is now encumbered by 180,000 pages of regulations and directives, with no guarantee that they further the common good . . . This *acquis communautaire* is always increasing in size, and no procedure exists whereby those who suffer the burden of regulation can eject the people who impose it."[205] It would seem that the way forward for governance on an international level lies in creating the same democratic feedback-mechanisms that function in democratic nation-states.

The Responsibility of the Church

The related processes of neoliberalization and globalization have led to what Rasmussen refers to as a sort of depletion, not only of the soil, but also of the soul of communities.[206] In order to restore appropriate relationships, both between human beings themselves and between human beings and nature, it is not enough to regulate the economy (or to encourage it to regulate itself) and to seek to strengthen forms of democratic political control on both national and international levels. Something else is needed, namely a strengthening of civil society. Without the "soul," without attachments to concrete people, in concrete places, cooperating for the common good, nature becomes increasingly vulnerable to plundering and the fabric of society disintegrates. This forms a basic conviction that drives the majority of scholars working in ecology and environmental ethics and, quite remarkably, unites those belonging to the left and the right of the political spectrum.

Scruton, for example, makes a passionate appeal for *oikophilia*, that is, for a love for the earth, exercised in concrete locales, in relation with others.[207] A comparable appeal is made by Rasmussen. As he argues, local, small-scale communities are greatly needed—precisely (and somewhat paradoxically) in the context of globalization. In quoting from the work of Sandal, he draws attention to the idea that a cosmopolitan ethic, in the context of globalization, requires the recognition that, in most cases, human beings live and interact with each other in smaller-scale contexts: "In an

204. Scruton, *Green Philosophy*, 305.

205. Ibid., 314; italics original.

206. Rasmussen, *Earth-Honoring Faith*, 179.

207. See Scruton, *Green Philosophy*, 326–75.

important sense . . ., an ethic of smaller-scale neighborly space matters *more* in a globalized world, not less."[208]

While Scruton and Rasmussen speak of civil communities in general, Northcott makes a more concrete application to church communities as places where human beings learn life-practices capable of sustaining and nurturing the goods of both the human and the non-human world. According to him, "[t]hese practices include: the lively and embodied worship of an embodied God; the nurture of children in stable families; the recovery of good work as craft and art, as service of others and of nature."[209] Northcott sees the fostering of environmental concern in the specific context of a church, defined as part of a particular social and cultural network, as one of the ways to actualize the well-known environmental slogan "think globally, act locally."[210] The appeals of Northcott, Scruton, and Rasmussen have been echoed by many other ecophilosophers and theologians as well. As Dalton and Simmons observe, "[m]any Christian ecotheologians think that concrete local and contextualized practices are the most effective way to confront the ills of globalization. The network of local efforts is the basis for hope."[211]

These appeals for local, church-based, environmental action have not gone unheeded—examples abound of ways in which church communities have become involved in environmental action, in programs in which not only the ecological dimension is addresssed, but also the social and spiritual dimensions of human existence. Stephen Jerie describes, for example, the case of the Roman Catholic Archdiocese of Bulawayo, in Zimbabwe. Located in the country's southern region, the Catholic Development Commission has articulated and set into action a two-pronged approach, namely, through involvement in the restoration of degraded lands, and in increasing the ecological awareness of local residents.[212] This approach is more top-down in its orientation and implementation. An example of a grass-roots movement can be found in Koinonia Partners, a Christian community located on a farm in the state of Georgia, US.[213] There, Christians live and work together in a community that is involved in both social and environmental action.

208. Rasmussen, *Earth-Honoring Faith*, 181; italics original. Rasmussen refers to Sandel, "Competing American Traditions," 7–12.

209. Northcott, *The Environment*, 324.

210. Ibid., 327.

211. Dalton and Simmons, *Ecotheology and the Practice of Hope*, 103.

212. Jerie, "The Role of the Church," 217–26.

213. See http://www.koinoniapartners.org/ (accessed July 21, 2016). This website is referred to in Yordy, *Green Witness*, 131n1.

Many more such Christian programs exist, either on their own, or as part of national or global networks, such as A Rocha, as I already referred to in chapter 2.

Bonhoeffer's concept of the church as one of the four mandates can help to strengthen, from a theological point of view, the function of the Church as a form of community within the larger society.[214] His ecclesiology is, of course, widely studied, and applications of it to the contemporary world abound. In large part, however, these applications often focus on the emphasis Bonhoeffer gives to the church as a site of resistance—for example, against injustices committed by states, or against racism.[215] Focusing on the specific role that Bonhoeffer saw for the church in the struggle against the Third Reich can be misleading, however, for these were times very much "out of joint," according to Bonhoeffer, that is, when the normal course of things was being profound disturbed. Care should be taken not to confuse this historical context with that of today.

This latter point is advanced and supported by Guillermo Hansen. After first asking whether or not it is appropriate to describe present-day neoliberal globalization as a situation that calls for a *status confessionis* from the church, he calls attention to how this famous Lutheran category enabled churches to oppose the absolutism of the medieval Roman Catholic Church, and the racist policies of South Africa's "Apartheidsregime."[216] According to him, "These examples shaped this confessional tradition, giving it a strong profile signaling freedom and resistance."[217] In contrast, Hansen is rather hesitant to identify the current trend of neoliberal globalization as a similar situation. Instead of trying to construct a new economic order, he argues that Christians would do better to focus on addressing the gradual fracturing of public space. Instead of trying to oppose globalization, they

214. I specifically refrain from calling the church a form of *civil* community, as that would lead to the question if the church is really best seen as a civil community. While this is certainly advocated by some (see Fergusson, *Church, State and Civil Society*), others strongly disagree (see Hauerwas, *The Hauerwas Reader*). Entering this debate would lead us too far away from the central point, which is that, regardless of whether one sees the church as a civil community or as a countercultural community, the church is a *community*—and as such, it has an impact on society, and on nature as well.

215. The potential of Bonhoeffer's ecclesiology as a resource for resistance has been often noted (see Rasmussen, *Reality and Resistance*). As a result, his concept of the church as a community of resistance is used in a wide variety of different contexts. See, for example, Wellman, "Bonhoeffer's Ethic of Resistance," 69–77; Thomas, "Life Together in a Life Apart World," 81–95; and Smith, "Discipleship in a Globalized World," 148–65.

216. Hansen, "Neoliberal Globalization," 167.

217. Ibid.

should exercise their citizenship in order to promote a social order based on peace, justice and equality.

As I would argue, Hansen is right in his observation: what is most needed in these environmentally rapacious and yet, by and large, peaceful times (at least in the Western world) is a focus on the church as a community, that is, on a collective body of believers capable of nurturing networks of interrelatedness and of recruiting its members to take part in protests and environmental action. Bonhoeffer's concept of the mandate can help to strengthen this focus.

7

Conclusion

IN THIS CONCLUDING CHAPTER, I WILL FIRST OF ALL LOOK BACK AND TO take stock of the work I have accomplished in correlating Bonhoeffer's theology with environmental ethics. I undertake this task in the first section, where I set out to answer the central research question. Secondly, I shall overview the results that this book has arrived at, indicating the relevance of this research for ongoing theological reflection on ecology. Thirdly, I will close with a description of the possibilities for future research on the monograph's topic.

Taking Stock of the Results Achieved

In chapter 1, I began by formulating the following research question: "In which way can a number of concepts from the theology of Dietrich Bonhoeffer be transposed and made relevant for contemporary discussions in the field of environmental ethics?" In response to this question, I examined a great number of concepts from Bonhoeffer's theology, bringing them into dialogue with current discussions in environmental ethics—this is the work that was carried out in chapters 2 through 6.

Chapters 2 and 3 explored concepts from Bonhoeffer's theology that could be situated under the general heading of the relationship between God (or more specifically, Christ) and nature. In chapter 2, I started off by treating four such concepts that deal with the relationship between Christ and the world in general (that is, not directly in reference to nature as such). The most prominent of these was Bonhoeffer's concept of Christ-reality, which, as we saw, gave shape to his proposal for overcoming certain false distinctions that precluded Christians from engaging with the whole of reality. As I made clear, Bonhoeffer bases his appeal on his assertion that, by entering the world, Christ directed all reality to himself, thereby overcoming the distinction between a "worldly" and a "spiritual" realm—in other words, for Bonhoeffer, reality is, in Christ, fundamentally undivided. At the same time, I also showed how Bonhoeffer acknowledges the existence of certain relative distinctions within reality, which guard his ontology from collapsing into a christological monism. As I argued, Bonhoeffer's assertion that the world as a whole is directed towards Christ bestows an eschatological dimension on his understanding of Christ-reality. In this connection, we discovered a number of parallels between his concept and contemporary research in New Testament theology, which stresses that the eschaton was inaugurated by Christ's advent in the world. I then correlated Bonhoeffer's concept of Christ-reality with the contemporary question of how to motivate Christians to take ecological action, especially in light of certain "escapist" tendencies at work in evangelical eschatology. In contrast to these tendencies, I presented Bonhoeffer's concept as a compelling alternative to a world-denying eschatology.

The second set of concepts that I explored in chapter 2 was that of the ultimate and the penultimate, which can be seen as one of the relative distinctions that Bonhoeffer articulates within the one, undivided Christ-reality. In understanding the ultimate in terms of justification by grace, we saw how Bonhoeffer dismissed both radicalism and compromise as false solutions for dealing with the divide between the ultimate and the present, fallen reality of the world. According to him, this tension is resolved, not in the attitude that the church happens to adopt, but in the person of Jesus Christ. In concrete terms, he develops the notion of the penultimate as a sort of third possibility, or alternative, insisting that the latter aims at (or prepares the way for) the ultimate, even while, at the same time, differing qualitatively from it. Just like with the concept of Christ-reality, I argued that the penultimate is defined in particular by an inherent eschatological dimension: it links up with the distinction in recent New Testament scholarship between the "already" and the "not yet" of Christ's eschatological Kingdom. I then correlated Bonhoeffer's pair of concepts with the connection between eschatology and ecotheology, drawing particular attention to certain trends in liberal eschatology. In particular, I used his thoughts on the penultimate in order to criticize the optimistic and immanent bearing of liberal conceptions of eschatology, arguing that his understanding of the merely preparatory nature of the penultimate can help relieve Christians of the (apparent) burden of having to realize God's Kingdom themselves.

Thirdly, I focussed on the further specification that Bonhoeffer gives to the relationship between Christ and the world through his discussion of the three moments of the incarnation, the crucifixion, and the resurrection. As I noted, this differentiation results in a particularly nuanced approach to the world. In correlating the concept with environmental ethics, I showed how this threefold definition of the Christ-world relation can provide a grammar that is finely-tuned and articulate enough to speak of nature's beauty and bounty without going so far as to underestimate (or conveniently ignore) the havoc and destruction that it causes. As such, I argued, the concept can help oppose those approaches to nature that adopt a dangerously myopic, or one-sided, point of view.

The fourth and final concept that I treated in chapter 2 was that of "the natural." As I showed, Bonhoeffer took a rather unique position relative to most other Protestant theologians by developing a robust appreciation of the concept of the natural, which was his way of taking the self-preserving process of life into account—that is, nature's tendency to restore equilibrium. I then correlated this concept with the Gaia theory, which has grown to be so popular in ecological circles. In particular, I argued that Bonhoeffer's concept of the natural can help provide an added theological weight to the concept: while it accepts the natural as a basic, biological category, it also resists the introduction of a pure and simple naturalism into the realm of Christian ethics.

Whereas the concepts articulated in chapter 2—especially that of Christ-reality—were foundational to Bonhoeffer's theology, allowing only for an indirect application to nature, chapter 3 dealt more directly with nature itself, or more specifically, with a cluster of concepts derived from Bonhoeffer's theology of nature. I treated five such concepts in all. The first was that of Christ as the hidden center of nature (specifically *after* the Fall). I brought this unique concept to bear in the context of environmental ethics by taking it as a way to overcome the Cartesian divide between subject and object, which separates human beings both from each other and from nature, helped facilitate the radical instrumentalisation of nature, and which is clearly one of the root causes of the current ecological crisis. Secondly, I focussed on Bonhoeffer's conception of the Fall, showing how he paints post-lapsarian nature in particularly dark colors. While I argued that his description of the world after the Fall is, in fact, somewhat *too* dark, I also made the case that the emphasis he gives to nature's fallenness can help call into question the comparatively uncritical appraisal of nature made by so often by contemporary ecologists.

Thirdly, I addressed Bonhoeffer's thoughts on Christ as the Redeemer of nature in connection with his theology of the sacraments—or more specifically, in connection with his assertion that the sacraments give shape to a sort of preview, as it were, of the coming redemption of nature. I correlated this view with the increasing attention granted to the Christian sacraments in environmental ethics, indicating how Bonhoeffer's (essentially Lutheran) assertion of Christ's real presence in the sacraments can function as a powerful motive for caring for creation. In addition, I argued that Bonhoeffer's concept fulfills a critical function as well: by limiting the sacraments to baptism and Eucharist, he helps resist the universal sacramentalism which—while popular in ecotheology—tends to affirm the *status quo*, and, as a consequence, makes it rather difficult to call unjust social structures into question. Fourthly and finally, I transposed Bonhoeffer's concept of the orders of preservation into the domain of environmental ethics. In particular, I showed how he developed this concept as a critical alternative to the concept of the orders of creation espoused by many German Christians—though Bonhoeffer affirms the existence of order, he also stresses that this order comes from above, that is, from God, instead of from below. In correlating this concept with the debate over the natural order in environmental ethics, I argued that it allows for the recognition of a certain order in the natural world, while also helping to criticize a hasty acceptance or romantization of nature—indeed, I showed how Bonhoeffer insisted quite emphatically that any order perceived in nature should be seen and understood in relation to Christ, and to him alone.

In chapters 4, 5 and 6, I focused on another general theme of Bonhoeffer's work, namely, on the relationship of human beings amongst themselves, and between human beings and non-human nature. Chapters 4 and 5 correlated four important themes of his theological anthropology with current debates in environmental ethics. In chapter 4, firstly, I began by addressing the first two of these themes: on the one hand, humanity's fundamental relationship with, or rootedness within, nature, and, on the other hand, its qualitative distinction from nature. Regarding the first theme, I showed how, throughout Bonhoeffer's work, he asserts the fundamental bodiliness of human existence. I indicated in particular how his emphasis on humanity's bond with the earth was influenced by the movement of the philosophy of life, but at the same time, I also showed how his focus on this bond differs from the latter insofar as it is both explicitly theological and directly grounded in Scripture. From here, I drew attention to how the appreciation of human bodiliness plays an important role in environmental ethics as well: in many different ways, humanity's attachment to other-than-human life is seen as imperative in the effort to overcome the perceived estrangement of human beings from nature. In transposing Bonhoeffer's train of thought into this debate, I argued that the significance of the particular way in which elaborates on mankind's connection to the earth lies in the specifically biblical and theological reasoning behind it. I then closed by arguing that this can further the acceptance of human bodiliness among

Christians, and that this, in turn, can serve as an additional motivation for environmental discipleship.

The second concept that I treated in chapter 4 was that of human distinctiveness. As I showed, even while Bonhoeffer stresses the fundamental bond between human beings and the earth, he also strongly asserts certain fundamental differences between human beings and non-human nature (or more specifically, animals). Throughout his work, he identifies a number of these differences. The most important of these can be seen in the strong emphasis that he places on human sociality—human beings, as he contends, are free *for* each other in ways that are purely and simply unavailable to other animals. On a more critical note, I referred to certain avenues of research showing how these distinctions are, in many important respects, theoretically inadequate—in particular, his understanding of human sociality as unique has been disproven, as have most of the other distinctions that he draws between human and non-human species. At the same time, I also argued that this in no way disqualifies the distinctions that Bonhoeffer sets up; if anything, they simply need to be reinterpreted in light of recent and ongoing ethological research. Regarding the theme of sociality, for example, I drew from research which shows that, while non-human species do indeed engage in certain forms of social relations and modes of behavior with each other, this sociality is far less developed—in degree—than that found in human beings. I then attempted to bring Bonhoeffer's account of human distinctiveness to bear on environmental ethics. Since anthropocentrism, which is inherent in Bonhoeffer's theology, has come under sustained criticism by environmental ethicists, I first of all defended the plausibility (as well as the viability) of an anthropocentric approach to nature, arguing that any thoroughgoing ecocentric alternative is not only philosophically unviable, but that it fails to motivate meaningful forms of environmental action and engagement. In this light, I made the case that an adjusted (or "weak") form of anthropocentrism is not only possible, but necessary. This paved the way for me to draw out the particular contribution that Bonhoeffer's theological anthropology is able to make in current debates. As I argued, his stress on sociality as something distinctly human can help to refocus attention on the social dimension of the ecological crisis—that is, on the closely intertwined relation between social and environmental problems.

In chapter 5, I correlated two other themes from Bonhoeffer's theological anthropology with environmental ethics: the theme of human mastery, on the one hand, and of loyalty to the earth, on the other. Firstly, in my account for Bonhoeffer's assertion that human beings are to *rule* over the non-human world, I argued that the way in which he effectively works this idea out is a far cry from an appeal for the ruthless exploitation of nature. Indeed, as I showed, he views humanity's excessive reliance on technology as a patent *failure* to rule the earth. I also showed how, while his early theology seems to be satisfied with a pure and simple condemnation of technology, in his later thought, he arrives at the more mature view of technology as an intrinsic (and inescapable) part of the world come of age. In this light, he argues that, instead of fighting against the inevitable, the current state of affairs should be accepted—*provided* that an appropriate, anthropocentric ethic come to govern technology's use and continued development. From here, I brought Bonhoeffer's thought into correlation with debates in environmental ethics concerning human mastery and technology. Firstly, I argued that the ancient idea of the *dominium terrae*, in spite of the many contentions surrounding it, doesn't need to be disqualified in light of the ecological crisis; on the contrary, it is a thoroughly adequate concept when viewed in light of nature's ambivalence. In the same view, I argued that Bonhoeffer's specific elaboration of this concept of mastery can help contribute to environmental ethics. Specifically, I made the case that his particular view of human mastery (which, as we recall, should only be exercised in recognition of God and of other human beings) can help to call the dominant Enlightenment paradigm (which effectively transforms the individual into a master of the universe) into question. Secondly, I argued that the maturation of Bonhoeffer's views with respect to technology can help redirect environmental ethics away from a fruitless (and insufficiently nuanced) condemnation of technology towards a more constructive engagement with the latter.

The second theme that I treated in chapter 5 was Bonhoeffer's imperative of remaining loyal to the earth. As I showed, the urge to love the earth was a defining feature of Bonhoeffer's entire theology, an appeal that gradually developed and matured throughout his theological development. We saw in particular how, over the course of time, he gradually shed some of the weight of the philosophy of life that had first informed his love and, in the latter's place, sought out a more robust Scriptural basis for his views. I then correlated his emphasis on human loyalty to the earth with similar appeals arising in contemporary ecology. I made the point that, whereas there is a striking similarity between these appeals, there is also an important, overriding difference: whereas environmental ethicists often draw from sources such as earth spirituality and the experience of nature in order to make their case, and while these often contain valuable insights, from a Christian perspective, Bonhoeffer would undoubtedly warn against such tendencies seeking to divinize the earth. Indeed, as I argued, his imperative to remain loyal to the earth helps to draw attention to this danger and to formulate a genuinely Christian alternative in its place.

In chapter 6, I shifted from Bonhoeffer's theological anthropology and focussed on two other concepts falling under the general theme of the relationship between human beings and nature: responsibility, and, closely related with the latter, the divine mandates. Concerning responsibility, I made the decision to focus exclusively on a single concept from Bonhoeffer's broader matrix of responsibility, namely, that of vicarious, representative action. My account of the development of this concept throughout the course of Bonhoeffer's corpus revealed just how fundamental a role it plays in the whole of his theology, being anchored at it is in the vicarious representation of Christ himself. While vicarious representation is primarily a concept concerning the relationships between human beings, Bonhoeffer makes clear that it can apply to things and states of affairs as well—though only in the form of being responsible *for*, and not being responsible *to*. Correlated with environmental ethics, I argued that viewing responsibility in terms of vicarious representation can offer a robust alternative to the popular conception of responsibility for future generations, which is fraught with philosophical difficulties. As I showed, Bonhoeffer's concept avoids these problems by focusing on the idea that suffering people, living here in the present, already furnish us with sufficient motivation for taking responsibility on their behalf. And since a large part of this suffering is caused by ecological degradation, it thereby becomes important to address this dimension of suffering (and responsibility) as well. An additional reason for this is the fact that, from the perspective of Bonhoeffer's conception of vicarious representation, it is possible to assign responsibility *for* nature and the environment *to* human beings.

Secondly, in chapter 6, I treated Bonhoeffer's concept of the divine mandates (viz., of marriage, work, state, and church), which he originally intended to serve as a blueprint for a new, post-war society. As I showed, this concept can be viewed as a further development of Luther's doctrine of the three "Stände." Though Bonhoeffer developed the concept against the backdrop of modernity, we saw how it was still quite traditional in nature, reflecting relatively old-fashioned Prussian ideals. In spite of this apparent drawback, I argued that the concept nevertheless bears a great deal of contemporary relevance for environmental ethics. First of all, I showed how Bonhoeffer's emphasis on the mandates as forms of God's commandments means that they function as a form of revelation—as such, they can help unmask unjust structures in society. While in his own time, Bonhoeffer used the concept as a tool to criticize a state that had become insatiably drunk with power, by shifting focus to the current context, I showed how it can also help to unmask the overwhelming dominance of the mandate of work which, through the doctrines of neoliberalism, has come to threaten and undermine the other three mandates. In this regard, I drew attention to the presence of a certain self-restraint at work within the mandate of work itself. As I argued, the best way forward is to embrace and strengthen the work mandate insofar as Bonhoeffer understood it, instead of simply condemning neoliberalism as a whole. Secondly, I asserted that, in order for Bonhoeffer's concept to remain relevant in today's context, the mandates would first need to be reformulated as *global* activities, or in other words, as a foundation for the establishment of global structures of accountability. This pertains specifically to the mandate of the state insofar as a globalized economy demands a measure of global, democratically mediated control. Thirdly and finally, I argued that Bonhoeffer's mandates can help grant a new impetus to the church to act as a *community* both in creating and sustaining networks of social interrelatedness, and in caring for nature.

The Relevance of this Research Project for Environmental Ethics

Having reviewed the major results of the project, I would now like to indicate what Bonhoeffer's concepts, when taken together as a whole, can contribute to the field of environmental ethics. This should allow us to organize each of the concepts according to a scale of priority, or of immediate practical significance, at least insofar as current ecological problems and dilemmas are concerned.

  As I indicated in chapter 1, the field of environmental ethics is remarkably wide and diverse. Keeping this in mind, the strategy that I have adopted has not been to develop an overarching perspective on the field as a whole, but rather to correlate certain concepts from Bonhoeffer's theology with a limited number of ecological debates and issues. At the same time, I also expressed the expectation that, rather than merely offering a loose collection of unrelated contributions, a more integrated approach could be developed on the basis of Bonhoeffer's theology. Taking a look back at the ground that we have covered, it is now possible to conclude that this goal has indeed been achieved—the correlations summarized above stand in a clear relationship to each other, and while I am not prepared, on the basis of his theology, to advance a wholesale "Bonhoefferian" approach to environmental ethics, I would argue that his theology *can* contribute in significant ways to key debates within ecology. In total, this contribution can be formulated along the lines of the following four general tasks: 1) generating motivation for environmental action and engagement, as well as forming a more ecologically sensitive attitude towards nature, 2) formulating an ecologically viable

Christian theology of nature, 3) revising Christian theological anthropology in light of the ecological crisis, and 4) reflecting on the relationship between sociality and ecology.

First of all, Bonhoeffer's theology can function as a valuable resource for the development of arguments capable of motivating people to take better care of nature. In chapter 2, I made clear how Bonhoeffer's concept of Christ-reality can be used to urge Christians to take part more actively in the concerns of the world—instead of shying away from taking responsibility for the earth, it compels them to work towards the "good" (defined as the reality of God made manifest in Christ) by conforming to Christ's threefold relationship to the world. This concept is undoubtedly the most important contribution that Bonhoeffer's theology can make in the context of ecology, for it links up directly with one of the most central issues in environmental ethics—namely, the problem of motivating people to abandon their environmentally destructive and careless behavior and to care for the environment. I addressed this issue in chapter 4 when I referred to Roger Scruton's observation of the need for a widely accessible argument explaining *why* people need to be concerned about the environment. Bonhoeffer's concept delivers such an argument. Though it is specifically addressed to Christians, it also sets Christian men and women free to engage wholeheartedly in the efforts of non-Christians to curb ecological destruction. Moreover, it never places them under the illusion that they themselves are responsible for the realization of God's Kingdom on earth—on the contrary, it clearly reveals that their task is, much more modestly, a mere preparation of the way for God's coming Kingdom.

Secondly, Bonhoeffer's theology contributes towards the development of an ecologically relevant theology of nature. In chapter 3, I argued that Bonhoeffer offers a surprisingly rich theology of nature, even in spite of its relatively underdeveloped state. One point that is especially valuable in this regard is his thinking on Christ as the center of nature. This is a centrality that, as we saw, remains hidden, and which only manifests itself in the sacraments, thereby offering a preview of nature's future redemption. This specific proposal for a cosmic Christology contains great promise for the formulation of a Christian theology of nature. In order to put the concept in context, I made the point that Bonhoeffer's emphasis on the cosmic scope of Christ's lordship in no way leads him to minimize—let alone deny— the importance of the historical Jesus; on the contrary, I showed how his Christology remains firmly committed to the Christian creeds. Given this groundedness in the creeds, I then argued that his cosmic Christology offers a viable alternative to, for example, the thoughts of Teilhard de Chardin, which are much more speculative and disengaged from the historical Jesus.

Also, in Teilhard's account, "sin" doesn't have nearly the same degree of prominence as it does for Bonhoeffer. In short, Bonhoeffer's cosmic Christology is considerably more "thick" in that it is able both to accommodate nature's fallenness and, at the same time, to recognize nature as already redeemed in Christ (even if this redemption still has yet to fully manifest itself). This "thickness" is also clearly discernable in Bonhoeffer's conception of the orders of preservation. As I showed, his assertion, that the order perceived in nature should always be seen in relation to Christ, opens up a middle way between an uncritical acceptance of nature "as it is," on the one hand, and a singular condemnation of every form of natural theology, on the other hand. In this way, Christ, by his threefold relationship to the world, becomes the criterion for deciding whether something is "natural" or not. In other words, nature is not purely and simply given, with Christ coming on the scene after the fact; no, for Bonhoeffer, nature is only fully revealed as nature in and through Christ alone. In the context of environmental ethics, it should also be noted that Bonhoeffer's theology of nature functions as a necessary complement to his understanding of Christ-reality (as well as related concepts), which I described in chapter 2, for it further develops an argument for people—specifically Christians—to care for nature.

The third general contribution to environmental ethics lies in Bonhoeffer's theological anthropology. In particular, I applied four elements of his anthropology to discussions bearing on the relationship between human beings and nature. As I showed, Bonhoeffer surprisingly refashioned certain elements from the philosophical and theological anthropologies of other thinkers and traditions. We saw, for example, how he adopts the general philosophical notion of bodiliness, only then to ground it in relation to Scripture. We also saw how he redefined the concept of the *imago Dei* in terms of an *analogia relationis*. After drawing attention to these renovated conceptual tools, I argued on behalf of the relevance of Bonhoeffer's theological anthropology with regard to ongoing debates in environmental ethics—for example, the debate concerning the appropriation of technology. At the same time, I also noted how the contributions that Bonhoeffer's thought is actually able to make are considerably weaker, or less significant, than those outlined in chapters 2 and 3. Regarding the theme of human distinctiveness, for example, we saw how *none* of the distinctions that Bonhoeffer drew between human beings and animals has stood the test of contemporary scientific inquiry. While I argued that it is important not to lose sight of human distinctiveness relative to animal life, Bonhoeffer's theology undoubtedly falls short here, for the only distinctions that we were able to keep were quantitative in nature, and not qualitative, as Bonhoeffer had argued.

As significant and important as his anthropology is, then, its contribution in the context of environmental ethics is relatively limited.

Fourthly and finally, I made the case that Bonhoeffer's theology can also contribute towards the development of a specifically Christian framework for taking responsibility, both in relation to nature and to society. As I showed, his concept of vicarious representation is valuable in the way that it stresses the qualitative uniqueness of Christ's vicarious representation, through which human beings are reconciled to God, while at the same time using it as a paradigm for authentic Christian living. This undoubtedly issues a radical call for taking responsibility both for society and for an endangered planet. In particular, it is able to provide a much needed alternative, or median path, between liberalism's dual-focus on the (moral) example of Jesus and social justice, and orthodoxy's focus on Christ's uniqueness and on individual salvation (though, to be fair, this presentation of either position is admittedly somewhat of a caricature). In addition, we saw how Bonhoeffer's conception of the divine mandates can be viewed as a concretisation of the way Christians can live out their lives responsibly. In this connection, I indicated certain ways in which this concept can contribute towards environmental ethics—for example, by emphasising that the mandates come from 'above' (as commandments of God), they help reveal unjust structures of power. Although Bonhoeffer's theology of responsibility can certainly make important contributions to contemporary environmental ethics, they too are relatively modest in nature. One specific limitation can be found in the fact that Bonhoeffer does not deliberately include nature in the realm of human responsibility, even though he provides the conceptual possibility of doing so. In addition, his concept of the divine mandates presents a number of problems, as I pointed out. Very much like his theological anthropology, then, the value of Bonhoeffer's theology of responsibility for current environmental ethics is relatively limited.

In sum, this book features two different categories of contributions. The first category consists of concepts (concerning the relationship between Christ and the natural world) that have the capacity to make the most significant contribution to environmental ethics. In contrast, the second category is composed of concepts (concerning Bonhoeffer's theological anthropology and his theology of responsibility) that would appear to have much less to offer. Setting this relative distinction to the side, however, one could still easily argue that Bonhoeffer's theology has a great deal to bring to bear on key debates within the field.

Possibilities for Future Research

This monograph helps open up a number of perspectives for future research, three of which I would briefly like to consider here, in closing.

First of all, I drew attention to the eschatological dimension of Bonhoeffer's theology. While I pointed out (primarily in chapter 2) that scholars have gradually come to acknowledge the presence of this dimension in his work, a thorough description of it has yet to be carried out. The partial exploration that I undertook in that chapter drew particular attention to the promise of Bonhoeffer's eschatology insofar as it provides an alternative to both escapist and immanent alternatives. While, in the context of this monograph, I focussed specifically on the potential significance of his eschatology for the field of ecology, it can readily be observed that it bears great promise for other contexts as well. Bonhoeffer's own examples of feeding the hungry and healing the sick, as activities belonging to the realm of the penultimate, could clearly be brought to bear in the field of social ethics, political ethics, and the ethics of care, for example. For this reason, it is crucial that more in-depth study be carried out on this aspect of Bonhoeffer's theology.

Secondly, this book has barely even scratched the surface of the potential contribution that Bonhoeffer's ecclesiology could make towards a renewed formulation of the church's mission, particularly in the context of the ecological crisis. Although I briefly touched on the subject in chapter 6, I only approached it in a very limited, *formal* way, that is, in relation to the divine mandates; as such, I have significantly restricted the present study from considering the full contribution that Bonhoeffer could make in this regard. A more thoroughgoing examination of Bonhoeffer's ecclesiology would very likely result in a much richer understanding of his potential contribution to environmental ethics, as well as to other contexts.

Thirdly, an important issue for further research concerns the relation between the theology of nature and the doctrine of Christ. This challenge was addressed in chapter 3, where I argued that Bonhoeffer's way of understanding Christ as the hidden center of nature helps to answer the question of how to overcome the subject-object divide within nature. However, there are many other possible contributions that could be drawn out from a more sustained reformulation of the theology of nature within the context of Christology, and not simply for the field of environmental ethics. To do so would necessitate going beyond Bonhoeffer, however, for his work only addresses the issue in a tentative fashion. One point that would be particularly important to address would be the question of how we ought to appropriate—christologically—the understanding of nature made available through the natural sciences.

Bibliography

Abromeit, Hans-Jürgen. *Das Geheimnis Christi: Dietrich Bonhoeffers erfahrungsbezogene Christologie*. Neukirchener Beiträge zur Systematischen Theologie 8. Neukirchen-Vluyn: Neukirchener, 1991.

Adams, Carol J. "'A Very Rare and Difficult Thing': Ecofeminism, Attention to Animal Suffering and the Disappearance of the Subject." In *A Communion of Subjects: Animals in Religion, Science, And Ethics*, edited by Paul Waldau and Kimberley Christine Patton, 591–604. New York: Columbia University Press, 2006.

Agamben, Giorgio. *What Is an Aparatus? And Other Essays*. Translated by David Kishik and Stefan Pedatella. Stanford, CA: Stanford University Press, 2009.

Althaus, Paul. *Theologie der Ordnungen*. 2nd ed. Göttingen: Vandenhoeck & Ruprecht, 1935.

Anderson, Bernhard W. "Made in the Image of God." In *Contours of Old Testament Theology*, 89–92. Minneapolis: Fortress, 1999.

Attfield, Robin. *The Ethics of Environmental Concern*. 2nd ed. Athens, GA: University of Georgia Press, 1991.

Auerbach, Bruce E. *Unto the Thousandth Generation: Conceptualising Intergenerational Justice*. Frankfurt am Main: Lang, 1995.

Axt-Piscalar, Christine. "Das Bild Gottes auf Erden: Zu Dietrich Bonhoeffers Lehre von der Gottebenbildlichkeit des Menschen." *Theologische Zeitschrift* 55, no. 2–3 (1999) 264–70.

Ballor, Jordan J. "Christ in Creation: Bonhoeffer's Orders of Preservation and Natural Theology." *Journal of Markets and Morality* 86, no. 1 (2006) 1–22.

Barth, Friederike. *Die Wirklichkeit des Guten: Dietrich Bonhoeffer's "Ethik" und ihr philosophischer Hintergrund*. Beiträge zur historischen Theologie 156. Tübingen: Mohr/Siebeck, 2011.

Barth, Karl. "From a Letter of Karl Barth to Landessuperintendent P. W. Herrenbrück, 21 December 1952." In *World Come of Age: A Symposium on Dietrich Bonhoeffer*, edited by Gregor Smith, 89–92. London: Collins, 1967.

———. *Gespräche 1959–1962*. Vol. 4 of *Karl Barth-Gesamtausgabe*. Edited by Eberhard Busch, Anton Drewes, and Hinrich Stoevesandt. Zürich: Theologischer Zürich, 1995.

———. *The Word of God and the Word of Man*. Translated by Douglas Horton. New York: Harper & Bros., 1957.

Barton, Stephen C. "New Testament Eschatology and the Ecological Crisis in Theological and Ecclesial Perspective." In *Ecological Hermeneutics: Biblical, Historical and*

Theological Perspectives, edited by David G. Horrell, Cherryl Hunt, Christopher Southgate, and Franscesca Stavrakopoulou, 266–82. London: T. & T. Clark, 2010.

Bayer, Oswald. "Christus als Mitte: Bonhoeffers Ethik im Banne der Religionsphilosophie Hegels." *Berliner Theologische Zeitschrift* 2 (1985) 259–76.

Bayertz, Kurt. "Eine kurze Geschichte der Herkunft der Verantwortung." In *Verantwortung: Prinzip oder Problem?*, edited by Kurt Bayertz, 3–71. Darmstadt: Wissenschaftliche Buchgesellschaft, 1995.

Beckmann, Klaus-Martin. "Die Mandatenlehre und die nicht-religiöse Interpretation biblischer Begriffe bei Dietrich Bohoeffer." *Evangelische Theologie* 28 (1968) 202–19.

Beder, Sharon. "Putting the Boot In." *Ecologist* 32, no. 3 (2002) 24–28, 66–67.

Beek, Abraham van de. *God doet recht: Eschatologie als christologie.* Spreken over God 2, 1. Zoetermeer: Meinema, 2008.

———. *Schepping: De wereld als voorspel voor de eeuwigheid.* Nijkerk: G. F. Callenbach, 1996.

Benktson, Benkt-Erik. *Christus und die Religion: Der Religionsbegriff bei Barth, Bonhoeffer und Tillich.* Translated by Christa Maria Lyckhage and Erika Goldbach. Stuttgart: Calwer, 1967.

Benz, Arnold. "Tragedy versus Hope: What Future in an Open Universe?" In *Technology, Trust, and Religion: Roles of Religions in Controversies on Ecology and the Modification of Life*, edited by Willem B. Drees, 120–31. Leiden: Leiden University Press, 2009.

Bergmann, Sigurd. *Creation Set Free: The Spirit as Liberator of Nature.* Translated by Douglas Scott. Sacra Doctrina. Grand Rapids: Eerdmans, 2005.

Berkhof, Hendrikus. *Christian Faith: An Introduction to the Study of the Faith.* Translated by Sierd Woudstra. Rev. ed. Grand Rapids: Eerdmans, 1993.

Berry, Robert James, ed. *The Care of Creation: Focusing Concern and Action.* Leicester, UK: InterVarsity, 2000.

Berry, Thomas. "Earthly Spirituality." In *Creation: A Reader*, edited by Jeff Astley, Ann Loades, and David Brown, 64–68. Problems in Theology 1. London: T. & T. Clark, 2003.

———. *Evening Thoughts: Reflecting on Earth as Sacred Community.* Edited by Mary Evelyn Tucker. Berkeley: University of California Press and the Sierra Club, 2006.

———. "The Gaia Theory: Its Religious Implications." *ARC: The Journal of the Faculty of Religious Studies, McGill University* 22 (1994) 7–19.

———. *The Sacred Universe: Earth, Spirituality, and Religion in the 21st Century.* Edited by Mary Evelyn Tucker. New York: Columbia University Press, 2009.

Berry, Thomas, and Brian Swimme. *The Universe Story: From the Primordial Flaring Forth to the Ecozoic Era—A Celebration of the Unfolding of the Cosmos.* San Francisco: HarperSanFrancisco, 1992.

Bethge, Eberhard. *Dietrich Bonhoeffer: A Biography.* Edited by Victoria J. Barnett. Translated by Eric Mosbacher et al. Rev. ed. Minneapolis: Fortress, 2000.

Bethge, Eberhard, ed. *Mündige Welt: 1. Weißensee, 2. Verschiedenes.* München: Kaiser, 1956.

Biehl, Janet, and Peter Staudenmaier. *Ecofascism: Lessons from the German Experience.* Edinburgh: AK, 1995.

Bismarck, Ruth-Alice von, and Ulrich Kabitz, eds. *Brautbriefe Zelle 92: Dietrich Bonhoeffer, Maria von Wedemeyer, 1943–1945.* München: Beck, 1992.

Bloch, Ernst. *The Principle of Hope*. Translated by Neville Plaice et al. Cambridge, MA: MIT Press, 1995.

Boersema, Jan Jacob. *Thora en Stoa over mens en natuur: Een bijdrage aan het milieudebat over duurzaamheid en kwaliteit*. Nijkerk: Callenbach, 1997.

Bonhoeffer, Dietrich. *Ethik*. Edited by Eberhard Bethge. 6th ed. Münich: Kaiser, 1962.

———. *Seminare, Vorlesungen, Predigten*. Vol. 5 of *Gesammelte Schriften*. Edited by Eberhard Bethge. Münich: Kaiser, 1972.

———. *Widerstand und Ergebung: Briefe und Aufzeichnungen aus der Haft*. Edited by Eberhard Bethge. Münich: Kaiser, 1985.

Bookless, Dave. "Christian Mission and Environmental Issues: An Evangelical Reflection." *Mission Studies* 25, no. 1 (2008) 37–52.

Bouma-Prediger, Steven. *For the Beauty of the Earth: A Christian Vision for Creation Care*. 2nd ed. Engaging Culture. Grand Rapids: Baker Academic, 2010.

Brennan, Andrew, and Yeuk-Sze Lo. "Environmental Ethics." In *The Stanford Encyclopedia of Philosophy* (Fall 2011 Edition), edited by Edward N. Zalta. http://plato.stanford.edu/archives/fall2011/entries/ethics-environmental/ (accessed July 21, 2016).

Brennan, Jason. "Dominating Nature." *Environmental Values* 16 (2007) 513–28.

Brink, Gijsbert van den. "Evolutionary Theory, Human Uniqueness and the Image of God." *In die Skriflig/In Luce Verbi* 46, no. 1 (2012) Art. #39, 7 pages. http://indieskriflig.org.za/index.php/skriflig/article/viewFile/39/588 (accessed July 21, 2016).

Brinkman, Martien E. *Schepping en sacrament: Een oecumenische studie naar de reikwijdte van het sacrament als heilzaam symbool in een weerbarstige werkelijkheid*. Zoetermeer: Meinema, 1991.

Brock, Brian. *Christian Ethics in a Technological Age*. Grand Rapids: Eerdmans, 2010.

———. *Singing the Ethos of God: On the Place of Christian Ethics in Scripture*. Grand Rapids: Eerdmans, 2007.

Brom, Luco J. van den. "The Art of a 'Theo-ecological' Interpretation." *Nederlands Theologisch Tijdschrift* 51 (1997) 298–313.

Bromiley, Geoffrey W. *Introduction to the Theology of Karl Barth*. Edinburgh: T. & T. Clark, 1979.

Brown, Wendy. "American Nightmare: Neoliberalism, Neoconservatism, and De-Democratization." *Political Theory* 34, no. 6 (2006) 690–714.

Brown, William P. "The Gardener and the Groundling: The Ecology of Resurrection." *Journal for Preachers* 32, no. 3 (2009) 33–37.

Brueggemann, Walter. *Genesis*. Interpretation: A Bible Commentary for Teaching and Preaching. Atlanta: Knox, 1982.

———. *Theology of the Old Testament: Testimony, Dispute, Advocacy*. Minneapolis: Fortress, 1997.

Brunner, Emil. "Biblische Psychologie." In *Gott und Mensch: Vier Untersuchungen über das personhafte Sein*, 70–100. Tübingen: Mohr/Siebeck, 1930.

———. *Der Mensch im Widerspruch: Die christliche Lehre von Wahren und vom Wirklichen Menschen*. Berlin: Furche, 1937.

———. *Die politische Verantwortung des Christen*. Kirchliche Zeitfragen 11. Zürich: Zwingli, 1944.

Brunner, Emil, and Karl Barth. *Natural Theology*. Translated by Peter Fraenkel. London: Bles, 1946.

Bryant, M. Darrol. "The Modern Myth of Mastery and the Christian Doctrine of Creation: A Journey in Ecology and Creation Theology." *Dialogue & Alliance* 9, no. 2 (1995) 56–68.

Burkholder, Benjamin J. "Christological Foundations for an Ecological Ethic: Learning from Bonhoeffer." *Scottish Journal of Theology* 66, no. 3 (2013) 338–56.

Burtness, James H. *Shaping the Future: The Ethics of Dietrich Bonhoeffer*. Philadelphia: Fortress, 1985.

Callicott, J. Baird. *In Defense of the Land Ethic*. Albany: State University of New York Press, 1989.

———. "Intrinsic Value, Quantum Theory, and Environmental Ethics." *Environmental Ethics* 7, no. 3 (1985) 257–75.

———. "On Norton and the Failure of Monistic Inheritism." *Environmental Ethics* 18, no. 2 (1996) 219–21.

Calvin, John. *Institutes of the Christian Religion*. Edited by John T. McNeill. Translated by Ford Lewis Battles. Vol. 1. Library of Christian Classics 20. Louisville: Westminster John Knox, 2006.

Capozza, Nicoletta. *Im Namen der Treue zur Erde: Versuch eines Vergleichs zwischen Bonhoeffers und Nietzsches Denken*. Berlin: Lit, 2003.

Chryssavgis, John. "The Earth as Sacrament: Insights from Orthodox Christian Theology and Spirituality." In *The Oxford Handbook of Religion and Ecology*, edited by Roger S. Gottlieb, 92–114. Oxford: Oxford University Press, 2006.

Clark, Adam C., and Michael Mawson, eds. *Ontology and Ethics: Bonhoeffer and Contemporary Scholarship*. Eugene, OR: Pickwick, 2013.

———. "Introduction: Ontology and Ethics in Bonhoeffer Scholarship." In *Ontology and Ethics: Bonhoeffer and Contemporary Scholarship*, edited by Adam C. Clark and Michael Mawson, 1–18. Eugene, OR: Pickwick, 2013.

Clayton, John Powell. *The Concept of Correlation: Paul Tillich and the Possibility of a Mediating Theology*. Theologische Bibliothek Töpelmann 37. Berlin: de Gruyter, 1980.

Clayton, Nicky, Nathan Emery, and Anthony Dickinson. "The Rationality of Animal Memory: Complex Caching Strategies of Western Scrub Jays." In *Rational Animals?*, edited by Susan Hurley and Matthew Nudds, 197–216. Oxford: Oxford University Press, 2006.

Clements, Keith. "Ecumenical Witness for Peace." In *The Cambridge Companion to Dietrich Bonhoeffer*, edited by John W. de Gruchy, 154–72. 2nd ed. Cambridge: Cambridge University Press, 1999.

Cloete, Newton Millan. "Hamartology and Ecology: A Critical Assessment of Dietrich Bonhoeffer's View on the Nature of Sin." Master's thesis, University of Western Cape, 2013.

Clough, David. "Interpreting Human Life by Looking the Other Way: Bonhoeffer on Human Beings and Other Animals." In *Bonhoeffer and the Biosciences: An Initial Exploration*, edited by Ralf K. Wüstenberg, Stefan Heuser, and Esther Hornung, 51–74. International Bonhoeffer Interpretations. Frankfurt am Main: Lang, 2010.

Cobb, John B., Jr. *Is It Too Late? A Theology of Ecology*. Beverly Hills, CA: Bruce, 1972.

Cochrane, Alasdair. "Environmental Ethics." *Internet Encyclopedia of Philosophy*. http://www.iep.utm.edu/envi-eth/ (accessed July 21, 2016).

Colyvan, Mark., et al. "Philosophical Issues in Ecology: Recent Trends and Future Directions." *Ecology and Society* 14, no. 2 (2009). http://www.ecologyandsociety.org/vol14/iss2/art22/ (accessed July 21, 2016).

Commission for Racial Justice. "Toxic Wastes and Race in the United States." New York: United Church of Christ Commission for Racial Justice, 1987.

Connor, William F. "The Laws of Life: A Bonhoeffer Theme with Variations." *Andover Newton Quarterly* 18, no. 2 (1977) 101–10.

———. "The Natural Life of Man and Its Laws: Conscience and Reason in the Theology of Dietrich Bonhoeffer." PhD diss., Vanderbilt University, 1973.

Conradie, Ernst M. *Christianity and Ecological Theology: Resources for Further Research.* Study Guides in Religion and Theology 9. Stellenbosch, South Africa: Sun, 2006.

———. "Creation and Salvation: Revisiting Kuyper's Notion of Common Grace." In *Creation and Salvation: Dialogue on Abraham Kuyper's Legacy for Contemporary Ecotheology*, edited by Ernst M. Conradie, 95–135. Leiden: Brill, 2011.

———. *An Ecological Christian Anthropology: At Home on Earth?* Aldershot, UK: Ashgate, 2005.

———. "Eschatological Dimensions of A 'Theology of Life.'" In *Christian Hope in Context*, edited by Aad van Egmond and Dirk van Keulen, 1:163–204. Studies in Reformed Theology 4. Zoetermeer, Netherlands: Meinema, 2001.

———. *Hope for the Earth: Vistas for a New Century.* 2nd ed. Eugene, OR: Wipf & Stock, 2005.

———. "Resurrection, Finitude, and Ecology." In *Resurrection: Theological and Scientific Assessments*, edited by Ted Peters, Robert John Russell, and Michael Welker, 277–96. Grand Rapids: Eerdmans, 2002.

———. "The Salvation of the Earth from Anthropogenic Destruction: In Search of Appropriate Soteriological Concepts in an Age of Ecological Destruction." *Worldviews: Global Religions, Culture, Ecology* 14 (2010) 111–40.

Crawley, J. N., M. E. Sutton, and D. Pickar. "Animal Models of Self-Destructive Behavior and Suicide." *Psychiatric Clinics of North America* 8, no. 2 (1985) 299–310.

Craycraft, Jr., Kenneth R. "Sign and Word: Martin Luther's Theology of the Sacraments." *Restoration Quarterly* 32, no. 3 (1990) 143–64.

Cunningham, David S. "The Way of All Flesh: Rethinking the *Imago Dei*." In *Creaturely Theology: On God, Humans and Other Animals*, edited by Celia Deane-Drummond and David Clough, 100–118. London: SCM, 2009.

Curry-Roper, Janel M. "Contemporary Christian Eschatologies and their Relation to Environmental Stewardship." *Professional Geographer* 42, no. 2 (1990) 157–69.

Dalton, Anne Marie, and Henry S. Simmons. *Ecotheology and the Practice of Hope.* SUNY Series on Religion and the Environment. Albany: State University of New York Press, 2010.

Darwin, Charles. *On the Origin of Species by Means of Natural Selection.* London: Murray, 1859.

———. *The Descent of Man, and Selection in Relation to Sex.* London: Murray, 1871.

Daub, Hans Friedrich. *Die Stellvertretung Jesu Christi: Ein Aspekt des Gott-Mensch-Verhältnisses bei Dietrich Bonhoeffer.* Münster: LIT, 2006.

Davis, John Jefferson. "Ecological 'Blind Spots' in the Structure and Content of Recent Evangelical Systematic Theologies." *Journal of the Evangelical Theological Society* 43, no. 2 (2000) 273–86.

Dawkins, Marian Stamp. *Through Our Eyes Only? The Search for Animal Consciousness.* Oxford: Oxford University Press, 1998.

Dawkins, Richard, *The Selfish Gene.* London: Penguin, 1977.

Dean, John F. *The Works of Love: Incarnation, Ecology and Poetry.* Dublin: Columba, 2010.

Deane-Drummond, Celia E. "Deep Incarnation and Eco-Justice as Theodrama: A Dialogue Between Hans Urs von Balthasar and Martha Nussbaum." In *Ecological Awareness: Exploring Religion, Ethics and Aesthetics,* edited by Sigurd Bergmann and Heather Eaton, 193–206. Studies in Religion and the Environment 3. Berlin: LIT, 2011.

———. "Ecology and Christology." In *Eco-Theology,* 99–113. London: Darton, Longmann and Todd, 2008.

———. *Theology and Biotechnology: Implications for a New Science.* London: Chapham, 1997.

Deane-Drummond, Celia E., ed. *Pierre Teilhard de Chardin on People and Planet.* Sheffield, UK: Equinox, 2006.

De George, Richard T. "The Environment, Rights and Future Generations." In *Ethics and Problems of the 21st Century,* edited by Kenneth E. Goodpaster and Kenneth M. Sayre, 93–105. Notre Dame: University of Notre Dame Press, 1979.

de Gruchy, John W. *Bonhoeffer and South Africa: Theology in Dialogue.* Grand Rapids: Eerdmans, 1984.

———. "Bonhoeffer, Apartheid, and Beyond: The Reception of Bonhoeffer in South Africa." In *Bonhoeffer for a New Day: Theology in a Time of Transition,* edited by John W. de Gruchy, 353–65. Grand Rapids: Eerdmans, 1997.

de Gruchy, John W., ed. *The Cambridge Companion to Dietrich Bonhoeffer.* 2nd ed. Cambridge: Cambridge University Press, 1999.

de Gruchy, John W., Stephen Plant, and Christiane Tietz, eds. *Dietrich Bonhoeffers Theologie heute: Ein Weg zwischen Fundamentalismus und Säkularismus?* Gütersloh: Gütersloher, 2009.

Dilthey, Wilhelm A. *Weltanschauung und Analyse des Menschen seit Renaissance und Reformation: Abhandlungen zur Geschichte der Philosophie und Religion.* Leipzig: Teubner, 1914.

Dinger, Jörg. "Mandate und Institutionen." In *Auslegung, Aktualisierung und Vereinnahmung: Das Spektrum der deutschsprachigen Bonhoeffer-Interpretation in der 5oer Jahren,* 244–53. Neukirchen-Vluyn: Neukirchener, 1998.

Donkan, Rupert. *Die Auferstehung Arabiens: Ibn Sauds Weg und Ziel.* Leipzig: Goldmann, 1935.

Dramm, Sabine. *Dietrich Bonhoeffer: An Introduction to his Thought.* Translated by Thomas Rice. Peabody, MA: Hendrickson, 2007.

Drees, Willem B. "Introduction." In *Technology, Trust, and Religion: Roles of Religions in Controversies on Ecology and the Modification of Life,* edited by Willem B. Drees, 1–8. Leiden: Leiden University Press, 2009.

———. *Is Nature Ever Evil? Religion, Science and Value.* London: Routledge, 2003.

Drees, Willem B., ed. *Technology, Trust, and Religion: Roles of Religions in Controversies on Ecology and the Modification of Life.* Leiden: Leiden University Press, 2009.

Drews, Paul. *Disputationen Dr. Martin Luthers in den Jahren 1535–1545 an der Universität Wittenberg gehalten.* Göttingen: Vandenhoeck & Ruprecht, 1895.

Du Toit, Cornel W. "Etsi Deus Non Daretur? Meta-Christian Values in a Post-Democratic World." *Journal of Theology for Southern Africa* 123 (2005) 61–73.

Duchrow, Ulrich. "Dem Rad in die Speichen fallen—aber wo und wie? Luthers und Bonhoeffers Ethik der Institutionen im Kontext des heutigen Weltwirtschaftssystems." In *Bonhoeffer und Luther: Zur Sozialgestalt des Luthertums in der Moderne*, edited by Christian Gremmels, 16–58. Internationales Bonhoeffer Forum: Forschung und Praxis 6. Münich: Kaiser, 1983.

Duggan, Lisa. *The Twilight of Equality? Neoliberalism, Cultural Politics, and the Attack on Democracy*. Boston: Beacon, 2003.

Dumas, André. *Dietrich Bonhoeffer: Une Théologie de la Réalité*. Geneva: Labor et Fides, 1986.

Edwards, Denis. "Deep Incarnation." In *Ecology at the Heart of Faith: The Change of Heart That Leads to a New Way of Living on Earth*, 58–60. Maryknoll, NY: Orbis, 2006.

———. "Eucharist and Ecology: Keeping Memorial of Creation." *Worship* 82, no. 3 (2008) 194–213.

Egmond, Aad van, and Dirk van Keulen, eds. *Christian Hope in Context*. 2 vols. Studies in Reformed Theology 4–5. Zoetermeer, Netherlands: Meinema, 2001.

Elkington, John. *Cannibals with Forks: The Triple Bottom Line of Twenty-First Century Business*. Oxford: Capstone, 1997.

Ellul, Jacques. *Le bluff technologique*. Paris: Grasset et Fasquelle, 1987.

———. *Le Système technicien*. Paris: Calmann-Lévy, 1977.

———. *La Technique, ou l'Enjeu du siècle*. Paris: Colin, 1954.

Erickson, Robert P. *Theologians under Hitler*. New Haven: Yale University Press, 1985.

Espinas, Alfred Victor. *Des Sociétés Animales: Étude de psychologie comparée*. Paris: Librairie Germer Ballière, 1878.

Evangelical Environmental Network. "An Evangelical Declaration on the Care of Creation: The Text." In *The Care of Creation: Focusing Concern and Action*, edited by Robert James Berry, 17–22. Leicester, UK: InterVarsity, 2000.

Falcke, Heino. "Welche Ansätze für eine Wirtschaftsethik finden wir bei Dietrich Bonhoeffer?" *Evangelische Theologie* 71, no. 5 (2011) 376–95.

Feil, Ernst. "Dietrich Bonhoeffer's Understanding of the World." In *A Bonhoeffer Legacy: Essays in Understanding*, edited by A. J. Klassen, 237–55. Grand Rapids: Eerdmans, 1981.

———. *The Theology of Dietrich Bonhoeffer*. Translated by Martin Rumscheidt. Philadelphia: Fortress, 1985.

Fergusson, David. *Church, State and Civil Society*. Cambridge: Cambridge University Press, 2004.

Finger, Thomas. *Evangelicals, Eschatology, and the Environment*. Scholars Circle Monograph 2. Wynnewood, PA: Evangelical Environmental Network, 1998.

Fiorenza, Francis Schüssler. "The Method of Correlation." In *Systematic Theology: Roman Catholic Perspectives*, edited by Francis Schüssler Fiorenza and John P. Galvin, 1:55–61. Minneapolis, MN: Fortress, 1991.

Floyd, Wayne Whitson, Jr. *Theology and the Dialectics of Otherness: On Reading Bonhoeffer and Adorno*. Lanham, MD: University Press of America, 1988.

Foucault, Michel. "The Confession of the Flesh." Translated by Colin Gordon et al. In *Power/Knowledge: Selected Interviews and Other Writings*, edited by Colin Gordon, 194–228. New York: Pantheon, 1980.

Fox, Matthew. *Illuminations of Hildegard of Bingen: Text by Hildegard of Bingen with Commentary by Matthew Fox*. Santa Fé: Bear, 1985.

Franz, Markus. "The Conversion of Social Life: Bonhoeffer's Mandates as Theological Dispositifs." In *Ontology and Ethics: Bonhoeffer and Contemporary Scholarship*, edited by Adam C. Clark and Michael Mawson, 133–49. Eugene, OR: Pickwick, 2013.

French, William C. "Natural Law and Ecological Responsibility: Drawing on the Thomistic Tradition." *University of St. Thomas Law Journal* 5, no. 1 (2008) 12–36.

Frick, Peter. "Bonhoeffer's Theology and Economic Humanism: An Exploration in Interdisciplinary Sociality." In *Being Human, Becoming Human: Dietrich Bonhoeffer and Social Thought*, edited by Brian Gregor and Jens Zimmerman, 49–68. Cambridge: Clark, 2010.

Gabriel, Andrew K. "Beyond Anthropocentrism in Barths Doctrine of Creation: Searching for a Theology of Nature." *Religious Studies and Theology* 28, no. 2 (2009) 175–87.

General Conference of UNESCO. "Declaration on the Responsibilities of the Present Generation towards Future Generations." November 12, 1997. http://portal.unesco.org/en/ev.php-URL_ID=13178&URL_DO=DO_TOPIC&URL_SECTION=201.html (accessed July 25, 2016).

George, K. M. "Towards a Eucharistic Ecology." In *Justice, Peace and the Integrity of Creation: Insights from Orthodoxy*, edited by G. Limouris, 45–55. Geneva: World Council of Churches, 1990.

Godsey, John D. "Barth and Bonhoeffer: The Basic Difference." *Quarterly Review* 7, no. 1 (1987) 9–27.

———. *The Theology of Dietrich Bonhoeffer*. Philadelphia: Westminster, 1960.

Gogarten, Friedrich. "Das Problem einer theologischen Anthropologie." *Zwischen den Zeiten* 7 (1929) 493–511.

Gosseries, Axel. "On Future Generations' Future Rights." *The Journal of Political Philosophy* 16, no. 4 (2008) 446–74.

Gottlieb, Roger S. "Introduction: Religion and Ecology—What Is the Connection and Why Does It Matter?" In *The Oxford Handbook of Religion and Ecology*, edited by Roger S. Gottlieb, 3–21. Oxford: Oxford University Press, 2006.

Gottlieb, Roger S., ed. *The Oxford Handbook of Religion and Ecology*. Oxford: Oxford University Press, 2006.

Gould, Rebecca Kneale. "Christianity (7h)—Natural Theology." In *Encyclopedia of Religion and Nature*, edited by Bron R. Taylor, 368–69. Bristol, UK: Thoemmes Continuum, 2005.

Granberg-Michaelson, Wesley. *A Worldly Spirituality: The Call to Redeem Life on the Earth*. San Francisco: Harper & Row, 1984.

Green, Clifford J. *Bonhoeffer: A Theology of Sociality*. Rev. ed. Grand Rapids: Eerdmans, 1999.

———. "Bonhoeffer's 'Non-Religious Christianity' as Public Theology." *Dialog: A Journal of Theology* 26, no. 4 (1985) 275–81.

———. Review of *Bonhoeffer*, by Eric Metaxas. *Christian Century*. http://www.christiancentury.org/reviews/2010-09/hijacking-bonhoeffer (accessed July 21, 2016).

Gregersen, Niels Henrik. "The Cross of Christ in an Evolutionary World." *Dialog: A Journal of Theology* 40, no. 3 (2001) 192–207.

Gregersen, Niels Henrik, and Willem Drees, eds. *Human Person in Science and Theology.* ESSAT Issues in Science & Technology. London: Continuum, 2000.

Gregor, Brian, "Bonhoeffer's 'Christian Social Philosophy': Conscience, Alterity, and the Moment of Ethical Responsibility." In *Being Human, Becoming Human: Dietrich Bonhoeffer and Social Thought,* edited by Brian Gregor and Jens Zimmerman, 201–25. Cambridge: Clark, 2010.

Gregor, Brian, and Jens Zimmermann, eds. *Being Human, Becoming Human: Dietrich Bonhoeffer and Social Thought.* Cambridge: Clark, 2010.

———. *Bonhoeffer and Continental Thought: Cruciform Philosophy.* Bloomington: Indiana University Press, 2009.

Gregorios, P. M. *The Human Presence: Ecological Spirituality and the Age of the Spirit.* New York: Amity, 1987.

Gremmels, Christian, ed. *Bonhoeffer und Luther: Zur Sozialgestalt des Luthertums in der Moderne.* Internationales Bonhoeffer Forum: Forschung und Praxis 6. München: Kaiser, 1983.

Grey, William. "Anthropocentrism and Deep Ecology." *Australasian Journal of Philosophy* 71 (1993) 463–75.

———. "Environmental Value and Anthropocentrism." *Ethics and the Environment* 3, no. 1 (1998) 97–103.

Grudem, Wayne. "Man in the Image of God." In ibid., *Systematic Theology: An Introduction to Biblical Doctrine,* 442–44. Leicester: InterVarsity, 1994.

Grundmann, Reiner. *Marxism and Ecology.* Oxford: Clarendon, 1991.

Smith, Ronald Gregor, ed. *World Come of Age: A Symposium on Dietrich Bonhoeffer.* London: Collins, 1967.

Gunton, Colin E. *Christ and Creation.* Grand Rapids: Eerdmans, 1992.

Griffin, Roger. "Fascism." In *Encyclopedia of Religion and Nature,* edited by Bron R. Taylor, 639–44. Bristol, UK: Thoemmes Continuum, 2005.

Habel, Norman C., and P. Trudinger, eds. *Exploring Ecological Hermeneutics.* Atlanta: SBL, 2008.

Habgood, John. "A Sacramental Approach to Environmental Issues." In *Liberating Life: Contemporary Approaches to Ecological Theology,* edited by Charles Birch, William Eakin, and Jay B. McDaniel, 46–53. Maryknoll, NY: Orbis, 1990.

Hagen, Joel B. "Teaching Ecology During the Environmental Age, 1965–1980." *Environmental History* 13, no. 4 (2008) 704–23.

Hall, Douglas John. *Imaging God: Dominion as Stewardship.* Grand Rapids: Eerdmans, 1986.

Hansen, Guillermo. "Neoliberal Globalization: A *Status Confessionis*?" In *Communion, Responsibility, Accountability: Responding as a Lutheran Communion to Neoliberal Globalization,* edited by Karen L. Bloomquist, 163–78. LWF Documentation 50. Geneva: Lutheran World Federation, 2004.

Hauerwas, Stanley. *The Hauerwas Reader.* Edited by John Berkman and Michael Cartwright. Durham, NC: Duke University Press, 2001.

Haught, John. "Catholicism." In *Encyclopedia of World Environmental History,* edited by Shephard Krech III, J. R. McNeill, and Carolyn Merchant, 1:200–203. London: Routledge, 2004.

———. *The Promise of Nature.* New York: Paulist, 1993.

Hardin, Garrett "The Economics of Wilderness." *Natural History* 78, no. 6 (1969) 20–27.

Hart, John. *Sacramental Commons: Christian Ecological Ethics*. London: Rowman and Littlefield, 2006.

Harvey, David. *A Brief History of Neoliberalism*. Oxford: Oxford University Press, 2005.

Harvie, Timothy. *Jürgen Moltmann's Ethics of Hope: Eschatological Possibilities for Moral Action*. Aldershot, UK: Ashgate, 2009.

Held, David, et al. *Global Transformations: Politics, Economics and Culture*. Stanford, CA: Stanford University Press, 1999.

Hempelmann, Reinhard. *Sakrament als Ort der Vermittlung des Heils: Sakramententheologie im Evangelisch-Katholischen Dialog*. Kirche und Konfession: Veröffentlichungen des Konfessionskundlichen Instituts des Evangelischen Bundes. Göttingen: Vandenhoeck & Ruprecht, 1992.

Hendel, Kurt K. "*Finitum capax infiniti:* Luther's Radical Incarnational Perspective." *Currents in Theology and Mission* 35, no. 6 (2008) 420–33.

Hessel-Robinson, Timothy. "Doctrine of the Lord's Supper: Modern Reception and Contemporary Possibilities." In *Calvin's Theology and Its Reception: Disputes, Developments and New Possibilities*, edited by J. Todd Billings and I. John Hesselink, 166–91. Louisville: Westminster John Knox, 2012.

Holder, Rodney D. "Science and Religion in the Theology of Dietrich Bonhoeffer." *Zygon* 44, no. 1 (2009) 115–32.

Holmes, Christopher R. J. "Bonhoeffer and Reformed Christology: Towards a Trinitarian Supplement." *Theology Today* 71 (2014) 28–42.

———. "'The Indivisible Whole of God's Reality': On the Agency of Jesus in Bonhoeffer's Ethics." *International Journal of Systematic Theology* 12, no. 3 (2010) 283–301.

Holte, Ragnar. *Die Vermittlungstheologie*. Uppsala: University of Uppsala Press, 1965.

Honecker, Martin. "Christologie und Ethik: Zu Dietrich Bonhoeffers Ethik." In *Altes Testament und christliche Verkündigung: Festschrift für Antonius H. J. Gunneweg zum 65. Geburtstag*, edited by Manfred Oeming and Axel Graupner, 148–64. Stuttgart: Kohlhammer, 1987.

———. *Die Kirche als Gestalt und Ereignis: Die sichtbare Kirche als dogmatisches Problem*. Münich: Kaiser, 1963.

———. "Zweireichelehre und Königsherrschaft Christi." In *Grundriß der Sozialethik*, 14–31. Berlin: de Gruyter, 1995.

Hoogstraten, Hans Dirk van. "Fundamenten voor een theologische milieu-ethiek: Bonhoeffers 'ethische theologie' sociaal ethisch bezien." *Tijdschrift voor Theologie* 31, no. 1 (1991) 42–64.

Horrell, David G., et al., eds. *Ecological Hermeneutics: Biblical, Historical and Theological Perspectives*. London: T. & T. Clark, 2010.

Huber, Wolfgang. "Freiheit und Institution." In *Folgen christlicher Freiheit*, ed. Wolfgang Huber, 113–27. Neukirchen-Vluyn: Neukirchen, 1993.

Hübner, Eberhard. "Eine marxistische Bonhoeffer-Interpretation." Review of *Von der Kirche zur Welt: Ein Beitrag zu der Beziehung des Wortes Gottes auf die societas in Dietrich Bonhoeffer's theologischer Entwicklung*, by Heinrich Müller. *Kirche in der Zeit* 16 (1961) 378–82.

Hübner, Jürgen. "Ökologische Verantwortung." In *Die Neue Verantwortung für das Leben: Ethik im Zeitalter von Gentechnologie und Umweltkrise*, 203–51. Münich: Kaiser, 1986.

Huizinga, Johan. *In de schaduwen van morgen: Een diagnose van het geestelijk lijden van onze tijd*. Haarlem, Netherlands: Willink, 1935.

Huntemann, Georg. *Die dialektische Theologie und der spekulative Idealismus Hegels: Ein Beitrag zur Geschichte des Kampfes um das finitum capax infiniti in der neueren Theologie.* Syke, Germany: Knauer, 1957.

———. *The Other Bonhoeffer: An Evangelical Reassessment of Dietrich Bonhoeffer.* Translated by Todd Huizinga. Grand Rapids: Baker, 1993.

Isherwood, Lisa. "The Tree, the Cross and Global Capitalism." *Feminist Theology* 10, no. 28 (2001) 93–106.

Jackson, Cecile. "Gender, Nature and Trouble with Anti-Dualism." In *Sacred Custodians of the Earth? Women, Spirituality, and the Environment,* edited by Alaine Low and Soraya Tremayne, 23–44. Oxford: Berghahn, 2001.

Jenkins, Willis. *Ecologies of Grace: Environmental Ethics and Christian Theology.* Oxford: Oxford University Press, 2008.

Jerie, Stephen. "The Role of the Church in Sustainable Environmental Management in Zimbabwe: A Case Study of the Bulawayo Archdiocese of the Roman Catholic Church." *Journal of Sustainable Development in Africa* 12, no. 8 (2010) 217–26.

John Paul II. "The Ecological Crisis: A Common Responsibility." In *Peace with God the Creator, Peace with All of Creation: Message of Blessed John Paul II for the celebration of the World Day of Peace.* January 1, 1990. http://conservation.catholic.org/ecologicalcrisis.htm (accessed August 15, 2013).

Johnson, Keith J. *Karl Barth and the Analogia Entis.* T. & T. Clark Studies in Systematic Theology 6. London: T. & T. Clark, 2010.

Jonas, Hans. *The Imperative of Responsibility: In Search of an Ethics for the Technological Age.* Translated by Hans Jonas and David Herr. Chicago: University of Chicago Press, 1985.

Joseph, Lawrence E. *Gaia: The Growth of an Idea.* New York: St. Martin's, 1990.

Jüngel, Eberhard. "Das Geheimnis der Stellvertretung: Ein dogmatisches Gespräch mit Heinrich Vogel." In *Wertlose Wahrheit: zur Identität und Relevanz des christlichen Glaubens,* 243–60. Theologische Erörterungen 3. Münich: Kaiser, 1990.

Justus, James, Mark Colyvan, Helen Regan, and Lynn Maguire, "Buying Into Conservation: Intrinsic Versus Instrumental Value." *Trends in Ecology and Evolution* 24, no. 4 (2009) 187–91.

Käfer, Anne. "Inkarnation und Schöpfung nach Martin Luther." In *Inkarnation und Schöpfung: Schöpfungstheologische Voraussetzungen und Implikationen der Christologie bei Luther, Schleiermacher und Karl Barth,* 10–84. Berlin: de Gruyter, 2010.

Kang, An Il. "Von der 'Nachfolge' zur 'Ethik der Verantwortung': Die Entwicklung des ethischen Denkens bei Dietrich Bonhoeffer." PhD diss., Ruhr-Universität, 2008.

Kant, Immanuel. *Groundwork for the Metaphysic of Morals.* Edited and translated by Jonathan F. Bennett. http://www.earlymoderntexts.com/pdfs/kant1785.pdf. (accessed August 21, 2014).

Katz, Eric. *Nature as Subject: Human Obligation and Natural Community.* Oxford: Rowman & Littlefield, 1997.

Kelly, Geffrey B. "Prayer and Action for Justice: Bonhoeffer's Spirituality." In *The Cambridge Companion to Dietrich Bonhoeffer,* edited by John W. de Gruchy, 246–68. 2nd ed. Cambridge: Cambridge University Press, 1999.

Keulen, Dirk van. "G. C. Berkouwer's Principle of Correlation: An Attempt to Comprehend." *Journal of Reformed Theology* 4 (2010) 97–111.

Kim, Sung Ho. "Max Weber." *Stanford Encyclopedia of Philosophy*. http://plato.stanford. edu/entries/weber/#EthConRes (accessed July 25, 2016).

Kim, Tae-Chang, and Ross Harrison, eds. *Self and Future Generations: An Intellectual Conversation*. Cambridge: White Horse, 1999.

Kings, Graham. "Canal, River and Rapids: Contemporary Evangelicalism in the Church of England." *Anvil* 20, no. 3 (2003) 167–84.

Kirchner, James W. "The Gaia Hypothesis: Conjectures and Refutations." *Climatic Change* 58, no. 1 (2003) 21–45.

Kirkpatrick, Martha. "'For God So Loved the World': An Incarnational Ecology." *Anglican Theological Review* 91, no. 2 (2009) 191–212.

Klassen, A. J., ed. *A Bonhoeffer Legacy: Essays in Understanding*. Grand Rapids: Eerdmans, 1981.

Klemperer, Klemens von. "Beyond Luther? Dietrich Bonhoeffer and Resistance against National Socialism." *Pro Ecclesia* 6, no. 2 (1997) 184–98.

Knights, Philip. "'The Whole Earth My Altar': A Sacramental Trajectory for Ecological Mission." *Mission Studies* 25 (2008) 56–72.

Kodalle, Klaus-M. "Das Leiden der Welt sucht seinen Träger: 'Stellvertretung'—ein irreführendes Konzept?" In *Dietrich Bonhoeffer: Zur Kritik seiner Theologie*, 99–112. Gütersloh: Gütersloher, 1991.

Körtner, Ulrich H. J. *Evangelische Sozialethik: Grundlagen und Themenfelder*. Göttingen: Vandenhoeck & Ruprecht, 1991.

———. "Schöpfungsglaube und Verantwortungsethik." In *Freiheit und Verantwortung: Studien zur Grundlegung theologischer Ethik*, 101–15. Studien zur theologischen Ethik. Freiburg: Universitätsverlag, 2001.

Koyama, Kosuke. "The Eucharist: Ecumenical and Ecological." *Ecumenical Review* 44, no. 1 (1992) 80–90.

Krause, Gerhard. "Bonhoeffer." In *Böhmische Brüder—Chinesische Religionen*, edited by Michael Wolter and Michael Schröter, 55–66. Vol. 7 of *Theologische Realenzyklopädie*, edited by Gerhard Krause and Gerhard Müller. Berlin: Walter de Guyter, 1981.

———. "The Humanity of the Human Person in Karl Barth's Anthropology." Translated by Philip G. Ziegler. In *The Cambridge Companion to Karl Barth*, edited by John Webster, 159–76. Cambridge: Cambridge University Press, 2000.

Kuikman, Jacoba. "Christ as Cosmic Tree." *Toronto Journal of Theology* 16, no. 1 (2000) 141–54.

Langdon, Adrian E. V. "Embedded Existence: Bonhoeffer, Barth, and Ecological Anthropology." *Didaskalia* 25 (2015) 59–77.

Lange, Frits de. "Against Escapism: Dietrich Bonhoeffer's Contribution to Public Theology." In *Christian in Public: Aims, Methodologies and Issues in Public Theology*, edited by Len Hansen, 141–52. Beyers Naudé Centre Series on Public Theology 3. Stellenbosch, South Africa: Sun, 2007.

———. "Aristocratic Christendom: On Bonhoeffer and Nietzsche." In *Bonhoeffer and Continental Thought: Cruciform Philosophy*, edited by Brian Gregor and Jens Zimmerman, 73–83. Bloomington: Indiana University Press, 2009.

———. *Grond onder de voeten: Burgerlijkheid bij Dietrich Bonhoeffer—Een theologische studie*. Kampen: Van den Berg, 1985.

————. "'Miteinander, Füreinander, Gegeneinander': Bonhoeffers Mandatenlehre in einer pluralistischen Gesellschaft." Lecture, Siegen, September 27, 1996. http://home.kpn.nl/delangef/artdbmandatduits.pdf (accessed July 21, 2016).

————. "'The Spiritual Force Is Lacking': Bonhoeffer on Secularization, Technology and Religion." Paper presented at the 8th International Bonhoeffer Conference, Berlin, August 2000. http://home.kpn.nl/delangef/dbberlin.htm (accessed July 21, 2016).

————. *Waiting for the Word: Dietrich Bonhoeffer on Speaking about God*. Translated by Martin N. Walton. Grand Rapids: Eerdmans, 1999.

Laslett, Peter, and James Fishkin, eds. *Justice between Age Groups and Generations*. New Haven: Yale University Press, 1992.

Lawrence, Joel. *Bonhoeffer: A Guide for the Perplexed*. T. & T. Clark Guides for the Perplexed. London: T. & T. Clark, 2010.

LeBlanc, Jill. "Eco-Thomism." *Environmental Ethics* 21, no. 3 (1999) 293–306.

Ledger, Christine. "Towards a Theology of Technology." *Interface: A Forum for Theology in the World* 7, no. 1 (2004) 124–29.

Lee, Jung Young. "Karl Barth's Use of Analogy in his Church Dogmatics." *Scottish Journal of Theology* 22, no. 2 (1969) 129–51.

Leonhard, Silke. *Leiblich lernen und lehren: Eine religionsdidaktischer Diskurs*. Praktische Theologie heute. Stuttgart: Kohlhammer, 2006.

Leopold, Aldo. *A Sand County Almanac and Sketches here and there*. Oxford: Oxford University Press, 1949.

Letcher, Andy. "'Gaia Told Me to Do It': Resistance and the Idea of Nature within Contemporary British Eco-Paganism." *Ecotheology* 8, no. 1 (2003) 61–84.

Levenson, Jon D. *Resurrection and the Restoration of Israel: The Ultimate Victory of the God of Life*. New Haven: Yale University Press, 2006.

Leys, Colin. *Market-driven Politics: Neoliberal Democracy and the Public Interest*. London: Verso, 2001.

Li, Huey-li. "On the Nature of Environmental Education: Anthropocentrism versus Non-Anthropocentrism––The Irrelevant Debate." *Philosophy of Educational Society Yearbook* (1996) 256–63.

Lindsay, Mark R. "Bonhoeffer's Eschatology in a World 'Come of Age.'" *Theology Today* 68, no. 3 (2011) 290–302.

Lovelock, James. *Gaia: A New Look at Life on Earth*. Oxford: Oxford University Press, 1979.

————. *The Revenge of Gaia: Why the Earth Is Fighting Back—and How We Can Still Save Humanity*. Santa Barbara CA: Lane, 2007.

————. *The Vanishing Face of Gaia: A Final Warning*. New York: Basic, 2009.

Lovin, Robin W. "The Mandates in an Age of Globalization." In *Ontology and Ethics: Bonhoeffer and Contemporary Scholarship*, edited by Adam C. Clark and Michael Mawson, 19–31. Eugene, OR: Pickwick, 2013.

Luther, Martin. *Luther on the Creation: A Critical and Devotional Commentary on Genesis*. Edited by John Nicholas Lenker. Translated by Henry Cole. Vol. 1 of *Luther Works*, edited by J. Pelikan and H. Lehman. Saint Louis: Concordia, 1955.

MacKenzie, Cameron A. "The Challenge of History: Luther's Two Kingdoms Theology as a Test Case." *Concordia Theological Quarterly* 71 (2007) 3–28.

MacKenzie, Donald, and Judy Wajcman. "Introductory Essay: The Social Shaping of Technology." In *The Social Shaping of Technology*, edited by Donald MacKenzie and Judy Wajcman, 1–49. 2nd ed. Buckingham, UK: Open University Press, 1999.

Maier, Harry O. "Green Millenialism: American Evangelicals, Environmentalism and the Book of Revelation." In *Ecological Hermeneutics: Biblical, Historical and Theological Perspectives*, edited by David G. Horrell et al., 246–65. London: T. & T. Clark, 2010.

Manoussakis, John Panteleimon. "'At the Recurrent End of the Unending': Bonhoeffer's Eschatology of the Penultimate." In *Ontology and Ethics: Bonhoeffer and Contemporary Scholarship*, edited by Adam C. Clark and Michael Mawson, 226–44. Eugene, OR: Pickwick, 2013.

Manrodt, David H. "The Role of Eschatology in the Theology of Dietrich Bonhoeffer," PhD diss., St. Mary Seminary & University, 1978.

Marshall, Paul A., with Lela Gilbert. *Heaven Is Not My Home: Learning to Live in God's Creation*. Nashville: Nelson, 1999.

Mayer, Rainer. "Die Bedeutung von Bonhoeffers Mandatenlehre für eine moderne politische Ethik." In *Dietrich Bonhoeffer heute: Die Aktualität seines Lebens und Werkes*, edited by Rainer Mayer and Peter Zimmerling, 58–80. Gießen: Brunnen, 1992.

———. *Christuswirklichkeit: Grundlagen, Entwicklung und Konsequenzen der Theologie Dietrich Bonhoeffers*. Arbeiten zur Theologie, 2nd ser., 15. Stuttgart: Calwer, 1969.

———. "Zuviel Staat oder zowenig Staat? Das Wächteramt der Kirche nach Dietrich Bonhoeffer." In *Dietrich Bonhoeffer: Beten und Tun des Gerechten—Glaube und Verantwortung im Widerstand*, edited by Rainer Mayer and Peter Zimmerling, 126–58. Gießen: Brunnen, 1997.

Mayer, Rainer, and Peter Zimmerling, eds. *Dietrich Bonhoeffer: Beten und Tun des Gerechten—Glaube und Verantwortung im Widerstand*. Gießen: Brunnen, 1997.

McFague, Sallie. *A New Climate for Theology: God, the World, and Global Warming*. Minneapolis: Fortress, 2008.

———. *Super, Natural Christians*. London: SCM, 1997.

McGrath, Alistair E. *Darwinism and the Divine: Evolutionary Thought and Natural Theology*. 2009 Hulsean Lectures. Oxford: Wiley-Blackwell, 2011.

———. *Nature*. Vol. 1 of *A Scientific Theology*. Grand Rapids: Eerdmans, 2001.

———. *The Re-Enchantment of Nature: Science, Religion and the Human Sense of Wonder*. London: Hodder & Stoughton, 2002.

McMillan, Franklin D. "Do Animals Experience True Happiness?" In *Mental Health and Well-Being in Animals*, edited by Franklin D. McMillan, 221–34. Oxford: Blackwell, 2005.

McMillan, Franklin D., ed. *Mental Health and Well-Being in Animals*. Oxford: Blackwell, 2005.

Menke, Karl-Heinz. *Stellvertretung: Schlüsselbegriff christlichen Lebens und theologische Grundkategorie*. Samlung Horizonte, Neue Folge 29. Freiburg: Johannes, 1991.

Metaxas, Eric. *Bonhoeffer: Pastor, Martyr, Prophet, Spy*. Nashville: Nelson, 2010.

Middleton, J. Richard. *The Liberating Image: The Imago Dei in Genesis 1*. Grand Rapids: Brazos, 2005.

Midgley, Mary. "Criticizing the Cosmos." In *Technology, Trust, and Religion: Roles of Religions in Controversies on Ecology and the Modification of Life*, 2009, edited by Willem B. Drees, 11–26. Leiden: Leiden University Press.

————. *The Ethical Primate: Humans, Freedom and Morality*. London: Routledge, 1994.

Migliore, Daniel L. "Eschatology and Ecology: The Witness of Reformed Theology." In *Christian Hope in Context*, edited by Aad van Egmond and Dirk van Keulen, 2:10–32. Studies in Reformed Theology 4–5. Zoetermeer, Netherlands: Meinema, 2001.

Mikkelsen, Hans Vium. "Kun den lidende Gud kan hjælpe: Dietrich Bonhoeffers relationstænkning." *Dansk Teologisk Tidsskrift* 59, no. 4 (1996) 266–87.

Miller, Daniel K. "Responsible Relationship: *Imago Dei* and the Moral Distinction between Humans and Other Animals." *International Journal of Systematic Theology* 13, no. 3 (2011) 323–37.

Moltmann, Jürgen. "The Alienation and Liberation of Nature." In *On Nature*, edited by Leory S. Rouner, 133–44. Boston University Studies in Philosophy and Religion 6. Notre Dame, IN: University of Notre Dame Press, 1984.

————. "Die Wirklichkeit der Welt und Gottes konkretes Gebot nach Dietrich Bonhoeffer." In *Die Mündige Welt: Weißensee 1959*, edited by Eberhard Bethge, 42–67. Münich: Kaiser, 1960.

————. *Ethics of Hope*. Translated by Margaret Kohl. Minneapolis: Fortress, 2012.

————. "God's Covenant and Our Responsibility." In *The Care of Creation: Focusing Concern and Action*, edited by Robert James Berry, 107–13. Leicester, UK: InterVarsity, 2000.

————. *God in Creation: A New Theology of Creation and the Spirit of God—The Gifford Lectures 1984–1985*. Translated by Margaret Kohl. Minneapolis: Fortress, 1993.

————. *Herrschaft Christi und Soziale Wirklichkeit nach Dietrich Bonhoeffer*. Theologische Existenz Heute 71. Münich: Kaiser, 1959.

————. "Theologie mit Dietrich Bonhoeffer: Die Gefängnisbriefe." In *Dietrich Bonhoeffers Theologie heute: Ein Weg zwischen Fundamentalismus und Säkularismus?*, edited by John W. de Gruchy, Stephen Plant, and Christiane Tietz, 17–31. Gütersloh: Gütersloher, 2009.

————. *Theology of Hope: On the Ground and the Implications of a Christian Eschatology*. Translated by James W. Leitch. London: SCM, 1967.

Moo, Douglas J. "Nature in the New Creation: New Testament Eschatology and the Environment." *Journal of the Evangelical Theological Society* 49, no. 3 (2006) 449–88.

Moses, John A. "Dietrich Bonhoeffer's Repudiation of Protestant German War Theology." *Journal of Religious History* 30, no. 3 (2006) 354–70.

Mostert, Christiaan. "Hope as Ultimate and Proximate." In *Christian Hope in Context*, edited by Aad van Egmond and Dirk van Keulen, 1:231–46. Studies in Reformed Theology 4–5. Zoetermeer, Netherlands: Meinema, 2001.

Muers, Rachel. *Living for the Future: Theological Ethics for Coming Generations*. London: T. & T. Clark, 2008.

Mulisch, Harry. *Voer voor psychologen*. Amsterdam: De Bezige Bij, 1998.

Müller, Heinrich. *Von der Kirche zur Welt: Ein Beitrag zu der Beziehung des Wortes Gottes auf die societas in Dietrich Bonhoeffer's theologischer Entwicklung*. 2nd ed. Hamburg: Herbert Reich Evangelischer, 1966.

Müller, Wolfgang Erich. *Der Begriff der Verantwortung bei Hans Jonas*. Frankfurt am Main: Athenäum, 1988.

Nash, James A. "Natural Law and Natural Rights." In *Encyclopedia of Religion and Nature*, edited by Bron R. Taylor, 1169–70. Bristol: Thoemmes Continuum, 2005.

Neugebauer, Matthias. "Die Theologische Lebensbegriff Dietrich Bonhoeffers im Lichte aktueller Fragen um Euthanasie, Sterbehilfe und Zwangssterilisation." In *Der Wert menschlichen Lebens: Medizinische Ethik bei Karl Bonhoeffer und Dietrich Bonhoeffer*, edited by Christof Gestrich and Johannes Neugebauer, 147–65. Berlin: Wichern, 2006.

Nickson, Ann L. "Freedom and Responsibility." In *Bonhoeffer and Freedom: Courageously Grasping Reality*, 116–46. Ashgate New Critical Thinking in Religion, Theology and Bibilical Studies. Aldershot, UK: Ashgate, 2002.

Nicolaisen, Carsten. "'Anwendung' der Zweireichelehre im Kirchenkampf: Emanuel Hirsch und Dietrich Bonhoeffer." In *Reaktionen*, edited by Niels Hasselmann, 15–26. Vol. 2 of *Gottes Wirken in seiner Welt: Zur Diskussion um die Zweireichelehre*, edited by Niels Hasselmann. Zur Sache 20. Hamburg: Lutherisches, 1980.

Nietzsche, Friedrich. *The Portable Nietzsche*. Edited and translated by Walter Kauffman. New York: Penguin, 1982.

———. *Thus Spoke Zarathustra (Selections)*. Edited and translated by Stanley Appelbaum. Mineola, NY: Dover, 2004.

Nissen, Ulrik Becker. "Responding to Human Reality." In *Being Human, Becoming Human: Dietrich Bonhoeffer and Social Thought*, edited by Brian Gregor and Jens Zimmerman, 191–213. Cambridge: Clark, 2010.

Northcott, Michael S. *The Environment and Christian Ethics*. New Studies in Christian Ethics. Cambridge: Cambridge University Press, 1996.

———. "Perils and Dangers: Climate Change and Theological Ethics." In *Environmental Ethics: Intercultural Perspectives*, edited by King-Tak Ip, 75–88. Value Inquiry Book Series. Amsterdam: Rodopi, 2009.

———. Review of *Environmental Ethics, Ecological Theology and Natural Selection*, by Lisa H Sideris. *Ecotheology* 10, no. 3 (2005) 403–5.

Norton, Bryan G. "Environmental Ethics and Weak Anthropocentrism." *Environmental Ethics* 6, no. 2 (1984) 131–48.

Nullens, Patrick A. "Dietrich Bonhoeffer: A Third Way of Christian Social Engagement." *European Journal of Theology* 20, no. 1 (2011) 60–69.

———. "Leven volgens Gaia's normen? De verhouding tussen God, mens en aarde en de implicaties voor ecologische ethiek." PhD diss., Evangelische Theologische Faculteit, 1995.

———. "Towards a Spirituality of Public Leadership: Engaging Dietrich Bonhoeffer." *International Journal of Public Theology* 7, no. 1 (2013) 91–113.

Nullens, Patrick A., and Ronald T. Michener. *The Matrix of Christian Ethics: Integrating Philosophy and Moral Theology in a Postmodern Context*. Colorado Springs: Paternoster, 2010.

O'Donovan, Oliver. *The Ways of Judgment: The Bampton Lectures, 2003*. Grand Rapids: Eerdmans, 2005.

Odum, Eugene P., and Howard T. Odum. *Fundamentals of Ecology*. Philadelphia: Saunders, 1953.

Oliver, Simon. "The Eucharist before Nature and Culture." *Modern Theology* 15, no. 3 (1999) 331–53.

O'Malley, Timothy. "Catholic Ecology and Eucharist: A Practice Approach." *Liturgical Ministry* 20 (2011) 68–78.

Ortega y Gasset, José. *La rebelión de las masas*. Madrid: Revista de Occidente, 1930.

Ott, Heinrich. *Reality and Faith: The Theological Legacy of Dietrich Bonhoeffer.* Translated by Alex A. Morrison. Philadelphia: Fortress, 1972.

Pangritz, Andreas. "Dietrich Bonhoeffers Kapitalismuskritik im Rahmen seiner theologischen Anthropologie." *Verantwortung: Zeitschrift des Dietrich-Bonhoeffer-Vereins* 23, no. 44 (2009) 5–12.

———. *Karl Barth in the Theology of Dietrich Bonhoeffer.* Translated by Barbara Rumscheidt and Martin Rumscheidt. Grand Rapids: Eerdmans, 2000.

Parfit, Derek. "Future Generations: Future Problems." *Philosophy and Public Affairs* 11, no. 2 (1982) 113–72.

Pattberg, Philipp. "Conquest, Domination and Control: Europe's Mastery of Nature in Historic Perspective." *Journal of Political Ecology* 14 (2007) 1–9.

Pattison, George. *Thinking About God in an Age of Technology.* Oxford: Oxford University Press, 2005.

Paul, Elizabeth S., Emma J. Harding, and Michael Mendl. "Measuring Emotional Processes in Animals: The Utility of a Cognitive Approach." *Neuroscience and Biobehavioral Reviews* 29 (2005) 469–91.

Pergamum, Metropolitan John of. "Preserving God's Creation." In *Christianity and Ecology*, edited by E. Breuilly and M. Palmer, 76–85. London: Cassell, 1992.

Pfeifer, Hans. "Dietrich Bonhoeffers 'Interim' Ethik: Untersuchungen anhand seines Geschichtsbegriffs." In *Dietrich Bonhoeffers Theologie heute: Ein Weg zwischen Fundamentalismus und Säkularismus?*, edited by John W. de Gruchy, Stephen Plant, and Christiane Tietz, 103–23. Gütersloh: Gütersloher, 2009.

———. "The Forms of Justification: On the Question of the Structure in Dietrich Bonhoeffer's Theology." In *A Bonhoeffer Legacy: Essays in Understanding*, edited by A. J. Klassen, 14–47. Grand Rapids: Eerdmans, 1981.

Picht, Georg. "The Concept of Responsibility: Introduction and Translation." *Religion* 28, no. 2 (1998) 185–203.

———. *Wahrheit, Vernunft, Verantwortung: Philosophische Studien.* 3rd ed. Stuttgart: Klett-Cotta, 2004.

Pierson, Russ. "Does God Love the World?" *Huffington Post.* August 5, 2013. http://www.huffingtonpost.com/russ-pierson/does-god-love-the-world_b_3239756.html (accessed July 21, 2016).

Plant, Stephen J. *Bonhoeffer.* Outstanding Christian Thinkers. London: Continuum, 2004.

———. "Dietrich Bonhoeffer (1906–1945): Jesus Christ and the Restoration, Preservation and Reconciliation of Creation." In *A Comparison on Recent Theological Movements*, edited by Ernst M. Conradie, 92–96. Vol. 2 of *Creation and Salvation.* Studies in Religion and the Environment 6. Berlin: Lit, 2012.

Plasger, Georg. "Hope in Our Lord Jesus Christ? A Dialogue with Jürgen Moltmann's Eschatology." In *Christian Hope in Context*, edited by Aad van Egmond and Dirk van Keulen, 1:247–63. Studies in Reformed Theology 4–5. Zoetermeer, Netherlands: Meinema, 2001.

Polkinghorne, John C. "Anthropology in an Evolutionary Context." In *God and Human Dignity*, edited by R. Kendall Soulen and Linda Woodhead, 89–103. Grand Rapids: Eerdmans, 2006.

Potts, Grant H. "Imagining Gaia: Perspectives and Prospects on Gaia, Science and Religion." *Ecotheology* 8, no. 1 (2003) 30–49.

Prenter, Regin. "Bonhoeffer and the Young Luther." In *World Come of Age: A Symposium on Dietrich Bonhoeffer*, edited by Gregor Smith, 161–81. London: Collins, 1967.

Preti, Antonio. "Suicide among Animals: A Review of Evidence." *Psychological Reports* 101 (2007) 831–48.

Primavesi, Anne. *From Apocalypse to Genesis: Ecology, Feminism, and Christianity*. Minneapolis: Fortress, 1991.

———. *Gaia and Climate Change: A Theology of Gift Events*. London: Routledge, 2009.

———. *Gaia's Gift: Earth, Ourselves and God After Copernicus*. London: Routledge, 2003.

———. *Sacred Gaia: Holistic Theology and Earth System Science*. London: Routledge, 2000.

Prüller-Jagenteufel, Gunter M. *Befreit zur Verantwortung: Sünde und Versöhnung in der Ethik Dietrich Bonhoeffers*. Berlin: LIT, 2004.

Przywara, Erich. *Religionsphilosophie katholischer Theologie*. Münich: Oldenbourg, 1927.

Ranke, Leopold von. *Über die Epochen der neueren Geschichte: Neunzehn Vorträge gehalten vor köning Maximilian von Bayern*. München: Duncker & Humblot, 1917.

Rappel, Simone. *"Macht euch die Erde untertan": Die ökologische Krise als Folge des Christentums?* Abhandlungen zur Sozialethik 39. Paderborn, Germany: Schöningh, 1996.

Rasmussen, Carl J. "Preserving the Natural: Karl Barth, the *Barmen Declaration*: Article 5, and Dietrich Bonhoeffer's *Ethics*." In *Theology and the Soul of the Liberal State*, edited by Leonard V. Kaplan and Charles Lloyd Cohen, 201–20. Graven Images. Lanham, MD: Lexington, 2010.

Rasmussen, Larry L. "Bonhoeffer and the Anthropocene." *Dutch Reformed Theological Journal* 55 (2014) 941–54.

———. "Bonhoeffer's Song of Songs and Christianities as Earth Faiths." In *Religion im Erbe: Dietrich Bonhoeffer und die Zukunftsfähigkeit des Christentums*, edited by Christian Gremmels and Wolfgang Huber, 186–93. Gütersloh: Kaiser, 2002.

———. "Cosmology and Ethics." In *Worldviews and Ecology: Religion, Philosophy, and the Environment*, edited by Mary Evelyn Tucker and John Grim, 173–80. Maryknoll, NY: Orbis, 1994.

———. *Dietrich Bonhoeffer: His Significance for North Americans*. Minneapolis: Fortress, 1990.

———. *Dietrich Bonhoeffer: Reality and Resistance*. Louisville: Westminster John Knox, 2005.

———. *Earth Community, Earth Ethic*. Ecology and Justice. Maryknoll, NY: Orbis, 1996.

———. *Earth-Honoring Faith: Religious Ethics in a New Key*. Oxford: Oxford University Press, 2013.

———. "Ethics of Responsible Action." In *The Cambridge Companion to Dietrich Bonhoeffer*, edited by John W. de Gruchy, 206–25. 2nd ed. Cambridge: Cambridge University Press, 1999.

———. "Introduction: Eco-justice—Church and Community Together." In *Earth Habitat: Eco-Justice and the Church's Response*, edited by Dieter Hessel and Larry L. Rasmussen, 1–22. Minneapolis: Augsburg Fortress, 2001.

————. "Life Worthy of Life: The Social Ecologies of Bonhoeffer and King." In *Bonhoeffer and King: Their Legacies and Import for Christian Social Thought*, edited by Willis Jenkins and Jennifer M. McBride, 55–68. Minneapolis: Fortress, 2010.

————. "The Whole of Earthly Life." In *Theology in Dialogue: The Impact of the Arts, Humanities and Science on Contemporary Religious Thought, Essays in Honor of John W. de Gruchy*, edited by L. Holness and R. K. Wüstenberg, 68–78. Grand Rapids: Eerdmans, 2002.

Rayson, Dianne, and Terence Lovat. "'Lord of the (Warming) World': Bonhoeffer's Eco-theological Ethic and the Gandhi Factor." *The Bonhoeffer Legacy: Australasian Journal of Bonhoeffer Studies* 2, no. 1 (2014) 57–74.

Regan, Tom. *The Case for Animal Rights*. 2nd ed. Berkeley: University of California Press, 2004.

————. *Deep Ecology*. Salt Lake City: Peregrine Smith, 1985.

Reist, Benjamin. *The Promise of Bonhoeffer*. Philadelphia: Lippincott, 1969.

Reynolds, Terrence. "Dietrich Bonhoeffer's Encouragement of Human Love: A Radical Shift in His Later Theology." *Union Seminary Quarterly Review* 41, nos. 3–4 (1987) 55–76.

Rieger, Joerg. *Globalization and Theology*. Horizons in Theology. Nashville: Abingdon, 2010.

Robinson, Frances M. C. "The Relevance of *Chaos* to Environmental Ethics." MAVE diss., Lancaster University 2001. http://www.lancs.ac.uk/depts/philosophy/awaymave/onlineresources/frances%20robinson.pdf (accessed July 21, 2016).

Robinson, John A. T. *Honest to God*. London: SCM, 1963.

Rölli, Marc. "Philosophische Anthropologie im 19. Jahrhundert: Zwischen Leib und Körper." In *Leiblichkeit: Geschichte und Aktualität eines Konzepts*, edited by Emmanuel Alloa et al., 149–61. Tübingen: Mohr/Siebeck, 2012.

Rollin, Bernard E. "Animal Happiness: A Philosophical View." In *Mental Health and Well-Being in Animals*, edited by Franklin D. McMillan, 235–41. Oxford: Blackwell, 2005.

Rolston, Holmes, III. "Naturalizing and Systematizing Evil." In *Technology, Trust, and Religion: Roles of Religions in Controversies on Ecology and the Modification of Life, 2009*, edited by Willem B. Drees, 67–86. Leiden: Leiden University Press.

Römelt, Josef. "Natur als Gegenstand menschlicher Verantwortung." In *Jenseits von Pragmatismus und Resignation: Perspektiven christlicher Verantwortung für Umwelt, Frieden undsoziale Gerechtigkeit*, 77–96. Vol. 3 of *Handbuch der Moraltheologie*. Regensburg: Friedrich Pustet, 1999.

Roskam, Willem. "Bonhoeffers posthumanistische christologie: Over ecologisch verantwoord burgerschap." *Radix* 40, no. 2 (2014) 110–20.

Roskos, Nicole. "Christian Theology and the Fall." In *Encyclopedia of Religion and Nature*, edited by Bron R. Taylor, 312–14. Bristol, UK: Thoemmes Continuum, 2005.

Ruether, Rosemary Radford. "Ecological Theology: Roots in Tradition, Liturgical and Ethical Practice for Today." *Dialog: A Journal of Theology* 42, no. 3 (2003) 226–34.

————. *Gaia and God: An Ecofeminist Theology of Earth Healing*. San Francisco: HarperSanFrancisco, 1992.

————. *Sexism and God-talk*. Boston: Beacon, 1983.

Ruether, Rosemary Radford, ed. *Women Healing Earth: Third World Women on Ecology, Feminism and Religion*. Maryknoll, NY: Orbis, 1996.

Ryan, Peter F. "Secularist and Christian Views of Human Nature and Its Fulfillment: Implications for Bioethics and Environmentalism." In *Human Nature in Its Wholeness: A Roman Catholic Perspective*, edited by Daniel N. Robinson, Gladys M. Sweeney, and Richard Gill, 57–79. Washington, DC: Catholic University of America Press, 2006.

Sandel, Michael. "Competing American Traditions of Public Philosophy." *Toward a New Public Philosophy: A Global Reevaluation of Democracy at Century's End, Ethics and International Affairs* 20 (1997) 7–12.

Santas, Aristotelis. "Subject/Object Dualism and Environmental Degradation." *Philosophical Inquiry* 21, nos. 3–4 (1999) 79–96.

Santmire, H. Paul. "Christianity (6c1)—Reformation Traditions (Lutheranism and Calvinism)." In *Encyclopedia of Religion and Nature*, edited by Bron R. Taylor, 341–43. Bristol, UK: Thoemmes Continuum, 2005.

———. "Ecology, Justice, Liturgy: A Theological Autobiography." *Dialog: A Journal of Theology* 48, no. 3 (2009) 270–71.

———. "Martin Luther, the Word of God and Nature: Reformation Hermeneutics in Context." In *Ecological Hermeneutics: Biblical, Historical and Theological Perspectives*, edited by David G. Horrell et al., 166–180. London: T. & T. Clark, 2010.

———. *Nature Reborn: The Ecological and Cosmic Promise of Christian Theology.* Minneapolis: Fortress, 2000.

Schaefer, Jame. *Theological Foundations for Environmental Ethics: Reconstructing Patristic and Medieval Concepts.* Washington, DC: Georgetown University Press, 2009.

Schaeffer, Francis A. *Pollution and the Death of Man: The Christian View of Ecology.* Wheaton, IL: Tyndale House, 1970.

Scharper, Stephen B. "The Gaia Hypothesis: Implications for a Christian Political Theology of the Environment." *Cross Currents* 44, no. 2 (1994) 207–21.

Schauffler, F. Marina. *Turning to Earth: Stories of Ecological Conversion.* Charlottesville: University of Virginia Press, 2003.

Schenk, Wolfgang. "'Finitum est capax infiniti': Zur Vor- und Interpretationsgeschichte dieser Formel unter Berücksichtigung des lutherisch-reformierten Gegensatzes und der Positions Karl Barths." *Communio Viatorum* 28, no. 3–4 (1985) 195–207.

Schlingensiepen, Ferdinand. *Dietrich Bonhoeffer, 1906–1945: Eine Biographie.* Münich: Beck, 2005.

Schmidt, Hans. "The Cross of Reality? Some Questions Concerning the Interpretation of Bonhoeffer." In *World Come of Age: A Symposium on Dietrich Bonhoeffer*, edited by Gregor Smith, 215–55. London: Collins, 1967.

Schwarz, R. "Luthers Lehre von den drei Ständen und die drei Dimensionen der Ethik." *Luther-Jahrbuch* 45 (1978) 15–34.

Schweiker, William. *Respsonsibility and Christian Ethics.* New Studies in Christian Ethics. Cambridge: Cambridge University Press, 1995.

Scott, Peter Manley. "Christ, Nature, Sociality: Dietrich Bonhoeffer for an Ecological Age." *Scottish Journal of Theology* 53, no. 4 (2000) 413–30.

———. "Postnatural Humanity? Bonhoeffer, Creaturely Freedom, and the Mystery of Reconciliation in Creation." In *Mysteries in the Theology of Dietrich Bonhoeffer: A Copenhagen Bonhoeffer Symposium*, edited by Kirsten Busch Nielsen, Ulrik Nissen, and Christiane Tietz, 111–34. Götingen: Vandenhoeck & Ruprecht, 2007.

————. "Postnatural Humanity? Bonhoeffer on Freedom and Order in Creation." In *Anti-Human Theology: Nature, Technology and the Postnatural*, 11–35. Revisioning Ethics. London: SCM, 2010.

Scruton, Roger. *Green Philosophy: How to Think Seriously about the Planet.* London: Atlantic, 2013.

Seeberg, Reinhold. *Die Anfänge des Dogmas im nachapostolischen und altkatholischen Zeitalter.* Vol. 1 of *Lehrbuch der Dogmengeschichte.* Leipzig: Deichert, 1922.

Seuring, Stefan, and Martin Müller. "From a Literature Review to a Conceptual Framework For Sustainable Supply Chain Management." *Journal of Cleaner Production* 16, no. 15 (2008) 1699–1710.

Sideris, Lisa H. *Environmental Ethics, Ecological Theology and Natural Selection.* Columbia Series in Science and Religion. New York: Columbia University Press, 2003.

Simmons, J. Aaron. "Evangelical Environmentalism: Oxymoron or Opportunity?" *Worldviews: Environment, Culture, Religion* 13 (2009) 40–71.

't Slot, Edward van. *Negativism of Revelation? Bonhoeffer and Barth on Faith and Actualism.* Dogmatik in der Moderne 12. Tübingen: Mohr/Siebeck, 2015.

————. "Theonomy and Analogy in Ecclesiology: Sources in Barth and Bonhoeffer for a Dynamic Ecclesiology." *Zeitschrift für Dialektische Theologie*, Supplement Series 5 (2011) 45–58.

Smedema, Ids J. *Grond onder de voeten: Karl Barths scheppingsleer in KD III/1 opnieuw gelezen.* Zoetermeer, Netherlands: Boekencentrum Academic, 2009.

Smith, David. "Discipleship in a Globalized World." *Scottish Bulletin of Evangelical Theology* 23, no. 2 (2005) 148–65.

Smith, Ronald Gregor, ed. *World Come of Age: A Symposium on Dietrich Bonhoeffer.* London: Collins, 1967.

Smith, James K. A. *The Fall of Interpretation: Philosophical Foundations for a Creational Hermeneutic.* 2nd ed. Grand Rapids: Baker Academic, 2012.

Sölle, Dorothee. "Die Dialektik von Angewiesenheit und Verantwortung (Auseinandersetzung mit Bonhoeffer)." In *Stellvertretung: Ein Kapital Theologie nach dem "Tode Gottes,"* 121–29. Stuttgart: Kreuz, 1965.

Southgate, Christopher. "Significance of the Cross and Resurrection." In *The Groaning of Creation: God, Evolution, and the Problem of Evil*, 75–77. Louisville: Westminster John Knox, 2008.

Spengler, Oswald. *Der Untergang des Abendlandes: Umrisse einer Morphologie der Weltgeschichte.* 2 vols. Münich: Beck, 1919–1922.

Starhawk. *Dreaming the Dark: Magic, Sex and Politics.* Boston: Beacon, 1997.

Steiner, Gary. "Descartes, Christianity, and Contemporary Speciesism." In *A Communion of Subjects: Animals in Religion, Science, And Ethics*, edited by Paul Waldau and Kimberley Christine Patton, 117–31. New York: Columbia University Press, 2006.

Steiner-Aeschliman, Sherrie. "Immanent Dualism as an Alternative to Dualism and Monism: The Worldview of Max Weber." *Worldviews: Environment, Culture, Religion* 4 (2000) 235–63.

Strandberg, Todd. "Bible Prophecy and Environmentalism." *Rapture Ready.* www.raptureready.com/rr-environmental.html (accessed March 17, 2013).

Tanner, Katryn. "Beliefs, Actions, Attitudes." In *Politics of God: Christian Theologies and Social Justice*, 1–34. Minneapolis: Fortress, 1992.

———. "Eschatology and Ethics." In *Oxford Handbook of Theological Ethics*, edited by Gilbert Meilander and William Werpehowski, 41–56. Oxford: Oxford University Press, 2005.

———. "Eschatology without a Future?" In *The End of the World and the Ends of God: Science and Theology on Eschatology*, edited by John Polkinghorne and Michael Welker, 222–37. Harrisburg, PA: Trinity, 2000.

Taylor, Bron R. *Dark Green Religion: Nature Spirituality and the Planetary Future*. Los Angeles: University of California Press, 2010.

Taylor, Bron R., ed. *Encyclopedia of Religion and Nature*. Bristol, UK: Thoemmes Continuum, 2005.

Taylor, Charles. *Modern Social Imaginaries*. Durham, NC: Duke University Press, 2004.

Teilhard de Chardin, Pierre. *The Divine Milieu: An Essay on the Interior Life*. Edited by Bernard Wall. Translated by Alick Dru et al. New York: Harper & Row, 1960.

Tennyson, Alfred Lord. *In Memoriam A. H. H.* London: Moxon, 1850.

"The Amsterdam Declaration on Global Change." Amsterdam, July 13, 2001. http:// www.colorado.edu/AmStudies/lewis/ecology/gaiadeclar.pdf (accessed July 21, 2016).

The Book of Concord: The Confessions of the Evangelical Lutheran Church. Edited and translated by Theodore G. Tappert. Philadelphia: Fortress, 1959.

Thomas, Günther. "Christus als Konnex von Schöpfung und Neuer Schöpfung: Dietrich Bonhoeffers realistische Eschatologie." In *Neue Schöpfung: Systematisch-theologische Untersuchungen zur Hoffnung auf das "Leben in der zukünftigen Welt,"* 344–82. Neukirchen: Neukirchener, 2009.

Thomas, John H. "Life Together in a Life Apart World." *Trinity Seminary Review* 25, no. 2 (2004) 81–95.

Thompson, Geoff. "'Remaining Loyal to the Earth': Humanity, God's Other Creatures and the Bible in Karl Barth." In *Ecological Hermeneutics: Biblical, Historical and Theological Perspectives*, edited by David G. Horrell et al., 181–95. London: T. & T. Clark, 2010.

Tietz-Steiding, Christiane. *Bonhoeffers Kritik der verkrümmten Vernunft: Eine erkenntnistheoretische Untersuchung*. Beiträge zur historischen Theologie 112. Tübingen: Mohr/Siebeck, 1999.

Tillich, Paul. "The Method of Correlation." In ibid., *Systematic Theology*, 1:59–66. Chicago: University of Chicago Press, 1950.

———. "Nature and Sacrament." In ibid., *The Protestant Era*, 94–114. Chicago: University of Chicago Press, 1948.

———. "The Problem of Theological Method." *Journal of Religion* 27, no. 1 (1947) 16–26.

Tinker, George E. "An American Indian Theological Response to Ecojustice." *Ecotheology* 3 (1997) 85–109.

———. "Creation as Kin: An American Indian View." In *After Nature's Revolt: Eco-Justice and Theology*, edited by Dieter T. Hessel, 144–153. Philadelphia: Fortress, 1992.

Tödt, Heinz-Eduard. *Authentic Faith: Bonhoeffer's Theological Ethics in Context*. Edited by Glen Harold Stassen. Translated by David Stassen and Ilse Tödt. Grand Rapids: Eerdmans, 2007.

Tracy, David. *Blessed Rage for Order: The New Pluralism in Theology*. New York: Seabury, 1975.

————. *The Analogical Imagination: Christian Theology and the Culture of Pluralism.* London: SCM, 1981.

————. "Theological Method." In *Christian Theology: An Introduction to Its Traditions and Tasks*, edited by Peter C. Hodgson and Robert King, 35–60. 2nd ed. Philadelphia: Fortress, 1985.

Treier, Daniel J. "Modernity's Machine: Technology Coming of Age in Bonhoeffer's Apocalyptic Proverbs." In *Bonhoeffer, Christ and Culture*, edited by Keith L. Johnson and Timothy Larsen, 91–111. Downers Grove, IL: IVP Academic, 2013.

Trilhaas, Wolfgang. "Natur und Christentum." In *Religion in Geschichte und Gegenwart*, edited by Kurt Galling, 4:1326–29. 3rd ed. Tübingen: Mohr/Siebeck, 1960.

Trowitzsch, Michael. "Luther und Bonhoeffer Zugleich: Eine Meditation über das Mittleramt Jesu Christi." In *Luther, Zwischen den Zeiten: Eine Jenaer-Ringvorlesung*, edited by Christoph Markschies and Michael Trowitzsch, 185–206. Tübingen: Mohr/Siebeck, 1999.

Truesdale, Al. "Last Things First: The Impact of Eschatology on Ecology." *Perspectives on Science and Christian Faith* 46, no. 2 (1994) 116–22.

Tulving, Endel. *Elements of Episodic Memory.* Oxford: Clarendon, 1983.

Turner, David L. "The New Jerusalem in Revelation 21:1—22:5: Consummation of a Biblical Continuum." In *Dispensationalism, Israel and the Church: The Search for Definition*, edited by Craig A. Blaising and Darrell L. Bock, 264–92. Grand Rapids: Zondervan, 1992.

Ulrich, Hans G. *Wie Geschöpfe leben: Konturen evangelischer Ethik.* Vol. 2 of *Ethik im Theologischen Diskurs.* 2nd ed. Berlin: Lit, 2007.

Vanden Berg, Mary L. "Christ's Atonement: The Hope of Creation." PhD diss., Calvin Theological Seminary, 2008.

Verstraeten, Johan. "The Tension between 'Gesinnungsethik' and 'Verantwortungsethik': A Critical Interpretation of the Position of Max Weber in 'Politik als Beruf.'" *Ethical Perspectives* 2, no. 3 (1995) 180–87.

Vilmar, August Friedrich Christian. *Die Lehre vom geistlichen Amt.* Leipzig: N.G. Erwert'sche Universitäts Buchhandlung, 1870.

————. *Dogmatik: Academische Vorlesungen.* Vol. 2. Edited by K. W. Piderit. Gütersloh: Bertelsmann, 1874.

Vischer, Wilhelm. "Der Gott Abrahams und der Gott Isaaks und der Gott Jakobs." *Zwischen den Zeiten* 9, no. 4 (1931) 282–97.

Visser, Douwe. *Het zondebegrip bij Dietrich Bonhoeffer: Een bijdrage tot de analyse van de ontwikkelingsgang van Bonhoeffers theologie.* Amsterdam: VU Uitgeverij, 1992.

Visser 't Hooft, Hendrik Ph. *Justice to Future Generations and the Environment.* Law and Philosophy Library. Dordrecht: Kluwer Academic, 1999.

Vosloo, Robert. "Body and Health in Light of the Theology of Dietrich Bonhoeffer." *Religion and Theology* 13, no. 1 (2006) 23–37.

Waal, Frans B. M. de. *Good Natured: The Origins of Right and Wrong in Humans and Other Animals.* Cambridge, MA: Harvard University Press, 1996.

Waap, Thorsten. "Gottebenbildlichkeit und Identität bei Karl Barth." In *Gottebenbildlichkeit und Identität: Zum Verhältnis von theologischer Anthropologie und Humanwissenschaft bei Karl Barth und Wolfhart Pannenberg*, 176–321. Forschungen zur systematischen und ökomenischen Theologie 121. Göttingen: Vandenhoeck & Ruprecht, 2008.

Waldau, Paul, and Kimberley Christine Patton, eds. *A Communion of Subjects: Animals in Religion, Science, And Ethics.* New York: Columbia University Press, 2006.

Wannenwetsch, Bernd, ed. *Who Am I? Bonhoeffer's Theology Through his Poetry.* London: T. & T. Clark, 2009.

Ware, Kallistos T. "Through the Creation to the Creator." *Ecotheology* 2 (1997) 8–30.

Waters, Brent. *From Human to Posthuman: Christian Theology and Technology in a Postmodern World.* Aldershot, UK: Ashgate, 2006.

Weber, Max. "Politik als Beruf." In *Gesammelte Politische Schriften*, edited by Johannes Winckelmann, 396–450. 5th ed. UTB für Wissenschaft. Tübingen: Mohr/Siebeck, 1988.

Weiner, Douglas R. *Models of Nature: Ecology, Conservation, and Cultural Revolution in Soviet Russia.* Indiana-Michigan Series in Russian and Eastern European Studies. Bloomington: Indiana University Press, 1988.

Weizsäcker, Carl Friedrich von. *Die Zeit drängt: Eine Weltversammlung der Christen für Gerechtigkeit, Frieden und die Bewahrung der Schöpfung.* Münich: Hanser, 1986.

———. *Zum Weltbild der Physik.* Stuttgart: Hirzel, 1943.

Wellman, David J. "Dietrich Bonhoeffer's Ethic of Resistance in George W. Bush's America: A Call to Progressive Christians in the United States." *Union Seminary Quarterly Review* 60, no. 1–2 (2006) 69–77.

Welz, Claudia. "Imago Dei: References to the Invisible." *Studia Theologica* 65 (2011) 74–91.

Wendel, Ernst Georg. *Studien zur Homiletik Dietrich Bonhoeffers: Predigt—Hermeneutik—Sprache.* Hermeneutische Untersuchungen zur Theologie. Tübingen: Mohr/Siebeck, 1985.

Wensveen, Louke van. "Christianity (7a)—Theology and Ecology (Contemporary Introduction)." In *Encyclopedia of Religion and Nature*, edited by Bron R. Taylor, 354–55. Bristol, UK: Thoemmes Continuum, 2005.

West, Charles C. "Ground under our Feet: A Reflection on the Worldliness of Bonhoeffer's Life and Thought." In *New Studies in Bonhoeffer's Ethics*, edited by William J. Peck, 235–73. Lewiston, NY: Mellen, 1987.

Westermann, Claus. *Genesis 1–11.* Biblischer Kommentar Altes Testaments I/1. Neukirchen-Vluyn: Neukirchener, 1974.

White, Lynn, Jr. "The Historical Roots of our Ecologic Crisis." *Science* NS 155, no. 3767 (1967) 1203–7.

Wiebering, Joachim. "Zwei Räume—Zwei Reiche? Bonhoeffers 'Ethik' in ihrem Verhältnis zur Tradition der lutherischen Sozialethik." In *Bonhoeffer-Studien: Beiträge zur Theologie und Wirkungsgeschichte Dietrich Bonhoeffers, im Auftrage des Bonhoeffer-Komitees beim Bund der Evangelischen Kirchen in der DDR*, edited by Albrecht Schönherr and Wolf Krötke, 73–85. Münich: Kaiser, 1985.

Wingren, Gustav. *Luthers Lehre von Beruf.* Forschungen zur Geschichte und Lehre des Protestantismus. Münich: Kaiser, 1952.

Winters, Anna Case. *Reconstructing a Christian Theology of Nature: Down to Earth.* Aldershot, UK: Ashgate, 2007.

Wolf, Ernst. "Bonhoeffers Begriff der Mandate." In ibid., *Sozialethik: Theologische Grundfragen*, 169–71. Göttinger Theologische Lehrbücher. Göttingen: Vandenhoeck & Ruprecht, 1975.

———. "Köningsherrschaft Christi und lutherische Zwei-Reiche-Lehre." In *Evangelische Ethik: Diskussionsbeiträge zu ihrer Grundlegung und ihren Aufgaben,* edited by Hans G. Ulrich, 75–97. Theologische Bücherei: Neudrucke und Berichte aus dem 20. Jahrhundert, Studienbücher 83. Münich: Kaiser, 1980.

World Council of Churches. "Final Document: Entering into Covenant Solidarity for Justice, Peace and the Integrity of Creation." In *Between the Flood and the Rainbow: Interpreting the Conciliar Process of Mutual Commitment (Covenant) to Justice, Peace and the Integrity of Creation*, edited by D. Preman Niles, 174. Geneva: World Council of Churches, 1992.

Wöhrle, Jakob. "*Dominium terrae*: Exegetische und religionsgeschichtliche Überlegungen zum Herrschaftsauftrag in Gen 1,26–28." *Zeitschrift für die Alttestamentliche Wissenschaft* 121, no. 2 (2009) 171–88.

Wright, Richard T. "Tearing Down the Green: Environmental Backlash in the Evangelical Sub-Culture." *Perspectives on Science and Christian Faith* 47, no. 2 (1995) 80–91.

Würthwein, Ernst, and Otto Merk. *Verantwortung: Biblische Konfrontation*. Kohlhammer Taschenbücher. Stuttgart: Kohlhammer, 1982.

Wüstenberg, Ralf K., Stefan Heuser, and Esther Hornung, eds. *Bonhoeffer and the Biosciences: An Initial Exploration*. International Bonhoeffer Interpretations. Frankfurt am Main: Lang, 2010.

Wynn, Mark. "Natural Theology in an Ecological Mode." *Faith and Philosophy* 16, no. 1 (1999) 27–42.

———. "Thomas Aquinas: Reading the Idea of Dominion in the Light of the Doctrine of Creation." In *Ecological Hermeneutics: Biblical, Historical and Theological Perspectives*, edited by David G. Horrell et al., 154–165. London: T. & T. Clark, 2010.

Yordy, Laura Ruth. *Green Witness: Ecology, Ethics, and the Kingdom of God*. Eugene, OR: Cascade, 2008.

Zentgraf, Martin. "Bonhoeffers Begriff der Mandate." In "Die Theologische Wahrnehmung von Institutionen: Eine Untersuchung zum Problem einer theologischen Theorie der Institutionen unter Berücksichtigung soziologisch-philosophischer und rechtswissenschaftlicher Institutionentheorie," 100–105. PhD diss., Friedrich Wilhelmsuniversität, 1983.

Ziegler, Philip G. "Dietrich Bonhoeffer: An Ethics of God's Apocalypse?" *Modern Theology* 23, no. 4 (2007) 579–94.

———. "Eschatology and Secularity in the Late Writings of Dietrich Bonhoeffer." In *Dietrich Bonhoeffers Theologie heute: Ein Weg zwischen Fundamentalismus und Säkularismus?*, edited by John W. de Gruchy, Stephen Plant, and Christiane Tietz, 124–38. Gütersloh: Gütersloher, 2009.

———. "'Voices in the Night': Human Solidarity and Eschatological Hope." In *Who Am I? Bonhoeffer's Theology Through his Poetry*, edited by Bernd Wannenwetsch, 115–45. London: T. & T. Clark, 2009.

Zimmerli, Walther. *Old Testament Theology in Outline*. Translated by David E. Green. Edinburgh: T. & T. Clark, 2000.

Zimmerling, Peter. *Bonhoeffer als Praktischer Theologe*. Göttingen: Vandenhoeck & Ruprecht, 2006.

Zimmerman, Michael E. *Contesting Earth's Future: Radical Ecology and Postmodernity*. London: University of California Press, 1994.

————. "Quantum Theory, Intrinsic Value, and Panentheism." In *Postmodern Environmental Ethics*, edited by Max Oelschlaeger, 277–308. Albany: State University of New York Press, 1995.

Index of Names

Abel, 81

Abromeit, Hans-Jürgen, 26n16, 31n40, 32, 32n44, 32n49, 35, 35n65, 36, 36n66, 36n68, 37, 79, 79n26, 82, 82n42, 82n43, 84, 84n54, 84n55, 85–86, 86, 86n62, 90n90, 137n86, 214, 214n28–15n28, 218n44, 221, 232n108, 234, 234n120

Adam, 78, 123, 124n26, 125, 132n60, 135, 136, 136n78, 174, 175

Adams, Carol J., 100n140

Agamben, Giorgio, 248, 248n177, 249

Althaus, Paul, 95, 95n113

Altner, Günter, 11

Anderson, Bernhard W., 140n99

Antaeus, 180–81, 181n78

Aquinas, Thomas, 3, 101n147, 112, 112n194

Aristotle, 152, 160

Attfield, Robin, 153–54, 154n158

Auerbach, Bruce E., 238n134

Axt-Piscalar, Christine, 136, 136n81, 137n84, 216n36

Bacon, Francis, 199

Ballor, Jordan, 96, 96n123, 96n124, 97n125, 97n127, 98

Barth, Friederike, 212, 212n18, 213, 213n24, 214, 214n27, 216, 216n34, 218, 218n43, 219, 219n49, 221–22, 221n58

Barth, Karl, 3, 3n11, 31–32, 39n78, 45, 50, 58, 64, 76n10, 77n19, 78, 81, 85, 85n60, 96–98, 96n124, 97n126, 102, 103, 103n150, 126, 138, 138n89, 139n94, 141, 162, 177, 184n94, 233, 234, 234n122, 235, 235n123, 236, 254

Bartmann, Bernard, 77n19

Barton, Stephen C., 62, 62n178, 63, 63n181, 63n183

Bayer, Oswald, 219, 219n48, 233n112

Bayertz, Kurt, 217n38

Beder, Sharon, 252n190

Beek, Abraham van de, 58n156, 58n158, 59, 59n164, 60, 140, 140n100

Beker, J. Christian, 28

Benktson, Benkt-Erik, 96n122

Benz, Arnold, 61, 61n172

Bergmann, Sigmund, 11, 11n42, 11n43, 13n51–14n51, 14n51, 16n59, 19n68, 20, 21n72

Bergmann, Sigurd, 201n172

Berkhof, Hendrikus, 12n47, 58

Berkhouwer, G. C., 12n47

Berry, Thomas, 70, 70n213, 109n177, 147, 147n137, 205–6, 205n187

Bethge, Eberhard, 1n1, 16n60, 35, 35n64, 42, 42n86, 50, 50n121, 50n123, 96n120, 97n126, 168n18, 187, 188, 189, 189n114, 189n119, 190, 228n89, 229, 230, 232

Bethge, Renate, 229

Biehl, Janet, 115n209

Birch, 113

Bismarck, Otto von, 218, 218n41

Bloch, Ernst, 99, 99n134

Blumhardt, Christoph, 193

Index of Subjects

evolutionary history, human beings
now responsible for, 241
expiation, Christ's act of, 28
"exploitative dominion," 178
exploitative relationship, between
human beings and nature, 194
eyes, development of human, 147

faith
change and non-identity in the
development of, 14
containing answers for the human
situation, 13
defining, 32
as either an *actus directus* or an
actus reflexus, 27
in God the Creator as a confession,
102–3
persevering in, 191
protesting against modern technology, 170
as the strongest weapon, 171n27
faithfulness to the earth, as counterpoint, 190
the Fall
Bonhoeffer's conception of, 105,
264
Bonhoeffer's description of open to
criticism, 81
ecological criticisms of the Christian doctrine of, 104
how "creation" became "nature,"
78–81
incomprehensibility of, 78
no enmity between human beings
and animals prior to, 174
reasserting the reality of, 104
fallen creation, 49, 79
fallen nature, winning the battle for
control over the earth, 166
fallenness
of human beings, 161
of the world, 30
false idols, 210
family ("Familie"), as a divine mandate, 223n66
fascist ideologies, Social Darwinism
and, 115

"fatherliness," of God, 123
feedback, systems of, 251
feeding of the hungry, clearing the
way for Christ's coming, 41
Feil, Ernst
on Antaeus, the giant, remaining
pagan, 181n78
on Bonhoeffer's reading Nietzsche,
192
on the cross as a simple sign of
salvation, 34
on God's image in Christ, 133n69
on homesickness for the other
world, 186n100
on the Incarnation, cross, and
resurrection, 34n61
on Jesus Christ as the sole mediator, 217n37
on the natural, 50
on orders of creation, 96
on the present world coming into
focus, 184
on the sacrament engaging human
beings, 87n72
on the theme of the world in *Discipleship*, 185
felt and considered preferences, distinction between, 157, 158
Feuerbach, insistence on the earthiness of human beings, 123n19
final judgment, expectation of, 239
finite, capable of bearing the infinite,
91
finitum capax infiniti, Luther's formula, 90, 107
"Finitum capax infiniti non per se sed
per infinitum," of Bonhoeffer, 91
finitum non capax infiniti, Calvinist,
90
Fiorenza, Francis Schüssler, 12, 14–15
Floyd, Wayne Whitson, Jr., 216n35
follower of Christ, suffering of,
212n20–13n20
For the Beauty of the Earth (Bouma-
Prediger), 113n198
"the forces of rebellion," Bonhoeffer
on, 226n77
formed nature, 197

nature ("Natur"). *See also* theology of
nature
  as anthropocentric, 5, 71, 161
  as a bearer of God's promises and
    as a fellow sufferer, 67
  becoming profoundly barren, 79
  Bonhoeffer on, 5
  bringing forth new forms, 100–101
  Christ as the center of, 73–98, 270
  Christ as the critical "middle" of,
    82–83
  Christ as the hidden center of,
    81–85
  Christ as the Redeemer of, 85–92
  as cruel, harsh and inhospitable,
    196
  dangerous and horrific sides of, 196
  depending on the history of hu-
    mankind, 79
  depending on the vicarious action
    of Christ, 86
  domination by (Western) male
    chauvinism, 148
  falling into disarray through hu-
    mankind's Fall, 103
  freed from its dumbness and rebel-
    lion, 89
  good and proper human dealings
    with, 101
  having its own relation to God, 98
  human beings as distinctive parts
    of, 118–63
  as a human responsibility, 238
  humanity's fundamental relation-
    ship with, 265
  humans called to master as not
    "pure" nature, 197
  as inherently restless, 110
  insights about the destiny of, 66
  interrelatedness with and depen-
    dence on, 146
  as intrinsically good, 101
  liberated from its ambiguity, 91
  lost the ability to praise God fol-
    lowing the Fall, 81
  moral ambiguity of, 115
  mute in the world after the fall, 80
  not having freedom, 82n43

  not included in the realm of human
    responsibility, 272
  not opposed to sociality, 102
  not purely and simply given, 271
  nothing divine in, 75
  as object, 99
  offering praise to God, 107, 108
  originating in God, 121
  as participating in the hope of final
    transformation, 67
  perceived christocentrically, 98
  primary goal to serve human be-
    ings, 98
  realistic interpretation of, 91
  rebelling against humanity, 79
  as redeemed in Christ, 271
  regaining the purpose that it had
    prior to the Fall, 89
  in relation to Christ, 73–117
  relation to taking the form of "stew-
    ardship," 163
  relative independence of, 71, 77–78
  revealed in and through Christ
    alone, 271
  rising up against man, 79
  ruthless exploitation of, 167
  as a sacrament, 109
  as sacred or divine, 72
  set free from its dumbness, 106
  shaped in advanced ways for hu-
    man purposes and ends, 197
  standing on its own, 100
  as a "state of affairs," 243
  subjected to spirit as a necessary
    precondition or foundation, 120
  theological conceptions of, 106
  theology of, 264, 269–70, 273–74
  worshiping the Lord, 77
nature and spirit, interrelatedness of,
  120
"The Nature of the Church" (lectures),
  32, 33–34, 212
nature philosophy, Schelling's, 99–100
nature's fallenness, remaining relevance of asserting, 104–5
nature's hidden center, 83
nature's redemption, sacraments as
  preview of, 106–10

Nazi Germany
    attacks on life carried out by, 51,
        127
    life as a mere means to an end,
        127n38
    marriage laws of, 145
    Social Darwinism and, 115
Nazi ideology, 249
Nazi regime, 207, 246
neoliberal globalization, indirect
    threat of, 247
neoliberalism, 247n168, 252, 268–69
New Age adherents, adaptation of the
    Gaia Theory by, 70
new earth, Bonhoeffer's perception
    on, 184n91
New Partnership for Africa's Develop-
    ment (NEPAD), 254n197
"new realism," 91
New Testament, about the inbreaking
    judgment of God, 60
"new" world, defined, 74
Nickson, Ann, 219, 220
Nietzsche, Friedrich, 51, 79, 192,
    192n133
nihilism, 48, 171, 186n102
Nike, scandal surrounding, 251–52
"No! An Answer to Emil Brunner"
    (Barth), 96n124
non-anthropocentric model, working
    out, 153
non-anthropocentrism, 154–57, 158
nonbeing (Nichtsein), 93
"none is good but God alone," 75
non-human animals
    having no morality, 142
    possessing consciousness, 141
    possessing episodic memory, 143
    reproduction as a conscious act
        among, 145
non-human beings
    human distinctiveness vis-à-vis,
        128
    lives of bereft of morality, 143
    not sharing sociality as humans
        do, 160
non-human creation, 78, 130
non-human nature

attributing intrinsic value to,
    155–56
existing for the purpose of serving
    human needs, 101–2
fundamental differences between
    human beings and, 266
non-human species, engaging in cer-
    tain forms of social relations, 266
non-religious Christianity, proposal
    for, 2
non-western, indigenous traditions,
    147–48
Northcott, Michael S.
    on church communities, 259
    on dynamic and changing character
        of the cosmos, 60n167
    on forms of relationality, 159
    on the Gaia Theory, 71, 72
    identifying ecological havoc as the
        result of technology, 200
    on Japanese belief compared to
        actions, 156
    on materialism, 203
    on natural law ethic, 111–12
    on nuanced treatment of the three
        moments, 68–69
    opposing unrealistic expectations,
        60
    on preference to empirical experi-
        ence, 114–15
    on the recovery of an ecological
        ethic, 105
    on sacramental approach, 110
    on technology, 200n166
    on teleological directedness of hu-
        man life, 203
Northern Europe, harsher natural
    conditions of, 168n18
Norton, Brian, 157–58
Nullens, Patrick A., 4, 61, 64, 195n143
Nuremberg laws, distinctions between
    "Jews" and "Germans," 145n133

"objective" process, 18–19
"objective" values of nature, articulat-
    ing, 155
Odum, Eugene, 114

Index of Scripture

Index of Dietrich Bonhoeffer Works

Made in the USA
Middletown, DE
25 May 2017